Francis Redfern

History and Antiquities of the Town and Neighbourhood of Uttoxeter

Francis Redfern

History and Antiquities of the Town and Neighbourhood of Uttoxeter

ISBN/EAN: 9783337367138

Printed in Europe, USA, Canada, Australia, Japan

Cover: Foto ©ninafisch / pixelio.de

More available books at **www.hansebooks.com**

HISTORY AND ANTIQUITIES

OF THE

TOWN AND NEIGHBOURHOOD

OF

UTTOXETER,

WITH NOTICES OF ADJOINING PLACES,

BY

FRANCIS REDFERN.

SECOND EDITION.

HANLEY:
ALLBUT AND DANIEL, PERCY STREET PRINTING WORKS.
LONDON:
SIMPKIN, MARSHALL AND CO.,
AND PUBLISHED FOR THE AUTHOR, UTTOXETER.

1886.

HISTORY AND ANTIQUITIES OF
UTTOXETER.

PREFACE TO THE SECOND EDITION.

When I first commenced enquiring into the History and Antiquities of Uttoxeter the ground appeared barren and unfavourable for cultivation. No special attempt had been made by any one to investigate any claims it might have to antiquarian and historical record, and it was generally supposed that all that could be said about it was, that it was pleasantly and healthily situated ; probably a town of high antiquity, and certainly one in which not many people grew rich. Its native poet, Samuel Bentley, who spent a life of comparative leisure in Uttoxeter, expresses his views as to its merits for historical recognition as follows :—" Very little more can be said about it than what the poet, Alexander Necham, says of another place, viz :

> " Hic locus ætatis nostræ primordia novit
> Annos fœlices, lætitæque dies.
> Hic locus ingenuus, puerilis imbuit annos
> Artibus, et nostræ laudis origo suit."

And which may be roughly translated : " This is the place where we spent our first happy years and joyous days. This is the place where boys are instructed in the liberal arts, and of our praise has been worthy." The opinion that Uttoxeter has not afforded scope for people acquiring wealth has been refuted in numerous instances, and I flatter myself that the First Edition of this book, the preparation of which was undertaken under circumstances the reverse of favourable for literary occupation, and during a period of exceeding poor health, proved that persevering enquiry, extending through a number

PREFACE.

of years, was sufficient to give discredit to the view formerly taken of Uttoxeter·as to its antiquarian, historical and general interest. Still, a revised edition of the work was highly desirable, and continued research has evinced that the First Edition could only be regarded as an instalment of what might be said as to the archæological and general interest of the town and neighbourhood. I have consequently re-written, with the exception of a few pages, the whole of the volume, carefully revising it, as far as I was able, and have made considerable additions of interesting and valuable material, consisting of descriptions of antiquarian remains and objects, biographical notices, curious old records, desirable accounts of families, old inns, obsolete trades, former superstitions and customs, historical and other facts, and a body of Teutonic and other earlier field names gathered from the old terriers of the parish.

I must thank Subscribers for their names in support of the undertaking, although it is truly desirable the number should have been more. I also feel it necessary to request their kind consideration towards me in the delay of the publication of the volume after its announcement, and to say that it is partly owing to long illness, compulsory absence from home, weariness and other reasons I need not mention.

I beg also to express my thanks to several gentlemen whom I have troubled with enquiries over the undertaking, and now venture to commit to what I hope may be the favourable reception of the public, a work which has engaged my attention about twenty-seven years.

FRANCIS REDFERN.

Uttoxeter, 1881.

CONTENTS.

CHAPTER I.
Introductory Remarks—Natural Scenery—Interesting Geological Notice—Etymology of Uttoxeter.

CHAPTER II.
The Celtic, Romano-British, and Anglo-Saxon periods.
Doomsday Survey of Uttoxeter—Its Feudal Tenure, &c.
Uttoxeter during the Civil War and Rebellion—Dr. Samuel Johnson's Penance—Peace of 1802—Royal Visits—Birth of W. J. Fox, Esq.—Peace Rejoicings.

CHAPTER III.
Lord Shrewsbury's Peerage—Trial for Alton Estates—Festivities at Uttoxeter on Lord Shrewsbury taking possession of Alton Towers.

CHAPTER IV.
History of Uttoxeter Church—Early period of a Church in Uttoxeter—Instance of Martydom in Uttoxeter, &c.—Altar-tombs—Church Inscriptions—Cemetery.

CHAPTER V.
History of Dissent in Uttoxeter—Quakers—Catholics—Independents—Wesleyan Methodists—Presbyterians—Primitives—Plymouth Brethern.

CHAPTER VI.
Distinguished Persons:—Thomas Allen—Dr. Lightfoot—Sir Symon Degge—Lord Gardner—Mary Howitt—Samuel Bentley—Captain Astle—Edward Rudyard, &c.

CHAPTER VII.
Extent of Uttoxeter—Its quaint appearance—Noted Buildings of Antiquity—Court Leet—Fires which have happened—Population since 1662—Persons noted for their longevity.

CONTENTS.

CHAPTER VIII.

Ancient Families:—The Mynors—The Degges Floyers—Normans—The Lightfoot Family—The Milwards.

CHAPTER IX.

Ancient Customs—Sacred Wells—Omens and Superstitions—Sports and Pastimes—Civil Usages.

CHAPTER X.

Antiquity of Uttoxeter Markets—Curious particulars of butter pots—Trial about Tolls, &c.—Manufactures and Trade—Printers and Books—Tradesmen's tokens.

CHAPTER XI.

Libraries—Mechanics' Institute—Town Hall.

CHAPTER XII.

Public Schools—Alleyn's Grammar School—Alleyn's will, &c.—National School—New Day School.

CHAPTER XIII.

Uttoxeter Charities.

CHAPTER XIV.

NOTICES OF PLACES IN THE NEIGHBOURHOOD OF UTTOXETER.

Loxley — Stramshall — Leigh — Fielde — Chartley Castle — Abbots Bromley—Woodford—Woodlands—Marchington—Houndhill—Draycott— Newborough — Hanbury — Faulde—Tutbury—Sudbury—Doveridge—West Broughton — Marston — Somersall — Eaton — Norbury—Alton —Tean—Croxden- Checkley—Rocester—Denston—Crakemarsh—Blount's Hall, Kingston—Needwood Forest.

LIST OF ILLUSTRATIONS.

The following Illustrations are by the late Mr. LLEWELLYN JEWITT, F.S.A. :—

LORD GARDNER'S HOUSE.
BIRTH-PLACE OF MARY HOWITT.
SAMUEL BENTLEY'S HOUSE.
UTTOXETER CHURCH.
  DITTO   OLD CHURCH, NOW TAKEN DOWN.
ALTAR TOMBS, UTTOXETER CHURCH.
REMAINS FOUND AT SUDBURY.
PORTRAIT OF THOMAS ALLEYN.
ANCIENT BUTTER-POTS.
TRADERS' TOKEN, WILLIAM CARTWRIGHT.
  DITTO   ROBERT GILBERT.
THE WHITE BEAR INN.
DR. JOHNSON AND CAPTAIN ASTLE.
AUTOGRAPH OF SAMUEL BENTLEY.
CELTIC CINERARY URN, TOOT HILL.
ROMAN URN, TOOT HILL.
DITTO VESSEL, HIGH WOOD.
CHECKLEY, "DANISH MONUMENTS."
  DITTO   FONT.
KINGSTON OLD CHURCH.
ROCESTER, INCISED SLAB.
  DITTO   "FRAME YARD."
  DITTO   SPEAR HEAD.
TORQUE, FROM NEEDWOOD FOREST.
ANCIENT HUNTING HORN.

LIST OF ILLUSTRATIONS.

BY MESSRS. BUTTERWORTH AND HEATH—
  STONE CELT FROM THE DOVE VALLEY.

BY MR. DORRINGTON—
  STONE CELT FROM LEIGH.

BY THE LATE MR. GILKS—
  BRONZE AXE SHAPED CELT.
  BRONZE ANGHARM CELT.
  FRAGMENTS SAMIAN WARE.
  TWO FRAGMENTS CASTOR WARE.
  A BOWL IN SALOPIAN WARE.

BY MR. W. J. POTTER—
  LOXLEY VASE.
  MANOR HOUSE.
  MICHAEL JOHNSON'S BIRTH PLACE.
  KNYPERSLEY HOUSE.
  OLD BUFFALO INN.
  UTTOXETER BRONZE CELT.
  AMULET.
  TWO FLINTS.
  PERFORATED STONE.
  BRONZE SIGNET RING.
  ROMAN GLASS BEAD.
  FRAGMENTS ROMAN POTTERY, UTTOXETER.
  QUERN.
  BENTLEY FORTIFIED HOUSE.
  SHELDON'S (ARCHBISHOP) HOME.
  SNAPE TOMBSTONE.
  BROKEN LOVER'S KNOT.
  CROSSES.

INDEX.

A.

	PAGE.
Abud, Rev. H.	192, 220
Abbots Clownholme	462
Agricultural Meetings	370—373
Algar, Earl	91—92
Altar Tombs	215
Ditto Legend respecting	217
Allen, T., Philosopher	256—259
Allen, W. S., M.P.	398
Alleyne's Grammar School	399
Ditto Will of	401
Ditto Orders of his School	408
Alton	450
Amulets	42—44
Anne, Queen, Bounty of	207
Ancient Watercourse	418
Antique Bell and Alphabet	453
Artists	287—289
Architecture, 14th century	306
Archbold, Memorial of	232
Ashenhurst, Col.	140
Astle, Capt.	282
Ditto his Library	285

B.

Bandoleers	147
Banks	423
Baal, Worship of	31
Barrow Hill	461
Bagot, Sir W.	157
Ball, E.	139
Beltine Fires	30—31
Bentley, S.	173
Bells	233
Bell, Curfew	234
Bentley, Samuel	263—271
Bishops, acquittal of seven	149—150

INDEX.

	PAGE.
Blue Coat Hunt	155
Blount's Hall	430
Blithard Mot	87
Bladon, Thomas	192
Bladon, James	286—287
Bookselling	382
Bowyer, Col.	140
British Torque	443
Brereton, Sir W.	134, 135, 143
Brethren, Plymouth	255
Bramshall	432
Bromley	438
Burrow Town	81—82
Bunting, Jabez, D.D.	253
Builder's Seal	292
Bull-baiting	353—355
Butter Pots	363—365

C.

	PAGE.
Campbell, C. M.	461
Cary, Rev. W.	438
Carlyle, Thomas	162
Cavendish, C. T.	197
Cattle Plague	373
Cauldon Canal	389
Celts	43—46
Cemetery	244
Checkley	454
Chief or Manor House	295
Cheese Fairs	366
Charities	413—423
Chartley	436
Ditto Roman Camp at	437
Charter to Uttoxeter	98
Cheshire Meadow	62
Charles I. at Uttoxeter	130
Ditto his propositions at Uttoxeter	130—133
Charles, Prince Edward	151
Church Goods	204
Chantries	213
Church, old	212—215
Ditto new	219
Ditto do. cost of erection	219
Chimes	233
Civil War	129
Cludd, E.	302
Cloyd, Capt.	144
Clipped Coin	144—145

INDEX.

	PAGE.
Copestake, Thomas and Henry	377
Copestake, J. C., M.D.	198
Copt Oak	47
Coaches	389—390
Congregationalism	248—250
Cook, Rev. J.	250
Cole, Rev., Effigy of, burnt	249
Common Oven	296
Court Leet	137, 296
Cope, F.	154
Ditto his stalwart ancestors	155
Communion Plate	243
Cotton Mill	379
Crakemarsh	445
Croxden	453
Crosses, Market and Wayside	369—370
Critchlow, S., Churches built by	385
Cromwell, Col.	143
Crowe, Eyre	162
Craig, W. Y., M.P.	197
Cumberland, Duke of	152—154, 160—161
Ditto do. Grant to Uttoxeter	153

D.

	PAGE.
Dawson, L., Will of	242
Dale Field Barrow	39
Danes, Slaughter of	442
Devonshire, Earl of	135
Degg, Sir Symon	207
Ditto do.	259—263
Ditto do. Estates of	335—341
Denstone College	463
Duke of Devonshire	264
Doomsday	13, 91
Doveridge	448
Dove Leys	461
Draycot	442

E.

	PAGE.
Eaton	450
Effigy	218
Egyptians	144
Elizabeth, Queen	79
Elm, a great	436
Enclosure of Uttoxeter Ward	109—128
Enclosures, Consequence of	109
Embroidering	38

INDEX.

F.

	PAGE.
Fast of 1795	176
Fairfax, Gen.	143
Faulde	444
Fever	311
Feudal Customs	352—353
Ferrars, Earls	92—101
Field names	87—90
Fitz Herbert, Walter	202
Fitz Herbert, Sir W.	202
Fire, great	301
Fiends and Ghosts	351—352
Flier, Thomas, Martyr	205
Flier, Family of	320—324
Flint, A. A.	192
Forges	375
Fosseways	53—79
Fox, W. J.	177—179
Fortified House	261
Forestalling	366
Frith Silver	296
Fulling Mill	376

G.

Gardner, Lord	266, 271—276
Gardner, Col.	234
Garlanders	345
Gaunt, John of	105—106
Gell, Sir John	134—136
Generosity, Instance of	440
Gentlemen disclaimed	344
George Elliot	220
Ghost laying	351
Goring, Lord	137
Gospel Oak	47
Gould, J. B., American Consul	254
Great Stone Bridge	82
Gresley, Thomas, Gift of	254
Gun, Wall	143

H.

Hanging Wicket	73
Hamilton, Duke of	145—146
Hawthorn, N.	165
Hall, J. P.	197
Harpdall, John	202
Hall, Old	300
Hanbury	443

INDEX.

	PAGE.
Hacket, Bishop	205—206
Hawkins, Mrs.	254—255
Heming, Mr., the Controversalist	208—211
Hermitage	301
Heraldic Visitation	343
Hiding Places	325
Hills, Gordon H.	216
Holland. W. R.	48
Hole-in-the-Wall	84—85
Howett, Mary	276—281
Howett, W.	280
Hobby-horse	438
Houndhill	441

I.

Inscriptions on Sundial	419
Ditto Churchyard	235—239
Inns	303—309

J.

James, Rev. J. A.	250
Jenny Shops	379
Jewellery Trade	377—379
Johnson, Dr. Samuel	162—174
Johnson, Michael	162—163, 167—168, 174 - 175
Joane Waste	205

K.

Kingstone	413
Knight, Ed.	358
Knighthood, Summonses for	344
Kynnersley, T. C. S.	161

L.

Lancaster, Earls, of	101—104
Lambert, General	146
Leaguer, the	143
Leigh	435
Lightfoot, Peter, MS. of	109
Lightfoot, Dr. John	329
Lightfoot, Rev. T.	329—332
Lightfoot, T., Memorial	227
Lightfoot, J. E., J.P.	440
Literary Institute	391—396
Loxley	425—430
Ditto Vase	76—79
Lover's Knot	334
Longevity, Instances of	313—315
Lucas, John F.	143

INDEX.

M.

	PAGE.
Madeley Holme, Roman Camp at	62—64
Marchington	441
Maypole	346
Markets	362
Memorial Chapel	440
Memorials in the Church	221—232
Methodism	251—254
Meteyard, Miss	378
Medicinal Waters	347
Mellor, Harriet	357
Mince Pie Hall	462
Milward Memorial	230
Milward, Sir T.	138
Milward Family	328
Ditto Stirrup Cup of	138—139
Moreton, Tumulus at	38
Moorhouse, do.	38
Mosley, Sir O.	142
Mural Decoration	435
Musical Society	359—361
Mynors, John, Memorial to	214
Mynors, Family of	316—320

N.

Naseby, Battle of	141
Needwood Forest	464
Newspapers	385
Newborough	443
Northampton, Earl of	135
Northburgh, Roger	200
Norbury	450
Noggins	381

O.

Oakley, Col.	143
Odery, Rev. R.	197
Offtman's Cross	46
Old Wood, Toot Hill, at	36
Old "Crown"	305
Oldfield Tablet	225
Omens	305
Overton, Roman remain found at	65

P.

Pamphili, Princes Doria	186
Parson's Counsellor	207

INDEX.

	PAGE.
Parish Register	240—241
Patriotic Fund	397
Peace Rejoicings	179
Pixley, W.	247
Pillar Stones	454
Pillory and Cuckstool	352—353
Plague, The	312
Portway	53—56
Popinjay, Game of	88
Poynes, General	140
Population	309
Protector, Lord	148
Presbyterian Church	248
Primitive Methodists	254
Prices	365
Printers and Printing	383—385
Prestwood	463
Pugin	255

Q.

Queen	177
Queen, Dowager	177
Queen, Autograph of	396
Quern	74

R.

Raleigh, Sir Walter, of Uttoxeter	101
Rebellion	160
Rocester	459
Ditto a Roman Station	65—73
Rosa Bonheur	463
Roman Catholics	255
Ditto Fortifications	73—74
Robin Hood	429
Ditto his Horn	429
Rudyard, E.	281
Runic Stone	47
Rupert, Prince	133, 138—139
Rykeneld Street	53—58

S.

Salter's Way	55—58
Saxon Graves	86
Ditto Fonts	350
Saxons	81
Ditto Sports of	84
Sayers, Capt.	142

INDEX.

	PAGE.
Saddler, M. Thos.	253
Schools	411—412
Scott, John, killed	137
Scotch Prisoners	147
Shrewsbury, Earl of, his death	195
Snape Headstone	333
Somersall	449
Souls' Day	355—356
Society of Friends	245—247
Stramshall, a Roman Fortification	61—62
Ditto	431
Stanhope, Lord	136
Stokes, Adrian	162
Sunday School Centenary	197
Sundial	411
Sudbury	447
Symond, Capt.	138

T.

Taylor, Herbert, M.D.	192
Talbot Peerage Case	181—195
Tapestry, fine	324
Tean	452
Ditto barrow	40—41
Tenures, curious	335
Thornbury, W.	172
Theatres	356—359
Tixal, Family of Hart, and others	325—327
Town Hall	397
Tolls, disputed	367—370
Toot Hills	29—38
Took Horn	276
Tokey, E.	304
Trade of Uttoxeter	373—386
Traders' Tokens	386—388
Turner, J., D.D.	282
Tutbury	444
Ditto Castle, pulling down	144
Tumulus Field	452

U.

Uttoxeter,	Derivation of	13—15
Ditto	Scenery of	16—20
Ditto	Surface Geology of	20—27
Ditto	A Roman Camp	49
Ditto	Roman Remains at	51—52
Ditto	In a State of Siege	129
Ditto	Extent of and Picturesque Buildings	290

INDEX.

V.

	PAGE
Vaughan, Sir W.	140
Vernon, John	250
Vernon, Lord	448
Vicarage of Uttoxeter	200
Ditto its Ordination	200

W.

	PAGE
Wall Croft	63
Warton, Sir G.	141
Watching, Saxon Custom of	146
Wales, Prince of, Marriage of	196
Warner, Family of	341—343
Water Supply	418
Wernerian Club	286
Well Worship	347—350
Wedgwood, Josiah	379
White Hart Hotel	161
Witches	351
Woodford	439
Woodlands	439
Woodseat	461
Works of Art	463

Y.

Yelts Barrow	39—40
Young Men's Association	398

CORRECTIONS.

Page 14, line 5 : For *antecedent*, read *subsequent*.

Page 29, line 24 : For *de*, read *du Tath*.

Page 31, line 21 : Omit *a* in *a gathering*.

Page 32, line 13 : For *Ashketons*, read *Ashkelons*.

Page 52, line 31 : For *sane*, read *lane*.

Page 73, line 6 : For *head*, read *heap*.

Page 76, line 22 : Omit *and*.

Page 92, line 31 : For *table*, read *sable*.

Page 203, line 29 : For *1,401a.*, read *140a. iv*.

Page 228, line 35 : For *nebutee*, read *nebulé*. In next line, read *sable* for *table*.

Page 263, line 5 : For *bent*, read *bend*.

Page 376, note : For *wane*, read *wave*.

From a Report of the British Archæological Associations to Staffordshire in 1872, referring to the Author, it states in a beautiful grouping "the hearty good will and cheery zeal of their poorer brother who met them at Uttoxeter, and laid aside his coopering for the day, catering for them in all reverence for that learning he would have more than compassed, had he but had their opportunities, &c."

HISTORY AND ANTIQUITIES

OF

UTTOXETER AND NEIGHBOURHOOD.

DEFINITION OF LOCAL HISTORY—GENERAL CHARACTERISTICS OF UTTOXETER—THE ETYMOLOGY OF ITS NAME—SCENERY AND GEOLOGY OF ITS NEIGHBOURHOOD.

Local History, considered in its most restricted sense, is a description of any single town or village, and as such it forms a portion of the topographical history of a county or kingdom. Yet, although, from being so understood, it is limited in its scope, it nevertheless treats on a great diversity of subjects and comprises many of the features which distinguish the pages of national history. It describes the natural characteristics of a neighbourhood; enquires into the origin of its occupation by early settlers; dilates on its antiquities and traditions, its general history, its distinguished worthies and notable families, and does not fail to assimilate all other information belonging to its especial province, or by which its interest and value may be enhanced. It may be conceded that it does not afford an opportunity for brilliant writing, and cannot, therefore, command the pen of a Gibbon, a Hume, a Macaulay, or a Motley. Still, it may be urged that it has engaged the abilities of men of superior intellect and eminent attainments in learning as Plot, Ormerod,

Hunter, Nicholson, Shaw, Borlaise, Sir R. C. Hoare, Fytton, the Lysons, and others, and that it frequently displays patient investigation, immense labour, varied and extensive knowledge and thoughtful writing, and that its general interest is frequently considerable. Its greatest charm, however, lies in the simple fact that it is Local History—the history of a locality with which one is intimately acquainted, and with which our sympathies are closely identified. There is much pleasure in knowing what has transpired and is interesting in any locality where Providence has fixed our lot, and most persons feel, as they ought, a just and worthy pride in being familiar with such knowledge, or of having the means of its acquisition within their reach. Some town, village, or hamlet, enshrines the early home of each and all of us. One of such spots, with its neighbouring hills, its quiet lanes, its pleasant meadows and peaceful and charming valleys, has been traversed by our feet more than others, and our memories are fraught with their reminiscences over many years, and, may be, our forefathers, for many generations, as well as others whom we have tenderly loved, sleep peacefully in the sacred enclosure of the Churchyard of the place which thus excites our liveliest sensibilities. The pages, therefore, of local history, descriptive as they are of all that relates to such beloved scenes, cannot fail being perused with delight, and of awaking some tender chord of affection and memory.

Such thoughts as the above find almost spontaneous expression whilst the attempt is for the first time being made to collect together the materials for a description and history of so interesting a town as Uttoxeter, or in preparing for publication a new edition of a history of that town—a town of great antiquity and noted for its former position in the honour of Tutbury; for its renowned markets; for the trying part it sustained during the civil wars of the seventeenth century; for its distinguished worthies, and on many other accounts having equal attraction and importance for the enquirer. Altogether the information relating to Uttoxeter and its neighbourhood is sufficiently varied, curious, and interesting, to raise them to considerable historical repute, not overlooking, at the same time, the simple attractions of the theme as they are poetically rendered by Samuel Bentley, the Uttoxeter poet, as here ensuing :—

" Uttoxeter, sweet are thy views !
  Each scene of my fond boyish days,
Past pleasure in fancy renews,
  While gratitude sings in thy praise ;
Here plenty with copious horn,
  Dispenses her bounties around,
And rosy thy sons, like the morn,
  In health and in spirits abound.
Thy buildings, what though they are plain,
  And boast no magnificent dome,
Enough for the wise may contain,
  Enjoying true pleasure at home ;
How happy thy poor, who enjoy
  Possessions o'er want to prevail,
Whose hills daily bread can supply,
  And sweet milky tribute the vale."

    The derivation of the name Uttoxeter has not hitherto been ascertained, and but few persons have attempted to give its etymology. Generally the subject has been admitted to be a perplexing question, and to be surrounded with difficulty. Still, the duty of fully facing it is not on that account in any way diminished. On the contrary, it increases the desire to seek its solution and stimulates the attempt. The name in Doomsday survey is Wotocheshede, which original form of its being written constitutes the perplexity to the etymologist. In writings in existence of a few centuries subsequent to the date of the survey, it occurs as Uttoxeshather, but Leland, Hollingshead, and Camden spelt it Uttoxcester and Uttoxcestre, and Camden declares that to be its Saxon name. It is scarcely necessary, in an attempt to arrive at the meaning of the word, to accuse the Norman scribes, or compilers of the survey, with the guilt of perverting the spelling of the name either on account of their antipathy to the Saxons or through their ignorance of the Saxon language, from which chiefly the names of places had been derived. In fact, to doubt their accuracy in this particular would render it necessary to drop the enquiry. So little, however, is this essential, that, on the contrary, it will be perceived that all antecedent ways of spelling Uttoxeter to that in Doomsday Book, for the most part confirms the value of that ancient authority. The modern spelling of the word is certainly somewhat misleading ; but Utcester, Ulcester, Uttok-cester, Uttoxceshather, and Tocester, Otteshather, Uttoxeshate, Tokestter, Wutokesher, Wittokshather, Uttexhautr, Taksettor, and Hutockeshather, all of which forms of the name are found in old writings have a near resemblance to the name as given in the Doomsday records. Wotocheshede has been supposed to be derived from *Wudu* (wood) and *Seade* (shade). * In early times Uttoxeter was well surrounded and shaded by woods, which circumstances has probably suggested such a derivation of the word. The same fact may have led to other derivations of the name, which may have been constructed from its modern spelling. On the supposition of it being a Saxon name in the form it is generally employed, it has been thought that the Saxon word *mattock*, the name of an implement, enters into its composition, and that, therefore, it implies that the place has been cleared of trees by the use of such an instrument. When, however, it is remembered that all places which have been disforested by the agency of a mattock are both on the Continent and in England called *field* or *felled place* it will scarcely be admitted that the word mattock has anything to do with the derivation of Uttoxeter. A highly esteemed writer who considers that Wotochesede proves nothing, and who endeavours to give a derivation of the name from Leland's spelling of it, which is Uttokcestre, proceeds to show that the prefix is from *Utt* (out), and *Token* being the regular Saxon particle of the verb *take*, Uttok comes, therefore, to mean an *outtake*. But recollecting that Uttoxeter was probably a British

---

* Ward's " Stoke-upon-Trent, ' in which it is said that the name as given in Doomsday Book is the most perplexing of Staffordshire names.

settlement, and that the Romans had a station at the place before its Saxon occupation, it is scarcely to be supposed that the Saxons would give it a name implying an outtake from a forest unless they themselves had effected it. Neither, for the same reason, can it signify an outtake from a chase. If the Saxons really gave Uttoxeter a name signifying an outtake at all, it would be more likely to mean an outtake from a camp. The Saxon word *stocca*, meaning the stem or trunk of a tree, is much more likely to be the origin of the prefix. If so, Uttoxeter may imply a town built of wood or on stocks, or surrounded by a stockade, where the Romans previously had a camp. Having now given several possible derivations of the word Uttoxeter, all of which, however, are unsatisfactory, it still remains to revert again to the Wotocheshede of the Doomsday survey. The form of the name now under notice, is, I believe, the real Romanised British name of the town—a name which it bore prior to our Saxon ancestors entering Britain, and all other ways of spelling it are but variations from the original word, and do not contain any Saxon element. The latter part of the word *cheshede* is evidently the Latin *sede*, which has the same meaning as *castrum*, a camp, when applied to a place occupied by the Roman stativæ. As to *Woto*, which is the prefix, and considering it along with Tocester, one of the old ways of spelling the name of the town, and which much resembles one or two of those previously given, it becomes evident that it is a variation of Toot, or Teut. Wotocheshede, with all its variations must, therefore, imply the Tootcester, or castra, situated near the altar dedicated to Teut or Toot. This explanation or derivation of the name has never before been given, and information and facts will be produced in subsequent pages which very highly favour its correctness.

Uttoxeter is situated on the eastern borders of Staffordshire * in Totmanslow south, and in the eccle-

---

* According to MS. notes of Sir Symon Degg, the word Staffordshire is derived from *stadeford*, the *strand*, *shore*, or *bank* of a *ford*. Another derivation is from *steaf*, a staff or pole, and *fa ran*, to go, and may mean part of a river which could be crossed on stilts. It might be derived from *stean* or *stone ford*.

siastical division of the See of Lichfield. It is distant from Stafford, the county town, about fifteen miles, and is one hundred and forty miles from London. The parish comprises Crakemarsh, Creighton, Stramshall (now ecclesiastically one parish), the Woodlands, and the liberty of Loxley, and, according to modern calculations, contains about 10,000 acres, 2,460 of which are in the township of Uttoxeter, 1,735 in Loxley, 1,066 in Crakemarsh, 1,274 in Stramshall, and 2,419 in the Woodlands.

Uttoxeter has an elevated position on the gravel, and to this circumstance is owing the salubrity for which it has become famed. The market-place lies in a central part of the town, and the main streets have a direct communication with it. The principal of these are High-street, having a northern direction, from which, at Uttoxeter Heath, are branch roads to Ashbourne and the Potteries; Carter Street and Balance Street towards the west for Stafford, Abbots Bromley, Rugeley, and Lichfield; the Doveridge Road on the east for Derby and Burton; and Schoolhouse Lane or Bridge Street on the south leading to Marchington and other villages, and in which is situated the fine passenger station of the North Stafford Line of Railway. The way to Stone is reached by Smithy Lane, or, as it is now called, Smithfield Road, out of High Street, and Tinker's or Susan's Lane out of Carter Street. There are two lanes taking a southward direction from Balance Street, which, although formerly but little frequented, have latterly become busy thoroughfares for traffic from the railway luggage station. These lanes are called Pinfold Lane, and Spicer's, Spiceall, or Petticoat Lane. The entrance to Carter Street from the market-place was formerly until about 1850 very narrow, being only half the width it is now, the causeway on the north side actually existing where the middle of the road is. Such places as Park Place, Fountain Terrace, Leighton Terrace, The Crescent, Sunny Side, and numerous other names, are quite modern, as well as all the residences now called villas.

The neighbourhood of Uttoxeter contains many sylvan and picturesque spots of much attractiveness, and it also affords prospects so beautiful that it would be difficult to find others in all respect to exceed them. The features of the landscape viewed in different directions from Dove Bridge are especially delightful. But the scenery around may be scanned to the greatest advantage whilst a stroll is being taken along Callimore Lane from the High Fields to the opposite extremity of Uttoxeter High Wood, and even down Moisty or, as old writings call it, Mister Field's Lane, and on to Marchington. These situations command charming panoramic views of considerable extent. To the south-west splendid glimpses are afforded of Needwood Forest Banks at points where its rich magnificence is not equalled anywhere else in its whole extent, and which swell more impressively and grandly upon the vision as they are approximated in the direction of the new church in the Woodlands. Looking north from the High Wood, Uttoxeter presents itself on an eminence with the fine spire of the parish church towering heavenwards above the human habitations and interests which cluster around its base. More to the north the prospect takes in the moorlands of Staffordshire, with the continuous range of the hills of Weaver, whose huge proportions

"Swell from each scene below,"

to about 1,500* feet above the sea. Although these hills have such an imposing look from a great distance, they lose much of their appearance of magnitude when the spectator sees them in close proximity above Wootton ; so true it is that

"Distance lends enchantment to the view."

This partial illusion is easily to be accounted for ; a gradually rising tract of country has to be gone over before their vicinity is reached. Besides these there are many other inviting patches in the landscape. Doveridge has a delightful appearance on the right, the spire of the village church is beheld

"Peering through tufted trees,"

---

* Pitt's Agriculture of Staffordshire. Later authorities give 1,154 feet above the sea level

and the declivity, crowned with Doveridge Hall, has a charming effect by the woody surface by which it is so appropriately adorned. Eaton Banks, a little more distant, deserve the poetic name they bear, and the neighbourhood would be devoid of one of its greatest charms without the woods which clothe their acclivities and summits—

"Painting with verdure all the scene."

Eaton woods were threatened with complete annihilation in 1797, subsequent to the death of their owner; the axe had made considerable havoc, but ere it was too late the exterminating summons appears to have been arrested, and consequently the portion of the woods now existing has been preserved for the admiration of all lovers of picturesque scenery. Thomas Gisborne, in his "Vales of Weaver," and Francis N. C. Mundy, in his "Needwood Forest," have emulated each other in lamenting the fall of the woods, which had begun, and in perpetuating expressions of their friendship with their deceased proprietor, Godfrey Clarke, Esq., in the following lines :—

> Ah! Eaton! soon thy woodlands gay
> Shall live alone in Mundy's lay,
> On Fancy's page immortal bloom,
> And spurn the sawpit's yawning tomb.
> Ofttimes the Bard, where Needwood low'rs,
> Sighed as he viewed your conscious bowers,
> Ponder'd o'er Clarke's untimely bier,
> And Friendship dropped a tuneful tear.
> Hence, Eaton, when thy woods dethron'd,
> Stoop from the heights they long have crown'd,
> Dryads and Fauns, a sylvan train,
> At eve shall mourn thy parting reign,
> In pale procession climb the steep,
> And o'er thy withering hours weep;
> Then shall the blue eye'd nymphs of Dove
> Glance at thy naked realms above,
> Lean on their silver oars, and hear
> The dulcet dirge with feeling ear.—*Vales of Weaver.*

> Yes Eaton banks, in vain I strive
> To hide the griefs your oaks revive;
> Bow thy tall branches, grateful wood!
> Afford me blossom, leaf, and bud.
> He, for whose memory these I blend,

> Thy late lost master was my friend.
> Fall, gentle dews ! fresh zephyrs, breathe !
> Spread, cooling shades ! preserve my wreath !
> Alas, it withers ere its time !—
> So faded he in manly prime :
> But virtue, scorning Friendship's aid,
> Rears its own palms which never fade.—*Needwood Forest.*

From the High Wood the valley of the Dove is exposed delightfully to view for some miles, and the river Dove is seen winding its way southward through luxuriant meadows, and by many a pleasant spot on its banks. In truth—

> What valley can with Dove compare
> For sylvan glades and pastures fair.

It is stated that Snowdon in Wales is perceptible with a glass from the High Wood in fine weather, and from there, and even from Uttoxeter Heath, on a clear day, Alton Towers, Hollington Stone Quarries, with a background of woods enclosing the vista, and the recently erected college of St. Chad's, Denstone, lying nearer, and all being places of much interest, may be seen with tolerable distinctness.

There are many charming woody declivities lying about Loxley, west of Uttoxeter, but they may be most favourably viewed on the way to Bramshall, and from the ridge on the west side of that village.

Perhaps the most interesting features belonging to the valley of the Dove by Uttoxeter are its vast extent and fertility. Here it expands into many thousand acres of the most productive meadow and grazing land. Leland testified that " there be wonderful pastures by the Dove." This characteristic of the valley has also given existence to various popular sayings, one of which is that

> " If a stick be laid down there over-night in spring
> It will not be found for grass the next morning,"

and in being taken as a standard by which to guage other land in the kingdom, it is said " it is nearly as good as Dove land." It has been further asserted, and probably without any exaggeration, that before the land in the county was cultivated, there was no fat meat in it but what came from the Dove. The wonderful qualities of the land so eulogised are owing to the floods of the river —" the British Nile "—which are sometimes sudden and of considerable extent, nearly inundating the whole valley, and carrying off sheep, and sometimes cattle, before any danger is suspected. A single night, by the melting of snow on the hills, or by a heavy fall of rain, which soon swells both the rivers Churnet and the Dove, as well as the Tean, which unite their separate volumes before reaching Uttoxeter, readily serves to cause the unexpected floods which produce the fertility which has given such fame to the land at Uttoxeter, and along the same valley for many miles. Hence the saying " In April Dove's flood is worth a king's good." *

> Down yon mid vale the British Nile,
> Fair Dove comes winding many a mile,
> And from her copious urn distils
> The fatness of a thousand hills.—*Needwood Forest.*

The geology of the neighbourhood of Uttoxeter, an account of which it may be thought ought to have preceded the description of its scenery, may not present many features of interest except to those who are engaged in a patient investigation of the science. To such there is much in its geology of no small amount of interest. Uttoxeter is situated upon what is geologically termed the *drift* formation, which belongs to the upper tertiary epoch and immediately beneath the materials of the alluvium. The whole of Europe, including this kingdom, except the highest parts, has been submerged beneath the sea, and the drift is regarded as evidence of a strong current from north to south. It consists of boulders and clay, large blocks of rock, and accumulations of gravel. The larger materials are considered to have been conveyed from their native position in the north in vast masses of ice, which, on dissolving, have deposited their stony freight at great distances south of where they are naturally found.

---

* See Plot's, Shaw's and Nightingale's Histories of Staffordshire, and Leigh's Lancashire, Cheshire, and Derbyshire.

The gravel contains small boulders which are supposed to have been deposited towards the close of the subsidence of the watery element. An extensive bed of fine drift clay lies near the surface at Uttoxeter Heath, and is of much thickness; but over a large extent of ground it has been mined and made into bricks, and its appropriation in that way has been going on many years. A brick —a memorial brick now in my possession—was dug up in 1869, with this inscription upon it: "This is the last brick that William Floads made in 1764." The clay of the Dove Valley, from which bricks are being made near the town, is of a more recent period, and trunks of bog oak are occasionally found in it, and one has been met with at Dove Bank Brickworks, the property of Mr. Lovatt, in an upright position, and leaning slightly towards the south-west. Another oak which was found prostrate at the bottom of the mine, which may be six feet deep, is eighteen feet long and two feet in diameter, and numerous other smaller ones have been met with, showing, as in other instances in the Dove Valley, that the valley level was at a remote period six feet lower than it now is, and had existing upon it a vigorous vegetable growth. At the town the gravel, I understand, attains a considerable depth over the clay, boulders are mingled in great quantities with the gravel, many being of considerable size. No fossils occur except such as have been detached from older rocks, and these are principally from the limestone formation, being chiefly encrinites and bivals. Close attention to the gravel works about has also detected several examples of Stigmaria Fecoides from the millstone grit, and a fine asteroid, apparently from the Silurian formation. A bed of sand from the red sandstone formation north has been washed on to the top of the High Wood, and the drift currents have also cast up in the same direction beds of gravel. What is very interesting, as illustrating the character of the glacial drift, is an extensive layer or bed of limestone lying at a little depth from the surface across the High Wood south of Uttoxeter, and deposited by a vast icefloe which had become stranded. Traces of it may be observed in a ditch, or rather antique British fosseway, by the side of a field a little south of the site of the old sandpit, now turfed over, near Balance Hill. It extends quite to the south edge of the High Wood. When in 1867 an attempt was made by the late Mr. Joseph Wilkins to obtain clay for brickmaking in a field there near to where the footpath from the High Wood joins the road to Scownslow Green, the bed of limestone was exposed and proved to have been deposited on a seam of grey clay. The great quantity of limestone pitched out fresh and sharp on the angles as if it had only then been dislodged from the rock, gave the place the singular aspect of a limestone quarry. The clay, being impregnated largely with carbonate of lime, proved worthless for brickmaking after much outlay had been expended on the enterprise, and the opening was re-filled with the limestone and clay and crumbling bricks, and re-turfed and deserted for its old purpose of pasturage. A large block of limestone, not less than a ton weight, lies, or rather appears to crop up, at the top of a field opposite the Farmers' Arms Inn, where it was left doubtless by a stranded iceberg. A smaller boulder appears at the bottom of the same field. Further interesting evidence of the glacial drift I observed in the spring of 1874, in a field north of Woodland Hall, where some draining was being carried on. A bed of pieces of sandstone lies there a little below the surface of the ground, and must have been conveyed to nearly the top of the hill in a block of ice from an outcrop of the new sandstone formation from probably the vicinity of Hollington, Alton, or Stanton, but most probably from the latter place.

The currents of the drift period have been considerably destructive of the marl in the vicinity of Uttoxeter, where there are now clay and beds of gravel, and the fine alluvium of the Dove valley. It remains, however, in the hills at each side the town, and in some places the rhœtic beds crop out from underneath it, and it also survives in Uttoxeter High Wood capped although they are in many places with gravel, sand, and clay and other *debris* of larger dimensions from early formations. A drift current has evidently proved almost effective in producing a channel at the west side of the High Wood southward, and after eddying, whirling and eroding for a long period, it left the landscape there as we now find it, consisting of numerous little hills resembling great tumuli, and finally the Dove Valley became scooped out, and from then till now has formed the oscillating watershed for a long period, of many hills and valleys which communicate with it. It is interesting to observe how precipitous the tertiary formation has been left at Eaton Banks, and also at the opposite side of the river Dove more south at Rough Cliff, at Woodford, and also in an interesting outlier some miles south-west of Sudbury.

The tertiary formation south of Uttoxeter has afforded an interesting fossil in the form of a tusk of the probosidian tribe. It was discovered beneath a bed of marl twenty feet in thickness during the process of an attempt to sink a well at Birch Cross, and it lay in what was described as a boggy sediment having the appearance of ink. The whole of the fossil animal lay entombed at the spot, but only the tusk, which is preserved by Mr. Hall, at Birch Cross, was obtained, and that only by being wrenched off by a horse and chain. The apparent futility of further trying to find water, and the danger to the house on any attempt being made to enlarge the space excavated for the well, rendered it necessary to leave the other part of the fossil in its primitive grave. The tusk is exactly 4 feet 2 inches in length, and $10\frac{1}{2}$ inches in circumference. About four inches have been broken from each end of the tusk, and some of the concentric circles have come off by exposure to the atmosphere. Its large size, concentric formation, weight, and slight curveture, indicate it to be probably the tusk of a mastodon. On being found it was covered with pyrites

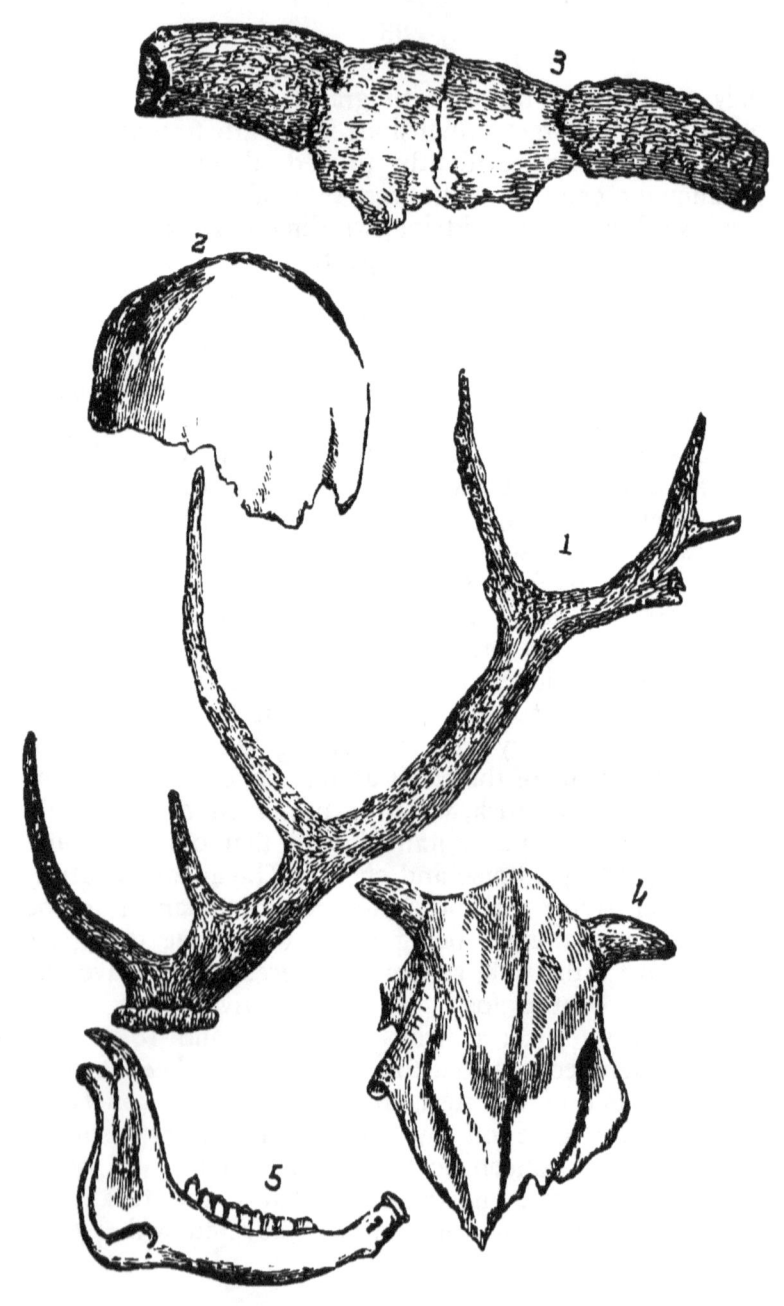

of iron. The late Mr. T. Bateman, of Youlgrave, to whom I sent an account of the fossil, was of opinion that it was a tusk of a mastodon, or Asiatic elephant, and, if so, was of greater antiquity than the remains usually found in bogs or near watercourses. He regarded its beautiful metallic appearance as singular, as it is more generally found upon fossils of the eocene, the lower tertiary, and the oolite days. I have myself met with the larger portion of the bones of the Irish elk in Uttoxeter High Wood at a depth of some 20 feet in the marl, and the antlers and head still remain there out of my reach.

The valley of the Dove and other alluvium or post-tertiary accumulations in the neighbourhood of Uttoxeter, contain and have yielded remains of much interest. At Rocester and Eaton antlers of deer have been found, as well as at Waldley near the brook there. A similar find has been made at Marchington. The floor on which the alluvium rests in the Dove valley appears from openings in various places to be strewed with leaves, hazelnuts and birchwood, and if the whole could be stripped off a truly surprising scene of extinct forms and early remains would probably be revealed. An example of the more interesting scenes which might be expected to present themselves was brought to light at the Eyes, Sudbury, in 1855, in the course of a new cutting for the river Dove being executed by Lord Vernon. At a depth of about six feet two trunks of bog oak, a fine antler, and skulls of the *Bos longifrous*, and the *Bos primigenus* were found; but what was more interesting still the discovery was made of a human skull having every appearance of being that of a female. The skull has been the subject of much comment by ethnologists, and the supposition expressed by myself in the First Edition of this book that it was Scandinavian, is confirmed by what has been said about it by Professor Huxley. In the alluvium at Marchington some years ago Mr. Sumner, in the course of some deep draining, came upon a large deposit of fresh water shells and large bones, of which, however, no specimens were preserved. Bog oak has been found near Rough Cliff, as well as in other places mentioned.

This slight reference to the surface geology of the neighbourhood of Uttoxeter cannot be dismissed without some regard being had to the oft-repeated belief that the district at an inconsiderable depth would yield a supply of coal. The ideas upon the subject have, however, for the most part been drawn from grounds which allow no such inferences. Some have supposed that thin layers of shale which are observed in one or two places, are the feather-edge, so to speak, of the outcrop of a coal formation; and very insufficient knowledge has been the cause of inducing others to infer that the locality was coal yielding simply on account of fragments of coal presenting themselves often when wells have occasionally been sunk, when, really, they ought only to have been regarded as evidence of having been conveyed from some distant outcrop of coal during the drift period. The opinion of Professor Ramsay expressed in a geological lecture which he delivered at Dudley in 1872, is more scientific in its nature, although it remains unconfirmed through the lack of sufficient enterprise. The professor stated that he should not feel the slightest hesitation in recommending a search for coal north-east of Cannock Chase; and in the neighbourhood of Uttoxeter, his belief in the presence of coal at a workable depth was equally strong, although nothing effectual has been accomplished. Efforts, stimulated by the above circumstances, have been attempted to test whether the vicinity of Uttoxeter is coalbearing, but they fell through for the want of sufficient funds. Mr. W. Vernon sunk a shaft to some depth on his land close on the north extremity of Rough Cliff, and he also bored in another part of the same property with the hope of meeting with indications of coal, but unfortunately he stopped vastly short of the necessary endeavour to in any degree test the important question. He did not get beneath the rock marl which lies there near the surface. A more serious attempt to sink a shaft for coal near Quee Lane, three miles south-west of Uttoxeter, was subsequently made about 1875. A shaft was constructed to a depth of fifty yards and bricked, and an endeavour was made to form a company with a capital of £10,000 in 1,000 shares of £10 each, to secure, if possible, the completion of the undertaking. The response to the circular issued to the public to take shares would appear to have been too limited to encourage any further prosecution of the design, and, after much anxiety, it also was abandoned, and for the present any intentions to obtain coal in the neighbourhood of Uttoxeter lie in abeyance. It is likely, too, that they will so long remain, if the opinion is correct that it would require a capital of some £80,000 or more, as stated by Mr. Cherry, F.G.S., to reach the coal measures underneath Uttoxeter. Of course, a boring experiment might be attempted for a few thousand pounds.

Numerous mineral springs exist near Uttoxeter. Penny-croft Well, Maiden's Wall Well, and Moat Spring are sulphurous, and the latter, which is situated in a boggy plantation near Buttermilk Hill, was formerly utilized as a bath, and bath buildings existed near the place on the rising ground opposite. A spring at the bottom of Pinfold Lane, on the premises of Messrs. Crichlow, is chalybeate, or contains iron; another near Draycot Mill is saline; one at Hanbury is vitriolic, and another at Draycot is alluminous. The character of some of these springs may be accounted for by being in the vicinity of gypsum beds.

CHAPTER II.

THE CELTIC, ROMANO-BRITISH, AND ANGLO-SAXON PERIODS.

> And this, then, is the place where Romans trod,
> Where the stern soldier revell'd in his camp,
> Where naked Britons fixed their wild abode,
> And lawless Saxons paced with warlike tramp.
>   JOHN BOLTON ROGERSON.

It has been common for topographical writers to express suspicion only that Uttoxeter was a British settlement before the Roman occupation of this island, but no one has yet attempted to furnish any information or reason in support of such a supposition. Of course there is no historical evidence to be had in its confirmation; but, at the same time, various interesting circumstances may be advanced which strongly favour it, and the researches and discoveries I have made and am about to relate will, it is hoped, add confirmation to the correctness of such an idea. The tribe which dwelt in this territory, according to Ptolemy, were the Cornavii, a term meaning "holy district or country of the priesthood," and strikingly indicative of the general prevalence of Druidical practices for which the then abounding woods and forests, in which they took place, and in which Strabo says they had their fortifications, were so favourable. The Cangi, or Woodlanders, who were herdsmen of this tribe, inhabited Cannock Chase, which, it is affirmed, joined Needwood Forest and extended even to the banks of the Dove.* So that it may reasonably be supposed that for the advantage of their flocks and herds of the extensive pasturage by the Dove, they would select so tempting a spot as Uttoxeter as the site of their residences in such huts as they erected.

However, there is decisive evidence both of the existence of the ancient Britons in the neighbourhood of Uttoxeter, and also of the observance of Druidical rites. These facts not only strengthen the likelihood of Uttoxeter having been a settlement of this ancient people, but are of considerable importance and invest the place with such interest, though in a smaller degree, as is possessed by the more imposing Celtic remains in the Peak of Derbyshire, and the relics of a similar nature in other parts. Toot Hill, on Uttoxeter High Wood, has associations of a similar interesting character, although it has only till now been mentioned as, probably, a Roman tumulus, or a place where Saxon Kings, or soldiers killed under Cromwell during the Civil War, were buried.

The name of Toot Hill implies that it was dedicated to the Celtic deity, Teutates, as an altar. At Petra, where he was worshipped, there was a tumulus as an altar, instead of a statue, to him. The name of this heathenish god is derived from De Tath or Deus Taautus. Tot, Toot, or Teut, is an Ætheopic word, signifying dog-star, and it is supposed that the Toth of Egypt, deified in the dog-star, was transferred to the Phœnicians who derived their astronomical knowledge from Egypt. The Phœnicians carried on commercial transactions with the island, particularly in tin, and it has been observed that the superstitious worship of this Deity was left by them amongst the barbarous islanders. At the same time the Druidic rites of the Celts have been accounted for as having been preserved amongst them from their common origin in the east. It has also even been surmised that some Egyptians had become established amongst them as among other rude nations, and had thus given a peculiar

---

* Whittaker's History of Manchester.

Egyptian character to the Druidic rites of this distant island. Stukely, in his "Stonehenge Described," conceives that the Druids came here from the east in the time of Abraham. * The chronological accounts fix the arrival of the Celts in Britain about one thousand six hundred years before the Christian era, and their migration across the Bosphorus and spread over the western parts of the old world upwards of two thousand years before Christ, or about the time when Abraham is supposed to have lived. The same heathenish deity was worshipped by the Greeks under the name of Hermes, and by the Romans as Mercury. †

Each of the fabled gods had offices assigned to him peculiar to himself. Teutates, amongst the Britons, was regarded as the god of messengers and travellers. The tumuli which were dedicated to him, as Toot Hill was on Uttoxeter High Wood, stood on elevated and precipitous places. The reason of this was, as Cæsar relates, that travellers might have guidance and protection along the roads and trackways, and become prosperous in their commercial enterprises.

On Toot Hill, as on all such eminences in the kingdom, the sacred, or Beltine fires, were kindled, and flamed thrice a year at the great festivities of the Druids, in honour of Baal, or the sun. One of a prodigious character was lit on May Eve on these hills, and produced a remarkable light over the whole country. Fires were again made on Midsummer Eve, and on the Eve of the 1st of November. The last was accompanied with sacrifices and festivities. On this day the people of the country, out of a religious sentiment inculcated by the Druids, completely extinguished their fires to re-kindle them the same eve, for the ensuing year, by a portion of the consecrated fire from the sacred altars. This was a duty which the head of every family was rigidly obliged to observe, and it was expected that by such observance

---

* Stonehenge described by Dr. Stukely.
† See Holwell's Mythological Dictionary on Toth, 1793.

good luck and prosperity would attend them till the return of the eve of the next 1st of November. For the privilege of obtaining the use of this holy fire, they had, it is stated, to pay an annual due to the Druids, which if they omitted to discharge by the last day of October ensuing, they had no prospect than to live without fire through the winter. No neighbour was permitted to give them any, or allow them the use of theirs—if they did, it was at the risk of excommunication, a fate, as ordained by this religious priesthood, worse than death.

At the sacred fires on the 1st of November it was customary for some person of distinction to take in his hands the entrails of the animal sacrificed, and walking barefoot over the coals thrice, carry them to the Druid who waited at the altar dressed in a whole skin. If he passed through the ordeal unhurt it was considered a favourable omen, and he was applauded; if otherwise, it was received as an augury of calamity to the whole community. The Midsummer fire and sacrifices were for the purpose of obtaining a blessing on the fruits of the earth now becoming ready for a gathering, as were those on the 1st of May that they might grow prosperously. Those of the last of October were a thank-offering for finishing the harvest. *

From Hollingbury being situated close to Toot Hill, it is not improbable that it took its name from another hill or altar dedicated to Belanus or Baal. This is the name under which the Celts worshipped the sun, and the worship of Tutates was generally united with it. In another part of the country there is a hill called Hilbury Hill contiguous to Toot Hill. Indeed, in the survey of Uttoxeter, taken prior to 1658 by Peter Lightfoot, physician, it is in one place called Hilbury or Hollingbury, indifferently. There are several mentions, moreover, of a Hollin Hall in descriptions of land on the High Wood as in the following instances:—"One tenement and barn and one close adjoining to the High Wood against Hollin Hall,"

---

* Toland's History of the Druids. Hones' Every-day Book.

and "One tenement and two closes adjoining to the High Wood and the lane over against Hollin Hall." These references without the slightest doubt are to Hollingbury Hall, and there may have been, as in other instances, an altar there to Belanus.

In the name of Ashcroft, a field near the High Fields, in a direct line with the High Wood, is also indicated another place of Druid worship. The Ash was a tree sacred to the Druids. In the most ancient of languages the word ash signifies fire, and the remnants of fires are to this day called ashes, and, therefore, the places where these fires, made chiefly of Ash, were kept, and have ash in the prefix of the name, as in Ashketons, and Ashfield, they may properly be concluded to be sites where these ancient rites were observed. There is also a meadow near Uttoxeter, which anciently bore the name of Beale or Bean meadow, but now only the latter, which may suggest the still greater prevalence in the neighbourhood of Uttoxeter, of the worship of Baal.

The doctrines of the Druids, out of which arose their rites just described, although the account may appear somewhat too favourable, have been remarked upon * as more refined and rational in their nature than those of most other religious bodies. They taught the immortality of the soul and a future state of rewards and punishment. Their morality was at once mild and strict, and their denunciation of the sins they specified was unremitting; but their opinions of the Deity were vague and erroneous. They had an imperfect perception of one pervading essence which revelation teaches Christians to worship under the name of God, but they worshipped the sun as a personification of His power, and used fire as an emblem of His nature in their worship; besides, they did not regard the Divinity as a being of such stainless purity as we reverence; still, this species of Baal worship— which originated in the East, where God himself, according to Scripture, (Hosea, c. ii, v. 16) was at one period

---

* Ireland illustrated.

worshipped under the name of Baal—was infinitely superior in simple and lofty truth to that of the Greeks and Romans. In course of time it became corrupted by teaching a plurality of gods. In many parts of the United Kingdom vestiges of the rites of the Druids may still be traced.

Having described some of the Druidical customs with which Toot Hill has been associated—on which indeed they have taken place—it only remains to be mentioned as a place of Sepulchre. Various modes of burial, very different to those in use at present, have been practised in times past. Some times Sepulchres assumed the character of vast barrows, as the Pyramids of Egypt; as the grave of Semiramis, upon which, as amongst the Etruscans, art and wealth were lavished without restriction. The tumuli, or loose tombs—meaning graves, which exist as artificial hills, are numerous in this kingdom, and many of them have been raised at the expense of much labour and time. They are chiefly of Celtic formation, but they have often been taken advantage of by the Romans and Anglo-Saxons for places of Sepulchre for themselves. * Toot Hill, as its name and associations show, is a Celtic grave-hill, and its somewhat oval form may indicate it to be of the most ancient type, and in age perhaps coeval with the Pyramids themselves. Having obtained permission to open it in May, 1860, I secured the aid of a man for a considerable part of one day, starting very early to the interesting research. I found myself from very early usage, a tolerable adept at the work both with the pick and spade. On the second day I employed two men to assist me, and we spent about three parts of the day in further digging into the mound. On the first occasion I opened it in two places in the centre, and also in two at the East end. At the base of the tumulus, in all those openings, I came across a bed of charcoal. I also discovered a piece of Roman pottery,

---

* Ten years' diggings in Celtic and Saxon Gravehills by T. Bateman, Esq., F.S.A.

at a depth of two feet, in one of the openings at the East end, it being part of a Roman Urn in Castor ware, of the form here represented, and interesting

ROMAN URN.

as showing that in this barrow interments of various periods have been made.

In the subsequent attempt I resolved upon cutting a trench nearly through the tumulus, beginning at the East end of it. In this opening, about ten feet below the surface, the layer of charcoal, of which I have before spoken, again presented itself, in an opening in the centre unaccompanied by any remains. In commencing the long trench, and about four yards from its outer extremity, a stone about eight pounds in weight was found lying at the South side of a small heap of human remains burnt to ashes, and from an appearance around them it is not unlikely they had been deposited in a cloth or skin. There was not a particle of soil mingled with them. They were about four feet below the surface. Exactly beneath these ashes on the floor of the tumulus, pieces of calcined bone, charcoal, and some portions of a Celtic cinerary urn of the type usually found in the Derbyshire and Staffordshire barrows, as shown in the engraving, were met with.

CELTIC URN.

I also found some pieces of yellow and red ochre and several flakes of flint, which might not have had any connection with the mound as a barrow.

The soil at the top of Toot Hill presents strong evidence of Beltine fires having been lit upon it, as, for about two inches in depth, the soil is burnt to redness all over its surface. The Eastern extremity of the barrow consists of a light loamy soil, whilst the rest portion of it is extremely firm, it being stiff gravelly clay. This is the more antique part of the tumulus, the other having doubtless been added at a subsequent period—probably during the Roman period, as in it I met with the portion of the Roman urn—and adding to its oval appearance.

The extent of Toot Hill at the base is about seventy feet by sixty-eight, and its height from seven to nine feet. The place overlooks the valley of the Dove, and was formerly in the depth of Uttoxeter ward of the Forest of Needwood. A number of trees are growing upon it, and it used to be enclosed with a holly fence.

Brends, the name formerly of land in the moor of Uttoxeter, may indicate the heathenish rite of interment by cremation. The name is probably derived from *brent*, meaning *burnt*.

Some time after opening Toot Hill on Uttoxeter High Wood, I explored another barrow on the property of the late John Beech, Esq., at the Old Wood, north of Uttoxeter. The opening of this took place on the 4th of July, 1863. The mound is situated on an elevated part of a field close to Old Wood farmhouse, and a hedge and ditch have been carried across its eastern margin. They were probably made when the land was enclosed from an extensive park, which was known as Madeley Park, and which, it is said, had belonged to the Foljambes. The barrow commences on the brow of the hill, on the north side, at about five feet deep, and it continues that depth part way along its western side, and then gradually diminishes in depth towards the south, until its outline is almost lost. I thought the best way of exploring the mound would be by taking a cutting, about six feet wide, across its middle. This I did, beginning on the northern and deepest part with the cutting. I felt doubtful whether I was dealing with a barrow, until I came to a slight sprinkling of charcoal, which at the north side lay about five feet beneath the surface. I kept the depth with which I started through the whole opening, but the layer of wood ashes gradually sloped upwards, thereby showing the natural surface of the hill to within a foot of the present surface of the barrow, and disappeared entirely a little way beyond its centre. My labours failed to bring me upon any interment. Within a few inches from the surface, about the middle, I, however, met with a fragment of a smooth tapering flint with bevelled edges, not serrated, which was burnt nearly to whiteness. I also, on replacing the turf, found part of a flint knife, which had been dug out near to where the other flint lay. By the layer of charcoal sloping to the surface, I think it is clear that a great part of the barrow had been destroyed.

Whilst proceeding with the work I obtained a clue to associations investing the mound having an interest beyond those it claims by being a barrow. Some of the children of Mr. Marson, occupier of the land, came to me to see what extraordinary work was going on, and one of them, now grown to womanhood, playfully asked me if I could run down "Toot'el Field." I exclaimed, "What field is that?" "Why," she replied, "this field." I was convinced that the field took its name from the mound, and that it should be named "Toot Hill," though I had not heard it called so; and I found, on enquiry, that it was supposed to be such, and this was confirmed subsequently by a perusal of a plan of that and adjoining property.

This Toot Hill is in a very elevated place, and its name-sake on Uttoxeter High Wood is observable directly south from it, and the scenery around for a great distance is of the most charming description.

I have already given the derivation of "Toot," but I will here add that the great prototype of this fabled deity is supposed to have existed far back in the darkness of time, and in antediluvian days, and that he was the erector of engraved pillars, one of which was standing in the time of Josephus, after having survived the Deluge, and that they preserved a knowledge of human and divine things, particularly of astronomy, and the great moral mystery of the world and its Maker. They are supposed to have been erected in Egypt by the descendants of Seth; and Syriad, the place where the historian saw one of the stones being rendered Osiris, or Sirius, favours the supposition. They are spoken of in the Book of Judges as "quarries," meaning graven stones. It is supposed that Pythagorus derived his knowledge of astronomy, and of the doctrine of immortality, from the inscriptions on these stones, veiled though they were in hieroglyphics; and that it is the sublime morality which they taught which lives in the writings of Plato to this day. *

---

* "Hermes Britannicus," by the Rev. W. L. Bowles.

Until the church was erected at Stramshall a tumulus stood on the open space opposite to where the spring is at the side of the church yard, and in 1860, one of considerable extent in a field at Moreton, near Houndhill, was partially destroyed, the soil being spread on the land. Some fragments of bone and a corroded piece of iron were brought to me from it, and I personally saw a considerable sprinkling of charcoal in the soil. There is also a tumulus at Lea Hill, Doveridge, having the name of fairy-ring. Its elevation, however, is but slight. An immense tumulus, infested with rabbits, exists close to Uttoxeter at the Moorhouse, it being about one hundred and twenty yards in circumference and ten feet in height. In the field immediately south of that containing the barrow, are also two interesting remains which have the appearance of hut-circles, in which, if so, there were dwellings of British erection. They are but a short distance from each other, are each twelve yards across, and are separately surrounded by a ditch about a yard and a half wide and nearly two feet deep. The edges of the remains are about two feet higher than the level of the land, but there is a depression in them deepening to the centre, rendering them concave or dish-shaped. Both places have trees growing upon them, and they are as much like each other as possible. From near the circles a deep fosseway proceeds up the ground in the direction of Woodland Hall, and at the lower part of the field adjoining the lane conducting to the house, the old way branches at a great depth in two directions to nearly the centre of the field where they slope out on to the elevated land. I do not know that any opinion can be formed of them except that they are British ways which conducted to the hut-circles and the Dove land, from the then frowning woods which covered the elevated parts of the district.

On November 28th, 1868, I opened a barrow in the Dale Field near Eaton Banks in the occupation of the late John Mynors, Esquire. The mound is not very large, and it had no reputation of being a barrow. It had been avoided by the plough at an early period, and that circumstance induced me to believe that it had been held in special regard on some account. On digging into it, the loaminess of the soil and fragments of charcoal convinced me that it was a barrow, and I subsequently found a piece of chipped flint, a small arrow flint point, and also an article of a more recent period in the form of a Saxon fibula. Owing to a defective spade I was unable to complete on this date the undertaking, which I resumed in March, 1870, when I met with a flint of larger dimensions, but of what class I am unable to determine, unless it was used to bore with. The Rev. Mr. Kerry calls it a scraper. It was certainly worked to a point which is broken off. The barrow cannot be more appropriately named than as Dale Field barrow.

On December 3rd, 1868, I proceeded to open a large mound in front of Loxley Hall at the top of the Park. Some fine elms grow round it, and it appeared a tempting object to the explorer of Celtic grave hills. Another large mound exists not more than thirty yards from it in " the Long Walk," and is known by writings not to have been there more than about sixty years in 1868. After some hard work in what had more the appearance of baked clay and gravel than anything else, and only meeting with traces of what was modern, I left the mound as a monument of recent date, and as not likely to afford any object to illustrate the early antiquities of this neighbourhood, and deemed it from its form an archery butt.

A very interesting discovery was made at the gravel pit at the Yelts, Doveridge, in 1869. On dislodging gravel from the face of the pit, the workmen broke into a cist in gravel containing two cinerary urns with only a slight mound of earth raised over them on the natural surface of the land. The urns were very much injured by water which had drained upon them through the gravel, and not being prized by anyone then cognizant of their discovery, they were placed in the garden of Mr. Oakden, of the Yelt's Farm, and there, in consequence of only being sun-dried, became totally destroyed by the action of the weather. The vessels were ornamented with the usual chevron pattern. It is of rare occurrence that cists are found containing urns beneath the base of Celtic barrows, as mostly the interments, with their accompaniments, are placed at the base, or high up in the mound itself. On the 26th of October, 1871, I opened a mound, supposed to have been a barrow, in a low-lying meadow west of the Yelt's farmhouse, but I discovered nothing in it except fragments of burnt sandstone and bits of mortar, and much of the soil had a black sooty look, but nothing appeared of a pre-historic age, or to indicate that the place had been used for funereal purposes.

On Saturday, July 29th, 1876, permission was accorded to me by W. Philips, Esq., of Heybridge, to open a barrow at Lower Tean, when the members of the archæological section of the North Staffordshire Naturalist Field Club assembled to witness the exploration. The mound is nearly eight feet in depth, and round the outside of the ditch with which it is encircled, it measures sixty-seven spaces. The south side of the elevation appears not to have been completed on some account, for it cannot be supposed that the unfinished state of the barrow is an appearance produced by the soil having been taken away. A trench was cut through the centre of the tumulus seven feet wide, and in the course of the proceedings six worked flints were discovered. These were probably cast into the barrow at the time it was raised, and intended, perhaps, as tributes of affection to the memory of the individual who was primarily interred there. Several of the flints may be flint chips, two or three arrow heads with perhaps a scraper. On further exploration on a subsequent date, several other flint articles were found, including a portion of a flint saw. The first object discovered was a portion of a rudely formed ring in jet. No human remains, except a tooth of perhaps a female, but certainly not of an old person, were met with. I present views of two of the flint articles—an arrow head and a flint chip which resembles some of the finest found in Denmark.

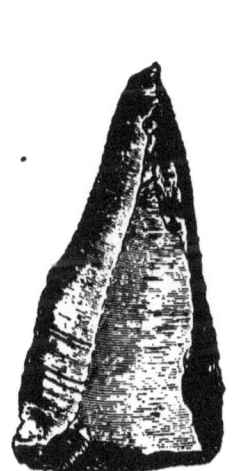

FLINTS.

There is the appearance of a barrow of not large dimensions in a croft in the rear of the house and garden of A. A. Welby, Esq., of Doveridge, on which trees are growing. There is a very large one overlooking the weir in the bend of the river Churnet. It can be seen from the carriage drive to Alton from the Quixhill Lodge, and there is also one not far from the farmhouse in Alton Park.

A flint of the Paleolithic period was found in Marchington Woodlands some years ago, and is in the collection of the late Mr. Molyneaux. It is a perforated flint, and was probably used as an amulet. A flint,

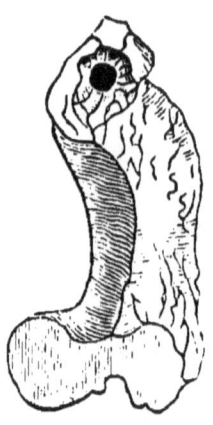

AMULET.

which might be designated a skinner of the same period was found in 1879 at Somershall, and presented to me by F. Bott, Esq. A portion has been worked out of it for the thumb, and is left smooth.

I have an arrow point which I found in the cemetery, a small flint which I found near Gorsty Hill, and a small peculiar flint from the surface soil at Mount Pleasant, all of the early period.

In the year 1878 a fine polished celt was found in the Dove Valley, near Ellastone, and by the kind permission of Captain Duncombe, of Calwich Abbey, to whom it belongs, I have had an engraving made which faithfully represents it on a reduced scale. Its size is seven inches in length by one inch and three quarters at

the widest end and tapering to about half an inch at the
end which would be in the wood haft in which it was

DOVE VALLEY CELT.

used. It is especially interesting in having a bevelled
edge similar to an axe or iron chisel. It is, of course, of
the neolithic period. Of the same age is a very interesting
celt which was found near Leigh by Mr. Garle, of Green-
snips. It is not in flint, but in a hard gritty stone, rubbed
smooth, and it has the rare, perhaps unique peculiarity, of

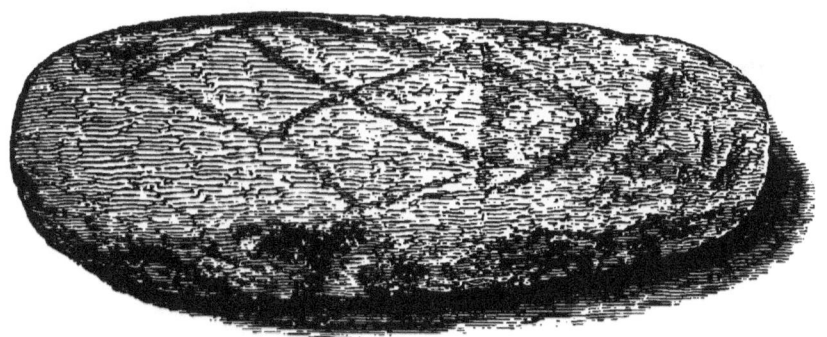

LEIGH CELT.

having upon it a portion of Celtic ornamentation. This
celt is seven inches long, two and a half inches across
the widest end, and two inches wide at the opposite
extremity. It appears to have been calcined. I possess

a finer flint weapon of the same class and period, but less polished, found in 1880 on the Alton estate, near the moat in Ribden, otherwise the moated tumulus there. The dimensions of the celt are six and a half inches in length; two and five-eighths in the widest part, and one and three-quarters at the narrowest end.

A fine stone axe was found in Sudbury Park in 1870. It is made out of marlstone or the lower oolite rock. It was shown at a meeting of the Midland Scientific Association soon after its discovery. I possess a stone hammer head from the Dove Valley south of Uttoxeter. It has had some bad usage, but it is of the form of one found in Dorsetshire and figured in the "Leisure Hour" for November, 1876, except that the perforation for the haft is nearer the narrower expanded end. Another interesting and very rare object of this period in my possession is an egg-shaped article made out of a quartz pebble and found at Marstone, near to Uttoxeter, it being probably a Celtic symbol of time and eternity. I also possess a peculiar article in stone of the same age found at Uttoxeter. Its length is three inches by a width of one-eighth under an inch. It is smooth and is worked from each side to a blunt point at one end. The other extremity has a diagonal slope on one side only, and through the centre of this is a perforation, and its form indicates that it must have been intended to have been fixed in a haft, unless its purpose was to be worn as a charm. The ensuing is an engraved view of the object.

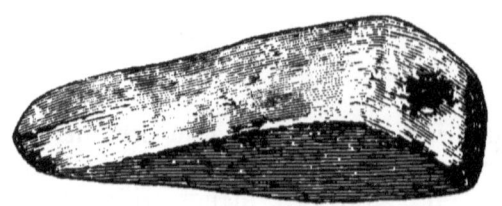

AMULET OR CELT OF UNIQUE FORM.

The neighbourhood of Uttoxeter has yielded a number of celts in bronze. These belong to the bronze age which immediately succeeded the neolithic, or new stone age, although the latter might overlap the bronze age as no doubt the manufacture of Paleothic implements overlapped the polished stone age. The oldest form of bronze celt is axe-shaped, one of which, now in my possession, was found at Somershall, and is here engraved. It is five inches in length and two and three-quarter inches across the edge, and weighs seven ounces.

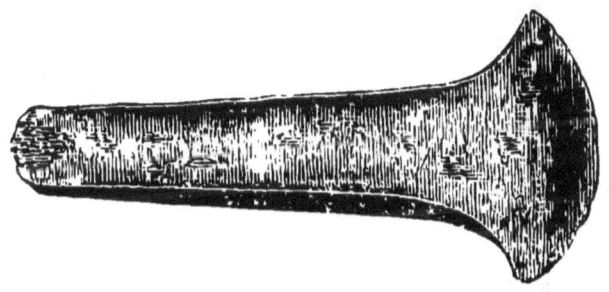

AXE-SHAPED CELT.

Another form of bronze celt, which I possess, and which has received the designation of angarm celt, was also discovered near to the same place. An engraving of it is given. Its length is five and a half inches, and two

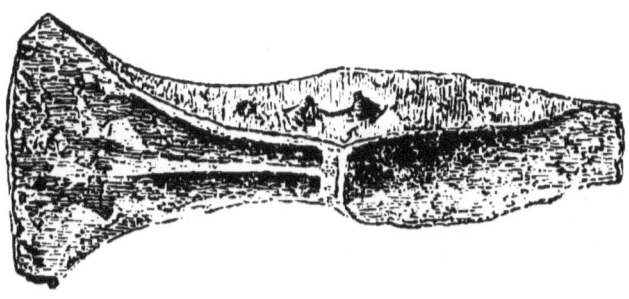

ANGARM CELT.

and a quarter inches across the edge. Its weight is nine ounce and three quarters. Another of exactly the same type, but finer in consequence of having been less used, was found near Swilcar oak, and was in the collection of the late John F. Lucas, Esq., of Bentley Hall. Another precisely similar was also found in the same district, and was in the collection of the late Mr. Molyneaux.

But I have a much finer bronze celt than any of those just specified, inasmuch as that it is over six inches in length and bears Celtic ornamentation. It was met with in the neighbourhood of Uttoxeter. The loop at the side by which it was fastened by thongs to its haft remains perfect. I present a sketch of it.

VIEW OF THE ORNAMENTED CELT.

These facts and the antiquities enumerated and only collected together during many years of incessant vigilance sufficiently attest the early and long settlement of the Britons in the vicinity of Uttoxeter. I know of no monoliths existing of the rude stone period nearer to Uttoxeter than Caldon Low, where there is an interesting one, not before mentioned anywhere, in a meadow, having the name of Offtman's or Hofton's Cross. It is a large unhewn stone marking evidently the site of an early interment on its south side.

Amongst objects in Nature, associated probably with Celtic times, is a remarkably antique oak known as " The Gospel Oak," at Hoar Cross, by the road side, midway of Hoar Cross village and Yoxall, at which, until Hoar Cross Church was recently built, funerals halted and set down the deceased, on their being conveyed to Yoxall Church for interment. With respect to a similar oak and custom near Penallt Church, Monmouth, Roscoe states. " Here is an evident continuation of the oak of Druidic and Celtic custom altered into Christian forms." This oak at Hoar Cross seems also to have been one of the Copt Oaks with the top cut off to admit of a cross piece of wood being fastened at the apex to render the tree an object of Celtic worship. The circumference of the oak at the base is about 32 feet. It is only recently it has been enclosed from the road side.

In 1870 I found what proves to be an interesting relic in the vicinity of Maiden's Wall Well, on Uttoxeter High Wood. Before attempting to introduce any notice of the object in these pages, I submitted it to the inspection of three gentlemen for their opinion upon it. Mr. Fradgley, architect, and the late Mr. Lucas, of Bentley Hall, deemed it to be of great antiquity, and the Rev. Mr. Kerry, of Puttenham, has not hesitated to declare it to be a portion of a Runic stone bearing Ogham characters. The stone itself is a piece of sonorous and dark tuff, probably from Andernach on the Rhine. Ogham letters are merely straight strokes arranged in groups along a line, as in the instance on this fragment, and mostly contain the name of the person in whose honour such stones were erected. * This antiquity is not, of course, so early as of the British period.

---

* See " Prehistoric Times " by Sir John Lubbock.

ROMANO-BRITISH PERIOD.

By discoveries which I have made, and purpose immediately to describe, it would appear that Uttoxeter and its neighbourhood are identified in a most important and interesting way with the Roman occupation of Britain, a fact which has hitherto been a subject of uncertainty and conjecture only. Erdeswick, the earliest writer of any consequence on the topography of Staffordshire, merely expressed his belief that Uttoxeter was a Roman station because it is situated about twelve miles east of Mere, which is a mistake, it being that distance nearly south-east; and Camden, on no better grounds, endeavoured to show that Uttoxeter was the Etocetum of Antoninus, a highly interesting circumstance if it could be clearly demonstrated, although he asserted Uttoxeter was a Saxon name. Whether Etocetum is at Uttoxeter or at Wall, near Lichfield, as is contrariwise also stated, I am unable to say, and must be content with relating what I have discovered, and leave suppositions to others better able than myself to work them out.

Arguing on the name of Uttoxeter, a gentleman, W. R. Holland, Esq., of Ashbourne, who resided a considerable time at Lichfield, writes to me as follows :—" I always connected Uttoxeter with Etocetum *said* to be near Lichfield at Wall, the next parish to which is Chesterfield. I cannot help thinking that Uttoxeter was Etocetum, or was named from it in some way. The root of the name would probably be Etox—perhaps a British word—the *etum* being a mere Latin termination, and the Etox would be pronounced Etok. To this add *cester*, Etoxcester, Ettoxcester, Uttoxeter. Compare the known case of Wroxeter to show how the *x* is arrived at. The Latin name was Uriconium. Drop the Latin termination, *onium*, and you have Urex. Add *cester*, and you have Urikcester,

Urixcester. Drop the *s*, and Urixeter, Uroxeter would ensue. I could follow out this analogy in lots of names —even York, Latin *Eberacum;* drop the *um*—Eborak, Evorak, Evork, York. The termination *eter*, at all events, I feel certain, is from *cestre*, *cester*, or *ceaster*, the Saxon form of *castrum*. The *s* is dropped in all words of this kind in the pronunciation, although retained in the spelling, unless the accent is on the syllable, as in Chester,—witness Rocester, Worcester, Gloucester, &c." These remarks, made in an endeavour to fix Etocetum at Uttoxeter, although I adhere to the derivation of the name I have previously attempted, are very valuable, and outweigh any other endeavours I am acquainted with to associate Uttoxeter with the Etocetum of Antoninus. But at least, judging from the termination of the name of the town as it appears in Doomsday Book, and in old writings, it may, under any circumstances, be confidently asserted that there was a Roman station at Uttoxeter, and in confirmation of that view the explanation of the word *caster* by Verstegan may be deemed conclusive. "This *caster*," he states, "is no ancient Saxon word, though found in Saxon writings; it is rather borrowed from the Latin word castrum, betokening a castle, fortress, *caster*, *cœster*, or *ceter*, being the termination of many names of places in England, do signify all one thing, and the places having such terminations had castles or fortresses built by the Romans."

That, there was a Roman station at Uttoxeter, I think I am able to show beyond the mere fact of it being indicated in the name of the town. At least I can point to a site which must have been in occupation by a body of Roman colonists, military or otherwise, a considerable time, although I am not able to mention any remains of masonry in association with it. The spot to which I refer is situated on the North side of Bradley Street, in the rear of a large stuccoed house standing back from the street. It is bounded on the East side by the playground of Alleyne's Grammar School, and on the West by the National School premises and some gardens. The ground at the back of the residence mentioned, swelled to a considerable height, and it appeared desirable to reduce a large space in conjunction with other improvements it was intended to carry out, and the work was begun in the Summer of 1876. The undertaking, however, did not progress much till the close of Autumn, when a space of ground was excavated to the depth of four feet and carried over an extent of about twenty spaces square. Every day numerous fragments of Roman pottery were found, and large quantities of bones and charcoal were discovered mingling with the soil over the whole area. The potsherds lay at a depth of from two to four feet.

The fragments of pottery are, for the most part, of a rude description, and may be assigned to the third century. A few pieces of Upchurch ware are amongst the collection, and also fragments which have belonged to vessels made from the white clays of Shropshire, and consequently called Salopian ware. The bulk of the fragments of pottery found have a brown or light red exterior. Some portions of the pottery recovered from the site bear rude ornamentations, particularly the handles of vessels. Several of the handles are adorned with round and elongated punctures which pass to the opposite side, and in one instance diagonal lines have been incised across the hollow of a handle. On the tops of two or three fragments of rims of vessels wavy lines have been executed in imitation of more archaic forms of fictile ornamentation. There is a very nice piece on the top of one pitcher so decorated. A piece of a rim of another vessel has a fringe which has been produced by a finger being pressed against it all round when in a plastic state. A fragment of the lower portion of a pitcher is rudely ornamented by a finger having been pressed upon it at intervals. Another fragment is adorned by a blunt tool having been used to push the clay each way, and so leave a ridge with indentations at each side. Perhaps the most interesting piece is one on which a potter's mark appears in the form of a raised square in divisions, unless it is a portion of ornamentation not continued on the fragment. Some of the fragments of pottery belonged evidently to clay-cooking pots, and the greasy appearance has not yet departed from the fragments of other food vessels. Some of the pottery, white as chalk and nearly as soft, is covered with a greenish yellow glaze, and one such portion is striated.

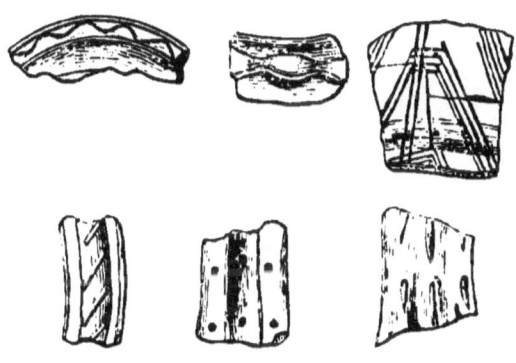

ROMAN POTTERY, UTTOXETER.

I cannot determine whether pottery in some primitive fashion was made on the spot, but there are reasons for supposing it might have been. A large quantity of grey clay lay in the soil in one place, and a portion which I found appears to have belonged to a large piece which had been subjected to flat ware mould pressing, but not carried through the entire process to make it into a complete vessel. It would appear that whilst it was in a moist state it was broken and flung aside.

In 1884, when new cellaring was being dug out for the Spread Eagle Inn, at Bear Hill, the neck of a bottle of Roman pottery, now in my possession, was met with. When deposited it would appear to have been full of liquid (wine), for the earth was quite black all about it. The other fragments of the vessel were not saved. I give small engravings of some of these fragments just to indicate their appearance.

The metallic articles found on the site in Bradley Street are not numerous. A portion of a bronze buckle was met with, and another metallic article recovered is a personal ornament, and possibly a portion of a fibula. It consists of two discs about half-an-inch across, and the ornamentation upon them resembles a Maltese Cross. This article, which is in copper or brass, has been enamelled or covered with a brilliant red paste, which has been nearly totally destroyed by the oxidation of the metal. There was also a personal ornament, broken from some other lost part, found in a white hard metal, bearing a geometrical design as well as a bronze button. At about four feet deep, and lying on the undisturbed gravel a piece of lead was found with a circular edge. A bronze handle of a Roman key was found in the Church Yard. All these articles are in my collection.

A fragment of a glazed stone vessel was also met with, it being a dark blue volcanic material, and used probably as the under part of a quern. One large and one or two small boar's tusks, probably used as ornaments, were also dug up, as well as pieces of corroded iron. I have found fragments of Roman pottery, including one bit of Samian ware only, over a space of more than seventy yards round; and some years ago a Roman coin was found on a cultivated part of the ground. At Dove Bank, not far from the place just spoken of as affording so much interesting evidence of Roman occupation, the greater portion of a little vessel of Roman pottery was dug up about the same time. Several large portions of a large Roman jar of Salopian ware were dug up close to Picknal Sane, in April, 1880. The whole of the relics are in my possession. But I have found fragments of Roman pottery in all parts of the town in gardens, the Cemetery, the Bank closes, and near the new junction.

There having been a Roman station at Uttoxeter, it is but natural to suppose that it was connected with other stations of varying degrees of importance by one of the Roman roads which traversed the province of Flavia Cæsariensis, whose head quarters was the famous Roman

City of Chester. It is generally allowed that this Roman way was the Rykeneld Street, or, as it is otherwise known, the Via Devana, or road to the town just named, and in the year, 1789, it was attempted to be traced from Leicester to Chesterton. It was found through Needwood Forest, and, it is stated, it was followed to within a mile South of Uttoxeter, and it has hitherto uniformly been said to have passed the town of Uttoxeter about a mile West of it, and not to have been traceable again except at Checkley and Tean. I have fragments of Roman pottery of my own discovery from Hanbury and Tutbury, referred to by Mr. Molyneaux, and from the vicinity of some cottages at Scropton lane end adjoining Tutbury, and I, for the first time, in a former edition of this work, pointed out that a Roman road passed through Tutbury, at the entrance of which interesting place from Burton, it gives the name " Portway Gardens," being itself the Portway, which probably proceeded through Fauld and along the deep and narrow old lane at Moreton. A " Portway-head " exists at Sudbury, and, in an old document relating to Dove Bridge, the way from Doveridge to Uttoxeter receives the name of Portway. A copy of this document will be perused with interest further on.

Before, however, proceeding further with the consideration of the direction of Roman ways near or at Uttoxeter, it may be useful to give some attention to their character. So far as my own observations go, I am led to state that they existed generally as fosseways whether they were used indifferently as great military ways or as provincial roads, and their origin is no doubt British. Such were some of the antique ways in Herefordshire, as described by the Rev. John Webb in his Memorials of the Civil Wars in that county. He speaks of them as " ditches," " narrow forest lanes," " antiquated hollow ways, deeper than the head of the horse or rider." The Wansdyke, from Bishop's Cannington in the direction of Bath, itself an old Roman way, has similar features—a high bank with a deep ditch. But I do not find the survival of the high bank or vallum, if that is meant, in connection with the deep fosseways in this neighbourhood except in one instance which will, in due course, be pointed out.

It is not for me to determine which of the old ways which converge upon Uttoxeter is the Rykeneld Street, but I think it will shortly be clear that it did not pass by the town so far West as has been stated. An old deep way, which may still be seen, proceeded from Moisty or Mister Lane near Marchington to Birch Cross, and the deep dyke accompanying the road through Marchington Woodlands, although it now forms the watershed of the land adjoining its course, has the reputation, as it has the appearance, of having been an old way in the direction of Uttoxeter. Until they were filled up large portions of the same fosseways existed at the side of the present road down the High Wood, and probably the part of the road extending between the two tollgates within a little distance of each other at the entrance to the town by the Brookhouse, is a short length of the same way now in use. Whether the name Maiden's Wall Well, which exists by the road side on Uttoxeter High Wood and Maiden Field is in any way illustrative of the ancient character of the road I dare not venture positively to determine, but as affording great probability to such a circumstance it may be mentioned that the fosseway along the great northern barrier, or Pict's Wall, is called Maiden Way. If such an interpretation is allowable, then it may indicate the way to be the Rykeneld Street, as the principal way, and it is interesting that the site of a Roman camp, about eighty spaces square, exists a little West of the Well, and comprises part of the Sand-pit Field in the rear of the red brick residence occupied by Mr. Wood. I have traced the outlines of three sides of it, and found several pieces of Roman pottery on the site of the place, as well as the bottom of an amphoræ, or leg of a skillet, in the Victoria Gardens near to. Whether High Street, or Old Street, which is the principal street in Uttoxeter, is a continuation of the same way, it would be difficult to say. But perhaps Portmantle Alley, forming a way close to the White Bear

Inn, and parallel, as far as it extends, with High Street, may be a name having an important meaning. I think the application of Port to the short passage or alley must be indicative of a portion of the Roman way. The late Mr. E. Brown, F.G.S., of Burton-on-Trent, traced a Roman road from Branstone, Burton-on-Trent, by Callingwood and probably by Newbrough, where a Roman coin has been found, and along Thorny Lane to Buttermilk Hill, which has been paved, and he contends that Etocetum was near to Uttoxeter South. I have examined the district thoroughly, however, but have not met with any surface evidence of any Roman town. It is not stated whether the road was found further in the direction of Uttoxeter, but it may be affirmed that either this way or the one previously referred to, must be the Rykeneld Street, and not the one followed in the last century through Needwood Forest to about a mile West of Uttoxeter, and what ensues will, I believe, confirm that idea. From the survey of Uttoxeter made, previous to 1658, by Peter Lightfoot, it is clear that the Rykeneld Street, under the names of Portway and Salter's Way, existed in the present Slade Lane emerging from High Street, or in its vicinity, although the designations have passed from all the parish books and plans or the parish now in use. Indeed Slade Lane, itself an ancient Saxon appellation, meaning narrow, is no doubt a part of the Via Devana, or Salter's Way. On first perusing the old survey, the names I have mentioned at once struck me on account of their undoubted interest. Still, there required a clue to the locality to which they are applied. After spending a considerable time in ascertaining what was meant by land, or fields, in "The Botham Field," "The Bromshulfe Field," "The Maiden Field," and other "fields," I came to the conclusion that the land on the South of Uttoxeter, went under the latter name, whilst that on the west had the name of Bromshulfe Field, and that on the North-East side of the town the name Botham Field. As certain fields in the Botham Field are stated in the survey to shoot or abut on, or adjoin the Portway, or Salter's Lane, I could arrive at no other conclusion but that Slade Lane was meant. Indeed the numbers of the plots of land under the heads of Portway and Salter's Lane, all lie along the course of Slade Lane, and Portway is mentioned some eight times in connection with the plots as in case of plot 33, "One little close adjoining the Portway." Plot 23 is described as at the lower mill, which existed in those days as a fulling-mill on the Tean brook, about midway of Uttoxeter corn mill and the cotton mill house, at the place called Bungalore. Other entries in which Portway occurs are as follows :—

 Plot 84. Another close shooting on the Portway.
 ,, 81. One little close shooting on the Portway.
 ,, 68. One close of pasture adjoining to the Portway.
 ,, 78. One close on the North side of the Portway.
 ,, 88. Two closes together near the Portway.
 ,, 79. One piece in close near the Portway.

I have stated that the lower mill was midway of Uttoxeter corn mill and the cotton mill house, now occupied by Mr. Povey, and Slade Lane makes directly for the spot. Plot 37, in which Portway occurs, is mentioned as lying by the Ashbourne way into which Slade Lane must have entered near Spath. The ancient road went up Stramshall, a most interesting place as we shall presently see, turning to the right at the church. After going some distance along this lane, which is really the Salter's Way, I find its old course only in fragments on either side of the present Hollington Road in slangs and pieces of fosseways, which are observable first on the right hand in several places, in one of which I saw some poplars growing (since cut down), and afterwards on the left or West side. At the right hand or East side of the road the fosse lies close to it, and where indications of the way appear on the West side of the lane, they occur just within the fields. These features continue on either side of the lane for a distance probably of a mile to what is called the Three Lane Ends where the Hollington Road bends slightly to the right. At this point a lane branches to the left, and another, a very modern one, called "Clay Lane," proceeds through the open fields to the High Farm House, now occupied by

Mr. W. Titley. This is the direction of the Salter's Way. The old fosseway exists just over the hedge at the right hand, close to the entrance of Clay Lane. It afterwards appears on the left hand side of the lane, where it causes some singular angles in the fences. The distance along Clay Lane to the High Farm House is but short, as it extends only through some three or four fields. The farm house is built on the site of the road, and when its erection took place the road proved to be paved. From this house the way passes through several fields having the name of Siches, which may be a corruption of strata, meaning paved way. A splendid portion of the Salter's Way passes through this land and also along the hedge side of a field of much length having the name of Holland's Wood, or probably, more correctly, Hollin Wood, and descending to and crossing a brook known as the Pingle Brook, from whence it passes by the back of the farm house at Madeley Holme. From there it is continued in Watery Lane which is now used as a road, and may be traced on to Fole Bank, where it is crossed by the present Hollington Road, on the North side of which it presents itself in the form of a deep ravine. From Fole, the way in its usual character of a deep fosse, keeps the companionship of the turnpike road to Checkley, and its course from this interesting village lies on the East side of Tean to the National Schools, beyond which point I have not attempted to follow it. But it would proceed through Draycot, where, on high ground in rear of the Post Office, there is evidence of a fortification with a circular trench at the top, and actually by the door of Dr. Garner, at Stoke.

Besides the documentary evidence given favouring the correctness of the view taken of the course of the Rykeneld Street, I have also discovered the sites of several Roman stations on the same principal route, which must, I think, place the line of its direction beyond all doubt. One or two of these have already been mentioned.

There are several branch ways joining the Rykeneld

Street, in the extent I have traced it, but which, to avoid confusion, it will be well not to mention till I describe the stations to which I have referred.

The Rykeneld Street, it should be explained, is supposed to have taken the name of Salter's Way in consequence of it having probably been the Packway of the Romans for salt out of Cheshire. Port is no less significant of it having been a portion of the same ancient way. The word is Teutonic, signifying *chief* or *principal*, and prefixed to way as under consideration, indicates it to have been what it really was, the principal way through the kingdom to Ireland.

I will not take the Roman stations in the order of the date of their discovery for description, but as they succeed each other on the line of what I have endeavoured to show is the Rykeneld Street. In so doing the station on the High Wood claims prior attention. This station, already mentioned, I discovered on March 15th, 1872, when, on going along the lane to the right hand from the top of Balance Hill to the High Wood, and allowing liberty to my habits of observation, I perceived a terrace extending across a field formerly known as the Sandpit field. The probability of it being the north side of a Roman camp at once struck me, and induced me to examine the adjoining fields to discover, if possible, traces of other parts of it, and just within the fields on the west or right hand side of the road, or lane, I found, though not in so complete a form, the west side of the camp. This I followed to the end of the lane by the cote, or cowhouse, and on passing through the stile I perceived the southern outline of it in the form of a slight fosse much broken up as far as it extends towards the east, and recently nearly effaced. Not satisfied with this very decisive evidence of the antiquity of the remains, I went to the far side of the field encompassed in the outline of the camp at the left hand side of the lane where I perceived a ditch had been newly cleaned out, and before I had proceeded far I found a piece of Roman pottery, it being a portion of the bottom of some kind of vessel. I have found other small fragments on the site, and in a field near to in which some draining was done in 1880, I met with a piece of pottery of the same period.

I have already referred to the interesting place in Bradley Street in Uttoxeter, where I found so large a quantity of relics of the Roman period, and there is a small quadrangular place in the croft or field adjoining the Hope and Anchor Inn, which may deserve ranking with similar remains.

Interesting as these remains of an early date are, they are exceeded by more important traces of primitive occupation at Stramshall in Uttoxeter parish, of which, I trust, a detailed account will meet with approval. I made my first discoveries there in January, 1872. Two years, however, previous to that date, I found a piece of Roman pottery in the bank of the road side shortly after passing by Stramshall Church on the way to Hollington, but I had then no idea that I should afterwards meet with such remarkable and interesting evidences of early occupation there. On the date above mentioned I was walking along the lane branching northward from the church, and happened to enter into conversation with Mr. Bullock, who occupies a house and some adjoining land on the right hand side of the lane, perhaps not much more than a hundred and fifty yards from the churchyard, and whilst I stood with him I was attracted by a little antique stone building standing at the remotest side of the garden, and I was told it was built over a well. Curiosity naturally led me to go to look at the place, and the extent to which the stone work is worn at the inner north side attests its great antiquity. The building over this well was destroyed in August, 1883. The well was cleaned out at the same time. It was found to be built round from the top to the bottom in stone, and to have at the bottom a sandstone flag, with a "*sump*," as described to me, in the centre, meaning a dish-shaped space of about a foot in width chiselled out, from which grooves radiate to the outer edge of the flag.

The building was of immense age, if not of the Roman period. But whilst viewing the well, the part of the garden in which it stands having recently been enclosed from the adjoining field, I perceived just east of the garden in the field mentioned, a site where I was told it was believed there had been an old house. Its appearance, however, did not corroborate that opinion, and I thought, instead, it rather bore the features of part of a Roman camp. On receiving permission to inspect it more minutely, I found there had been some digging on the spot for rabbits for which drain tiles had been laid in the earth for them to run into, and amongst the soil scattered about I found a few pieces of Roman pottery. I also found several pieces in the soil about the well, and which soil lies for about a foot in thickness over a pavement of small boulders. With the concurrence of Mr. Carrington, of Pointhorn, the owner of the land, and Mr. Bullock, the tenant, I took the earliest opportunity to explore the site to some extent with the spade. I made five openings at a considerable distance from each other, and in all I found portions of Roman pottery, some of which indicate a rude species of manufacture. One of the pieces is of a light coloured or white soft paste, covered with a green glaze. It may be the handle of a lamp, or even the pointed bottom of a small amphoræ. Another fragment amongst the numerous pieces which I dug out is part of the rim of a vessel bearing upon it chevron ornamentation. There are also portions of the rims of other vessels, one of which bears indistinctly the initials of the maker's name. A portion of another vessel which I discovered must have been of a singular shape, but it is without ornamentation and is vitrified. The varieties of potsherds which I found on the place comprise brown, white, blue, and black descriptions, but not any real or imitation Samian.

On the contrary side of the road I found in a field round the margin of a pit of water, several pieces of Roman pottery, one of which is a handle of a vessel, and in the then large cabbage garden, since turfed over, just

west of the church, I have obtained many portions of the
same kind of earthenware. At the entrance of Stramshall from Uttoxeter, in the garden and land adjoining the
first house on the west side of the road, a number of
pieces of Roman ceramic ware have been dug up since
the rumour of my first discoveries spread, and were presented to me by the late occupier of the house and land,
and from whom I also obtained a small Roman coin in
copper, found at the same place, but too much defaced
for any novice to assign to it its legitimate reign. The
fragments of pottery met with in this part of Stramshall
are of a different make to the many pieces found at
the previously mentioned sites at the same place. One
or two portions are of a red description almost resembling Samian ware both in colour and texture.
Other fragments of a dark colour are very hard, which is
not the case with the pottery found in the cabbage garden
and on Mr. Carrington's land. The area of occupation
at Stramshall by the Romans was evidently considerable,
and in some parts for military purposes remarkable and
interesting. The north side of the extensive space was
bounded by a vallum and fosse extending up the land by
Mr. Bullock's house and the whole length of the field
from which the churchyard is enclosed, and curving at
the top of the field and through the hedge, into the road
leading to Beamhurst and in the direction of the land on
the opposite side of the same way where there are three
terraces. The width of space of ancient occupation on the
south side of the village from the road appears to have
been about equal to that on the north side, and remains
of terraces are perceptible on the same side opposite to
the church and adjoining garden, the east edge of which
is a terrace defaced by cultivation. The remarkable
terraces on the west side of Stramshall exist on the south
side of the present road in a large pasture field adjoining
the Hill farm house, occupied by Mrs. Baker. They
extend across the whole field, their length being one
hundred and fifty-four spaces. The height of the first
escarpment is about four feet six inches, and the second

and third about three feet each. The first platform is thirty-nine spaces wide, and that of the second and third eighteen respectively. Along the front of each platform evidence exists of there having been vallums, and along the first there is also a fosse, and I think that, instead of their having been terraces for cultivation at a remote period, there cannot be a doubt that they are remnants of a fortification constructed either by the Romans or Britons. Indeed, I have no hesitation in saying that the name of Stramshall itself, from the various ways it is spelt, not only implies a stronghold or fortified hill, but also a Roman *chester* or camp, both of which ideas admirably accord with the appearance of the place and the discoveries I have made. In the old Uttoxeter survey we have *Strongshall*; elsewhere in more ancient records, *Straguceshol*, *Sterangricheshull*, Stronshall, all clearly implying a *chesterhold* or fortified camp. It is noteworthy that the land there is called the Ransoms, which may imply that a battle has been fought and won there and the place of occupation saved. Indeed, there is a tradition in Stramshall that it has been the scene of a great battle, some saying that it occurred on the top of Stramshall, and others on Stramshall Green.

The Rykeneld Street has already been described from Stramshall to Madeley Holme, where there is a Roman camp, and where, probably, there was subsequently a Saxon town, and earlier there was probably a British Settlement at the place; for overlooking the Madeley field there is Toothill, of which I have already spoken. My attention for several years has been particularly fixed upon Madeley field, and various reasons have induced me to pay it numerous visits. I was in the first instance much interested by the name of a field connected with the Old Wood farm, the property of the late Mr. Beech, in whose deeds it is called "Cheshire Meadow." Mr. Beech informed me that during draining operations in the field, foundations of buildings were met with, and also moulded and carved stone work, and putting the name of the field, its appearance, and traces of masonry together, I drew the inference that it must have been a site of permanent Roman occupation. The field has a very uneven surface. I was further confirmed in my convictions of the great interest of the situation by an adjoining meadow, which lies by the side of Cheshire meadow and the Madeley field, having the name of Wall Croft, whilst the Madeley field itself also appeared to have been a place of much pre-historic interest. I found that this field is separated from the Wallcroft by a deep fosseway and an elevated vallum, which undoubtedly gives the name to the croft. This fosseway, which is hid by a plantation of trees is, I believe, the continuation of one from the vicinity of the three terraces on the west side of Stramshall. It starts from just above the terraces, and is intersected by the present road from Stramshall to Waterloo. It is very evident in the form of a deep gorge just west of the cottage on the high bank side of the present road, and the Spring-field house is built upon a portion of it. From there it proceeds down the brook course which is claimed by the representatives of the late Mr. Smith, of Beamhurst, but along which the trustees of roads actually claim a right of road, notwithstanding the excellent road adjoining the brook. Fragments of the old fosseway are perceptible in places on either side of the road through Beamhurst, and particularly near Beamhurst Hall, where it exists in a farm yard, and further on where it has been utilised for a pond, and since partially converted into a garden. It was formerly more evident along side of the brook through Beamhurst, and where it turns in at the Madeley farm house it retains its primitive character, and points direct for the splendidly perfect fosseway and vallum in the plantation which divide the Wallcroft from the Madeley field, and it shows that there were two ways of communication between the site of Roman occupation at Madeley Holme and Stramshall. The fosse does not exist in a perfect form quite to the east side or end of the large Madeley field ; still it has evidently gone to the end of it where it winds to the left at the head of

Cheshire meadow in the form of a deep excavation which gradually slants out on to nearly the centre of the field side, and showing that the fosseway was made for some special purpose relating to the land, and fully explained by its designation of Cheshire Meadow.

In whatever way Cheshire Meadow may have been occupied—whether by Roman residences or otherwise—it is clear there is the site of a Roman camp at the south east angle of the Madeley field adjoining. As far as it remains entire it appears in the form of a raised quadrangular terrace. I made slight explorations of the place in September, 1871, and in the eastern margin of the camp I dug out numerous fragments of late Roman pottery and a corroded piece of iron. Slight as these discoveries were they proved of no small degree of interest, affording as they did decisive evidence of the interesting associations of the neighbourhood. During the day Mr. W. Vernon, of Fole Mills, very kindly came to render me assistance, and interested himself by digging into what he conceived were the sites of roads which he found were paved. The pavement in some parts consisted of iron slag. The only article he found for preservation was an iron fibula resembling one which I found in the Dale Field barrow. There is a large hollow space near the camp which proved to be paved with large boulders.

Traces of roads exist all over the Madeley field, if not foundations of buildings. Large stones also used to lie about near the vicinity of the camp, and there were also rows of flat stones placed in the earth edgways. When I first became acquainted with the field I met with one stone with a single moulding on one edge. A desire, however, by a late tenant to improve the field has led to all the stones being taken up and carted away, the fragments of fences to be destroyed, and other traces of early occupation to be erased.

The Saxon occupation of Madeley Holme is, I infer, indicated in the name of a field close to Madeley farm house, it being called "The Townsend," meaning the end of the town, unless the name has been acquired in consequence of prior occupation by the Romans. A little north of the camp at Madeley, at Overton, evidently an old inhabited locality, a circular leaden case was found during some draining operations. It was about sixteen or eighteen inches across and about nine inches or perhaps a little more, in depth. It was probably a sepulchral urn case of the Roman period, but, although it was offered to me for purchase, it was too much injured with the pick and spade for me to care to possess it. A writer in the " Reliquary" states that wherever the word "over" occurs either as a prefix or affix in a word it denotes that there were Roman residences there.

A branch Roman fosseway proceeds from the north west angle of the Madeley field by Hollington to Rocester, and forms a junction with the Salter's Way. A Roman camp situated at an angle so contrived, must have been of some considerable importance. The way is complete to Hollington, but afterwards it is met with only in fragments. It exists close to the foot road at Pointhorn (from probably "pont," a bridge, there being a stream in the valley, over which there may have been a bridge), and it may be seen in other places betwixt there and Rocester. This old way on the east side of Rocester exists as a fosseway parallel with the present new road to the top of the hill, and beyond there, from whence it proceeds to Little Chester, it is now used in its primitive state, as far as I have seen it, as a fosseway for the most part, that is, a narrow road with deep sides to it.

Rocester, during the Roman period, was an important place, which I am enabled to infer from the results of my attention to it for archæological purposes over many years. Very little has hitherto been said about it in illustration of its character at the remote period under consideration, beyond that, in the year 1795, when some improvements were taking place at the cotton factory some pits were discovered in which a brass spear head and some Roman coin were found. The father of the present lodgeman at the factory fell into what he described as a cellar in the Frame Yard, not far from the door of the farm house opening into it. Another man informed me that when he was employed on the premises of the mill about forty years ago (this 1880) he suddenly came upon a human skeleton which was, as he described it, drawn together, or in a flexed position, and it was preserved in a cupboard in the mill lodge many years. I possess an eliptical quern for crushing corn which was found in the earth near the mill, and it is about thirty-eight pounds in weight, its small circumference being 28 inches, and its larger circumference 32 inches. It is stated that when the National Schools were erected many fragments of Roman pottery were recovered, and from descriptions of them given to me they were probably Samian ware, and a portion of a coarse vessel then discovered found its way to Stoke Museum.

When a large space was excavated for an extension of yard room and for a new engine and boiler at the factory I found in the soil taken away, and large portions of which I turned over with a spade for the purpose, many pieces of Roman pottery. Across the area of ground lowered there appeared to have been a wide and deep gutter filled with black soil. From the ground added to the churchyard at the time of the erection of the new church, I have many fragments of pottery. In 1871 an excavation was made in the centre of this space for sand for the new church, and it was during the progress of getting sand that the pieces were discovered. One nice piece is the bottom with a portion of the side of a Samian bowl. The fragments of pottery thus collected together, I will endeavour to classify.

Several pieces I possess from Rocester are of Samian ware, which is red, and was deemed the most valuable class of pottery amongst the Romans. One piece is the bottom of a Samian bowl with the name of the maker stamped across the inside. The name is OF. IVCVN. As already mentioned, another piece consists of the bottom and a portion of the side of a Samian bowl bearing part of the figure in relief of a lion, and which probably was represented in connection with some description of sport. This piece of pottery does not perpetuate the name of its maker. Part of the side of a Samian bowl has a representation of some Phallic rite, and is very obscene, and both it and another fragment have the prevailing ornamentation on them of a border usually existing on Samian pottery, and which is shown further on in an engraving of an interesting fragment from Barrow Hill adjoining with a representation of Minerva.

Another description of Roman pottery much in use at Rocester was of a light colour, and was probably of Salopian manufacture, for Roman potworks existed in Salop at that remote period, where the white clays of the county have ever since been in requisition for earthern vessels. The larger proportion of the pieces which I possess of this kind of ware, indicate that it consisted, for the greater part, of larger vessels for domestic purposes and for hard usage. Several pieces are massive, and are probably part of an immense amphoræ. Others are wide necks of vessels which have had handles to, and they have ribs or mouldings round them. Part of a shallow bowl, consisting of a mixture of dark coloured sand with white clay, has a fine broad rim with a moulding round the inner edge, and was about nine and a half inches across. The rim of another portion of a vessel, which was about seven and half inches across, widens downwards by sloping from the side of the pitcher. Another fragment of a similar domestic article, being nearly half of it, has a flat projecting rim with an outer and inner groove extending round it. The vessel was about six inches wide by two inches deep at the outside. Perhaps the most interesting portion of light coloured pottery I possess from Rocester is part of a mortariam. It bears an inscription as follows: L. FECIT. This however, is not the complete original inscription. The other part was on the opposite side of the utensil which has not been recovered. The whole of the letters stamped upon the rim would be these :—DIVIXTUL. FECIT. It is simply the name of the maker, the latter part being the Latin word for maker. This potter has hitherto only been known as a maker of Samian pottery, and much interest consequently attaches to my massive piece of a mortariam, by showing that its manufacturer produced a different kind of pottery beside Samian. I have amongst other fragments of this description of pottery from Rocester, a small part of a rim only on which the maker's name is stamped, but the characters, which are much defaced, do not appear to have been of the ordinary Roman type. Another small bit is decorated with elongated indentations made apparently with the thumb nail.

I have likewise many fragments of Roman pottery from Rocester of the class which was made at Castor in Northamptonshire, the Durobrivæ of the Romans. This kind is of a grey or bluish colour; mostly of a good form, but, except in two or three of the examples I possess, without ornamentation. Projections have been made on the side of one vessel by pushing the paste outwards by a finger when it was in a pliable state. This little pot was only $2\frac{3}{4}$ inches wide by two inches deep. The others varied from being nine and a half inches across to seven inches wide. One fragment must have belonged to an elegant vase. The top part consists of mouldings and hollows with bars laid perpendicularly in slip across the principal hollow. The upper portion of another vessel bears a carefully executed zigzag or chevron adornment, and another small fragment is carefully cross-hatched.

I have only met with one or two pieces of red (not fine Samian) pottery at Rocester, one portion of which has belonged to a shallow vessel about nine inches wide and two inches deep, and it has scarcely any rim. Another represents a pitcher eleven inches across and three inches deep with a broad rim. It is smooth outside, but the inside is rough, and has been subjected to much abrasion by, probably, having been used for bruising vegetables in connection with culinary processes.

Only one moderately sized piece of black Upchurch ware (so named from such pottery having been made at Upchurch, in Kent) has been met with at Rocester by myself, and the piece seems to have formed part of a jar or urn like pitcher about seven inches across.

The wide nozzle of a bottle shows, where the fracture has occurred, a most interesting feature in the manufacture of such vessels. The bulb of the bottle, or amphoræ has evidently been made from a light red paste, whilst the neck and mouth of the same is of a coarse deep red material. As the fracture has occurred at the juncture of the two, it reveals the fact that they have actually been screwed together. I rather imagine that the nozzle has been manufactured first with a worm round a portion, and then, after being baked, screwed on to the body of the vessel whilst in a plastic state and which has been smoothed off over it. I have several wide necks of amphoræ with mouldings round from Rocester, the mouth of one expanding to about three inches wide.

I have also found at Rocester a red flue tile with the impression upon it of the thumb of the maker showing all the marks of the skin. I also possess a signet ring in bronze from there and a fine large bead in imperfectly vitrified blue glass.

ENGRAVINGS OF RING AND BEAD.

Two spear heads have also been found there, a drawing of one of which of a barbed form I have seen at the "Salt Library."

Large lumps of lead, resembling clogs, were also dug up near the factory, but they were melted down before I heard of them. I have likewise found fragments of querns, and horns of animals which are associated with the Roman period at Rocester.

The era of Roman occupation at Rocester included " The Frame Yard Field," the church yard, the garden east thereof, the vicinity of the factory, but how much space south of the Frame yard field, on the contrary side of the road, I have had no means of ascertaining. The field west of the church and churchyard bears surface evidence of early occupation, but as yet I have not had an opportunity of observing whether it contains evidence similar to other parts mentioned of the Roman period. The Frame yard appears to have been circumscribed by a vallum, a portion of which appears at the south-east angle of the field. Another remain in the field is highly interesting. It is a quadrangular place of about forty-five spaces each way. It is excavated below the level surface of the land, except that a platform exists in the centre of about fourteen yards across, apparently with walks to it, from the four sides and forming a junction with a walk encircling the central elevation. Along the four sides there is evidence of other walks, and by the outer edges of the quadrangular enclosure there are elevations in the form of vallums, which swell out at the south-east and south-west angles to two large circular mounds. In the centre of the south side an opening exists to admit to the enclosure. It may possibly be the pretorium of a camp. Near the mill I observed in the ground some masonry. A field opposite to the mill is called " the camp hole."

I feel persuaded that Rocester, at the close of the Roman occupation of this kingdom, was overrun by those barbaric hords, Picts or Scots, by whose ravaging hands so many other Roman British towns, villas, and camps were subjected to destruction. I cannot otherwise account for human remains being found in almost every place where excavations of some two or three feet deep have been attempted, and of their discovery having been made in what are described as drains of brickwork, but which were probably flues. Such discoveries were come upon when the large excavation was effected for sand for the new church in 1871, in the centre of the part recently enclosed from the Frame yard for the church yard. I found a consideration of this place of very considerable interest. Resting upon the gravel was a depth of from two and a half to three feet of rich black soil, and decided traces of ancient occupation were perceptible at the juncture of the soil and gravel, in the existence of numerous pieces of sandstone, and nearly commingling with them, on the south side of the opening, were remains of two persons, one full grown and the other of a child. On the west side of the excavation at a similar depth another human body, or rather skeleton of one, was discovered. Numerous fragments of Roman pottery lay scattered in the superincumbent soil, one piece being the bottom of a fine Samian bowl with a portion of the side retaining part of the embossed impression of a lion as referred to already, and, what to me appeared singular, the gravel of the original surface with which the pieces of sandstone and the human remains were contiguous, appeared to have been burnt to whiteness and cracked into small fragments by the action of intense heat. The inference which I drew was that the remains were those of Romano-British individuals who had met with sudden and violent deaths, and whose houses, which might for the most part have consisted of wood, had been consumed by fire. It would also appear that everything valuable and perfect was carried away, as nothing but what is fragmentary, so far as I am aware, has hitherto been met with. I made a sketch of a section of the excavation, showing the position of the human skeletons and the form of the pieces of stone at the meeting of the gravel with the black soil.

At Barrow Hill, close to Rocester, there is a Roman camp (if it is not a British fortification,) which was pointed out to me in July, 1871, by Captain Dawson, who has numerous corroded Roman coins from the place. It is square and of considerable extent. The north and west sides are perfect, and a large portion of the original glacis, of greater elevation than any other remaining portions, exists at the rear of the farm buildings adjoining the Ashbourne Road. In a large heap of gravel, or refuse heap, at the north-west angle of the camp in the adjoining field, several pieces of Samian ware and other varieties of Roman pottery were dug out under the direction of the late John F. Lucas, Esq., of Bentley Hall, in the year 1870. I present an engraving of a fragment of a Samian bowl, which bears a figure of Minerva.

SAMIAN WARE.

A little Samian dish, which is six inches wide and three quarters of an inch deep, was also found here. Other engravings represent two fragments of Roman pottery

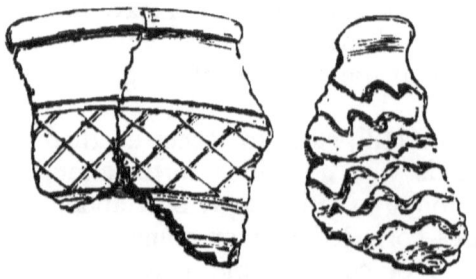

CASTOR AND UPCHURCH WARE.

in Castor and Upchurch ware, and a bowl of Salopian ware, which I built up from fragments, and all of which are from the same refuse heap. A circular fibula also was found at Barrow Hill. All these relics are in the possession of Captain Dawson.

SALOPIAN BOWL.

An old fosseway has passed close by the refuse head at Barrow Hill, and portions of it are perceptible as far as Uttoxeter.

Near the Roman way which came by Buttermilk Hill, several interesting remains exist either of that or an earlier period. There is, or was, one near the new church and another one lies not far from Buttermilk Hill, and is known by the name of the moat. There is a fine fortified Roman camp near Hanging Wicket House, in the same vicinity, which, as *Wic* signifies fortress, probably took its name from the camp. I think I have designated it a Roman camp advisedly, for on digging into it in numerous places in 1872, I found several pieces of Roman pottery, one piece being coarse dark blue and another red. I also met with one piece of glass with three lines upon it. At the side near the north-west angle at a slightly rising part of the surface, I dug into a material consisting of sand and clay, prepared for pot making, and mixed up with it were broken pieces of baked clay with a smooth surface. I am unable to conceive the fragments to have formed any article of use except a clay hearth. At the various spots where I slightly explored large and small pieces of stone lay at a depth of about one and a half feet. The fortification is in two divisions by large fosses. The western division is seventy-two spaces by sixty-six; the other division is fifty-two by sixty-six spaces. The very singular tradition exists that Uttoxeter existed first at this fortification. The roads formerly conducting from Buttermilk Hill were of very great width. The one existing opposite to the fortification at Hanging Wicket had spaces to it at each side some seven yards wide. When the wastes at each side the road beyond the lower parts of Uttoxeter High Wood were being enclosed in 1881 and 1882, and laid to the property of J. E. Lightfoot, Esq., the upper part of a quern, here shown in an engraving, of the Roman period was found in the hedge bank during the process of stocking up the hedge and levelling the bank. The stone is nine and a half inches in length, and eight and a half in width, whilst it has a thickness of four inches.

QUERN.

The stone is volcanic from Andernach. The surface is convex and is full of punctures to make it rough for bruising or grinding corn. The socket or stone bowl or dish in which the stone was made to revolve was not discovered. I give an engraving of it, as it is in my possession. I have found several fragments of stone dishes in different places which had been used for such purposes.

There was a quadrangular camp with a fosse existing in a field close to the New Road, and in the third field from the Three Tuns public-house on Uttoxeter Heath. Recently a new house has been built on the site, and only a small portion of the fosse is perceptible. I have called it a camp, and in confirmation of the opinion

I have formed of it I possess part of the handle of a Roman vessel from it. The fragment is perforated with holes similar to handles I possess from the site in Bradley Street. The place is spoken of in Lightfoot's old survey of Uttoxeter as one where there had been a moated house, which is decidedly a misconception.

Whether all these camps, for the first time pointed out by myself and described, were occupied for the protection of the Via Devina, or as outlying posts to the more important and permanent camp at Rocester, or some of them for only temporary purposes, are points I am unable profitably to discuss. The remains at Denstone, north of Rocester, known as Cromwell's Green, with a double ditch, may be assigned to the Roman period, as, on examining the site in 1873, I found, where some turf had been removed, a piece of Roman pottery.

The mention of a few more particulars will conclude the consideration of the period under notice. In the year 1788, during the time Uttoxeter High Wood was being enclosed for cultivation for the advantage of the parish, a Roman metallic sacrificial vessel

was found, of which Mr. Samuel Bentley, the poet, made a drawing which he sent to the "Gentlemen's Magazine," in which an account of the relic with an engraving appeared. Part of the vessel was corroded away. The present engraving is a representation of the one in the "Gentlemen's Magazine."

I possess a Roman brass coin, small and of considerable thickness, which was found on Uttoxeter Heath.

An interesting coin was found on the premises of the Uttoxeter Brewery Company in the summer of 1872, when excavations were being made for the foundations of new offices opposite to the Town Hall. It is what appears to be usually called a Minimi, a species of coin fabricated by the native inhabitants of this island in rude imitation of the previous currency of the Romans, who had abandoned Britain for the protection of their own empire.

Picknal Lane, north-west of Uttoxeter, is an antique fosseway coeval with other old ways described. In one direction it passed over Uttoxeter Heath to probably Stramshall, and south-west it proceeded up the dimble from the railway crossing at the bottom of Picknal Lane, and went by Loxley Bank, Loxley Green, and up Fishbrook Lane by Leese Hill over the Blythe by where the ancient forges were near Grindley, and near which place there is a space enclosed by a moat.

A beautiful Samian Vase, with the lily and anthemun pattern upon it, in black upon a red ground, and being about three and a half inches wide and three deep, and is said to have been found at Loxley in the middle of the last century or soon after. But I will give its history, which appears to me to have the stamp of truth and correctness upon it. It is related that it was found in a broken state by Thomas Kynnersley, Esq., who put it together and thought much of it, believing it to be ancient and of Roman workmanship, and he resolved to have a few copies made in resemblance of it. For this purpose it is said it was put into the hands of the late Josiah Wedgwood, who is stated to have made the required number of copies, of which that from which the engraving is taken is held to be one. This copy, it is continued, was given to Mr. White, Mr. Kynnersley's butler, from whom its history was originally derived, and he, at his death, gave it to another old servant, the gardener, named John Foster, who is well remembered as having subsequently been clerk at Bromshall

LOXLEY VASE.

Church, dying there at the age of 90 years or more. By the old gardener it was given to his nephew, Mr. Foster, of Endon, who has it now. The vessel has, on my account, been shown at the establishment of Messrs. Wedgwood, and the opinion there is such as to confirm the view here given. If it had been manufactured by them for commerce they would have had copies by them, besides models and memoranda, but having none of these they believe it must have been made for some private gentleman in imitation of some interesting relic, as they were frequently making copies of such out-of-the-way objects without keeping any record or models of them. I give an engraving of this beautiful vase which will not fail to be admired.

There is an antique fosseway through Loxley Park from the direction of Uttoxeter, and it was doubtless over this way that Queen Elizabeth in 1575, and King Charles twice in the subsequent century, passed to Stafford. In or about the year 1772 a petition to Parliament was presented for the improvement of this road, and as it gives a striking picture of the fearful state of one of the most primitive roads then existing, a transcription of it, whether it was an old Roman way or not, cannot fail being welcome.

" *To the Honourable the Commons of Great Britain in Parliament assembled.*

" The humble Petition of several Gentlemen, Clergy, Freeholders of the County of Stafford, of the Mayor, Gentlemen, Tradesmen, and Inhabitants of the Borough of Stafford, in the County of Stafford, and of the Gentlemen, Tradesmen, and Inhabitants of Uttoxeter, in the said County of Stafford, sheweth :—That the road leading from the said Borough or Town of Stafford to the Town of Uttoxeter aforesaid, is in many parts thereof become so very deep and founderous, that during many months in the year the same is very inconvenient and dangerous for horses, and nearly impassible for carriages, and in many places so very narrow that carriages cannot safely pass each other, and in time of floods the overwhelming of the rivers Trent and Blythe renders the passing so extremely dangerous as to stop all communication between the said Town of Stafford and the said Town of Uttoxeter, without going many miles about. And the said road cannot be kept in repair by the ordinary methods prescribed by law.

" And your Petitioners further shew that the repair of the said road will be of great public utility, as thereby a free and open communication will be obtained between the Town of Shrewsbury and the Towns of Derby and Nottingham, nearly in a direct line, by means of turnpike roads.

"Your Petitioners therefore pray that leave may be given to bring in a Bill for more effectually repairing, widening, turning, altering, amending, and keeping in repair the said road. And also for building bridge or bridges over the rivers Trent and Blythe, so as to render the passing over the said rivers safe and commodious to travellers, with such powers and authorities and under such regulations as to this Honourable House shall seem meet."

If the petition was presented it was not for some time granted. *

---

* The original is in the possession of W. Jones, Esq., of Stafford.

THE ANGLO-SAXON PERIOD.

During the Saxon Heptarchy Uttoxeter was included in the Kingdom of Mercia, from Myricnarac, * signifying in the Anglo-Saxon Language, the Woodland Kingdom, and therein agreeing with Coitani, the latinized name of the old British inhabitants, meaning woodland men or foresters. Uttoxeter, having been a Roman station, was occupied by the Saxons at an early period of their acquaintances with this island. Before the villages came into existence, most of which have had a Saxon origin, the stations of the Romans, although partially demolished by the Picts, were invariably seized upon by the Saxons for dwelling places. This fact accounts for their hybrid character, causing no little perplexity in their derivation (especially when coming through Norman writers), of many Saxonized Roman towns and villages.

In fact, if Uttoxeter is not a Saxon name, but one of higher antiquity, there is tolerably clear evidence of it having been an important place in Anglo-Saxon times. Indeed it had the distinction of then being a borough town, for the words "The burrow town" of Uttoxeter, occur in an old writing of the latter end of the sixteenth century or the beginning of the seventeenth. There is no date to the writing, but the signatures are of persons who were then living. The writing itself relates to Dove Bridge which it very strikingly mentions as "a great Stone Bridge." It is not to be supposed that Uttoxeter was a borough town in the sense of those borough towns which send men to Parliament. The word *borough*, as applied

---

* Macpherson's Annals of Commerce.

to Uttoxeter, is a monument itself, we are told, older than all written records of the state of society, in which, in these islands, the institution originated. * The word borough is from the Anglo-Saxon *byrig*, *byrg*, *burk*, like the German *burg* of the present day, and was the general name for any place, large or small, fortified by walls or mounds. The state of the age, the prevalence of warfare both on a large and petty scale, and on the constant liability to foreign incursion, made walls and trenches necessary to the security not only of trading towns but of isolated mansions, and *burg* or *borough* was the name for all. Uttoxeter was probably surrounded by a fortification. Hollingbury, on Uttoxeter High Wood, shows clearly by its name that there was a residence there in Anglo-Saxon times, defended in some way by a fortification. Independent of the fact preserved in the old document there is a general impression that Uttoxeter, in some sense, is a borough town, and, prior to the ancient writing falling in my way, I have been questioned if such was not the case, and why, therefore, did it not return a member to Parliament. I think this circumstance shows the vitality and strength of tradition, and it may be added its reliability often, and how worthy the tradition of any thing is of being enquired into and traced, if possible, to its origin. As the writing is highly interesting and valuable, and not very long, it perhaps could not be more appropriately introduced than at this place. It is entitled "A true copy of a writing which was *formerly* made concerning the two meadows commonly called the Broad Meadow and Netherwood." It occurs in the original copy of Peter Lightfoot's Survey, in the peculiar writing of the seventeenth century, and the original was made at a Court Leet of the town.

"Whereas a Great Stone Brigde standeth upon the river Dove in the confines of the counties of Stafford and Derby called Dove Bridge which is as common a portway and as much occupied as annie passage in these parts of the Rellme, which said bridge is and by all tyme whereof the memory of man is not to the contrary, hath bin

---

* Verstergern Restitution of Decayed Intelligence.

only supported, upholden, and maintained by the inhabitants and residents within the Lordship of Uttoxeter. And whereas allso the same tenants and inhabitants of their good and godley disposition as well in sparing the burden and charge of the poor, as allso for the maintainance of the *burrow town of Uttoxeter* which would grow to utter ruin if the said bridge decay, have devised and frequented of longe tyme by and with a common consent amongst themselves to save and preserve the aftermath of their common meadows until they were well replenished and furnished with grass and then taken cattle to agishmont into the said meadow by the weeks after a reasonable rate to the good liking of all well disposed people, and the same money so raysed and so used and employed to the repair of the said bridge as oft as need did require. And forasmuch as the said inhabitants have by experience tasted and found how good and beneficial this practice hath proved, it is at this court ordered, established and decreed that every mannar of person or persons which hath or hereafter shall have annie ground of estate or inheritance or otherwise within the precincts of this manor shall at all and any tyme and tymes and from hence and hereafter and from tyme to tyme *for ever* not only permit, suffer and allow the said common meadow to be used, occupied, holden and kept in severaltie for the common utility and profit of the same inhabitants as afore is said, but allso shall suffer and allow the said meadow to be rated, rented and agished and the money thereof raysed to be employed according to the purport, true intent and meaning hereof upon payne everie person that doeth either practice, procure, or command annie wayes or means to the contrary, to forfeit for everie tyme ten pounds *toties quotios*.

Signed by,

Anthony Kynnersley, Ralph Mynors, Ffrancis Mynors, John Norman, William Startyn, Richard Startyn, Richard Wilshaw, Lawrance Heath, Edward Chamberlain, Ffrancis Poker, Thomas Holbrooke, John Berd and others.

Salter's way, otherwise Portway, applied to Slade Lane, are decisive as to their application to the Rykenald Street, but Port as applied to the Doveridge way, in the old Plan of Uttoxeter, must have another meaning, being probably equivalent to the word borough, as the burrow town of Uttoxeter, and was consequently the borough way.

But there are also several other interesting circumstances which clearly identify our Saxon ancestors with Uttoxeter. Accounts are preserved, accompanied with pictorial representations, of the amusements of the Saxon people, amongst which was that of seeing bears exhibited. A scene of this description, as having taken place in an

Anglo-Saxon ampitheatre, is given amongst the Harleian manuscripts in the British Museum. The word Bear Hill, applied to the open space at the East end of Uttoxeter Market Place, and which it had more than two hundred years back, implies that this pastime was common in Uttoxeter amongst the Saxons, and that either the bears were kept at Bear Hill, or that the sports with them took place there, or both. As the Saxon people of the town were not likely to import these creatures for the purpose, it may be presumed they obtained them from Needwood Forest, where, as well as in other English Forests, they existed in common with the wild boar and wolf. That there is no mistake in the correctness of the word here being *bear* and not *bare*, meaning uncovered or unoccupied, the following extracts from the ancient terrier of the town fully substantiates the antique way of spelling bear being preserved. The entries are :—

"Thomas Moor had one little cottage at Beare Hill."
"Francis Morris had a cell at Beare Hill."

As a proof that the wolf inhabited Needwood Forest and other woods near Uttoxeter in Saxon times, it may be cited that there is a piece of land near Uttoxeter having the name of Wolf Hurst. The word is Saxon: *Wolf* being the Saxon name of the animal itself, and *Hurst* that of wood or forest. The wolf, in fact, was the plague and terror of the island.

Uttoxeter is also associated with Saxon times by what is implied in a curious monosyllabic compound, thought to be the nickname of the place, at the East end of Silver Street. The word is *Hole-in-the-Wall*, in which the Alwynehall may be traced, implying that one Alwyne, a Saxon thane, had his residence there. A similar derivation has been given to a *Hole-in-the-Wall* at Mavesyn Ridware. This little circumstance is of interest, as it probably points out the locality where one of the Saxon nobility lived, and who was possibly one of the influential local functionaries of the day. It may be useful to add, that the thanes were of several orders, although it would be useless to inquire of what degree the Alwyne was who may be supposed to have lived at the *Hole-in-the-Wall.* The King's thanes or attendants were of the first order; then the thanes of the Aldermen and Earls, who were of the highest degree of the Saxon nobility, and next the inferior thanes who were of the landed gentry. Thanes were amongst the members of the Saxon Whitenagemont, or Parliament, or meeting of wise men. One of the qualifications of a Saxon thane was the possession of a certain amount of landed property, five hides of land being required to qualify one of the highest order. One of the laws of Æthelstan declares that if a ceorl, or commoner, shall have attained five hides of land in full property, with a church, a kitchen, a bell house, a burgate seat, and a station in the King's hall, he shall henceforth be a thane by right. Perhaps the Alwyne at the Hole-in-the-Wall was the thane of an earl—possibly of Earl Algar.

But places having the name of Hole-in-the-Wall are really numerous. There is such a place at Bradley, near Ashbourne, and "Nature and Art" states that the Hole-in-the-Wall, so common in military towns, was probably a snug recess in the town walls devoted to sutting purposes. It is also said to have been a round hole in the wall in the debtors' prison in Fleet, through which they were permitted to receive alms. The hole-in-the-wall is a familiar name for a refreshment room in the house of representatives at Washington. At the same time the spot at Uttoxeter may have acquired the name from the circumstance mentioned and not from the customs from which it has arisen at the other places referred to.

We are further reminded of the Saxon character of the town by the principal entrance to the Church yard being called "Light Gate." The word Light, in this way of implying it, is corrupted from *Lice,* the Saxon word for carcass or dead body, and Lich Gate was therefore the name given to the South entrance to the Church yard at Uttoxeter by the Saxons, it being then, as now, the entrance through which funeral processions conveyed the dead. *Lich* watching, or sitting with the dead, which is a custom still observed in some places, was originated by the Saxons, but the practice is not continued at Uttoxeter.

There is also additional evidence of the relation the neighbourhood of Uttoxeter bore to Saxon times by the existence of a Saxon grave a little south of the town. It is in a field east of, and almost opposite to, that in which are the remains which I have named hut circles, and it is indicated by a clump of trees in an open field observable on the left of the foot-road going to Woodford. This interesting site of Saxon Christian burial is marked by a mound in the form of a cross The four radii of the cross, which agree with the four cardinal points, are each about ten yards long, two feet high, and about two yards and a half wide. The place, as mentioned, has trees growing upon it, and an oak stands at the intersection. Owing to this interesting remain being now exposed to the trampling of cattle, it is liable to become, in time, trodden out of existence. When I first discovered the site it was enclosed by a good hawthorn fence.

But what is equally, if not more interesting, there is what has every evidence of being a Saxon cemetery in Uttoxeter parish at Low Fields, where it has hitherto been supposed there was only an ordinary tumulus. A slightly raised mound of this character, and of but small extent, certainly exists in the field just on the north-east side of the place hitherto supposed to be a low, but now the trees and impenetrable brushwood have been cleared away from the site conjectured to have been a barrow, it proves to be an extensive cemetery enclosed by a circular ditch and fence. Over the surface of the enclosure there are slightly raised earthern banks in the form of a cross, and which must indicate it to be a Saxon Christian burial ground. One of these remains has the name of Robin Hood's butts, and the land on which they exist is so denominated in an old survey of Uttoxeter parish. The position from which he is stated to have shot his arrows from his trusty bow, is placed at the White Gate at Stubwood. There is a prevalent tradition also, that a great battle has been fought at Low Fields in remote times, and that the contest surged in that direction from Rocester, and it is said that fragments of swords have been dug up thereabouts.

There is a remarkable remain on the Dairy-house Farm, in the parish of Leigh, but to what period it belongs I am not prepared to determine. It is forty yards square with a double ditch on three sides, and a treble ditch on the east side. The number of ditches would seem to indicate an early period for the fortification, but remains have been found in it which belong to the eleventh century. When a drain was being carried across the remain some thirty years back relics of what appeared to be steel chain armour were found (of which I have a small portion) and also a large sheet of what is supposed to have been chain armour in gold. The links of which this relic consist are riveted together, and have on them a representation of a snake's head. Other interesting remains found were shoes with long points curling up and supposed to have been fastened at the knee. The place is called Blithard Moat or Mot.

Indeed, the neighbourhood of Uttoxeter appears to have become thoroughly Saxonised, for the hills, fields, lanes, and brooks in the parish, and adjacent places, have received names from the Saxon language, which they have retained through the changes of many generations. Of course there are a few exceptions, as in the name of the Dove, which is derived from the British word *dwr*, meaning water, and in the Tean, or Tain, which is from the British word *terne*, signifying violence, force. Caverswall or Carser, and Carris, as in Carriscopice, may be from the British word *caer*, a field or fortress. The Alders and Aldersbrook must contain the British word *ald*, meaning old. But in Marriotholme, Sweathholme, and Clownholme, the "Gentlemen's Magazine" informs us we have the old English word for holly. The word *holme* also means land surrounded by water, and also the pitch of a hill. In Hanging-wicket there is the Saxon word for gate; or as before hinted, it may be from *wic*, a fortress. All the following words or names applied to places about

Uttoxeter, but to land chiefly, are derived from the Saxon language. Beam or Bam, in Beamhurst, means woody. Haugh *(Norse)* in Culverhaugh, implies a green plot in a valley—a sepulchre. Wiggins signifies the mountain ash. Marsh, in Crakemarsh, means Fenny or Watery. Stonyford, applied to some place in the lower part of the Rycroft land, is from stane, stony. Eaton means a watertown. Wingfield and Wingfield-lake may mean to win peace—a battle. In Popingham, otherwise Popinjay, as it is now commonly called, is the old word for home. The former word appears in old documents, but Popinjay, as the place is now called, may some three or four hundred years ago or more, have been a public-house with the sign of the Popinjay, which is an old pastime which consisted in shooting with a cross bow at an artificial parrot. Or it may have been a place where people met to shoot for games at the Popinjay. Hockley signifies a dirty pasture. Muckle Brook, a name in old documents for Hockley Brook, implies dirty brook. In Slade, which is applied to Slade Lane or Salter's Lane, there is the Saxon meaning for a long flat piece or slip of land. I have heard Lannock applied, at Uttoxeter, to a bucket ear, and as it implies something narrow it was properly used. It also means a narrow slip of land, and hence we have also lant. In Cliff, in the compound Rough Cliff, there is the Saxon for the side or pitch of a hill, a rugged mountain. Its appropriateness will be apparent to all who have seen Ruff-cliff. There is Shaw, the Saxon for wood, and also Field for *felled place*. Wodens near Combridge is also Saxon, and indicates a site of the worship of Woden, the Mars of the Northern nations.

The antique names of fields, either altogether or in their prefixes or suffixes, in the parish of Uttoxeter, as preserved in two old surveys of the respective dates 1658 and 1774 are so curious, that, although I am unable to give their derivation in many instances, I shall be doing a good service to local word lore, and thereby to ethnological enquiries by printing them, especially as they are for the most part, if not altogether, dropped out of use by modern overseers of the parish. In the part of the survey relating to Uttoxeter are the following field names:—The Bottoms; Arbour, *a place of refuge;* The Patch; Hazzlewall, meaning a *stockade;* Emath; Mastels; Callcroft; Catchinene Croft; Kiddlestich or *Sich;* Mothams; Bratches; Brickley Meadow; Gill Hill, a *ravine;* Jackmore Lant; Dow Lane; Owley-moor; Eastmoreton, a *fen;* Willigs; Alders; Holloway Close; Ouze, *a small lake;* Stockley Croft, *a fortress;* Amberlands, the *Amber* or sacred stone where religious rites were performed—the abode of gods; The Breach; Stocking, *a stockaded place;* Riddings, *the Thirdings;* Hatchet Wood, a *hitch gate* in the neighbourhood of a forest; The Sling; Insich; Buddie Close; Perryfall's Close; Grisslesich; Beale Meadow, *the Celtic Bel or Belan;* The Crich; Clames Croft; Wiggan Lands; Rackyard, where the punishment of the rack was inflicted; Fflambolt's Meadow; Conygree, *a rabbit warren;* Walesfield; Neephurst; Fauston Fields; Owfast; Ridnall; Shields Acre; Siches or Mue Acre; Marlow; Warlow Riddings; Little Shell Croft; Hobheys; Spurn Nook; Quoynes; Hatch Gate; Tommey Fields, from Tomen, Celtic, *a Temple;* Nobleworth, the Anglo-Saxon, *weorthing,* a place warded or protected; Sweath Holme Knowle; Tinset Park, which may be from the Norse *Things,* as in Tinwell, a place of judicial assembly of North men, and others.

In Stramshall and Creighton, which are in Uttoxeter parish, the following field names occur in the survey of 1774:—Grimmer Meadow; Marrish Ground; Crimbles; Low Sernshaw Balk; Glednall; Crenibles; Flash; Gommersley; Barnard Fold, *the enclosure for the bear or crop, and it enclosed the settler's home;* Butterley; Stings; Hash; Grif; Rossel and Rosser, *the Celtic, probably for moor,* hence Roston is the Moor Town; Little Shines; Pale Flat; Pikes; Homson Piece, *from Ham, a home;* Six Days' Nath; Hiversley; Wotrains; Stakes; Hemp Crafts; Brimsholme; Gibb Meadow; Gussott; Weting; Hood Croft; Lower Barrow Piece; whilst in Crakemarsh, in the same parish, are these names of fields:—Nattspiece; Smithoms; Oe Meadow; Honey Spot, and Chapel Yard.

In Loxeley and the Woodlands, in Uttoxeter parish, there are field names as ensuing:—Crze Croft; Sich; Hankay; Stear Field; Far Blakeley, *from the Celtic, blaique, a hill:* Ami Hills; Long Bentley; Leppen Wall or Loppen-wall, *a stockade;* Great Langley; Older Carr, *from Caer or Car, a fortress or castra;* Intake; Cop Hill Flat; Cuckoldshaven; Duckstone Piece; Ashendun Croft; Birchen Croft; Great Derndale or Dundale (celtic), may mean a *wooded valley, or a place of meeting,* a hill or barrow which, with the surrounding grove, formed a Celtic Temple;* Hobhey Croft; Range Flat; Wiggin's Croft; Buddy Meadow; Muckley Close; Fell Croft; Swenteen-acres; Hopyard; Sweathholme, and several others less interesting. Godstone, near Field, as well as Garstone more North, may be from *Maen Gorsed* (or Stone of Assembly) at which the Druid Priests assisted, and traditions and poems were recited. Cuckholds and Duck Stone perpetuate the name of customs which modern civilization has extirpated.

---

* See Naology by John Dudley, M.A., Rivington, 1846.

THE FEUDAL TENURE OF UTTOXETER.

Hitherto we have scanned the pre-historic period relating to Uttoxeter, and it has proved itself not altogether barren of many matters of both local and general interest. We are now arrived at that period when local history receives the aid of authentic records, namely, when the survey of the kingdom was taken, by appointment of William the Conqueror, and contained in the Doomsday Book, which was finished about 1086. The accounts of places are in a contracted form in the mixed Latin of the time. Written out in full and plain English, the portion relating to Uttoxeter is as follows:—"Wotocheshede belongs to the king. It formerly belonged to Earl Algar. It has half a hyde of land. The arable land is ten carucates, with two in demesne and one servant, twenty-four villans, eleven borders, with eleven carucates. There are also sixteen acres of meadow land, and a wood two miles long and broad.

"It was worth seven pounds in the time of Edward the Confessor; it is now worth eight pounds."

A *hide* of land was one hundred and twenty acres. The arable land designated *carucates* was plough land, a *caruca* being as much as was tilled in a year. The villans, who took their name as a class from *villa*, a country farm, were employed in tillage, and are supposed to have been formed by the coalition of the conquered Britons, called Thralls, and of the free Saxon Ceorls. ✻ The borders, or boors, were inferior to the villans, and held small quantities of land on the borders of manors on a base and uncertain tenure.

✻ Harland's History of Manchester, 1860

It must not be supposed that the Doomsday Survey gives a complete account of all the land in Uttoxeter, and a perfect enumeration of all the inhabitants in the parish, for it was not a parochial survey. It was limited to estates upon which the Crown had claims, and therefore was a mere rent roll of the particular lands which owed rent, suit, or service to Edward the Confessor or William the First. *

It is singular that the name of Earl Algar is found in the survey, as he died seven years before the Conquest, and was succeeded by his sons Edwin and Mercar, Earls of Mercia and Northumberland, who took up arms on behalf of their countrymen in 1071. Edwin, who had become owner of Uttoxeter, on the death of his father, was betrayed to the Normans, and his estates were confiscated by the King. † This was a fate to which many Saxon noblemen were compelled to submit whether they were favourable or not to the accession of William the Conqueror. The King, however, did not long retain Uttoxeter, but along with seven lordships in Staffordshire, and numerous others in Derbyshire, Warwickshire, Nottinghamshire, and Leicestershire, gave it to Henry de Ferrars, Ferers, Ferries, or Ferrarii, son of Walkeline de Ferrariis, a baron of great wealth and power in Normandy, who accompanied the King. ‡ The name of Ferrars was taken from his emyloyment, which was that of shoeing horses—not that he himself was a farrier, but was appointed to direct and superintend that business in the nature of *præfectus faborum*. So when, at the time of the Crusades, it became the custom for families to take coat armour hereditarily, a charge of six horse shoes table, on a field argent, was assumed by this great house. But in fuller elucidation of this point I cannot do better than give some remarks of a popular writer on antiquarian and heraldic subjects. § He writes :—

---

* Gentleman's Magazine, vol. 95, and Sharon Turner's Anglo-Saxons.
† Henry's History of England, and Ward's History of Stoke-on-Trent.
‡ Erdeswick.
§ Mr. L. Jewitt, F.S.A.

"Whether De Ferrars did hold the office of chief of the farriers, and whether or not in virtue of that office he assumed the badge of the horse shoe, or whether it was assumed as a "canting" badge (*armes parlentes* becoming pretty general as early as the reign of Henry II.) from its name *fer de cheval* for Ferrars, as is generally believed—certain it is that the horse shoe was borne by the family of Ferrars in a variety of ways, and that it is identified with them throughout the period in which they held lands in this county. Mr. Planché, Rouge Croix Pursuivant of Arms, has laboured hard to prove that the Ferrars are not originally entitled to the distinction of the horse shoe, and that it was only borne by them after an alliance with the Marshalls, Earls of Pembroke, but I have no doubt in my own mind that he is wrong in the conclusion he has arrived at. Three or six horse shoes are described as the arms of Ferrars—called, of course, by the early heralds, "ferres de cheval"—thus the play on the word "ferres" for Ferrars is easily seen Another bearing of the word Ferrars is "Vaire, or and Gules," and I conceive that here (although such a supposition has never heretofore been started by any writer)—is another instance of the "canting" or playful bearings. Vaire being spelt and pronounced "VERRE" is so close an approximation to "Ferrars" as to warrant one in supposing that to that circumstance it owes its adoption as an heraldic bearing of that once powerful family. Again, on a Norman pitcher, recently discovered by me near Duffield, are, besides five horse shoes, two buckles, which were probably also adopted as a badge from the resemblance of the name "fer-mailles" or Fermaux to "Ferrars."

"It might be pushing the idea too far to suppose that the pitcher just described proves that the proper heraldic bearing of the Earls of Ferrars and Derby was five horse shoes instead of three or six; but I think there is reason to suppose this to be the case. In the first place five is equally as legitimate and usual a number as six, and is one which fits the shape of the shield quite as well. It is evident from the disposition of the horse shoes on this jug, that the potter had some special end in view in placing five found it; for he has put four of an uniform size, and then to complete the requisite number has had to crowd in a small one by the buckles. The pitcher here described was found in the remains of a Norman pottery, on lands formerly belonging to the Ferrars, and not far from their chief residence, Duffield Castle. It has been carefully engraved and described in the "Reliquary," vol. iii., page 216."

"It has generally been believed that the Normans were the first to introduce the practice of shoeing horses into England—but this has long been disproved, and I have myself found iron horse shoes with undoubted Roman remains. That the Normans attached great importance to the art of farriery there can be no doubt, for besides the grants to the Ferrars it is recorded that the Conqueror gave to Simon St. Liz, the town of Northampton to provide shoes for his horses, that Gamelhere held land in Cuckney, Nottinghamshire, for the service of shoeing the King's palfrey upon four feet, with the King's nails, or shoeing materials, as oft as he should be at his manor of Mansfield, and if he put in all the nails, the King should give him a palfrey of four marks, or he was to have the king's palfrey giving him 5 marks, as he was also to do if he lamed the horse, pricked him, or shod him straight, that Henry de Avering held the manor of Norton (Essex) by the sargentry of finding a man with a horse value ten shillings, and four horse shoes, one sack of barley, and one iron buckle, as often as the King should go with his army into Wales, at his own expense, for forty days."

"The horse shoe was painted on the wooden foot quintain and occurs heraldically on the seal of Walter Marshall, Earl of Pembroke, 1246, in the arms the company of Farriers, and those of the families of Birlace, Cripps or Crispe, Ferrars, Romdall, Shoyswell or Shoeswell, and others. It also forms the arms of the town of Oakham, in Rutlandshire, and here again its connection with the Ferrars is remarkable, for the manor, with its regal hall, was held by them, and they had the privilege, which is still retained as a right, although compounded for by money, of claiming from every Peer of Parliament the first time he passes through the town, a horse shoe to be nailed on to the Castle gate, and if he refuse, the bailiff of the manor has power to arrest him and take one by force from his horse's foot. In the fine old hall at Oakham a number of these horse shoes, many of them with the names of the peer from whom claimed, are preserved."

Henry de Ferrars was held in great esteem for his political knowledge, abilities, and integrity. The bestowal of these extensive possessions upon him by the King was for the eminent services he had rendered to this monarch. In the settlement of these lands in the honor of Tutbury (by which is meant an estate consisting of several lordships—as the lordship of Uttoxeter—manors and Knight's fees), upon this noblemen, the King reserved to himself, or the crown, certain privileges and payments. He nevertheless, on certain conditions, allowed portions of the same lands to be again given to others for their services, as will be subsequently perceived. Henry de Ferrars was one of the commissioners appointed to take the general survey of the kingdom. He died in the interval of the years 1080 and 1090. He had by his wife, Bertha, three sons, Eugenulph, William, and Robert. The two former died during the lifetime of their father, so that he was succeeded by Robert in the possession of Uttoxeter.

To Robert de Ferrars, who was a nobleman of enlightened views, Uttoxeter was indebted, in common with other immediate parts of the honor of Tutbury, for some of its earliest advantages, arising from improvements in agriculture and trade. With a view to the cultivation of some newly enclosed parts of Needwood Forest, and the consumption of their produce, he enlarged Uttoxeter and Tutbury and built Newborough. Uttoxeter, according to the Harleian MSS., had 127 Burgages, Tutbury 182, and Newborough 101, the occupiers of which got their living by some handicraft or trade of merchandise. At Uttoxeter, iron was manufactured, whilst bleaching was pursued at Newborough, and woolcombing at Tutbury. Thus Earl Robert intended the agricultural and trading populations of the district to be mutually advantageous to each other; the former to supply the latter with necessary food, whilst they in return were to supply the former with the requisite articles of clothing and implements of husbandry. Uttoxeter also gained other benefits under this wise and beneficent Earl; he made it a free borough, by which is to be understood that the inhabitants were exempt from servile offices to the lords of the honor. He also granted unto them other privileges which they had not before enjoyed. They were made free of tolls, tonnage, package, poundage, and other exactions within their possessions. * Liberty was given them to cut wood within the Uttoxeter Ward, or division, of the forest, for fuel, buildings, and fences; known as fire-boot, house-boot, and hay-boot, as also to depasture horses and cattle in the forest, and to turn swine therein to consume the acorns, for which a sum of money was paid called pannage. † In the survey of Uttoxeter by Peter Lightfoot, some portion of land on Balance Hill bore the name of Swine-pits, either from the woods having at some period extended as far, and in which swine were turned, or from swine having been collected there out of the forest, or fed there with acorns collected for them. The Doomsday Survey contains some curious items respecting the feeding of swine on acorns, which show their value, and how greatly they were depended upon as a source of profit and food. The return for Middlesex was 16,535 hogs, for Hertfordshire 30,535, and for Essex 95,991. But more curious is it that a nobleman, by his will, left 2,000 swine to two daughters; another devises 100 swine and a hide of land to his relations, and 200 swine to two priests, in equal proportions for the good of his soul; whilst another disposes of land to a church, on condition that 200 swine were fed for the use of his wife.

---

* Harleian MSS.
† History of Tutbury, by Sir Oswald Mosley.

Robert de Ferrars also granted to the Monks of Tutbury Priory right to make a trench in the moor of Uttoxeter to preserve their fields, and gave them the branches of the willow and osiers which hung over the water for the improvement of their wet lands, which were often injured by floods.

It does not appear who was the wife of this Earl, but beyond the great improvements which he made in the Honor of Tutbury, in which Uttoxeter so largely participated, it is mentioned of him that in the reign of King Stephen, he accompanied William Percival, Earl of Nottingham, and other noblemen who undertook to repel the invasion of David, King of Scotland; and in consequence of the personal valor he then displayed, King Stephen created him an Earl. He died in the year after this memorable event, in 1139.

He was succeeded by his son Robert, who in his father's life-time styled himself " Robertus junier, comes de Nottingham." He succeeded his father as Earl of Ferrars, and is said to have been the first who assumed the title of Earl of Derby, he being created to that dignity by King Stephen in 1141. But it is also said that he was the *First* Robert who was thus distinguished by Stephen for his conduct at the Battle of the Standard. This Second Robert died in 1184, in the thirtieth year of Henry II. He was succeeded by his son William, Earl of Ferrars and Derby, who married Margaret Peveril, and through her inherited estates, to one of which " Higham Ferrars," he added his name. He is said to have died at the Seige of Acre in 1190. His son the Second William married a daughter of Hugh Kevillioc, Earl of Chester, and died in 1247. He was created Earl of Derby by King John in the first year of his reign. He was succeeded by his son, the third William, who married Sibilla, daughter of William Marshall, Earl of Pembroke, who in his turn was succeeded by his son Robert, the last Earl, whose course of infidelity to his sovereign, and reckless and open rebellion, ended in his attainder and the confiscation of his lands, which in 1266 were given by Henry III. to the Earl of Lancaster.

King John was greatly indebted to the Second Earl William, for his faithful attachment, and by a special charter created him Earl of Derby. On this occasion the King himself girded him with a sword, and not only had he in the same charter a grant of every third penny in all pleas before the Sheriff of the County of Derby, but in the same year and afterwards the honor of Tutbury was extended by the addition of other manors and grants of land. When the Pope had deposed King John, this Earl proved his fidelity to him by becoming surety for his fulfilment of those conditions to which the King was obliged to submit. As an additional return for the royal favours he had received, he accompanied the King to Poicton, and both aided him and his successor Henry III. against the rebellious barons, betwixt whom, some years afterwards, from the estimation in which he was held as a peace-maker and lover of justice, he was chosen arbitrator in their quarrels. He died in the year 1247.

His successor, William de Ferrars, Earl of Derby, did homage for Chartley, and it was during his life that some of the wild cattle of Needwood Forest (derived from Neat's Wood, or wood of cattle) were driven into the park at Chartley, where their kind have remained more than 600 years. He was well acquainted with the laws of his country, and, like his father, possessed those qualities which commended him to the esteem of all who had the privilege of his friendship. It was this Earl (who died from the effects of an accident in 1254, and was buried in Merevale Abbey), who granted the following charter to the Burgesses of Uttoxeter, which is dated August 15th, 1251.*

"To all men that shall see or heare this present deed, William de Ferrars, Earle of Derby, sendeth greeting in our Lord : Know ye, that we have granted and by this present deed confirmed for us and our heires, to all our burgesses of Uttoxeshather, that they hold from henceforward a free burgage and burgages with appurtenances in the same towne of Uttoks, as some of them have formerly bin assessed, and others hereafter shall happen to be assessed with free ingresse and egresse, to be held of us and our heires to them and their heires

---

* Uttoxeter Chronology in MSS.

or assigns and their heires for ever, as freely and as decently they shall and may hould as free burgesses, with all liberties, free commons, and easments to a free burrow belonginge, yielding to us yearely and to our heires for every burgage by itself twelvepence sterlinge at two terms of the yeare, viz. :—the halfe at the Annunciation of our Ladie and the other halfe at the feast of St. Michaell, for all secular service, custome, and exaction to us and our heires belonging. We have granted alsoe to the said burgesses and to their heires as is above said, that they maye take within themselves upon the burgages aforesaid chapmen and other free men whom they will, fufeoffing them or granting them other easments within the said borrow without hurt to the said borrow, and without hinderance to us and our heires, saving our service in all. And further we will, that none use anie trading within the said free common or libertie of the said burgesses without reasonable toll and usual. We have granted alsoe to the said burgesses and their heires as aforesaid, and to all being within their commonaltie that they shall be within all our propper lands and libertyes free from tolle wheresoever they shall pass for ever, saving other men's charters and liberties made and used before this deed. All these things aforesaid we have granted within the said commonaltie of the foresaid burgesses for ever, saving to us and our heires a reasonable tolle of all our said burgesses and their heires or assignes, and of all within their commonalties being, when as our lord the King that for the time he shalle taxe all his borrows throughout England so as the said taxe be gathered by the hands of two burgesses to the use of us and our heires, and also saving to us and our heires the ovens and market with their profits, and the places of the borrow and market, and of the court-leet alsoe from them, with pannage and all other our liberties without our said borrow, but soe as the said burgesses and all within their commonaltie being, have common and herbage within the warde of Uttokes, *whereat the men of the said town had wont formerly to outcommon without our offences*, soe as it may be lawfull for us and our heires to make our profit of all our lands and tenements, meadows, pastures, woods, marches, moores, and in all other places within the foresaid towne and ward without contradiction of the said burgesses or their heires. And if it happen anye burgage by annie means or by fire to be in lacke of occupation or service by the space of one yeare belonginge to us or our heires, that for want of a tenant, the whole commonaltie of the burgesses of the said town straight after the yeare, take the said burgage into their hands, and make the best profit thereof, and answer to us and our heires for the farm and service without annie challinge of him or his, who first held the burgage; wherefore we will and grant for us and our heires, that all things aforesaid be observed and kept to the said burgesses and their heires for ever. In witness whereof this my present writinge with the strength of my Seal for me and my heires I have confirmed.

"These being witnesses: Hugh de Meynnell, the steward, Robert de Esseburn, Robert de Punchardung, Richard de Mortimer,

Jeffrey de Caudraye, Robert de Merington, Thomas (then rector of the Church of Uttoks), Robert de Stretton, clearke, Jordan de Grendon, John de Twyford, clearke, and William de Rolleston. Dated at Uttoks on the day the Assumption of our lady, in the year of the raigne of King Henry, Sone of King John, the thirty sixth, and done in August, 1251." *

The last Earl of Derby to whom Uttoxeter belonged, was Robert de Ferrars, son of the latter William. The loss of his father whilst he was under age was a great misfortune to him, for he grew up without the influence of paternal authority. He was naturally of a perverse mind, and a knowledge of his extensive possessions was not likely to be favourable to its subjection. On attaining the age of twenty-one years, he openly rebelled against the King, his extensive estates furnishing him with a considerable number of followers; and in consequence of the depredations he committed a large army was sent against him under the King's eldest son Edward, who demolished Tutbury Castle, laid waste the country round with fire and sword, and involved the peaceful occupiers of the district in great suffering and loss. Uttoxeter being one of the most considerable places within a few miles of the Castle, the possessors of its burgages influential, free from all servile offices, but bound to attend the superior lords of the honor in time of war, most likely felt the infliction of the chastisement upon the Earl in a severe degree. Still the loss he thus sustained and the misery he entailed upon the guiltless occupiers of the land, had little effect upon him; he continued his rebellion until at length, for his misdemeanours and crimes the King resolved to punish him. Seeing his doom, he flung himself upon the mercy of his Sovereign, who generously pardoned him. He was bound by the most solemn stipulations to rebel no more, but in their very face he soon reappeared in arms against the King. His tenure of power, however, was short. His forces were routed by Almaine, the King's eldest son; he himself was captured and cast into prison, in London, and his lands, by two grants dated June and August, 1266, were given to Edward, Earl of Lancaster, son of Henry III.

---

* A translation by Peter Lightfoot early in the seventeenth century.

It would be out of place here to follow this Earl through his useless litigations for the recovery of his confiscated estates after his imprisonment of three years; but it must be observed that soon after he became of age, and previous to the year 1262, he gave to John Tunley one hundred and twenty acres of land upon the Brends of the ward of Uttoxeter, with timber growing thereon, to be held of him and his heirs, unless they should be religious men or Jews, freely, with house-boot and hay-boot, throughout the ward of Uttoxeter, and rights of common in the forest of Needwood. He also gave liberty the same year, by his letters patent, dated at Yoxall, to Sir Walter Raleigh and his heirs residing at Uttoxeter, to hunt and course the fox and hare within the precincts of his forest of Needwood, with eight braches (a particular sort of hound, perhaps the beagle) and four greyhounds. *

In the Duchy Court of Lancaster a Seal is preserved of this last and truly unfortunate Earl of Derby, of the noble family of Ferrars. The obverse represents the Earl in full armour, clothed in a suit of chain mail, with hauberk closed, and sword drawn. He bears a heater shaped shield emblazoned with his arms, vaire *Or* and *Gules*, and the trappings of his horse are charged with the same bearing. The figure is surrounded with the legend ROBS FIL' ET HERES DNI WILL'I DE FERRAR' QVDA COMITIS DERBEYE. The reverse bears a heater shaped shield of the then arms of Ferrars, vaire *Or* and *Gules*, hanging upon a tree, the foliage surrounding the shield being truly elegant and highly characteristic of the early English period. Around the seal is the legend SIGILLVM ROBERTI DE FERRARIIS COMITIS DERBEYE. The seal is one of the most beautiful and perfect of its period.

Uttoxeter must now be considered as having become transferred to Edmund, Earl of Lancaster, who was a

---

* As noticed by the Athenæum in 1881, this fact is confirmed by a charter of the convent of Strikeswold, Lincolnshire, purchased by the British Museum from the Rev. Canon Greenwell, of Durham.

branch of royalty. This Earl claimed various privileges for Uttoxeter, (as also for Tutbury,) which were view of frankpledge, infangthef, the right of erecting a gibbet and of receiving waives; also a free warren, a market once in seven days, on Wednesday in each week, and an annual fair on the eve and nativity of the blessed Virgin, all of which liberties, rights, privileges and customs had been held by Robert de Ferrars, the last Earl of Derby.

The events of the life of Edmund, Earl of Lancaster, may be comprised in a very brief summary. In his youth he was invested by the Pope with the fictitious title of King of Sicily, probably with the idea of deriving a large revenue from this country. Subsequently he was created Earl of Chester, and at the death of Simon de Montfort, at the Battle of Evesham, that nobleman's lands, with the honor of Leicester, were granted to him. He accompanied his brother, Edward I., to the Holy Land, but returned in safety. In the twenty-fourth year of this King, he was sent, with the Earl of Lincoln, with twenty-six bannerets to Gascoigne; they set down near Bordeaux, but seeing no likelihood of its surrender, they marched, after some skirmishes, from thence to Bayonne, where they were honourably received. Having, however, many soldiers with them whom they could not keep together, owing to the exhaustion of their treasures, he grew much troubled in mind, and thereby falling sick he died at the feast of Pentecost, in the year 1296. He commanded that his body should not be buried till his debts were paid; after which, truce being made, his body was carried to England and buried in Westminster Abbey. A monument was erected to his memory, of which there are plates in Gough's Sepulchral Monuments of Great Britain.* This Earl was twice married; by his second wife, Blanche, he had three sons—Thomas, Henry and John, and one daughter.

Thomas, second Earl of Lancaster, the most powerful and wealthy subject in Europe, did much to improve the

---

* Shaw's History of Staffordshire.

country surrounding the castle, which he found still suffering from the injuries sustained during the rebellion of the first Earl, and he also repaired and beautified the castle at Tutbury. In the second year of Edward II. he had confirmed to him by royal grant the weekly market, on Wednesday, and the fair at Uttoxeter. In the tenth year of Edward II., he was in the Scotch wars, and was commanded to raise two thousand foot, well armed, out of his own lands and fees, and to bring them to Newcastle to the King within one month of the feast of the nativity of St. John the Baptist. He retained Sir Hugh Meynell to serve him in peace and war. * He lived in a state of great splendour, and well would it have been for him if his views had been confined to the improvement of his estates and the sumptuousness of his hospitalities. He became General of a Confederate Army against Edward II.; various recriminations, and some not the most honourable, were inflicted upon him; ultimately he was taken prisoner, and after having been condemned by a counsel of the King's officers, and not by a body of noblemen, he was beheaded at Pontefact in March, 1320, amid great indignities, and in the sequel *canonized*. †

Uttoxeter now became a demesne of the crown, although but for a short time, for after having been consigned, with the rest of the estates of the late Earl, to the custody of Roger Beler, who was attached to the King's person, the period approached for those extensive possessions to revert to the brother of Thomas, Earl of Lancaster. King Edward became the Royal captive of Henry, Earl of Lancaster, but afterwards falling into less humane hands, he was barbarously put to death. The claim of Henry de Lancaster to the estates of his brother was admitted by Prince Edward, who assumed the administration of the State. It was also again recognised in the first year of Edward III., and an Act of Parliament was passed for revising the attainder of Thomas, Earl of Lancaster, upon the ground that he had not been tried by

---
* Shaw's History of Staffordshire.
† Dunstanborough Castle, amongst plates after J. M. W. Turner.

his Peers according to law and Magna Charta. In the same year, 1327, an inquisition was taken of the lands of the late Earl left at his death, and Uttoxeter is particularly mentioned in connection with those in Staffordshire.

The principal residence of Henry, Earl of Lancaster, was at Leicester. Very few transactions of his life are upon record connected with the honor of Tutbury. He died in 1345, leaving by his wife Maud, Henry who was created Earl of Derby, and subsequently Duke of Lancaster, who was the first English subject, except those of royal descent, who was invested with the ducal title since the Conquest. A considerable part of his life was passed abroad in the service of his country, in which he proved himself one of the greatest warriors of his age. He had, however, in his father's lifetime so distinguished himself as to be made Captain General of the King's army in Scotland. * His chivalrous exploits formed a theme of exultation to every Englishman, and produced a paralyzing dread in the hearts of his opponents. His life was terminated by the plague at Leicester, on the 24th of March, 1361. This nobleman left two daughters, Maud and Blanche, co-heiresses of his extensive possessions. Those which formed the earldoms of Derby and Lancaster fell to the share of Blanche. Uttoxeter was included in this division, it being in the honor of Tutbury. This lady became the wife of the famous John of Gaunt, who inaugurated an area of almost fabulous splendour at his Castle at Tutbury, which he had restored to its former strength and beauty after it had lain in ruins and neglect since the death of Thomas, Earl of Lancaster. The whole of the honor felt the benefit of the change; husbandry and trade received an impetus, and the deadly nightmare of depression for forty years, produced by circumstances already described, and the absence of the princely earls from their turreted home for that period, at once fled. At this time, namely, in 1370, Uttoxeter had one hundred and forty burgages which made a rental of

---

* Shaw's History of Staffordshire.

£7 2s. There were also two forges and a plot of land rented at 2s. 6d. a year. The rent of assize of free tenancy, with one bow and one sparrow hawk, were valued at £15 8s. 11d. A meadow, called Wolricheshey, was let at 6s. 8d. The rent of assize of free tenants amounted annually to £24 6s. 8d. The free fishery in the Dove, with another fishery in the Pool of Uttoxhather, was estimated at £1 5s. a year. There was a payment of 12s. by ancient custom at the two great courts; and at the feast of St. Martin, another payment of 5s. as a poll tax of young men. Twenty acres of land and one rood of meadow were valued at £1 5s. annual rent. The pleas and perquisites of the court produced £1, and a watermill there was rented at £5 6s. 8d. The sum total being £61 5s. 5d. At this time Needwood Forest was divided into five wards, of which Uttoxeter had one. In the Uttoxeter ward the sale of lime-tree bark was valued at 6s. 8d. a year; the pannage of hogs at 6s. 8d. and the perquisites of the wood-mote at 5s. There was in this ward a hay, called the moor of Uttoxeter, which was worth in herbage and acorns £2 a year, and the amount of the ward was £3 18s. 4d.

After the death of his first wife, John of Gaunt, who had become Duke of Lancaster and Earl of Richmond, married Constance, Queen of Castile, and subsequent to the demise of this lady, Catherine Swinford became his third wife. John of Gaunt died on the 3rd of February, 1399. By his Duchess Maud, he had one son, Henry, who was created Duke of Hereford. But instead of being peacefully permitted to succeed his father in the Lancastrian estates, King Richard II., who had already followed him with persecution into banishment, seized upon the goods of John of Gaunt, and issued orders for the rents and revenues of his possessions to be received for himself. The nation, however, was greatly incensed with the King's behaviour towards the Duke of Hereford, and as he passed through the city of London, on horseback, on leaving the kingdom, he was followed by forty thousand persons, who bewailed his fate and their own in the most moving manner. The Duke's attorney insisted upon the right of the claim, which Richard would on no account listen to. The imbecility and incapacity of the King, together with his repeated instances of oppression and tyranny, at length completely alienated the affections of his people, and by almost universal consent he was judged no longer worthy to manage the affairs of the realm. By the advice of Parliament he resigned the throne, and the Duke of Lancaster, son of John of Gaunt, was chosen king in his stead, by the name of Henry the Fourth. Consequently, Uttoxeter was now connected with the Crown by right. Still,

"Uneasy is the head that wears a crown."

Henry IV. had several disaffected subjects in different parts of his kingdom. His policy, however, in attaching to his interests a large number of his feudal tenants, served him most effectually in suppressing rebellion amongst the noblemen, whose fidelity was thus relied upon in the several offices to which they were appointed. Amongst these were Sir Nicholas Montgomery, of Sudbury (an ancestor of Lord Vernon), who held the office of constable of Tutbury Castle, and warden of the chase of Needwood, with a salary of £20 ; Sir John Bagot, Knight, who for other services received forty marks from Uttoxeter ; together with Sir John Gresley, Baronet, and Sir Avery Lathbury The most formidable of the King's disloyal subjects was the Duke of Northumberland. Although defeated, he maintained considerable influence in the North of England, from whence he issued a proclamation, a copy of which found its way into Staffordshire, where with several gentlemen and others, the newly-elected king was supposed not to be in great favour. Riotous proceedings were commenced against the King's tenants and officers in this country, and they were continued even after the Duke of Northumberland was slain and the rebellion at an end. Two of these gentlemen were Hugh de Erdeswick and Thomas de Swinnerton, who armed a number of men and made a violent attack upon John

Blount, steward of the King's manors at Newcastle-under-Lyme. He was son of John Blount, to whom John of Gaunt gave Barton Park upon the outlawry of Bakespur, whose cause the family of Erdeswick, who lived at Sandon, espoused. Hugh de Erdeswick made a second attack with an armed force upon John Blount, at Lichfield, and nearly succeeded in murdering him. In the first attack the Mayor of Newcastle was intimidated from taking proceedings against the parties for fear of losing his life. For a second attack by Erdeswick, a warrant was issued for his apprehension by the chief steward of the Duchy, and he and his attendants were bound to keep the peace. On that very day, however, he and three brothers of the name of Mynors, of the ancient family of that name then at Uttoxeter, armed themselves and attendants with lances, and made attacks on numerous others of the King's tenants and servants with the intention of killing them. Amongst these other victims of their malice were persons at Rolleston, Dunstall, Newcastle and Marchington, who saved themselves by a spirited resistance or a lucky escape. At Uttoxeter they broke open the house and destroyed the furniture therein of an old forester, named John Passman, a faithful servant of the Duke of Lancaster. They also threatened the life of the miller at Uttoxeter Mill, if he continued longer to work there, and attempted to kill Thomas de Belton, a tenant of the Duchy. These tumultuous proceedings lasted about a year, when they were suppressed by legislative interference.

After the lords of the Honor of Tutbury had been raised to the throne, a great depreciation took place in the value of their lands and possessions. The reason of this was that in consequence of their absence from the castle, there was a less demand for the produce of the neighbourhood. From the survey taken in the reign of Henry V., preserved in the office of the Duchy Court of Lancaster, it appears that Uttoxeter continued in the Honor of Tutbury. The same survey, which is contained in a beautifully engrossed vellum book, called the "Coucher," shows that Uttoxeter had suffered from the same cause. The number of burgage houses at Uttoxeter had decreased from one hundred and forty to one hundred and thirty-eight, and the rents from £7 2s. to £6 17s. 8d. The two forges, which are mentioned in a previous survey, appear to have been abandoned, as no mention is made of them in the "Coucher."

On Edward IV. gaining the ascendency over Henry VI., he granted the Honor of Tutbury, which he dissevered from the rest of the estates of the Duchy to George, Duke of Clarence, who is chiefly known for his whimsical choice of being immersed in a butt of Malvoisie wine. King Edward, however, annulled the grant, owing to the Duke joining the Earl of Warwick in a rebellion against himself, and issued a warrant in the thirteenth year of his reign to resume the possession of these estates, which were accordingly granted in that year to Thomas, Archbishop of Canterbury, and other trustees, to hold for the King during his absence in France.

The chase of Needwood now began to be regarded as a royal forest, but the keepers of the various wards rendered themselves exceedingly disagreeable to the occupiers of the lands on the borders of the chase, by heavily amercing them, for driving the deer back within their boundaries, from whence they often escaped, and did much damage to the crops. But when it was shown that the levy of these fines was unjust, and the keepers thereby lost this means of enriching themselves, they did not hesitate to commit unwarrantable havoc with the timber growing within the forest. In the reign of Henry VIII. one of these officers was detected in an offence of this description. As a consequence of this, further enquiries were made into the extent of the evil, when it was discovered that keepers of the various wards had cut down and sold large quantities of timber, and the keeper of Uttoxeter ward eight hundred and forty-one loads in a single year. In the first year of the reign of Queen Elizabeth, Uttoxeter ward was disforested, and the deer in it destroyed: but at the same time it contained more and better timber than any other.

The first most extensive dismemberment of the great possessions of the Earl of Lancaster, was effected by James I., by making grants of various lordships in Derbyshire. King Charles I., whose scruples were less and necessities greater than those of his predecessor, did not hesitate to make grants of his territories lying in the vicinity of his castle. The manor of Uttoxeter and other appendages of the Duchy of Lancaster, were disposed of on May 24th, 1625, to Lord William Craven, Sir George Whitmore, Sir William Whitmore, and Mr. Gibson. These gentlemen immediately caused a survey of the manor of Uttoxeter to be made, and re-sold it to the inhabitants of the town for £3,120, who conveyed to the various occupiers their interest in the same. The timber then growing in Uttoxeter High Wood was about this time sold for the king's use, by Sir Edward Mosley, the Attorney General of the Duchy, to Thomas Degg and Richard Startin, who again sold it in lots to others. In 1635, an attempt was made to enclose * the Uttoxeter ward of the forest of Needwood, upon which the inhabitants of Uttoxeter had inherited common rights from time immemorial. An account of the whole proceedings was written at the time by Mr. Peter Lightfoot, and the MS. has fortunately been preserved. The document gives quite a different complexion to the case than another brief one which has appeared. The commencement of the business was evidently attended with difficulty from the great injustice which was about to be inflicted upon the town, and hence it was undertaken with no little cunning. It would have been quite legitimate to have proposed the enclosure of the ward to those who owned common rights upon it, offering therewith just terms for

---

* With respect to enclosures made about this time the "Athenæum" of October 28th, 1876, observes :—" For by reason of these enclosures, many subjects have no ground to live on, as they had before time—not all enclosures, but only such as turneth common and arable fields into pasture, and violent enclosures of commons without just recompense of them that have right to common therein. The enclosures of the sixteenth century laid the foundations at once of modern English agriculture and modern English pauperism. They displaced a primitive system of husbandry which was incompatible with good farming, but they did so with small regard to the rights of the commoners."

acceptance or refusal ; but without this and in disregard
of the almost unanimous opposition of the inhabitants to
the enclosure of the ward in which they had rights equally
with the King, it could scarcely have been just and fair.
How the ground was broken the worthy old townsman,
Peter Lightfoot, amply informs us. He tells us that two
strangers are alleged to have appeared on the scene. They
are said to have been travelling upon the road, doubtless
the one on the High Wood, and having, as stated, heard
of the taking in of the Leicester forest, and other commons
on the King's tythe, they sought an interview with Sir
Edward Mosley, of Rollestone, to induce him to adopt
steps to take in the greater share of Uttoxeter ward for the
King, and to permit them, with some others, to deal for
it for the good of the poor, a most kind purpose, if sincere,
and clearly showing that they were not such great
strangers in Uttoxeter. So they laid the plot, but as it
was not likely that the freeholders would consent to forego
their rights, Sir Edward Mosley proceeded against the
projectors and several other persons who, with one or
two exceptions, were prepared to accede to it, in the hopes
of personal gain and not for the benefit of the poor. It
appears that the bill, the answers to it, and the subpœners,
were served and the *answers made in one hour by one hand*,
most of the parties being of one side. The bill was dated
the 9th day of February, 1635. It states the extent of
Uttoxeter ward to have been five hundred acres, and to
have been known by certain boundaries and motes. The
ward was claimed for the King to the exclusion of any
right or interest therein of any one else, and the inhabit-
tants of Uttoxeter were accused of having destroyed the
deer and birds of forest with which it is stated it had been
replenished by the King, and that without their having
had any liberty of warrant to do so. Therefore, Lawrance
Dawson, John Dynes, John Carter, Edward Ouldfield,
Edward Moor, Robert Gilbert, Luke Bushbey, Thomas
Mastergent, Peter Lightfoot, and Richard Ouldfield were
commanded on threats of pains and penalties to attend
the Duchy Court and abide its decision. With the

exception of Peter Lightfoot they all returned answer admitting the King's rights and submitting to the court, but requesting that as they had possessed common rights of pasture thereon *for time out of the mind of man*, their rights might be compounded for, for the benefit of the poor inhabitants of Uttoxeter. Mr. Peter Lightfoot was dismissed, as the court were not willing to hear any contradiction. Subsequently a commission was appointed consisting of Sir Edward Mosley, Sir Edward Vernon, Elbre Woodrooffe, Thomas Holland, and Thomas Ayloff, Esq., to compel the remainder of the inhabitants to abide by a similar decree of the court, a proceeding which was utterly unnecessary if the town had no claim on the ward; and as a temptation to secure the fuller acquiescence of the town, a portion of the ward was offered to them, not, however, without their being given to understand that they had no right to any. But at this juncture of the proceedings the King happened to visit Nottingham, when the town resolved to petition him on the business. A sum of money was consequently collected for the expenses of the undertaking, and two townsmen of Uttoxeter, named William Sherwin and William Poker, individuals quite unworthy of public confidence, were delegated to convey the petition to his majesty, the Earl of Essex having previously promised to present it to him, and if this had been done Uttoxeter would now most probably have been enjoying the benefit of the whole ward. But these two traitorous and subservient persons, in whom the people of Uttoxeter had undertaken to repose so much confidence in an important trust affecting the town through all future time, never attempted in the slightest way to perform the commission which had been committed to them to execute. In the mean time Sir Edward Mosley visited Uttoxeter, and by the use of many threats caused a few others to assent. In consequence of the commission and their intimidations, some twenty-two more names only were returned, by William Poker and William Sherwin; but it is evident that most of the names were falsely certified by these two officious parties. In reality only fifteen out of two hundred and fifty commoners submitted, and those only on condition that they might have the apportioned part of the ward themselves. It was assumed, however, that there were no dissentients: it was also as strongly averred that no part of the waste had been commonable with cattle: it was therefore decided, as from the first it had been determined, to enclose the largest and best part for the King, and leave the rest to the inhabitants. The division was accordingly effected, but some time afterwards, and before any fresh use had been made of the land, the fence was in part destroyed by the ruder sort of men and women, which called forth an injunction to restrain commoners from attempting to depasture on the King's share. Whether the ward did really contain five hundred acres appears doubtful. In the accounts to which reference has been made, it is stated by the townspeople to have been only three hundred acres, and in the old survey of the town the common or waste on the High Wood is put down to be 369a. 2r. 5p. This latter statement is evidently the result of an actual survey and is reliable, but whether it is intended to comprise the whole of the ward or only the portion assigned to Uttoxeter, is not specified. It was probably the total of the acres of the whole ward as made by the survey appointed to be undertaken by the Duchy Office, which possibly fell short of its actual extent. The King's moiety, whatever its dimensions were, was granted in 1639, to Mr. Nevil, one of the officers of the King's bedchamber, and for several years he received the rent arising from it without any interruption, but a few years before the commencement of the civil war, a party of soldiers who had been impressed against their will, burnt the rails, destroyed the fences, and laid the ground waste. For this trespass several of the townspeople were prosecuted in the Star Chamber, and had not the political convulsions which immediately arose put a stop to the proceedings, the greater part of the inhabitants would have been subjected to a continuance of vexatious law suits respecting it*—law suits

---

* See Sir Oswald Mosley's History of Tutbury for this last fact.

not very just in their nature when their object was to punish people of the town for the deeds of others for whom they could not have been responsible.

The part of the common on the High Wood which had been assigned to the inhabitants of Uttoxeter, together with the waste or common on Uttoxeter Heath of 64a. or. 35p., making in the whole 250a.* was enclosed in the year 1788, by Act of Parliament, for the purpose of aiding the poor-rates of the parish which then pressed heavily upon it. The enclosure was effected under the directions of a body of trustees, by whom the old workhouse was built, as appears from an inscription on a large circular tablet in sandstone (now in my back yard where I reside in Carter Street) which was placed high in the front of the building, the record being as follows :— "This workhouse was rebuilt by the trustees for enclosing the common within the constablewick of Uttoxeter, 1788, Thomas Garner, builder." This workhouse was taken down and the present one erected about the year 1840. It occupies three roods of land, and cost £3,900, and accommodates two hundred. Before either of these workhouses were erected a number of old houses in Special Street, close to the brook, were used for the accommodation of paupers.

The annual proceeds of the enclosed lands, now known as the High Wood Trust, amount to about £260 per annum, and it is for the relief of the poor in the constablewick of Uttoxeter only. In 1867 the constablewick of Wills Lock participated in the advantages of the trust, but a public meeting was convened to protest against the irregularity, and a deputation was appointed to wait upon the trustees, who admitted their error and made it satisfactory that the like should not occur any more. In 1868 the sum of £580 5s. was applied from this trust in relief of the poor-rates for the year.

---

* The Survey of Uttoxeter of 1658 states that the parish had 433a. 3r. op. in commons, greens, lanes, and ways. A Survey of the year 1774 records that Uttoxeter had on the High Wood 159a. 1r. 3p., and in the Woodlands 200a. 3r. 5p., more, all belonging to the poor.

As Mr. Lightfoot's document, from which some of the preceding information is derived, and which indeed gives the spirit of the paper itself, is so interesting as bearing upon the subject of the rights of the commoners of Uttoxeter, was deemed a work of *much toyle* and was intended for perusal *in times to come*, it will be considered important that it should find a place in these pages for permanent preservation. It is as following :—

"A true relation of certain transactions and passages which doe concerne the enclosing of parte of the common or waste grounds called Uttoxeter Wood.

"Set down purposely to show times to come how by those cunning plottings and contriveings they may find out the toyle and be taught how to prevent them if any such thing should set on foot hereafter.

"The timber of the said common (being very much) was about the year (1625) sold by the offices of the Duchy (one of which was Sir Edward Mosley, Knt., attorney) unto Thomas Degg and Richard Startin, who sold it by piece to all that pleased to buy it, so that in a short tyme all was fallen, and the ground made plaine. Not long tyme after projectours began to worke, and firste two strangers, who, as they travelled upon the road, did heare of the taking in of Leicester forest and other commons upon the king's tythe, and therefore wrought with Sir Edward Mosley, their attorney of the Duchie, living at Rollestone, that he would set the matter on worke and take in the greatest share for the king, and admit these two and some other parties to deal for it (as they did pretend) for the good of the poor. This could not be done without the consent of the freeholders, and to gain their consent was thought impossible. Therefore, Sir Edward Mosley thought good to proceed by bill against the projectours, or their partners, and with us (Mr. Lightfoot being one) put in some who (were feared) would oppose. So those that were parties would give their consent, and the others before they would figure in a suit against the king (which then to do was dangerous) would yield also. This plot, thus layde soe cunninglie was followed as roundly, for presently a bill and an answer to that bill and subpenas came all at one time, and the subpenas were served and the answers signed too all in one hour, the bill and answers being made both by one hand, and indeed the game plaid, most of the parties being of a side."

The bill was this:—

"9th February, 1635. To the Right Honourable Edward Newburgh, honourable councellor of his Majestie's Duchy of Lancaster, and one of his majestie's most honourable privy councellers, Humbly informeth and showeth unto your good lordship, Sir Edward Mosley, Knt., attorney general of his majestie's Duchy of Lancaster, whereas the king's most excellent majesty and his most noble projectours in right of the the Duchy of Lancaster were seized in their demesne as of fee of and in great parcel of land or waste commonly called or known by the name of Uttoxeter ward being one of the wards of his majestie's said forrest or chase of Needwood and parcel of the honor of Tutbury which is a member of the said Duchy of Lancaster; which ward or waste containing the quantity of five hundred acres thereabouts, which said waste or ward is known by certain motes or bounds, and is parcel of the said forest or chase whereout divers rents, dues, and yearly proffits have arisn, and accrued to his said majesty, and hath been also heretofore replenished and stored with deare and other beasts and birds of forrest chase and warren which now and long heretofore, are and have bin soerly destroyed and extinct therein by the inhabitants thereabouts, without any knowledge, preceipte, or warrant of his majesty or of any his said projectors or predecessors, the same now lying waste and unmanured, but may, when his majesty pleases, be replenished againe with deare, which land and waste his majesty and his most noble projectors as in right of their Duchy of Lancaster being the undoubted owners, and his majesty having a gracious purpose to improve the land for the good of his people and the whole commonwealth. So it is. May it please your Lordship that Lawrence

Dawson, John Dynes, John Carter, Edward Oldfield, Edward Moor, Robert Gilbert, Luke Bushby, Thomas Mastergent, Peter Lightfoot, and Richard Oldfield, and divers other unknown persons, who, when their names shall be known, his majestie's said attorney prayeth that they may be inserted and made defendents to the information clayming either some interest or tythe in or unto the said waste or ward called Uttoxeter ward or some part thereof or common of pasture there, where, in truth, they have no estate, right, tythe, or interest therein or thereunto. And yet the said inhabitants doe oppose and interrupt his majestie in the said works so intended by him to the great wrong and prejudice of his majestie. For consideration whereof may it please your good lordship to award thus his majestie's writt of privie seal to be divided to the said Lawrence Dawson, John Dynes, John Carter, Edward Oldfield, Edward Moor, Robert Gilbert, Luke Bushby, Thomas Mastergent, Peter Lightfoot, and Richard Oldfield, commanding them and every one of them at a certain day and under a certain paine therein to be lymited, personally to be and appear before your good lordship in his majestie's Duchy court of Lancaster, then and there to answer the information and further to stand and abide all such order and decree as shall seem to your Lordship to stand with equitie and right, and his majestie's said attorney shall dayley pray for the increase of your lordship's happiness.

"Ed. Mosley.

" 28th April, 1636.

" The answers made by all, but only Peter Lightfoot excepted.

" The jointe and severall answers of Lawrence Dawson, John Dynes, John Carter, Edward Oldfield, Edward Moor, Robert Gilbert, John Bushby, Thomas Mastergent, and Richard Oldfield, defends to the information of Sir Edward Mosley, Knight, Attorney General of his highness duchie of Lancaster Courght.

" May 14th, 1636. All advantage of exception to the uncertainties and insufficiences of the said information to these defendents and every of them, now and at all tymes hereafter being framed and reserved for answer to soe much thereof as anie may concern these defendents to make answer unto, they are hereby for themselves personally make answer, as following :—And first these defendents doe confess that they thinke it is true that the king's most excellent majestie and his projectors in right of the Duchie of Lancaster now siezed in their demesnie as of ffe of and in a parcell of land or waste commonly called by the name of Uttoxeter ward or Uttoxeter woods, containing about 300 acres in the judgement of the deffendents and noe more, and that the same was one of the wards of his majestie's chase of Needwood and part of the honour of Tutbury, but what rents or proffits thereof have arisen out of the same to his majestie or projectours, the same have been replenished with deare and other beastes and birds of fforest, chase and warren, and how and by whom the same have been destroyed, their deffendents know not. But these deffendents doe sundrie of themselves personally say that every of them and as they take it have lawfully and respectively seized of a messuage and certain lands and tenements thereunto belonging in Uttoxeter aforesaid, and that they and all those who so state they respectively of and in their said several messuages and land thereto belonging have *time out of the mind of man* had and used to hand for themselves, their farms and tenements thereof, common pasture upon the said ground called Uttoxeter waste or Uttoxeter wood for all manner of cattle commonable at all tymes of the yeare as to their said respective messuages and lands appertaining, which these deffendents hope under the favour of the honourable court they shall enjoy. And these defendents doe further for themselves severally saye that if his majestie as lord of the said waste do improve the land and take any part thereof into his own hands from these defendents and the rest of the commissioners there, these defendents have under the favour of the honourable court they shall and may be admitted to compound for the same with his majestie, so and for the benefit of the poor inhabitants of Uttoxeter who have little or no other means to keep their kine upon, for the necessary proportion of their houses, and if that, the same, or any part thereof doe happen to be taken from them and enjoyed in severalty by others, it will tend to the improvement of dyvers good people, whereof these defendents hope this honourable court will take consideration of. Without that anie other matter or thinge in the said information contained materiall or effectuall in the law for these défendents or any of them to make answer unto and not therein or thereby well and sufficiently answered unto, confessed and avoyded, traversed, or denied, is true. All and every which matters and things these defendents and every of them are readie to averre and prove as this honourable court shall award. And humbly pray to be hence dismissed, which their honourable court and charges in this behalf wrongfully sustaine.

"ALESTRIE.

" Upon this there was a proceeding to enforce others to the like submission, the court not being satisfied with those few, and myself (that is Perer Lightfoot the writer) standing out after a little time, was dismissed the court, they being unwilling to heare anie contradiction.

" 15th May, 1636.

" Sir Edward Mosley, Knight, Attorney, and Thomas Mastergent, and the inhabitants of Uttoxeter, defendents.

" Whereas the court was this day informed by Mr. Bannester and Mr. Ayeloffe as councell with his majestie that divers ffreholders and inhabitants of the said town of Uttoxeter being thereto so pressed with process to answer an information exhibited in the courte that they in all obedience accordingly have done the same and submitted themselves to his majestie's pleasure. And also the court being moved upon the said answer that all the other resiants, inhabitants, might be bound by a decree to be made soon, the said answer, Sir Edward Mosley, Knight, his majestie's attorney of the duchy, informed the court that they were willing so to be, and likewise submitted themselves there unto, it is therefore this day ordered

that all the said other inhabitants and resiants that are commoners there which have not answered to the said information, shall acknowledge the same by some instrument under their hands to satisfie the court of their said submission, or otherwise to answer forthwith to the said information and abide the censure and judgement of the court concerning the promises.
" Ed. Mosley.

" The commission to that purpose.

" Charles by the grace of God, King of England, Scotland, France and Ireland, defender of the faith, and to our trustie and most beloved Sir Edward Mosley, Knight, our attorney general of our duchie of Lancaster, Sir Edward Vernon, Knight, Symon Every, Esq., solicitor general of our said duchie, Walter Vernon, Ellibe Woodroffe, Thomas Holland, Thomas Ayloffe, Esqrs., and to eveie of them greeting. Whereas we by the advice of our councellor and councel of our said duchie of Lancaster are resolved for the increase of our revenew and other good reasons, causes, we thereunto moving to make an improvement upon Uttoxeter els Uxater ward, some times one of the wards of our forest or chase of Needwood of the possession of our said duchie in the county of Stafford, to which end an attorney general of our said duchie hath exhibited an information unto our said court against the ffreeholders, inhabitants, resiants, and all others that clayme or pretend to have common or be commoners upon our said ward to which divers of them have answered and submitted themselves to our pleasure, whereas our said court taking notice by motion made on our behalfe in eastern terme last, did order that all the said inhabitants and resiants and other the said claymers or pretenders to our common in our said ward which had all then answered the said information should acknowledge· these covenants by some instrument or writing under their hande to certify our said court of their submission or else forthwith to answer the said information and abide the censure and judgement of our said court concerning the promises. Know yea therefore that wee espetially trustinge in your wisdoms, judgments, discretions of our service in the premises have assigned, nominated, and appointed, and by these presents doe give unto you our said commissioners or annie two or more of yee full power and authoritie to summon and call before you or annie two or more you afore said all the said inhabitants and commoners or pretenders to have common on the said ward which have not answered the said information before yee and to take their consents and submissions according to the direction of the before mentioned order. And also to treat with and settle agreement betwixt us and the said inhabitants, tenants, commoners, or pretenders to any common upon the said ward for a fit and reasonable proportion of the said to be let out, enclosed and improved for our best benefit [*In the bill it is a gracious purpose the land for the good of the commonwheal* ✱] advantage and avayle from the waste of the said ward, and for the better enabling of yea our commissioners or annie two or more of yea as aforesaid to perfect and effect this our service for our best benefit and advantage. We doe hereby also give unto yee or annie two or more of yee as aforesaid full power and authority to nominate, collect, and chose one or more able and sufficient surveyor or surveyors and to give to such surveyor or surveyors full power and authoritie to make perfect and dyrect admeasurement of all the said ward or waste ground and set out, sever, divide, and distinguish the same by meers and marks from other grounds adjoining to it. And having by a treatie which the said tenants, inhabitants, commoners, or pretenders to have common in the said ward or waste agreed upon a portion thereof to be set out for us or for our use from the rest of the said ward or waste in severaltie, our will and pleasure is that you do cause such a proportion or parte to be severed, divided and distinguished from the rest of the said ward or waste as shall by your agreement contayned unto the said tenants, inhabitants, commoners or pretenders to have common in the said ward by suffyent notorious meers, bounds, or

---

✱ This and any other notes in brackets are by Mr. Lightfoot.

marks. And we doe hereby also give unto yee our said commissioners further power and authority to enquire of, do, performe, execute as well by your own view as by examination of witness upon oath and by impannelling and swearing of one or more sufficient jury or juryes and by all and every other fitt and legall ways and means which to you or any two or more of ye as aforesaid shall seeme best and fitte, shall such matter and things as may anny way conduce to the advancement and furtherance of our service in the promises. And for the better enabling of ye our said commissioners to peform this service for us we shall and command our sheriffe of our countrie of Stafford that at such day, tyme and place, days, times, and places, as ye or annie or two or more of you as aforesaid shall appoint to have the cause to come before yee such and so many lawful and honest men of the said countrie as will make up or more sufficient jury or juryes. And of your ffacts, doings, and proceedings herein, together with these our letters, wee will and require you or anne two or more of you as aforesaid to certify our said chancellor and councellor of our said duchie in our duchie chamber at our pallace of Westminster in meuse (month) Michls next coming or sooner if you can conveniently not fayling hereof as we especially trust you. Given at our said pallace under the seale of our said duchie the ninth day of July in the twentieth year of our ragne.

"H. GERRARD.

"'Thus farre the first petitioners, John Carter, Edward Oldfield, and one or two more stood in good hope to gaine what they looked for, when, whilst those things were in doing the King came to Nottingham and means was made by this town to the corte of Westminster to petition the King concerning the business. A petition was drawne, a large summe of money was ggathered to beare charges and William Sherwin and William Poker undertook to wait upon the Earl of Essex who promised to deliver the petition to the King and to solicit for the towne which with longing desire *(as he himself told me—that is told*

Peter Lightfoot) he waited for. But these two petitioners, though they were at Nottingham all the tyir yet came not at the corte, not did anything at all in the matter, but turned and fell into them that submitted and justified that submission as twentie ffrehoulders *(as shall appear hereafter)* who never gave their consent, none were acquainted with it, but at the doore of the parliament in the lobbie there did utterly renounce the same afterwards. Sir Edward Mosley with some of the commissioners came to the towne here and with sad and manie threats procured the subscription of some more than was before and returned up the same as following :—

" May it please your lordship.

" According to the tenour of a commission forth of the duchie chamber to us and other our fellow commissioners who clayme or pretend to have common in that waste, ground, or ward called Uttoxeter els Uxater ward being one of the ffive wards of the fforest or chase of Needwood, and whereas by an order in the said commission mentioned, it was ordered that they should submit themselves to the answer of Lawrence Dawson and others an information exhibited against them and likewise signified soe much by some instrument under their hands these are to certify your lordship that they are contented so to do as it may appear by the contents thereof hereafter following.

"SIMON EVERY, THOMAS AYLOFFE.

" Whereas by an order forth his majestie's court of Duchie chamber *Tercinno Pasche* in the twelfth year of his majestie's reign upon particular information of Sir Edward Mosley his said majestie's attorney general of the Duchie, that the freehoulders, tennants, and inhabitants of the towne of Uttoxeter were willing to be bound by a decree to be made upon an answer in that honourable court by Lawrance Dawson and others to an information by the said attorney there exhibited and submitted themselves to his majestie's pleasure touchinge the same as they the said Lawrance and others hath done, it was ordered by the court that they should acknowledge the same by some instrument under our hands. We the said freehoulders, tennants and inhabitants, whose names are hereunder written, in all obedience to the said order doe hereby testifie and declare that we willingly doe assent and joine with them in their submission to the said order and deqree of this honourable court to be bound by the same, and hereby witness it under our hands this 21st day of September, 1636.

"Thomas Mastergent, William Spragg,
"Humphrey Hill, John Townsend,
"John Carter. John Dynes.
"William Heaton,

"We whose names are underwritten agree to the answers of our neighbours, viz., William Poker, William Sherwin, William Heaton, William Spragg, Thomas Wilshaw, Ffrancis Chamberlain, Richard Bakewell, James Keeling, Thomas Newton, Francis Tomlinson, Ralphe Grey, John Sherratt, Robert Bakewell, Francis Allen, Richard Wood, William Barns, William Bath, Anthony Basford, Ralphe Wilshaw, Richard Burton. Humphrey Moore, Humphrey Hill.

"These men's names herein mentioned are testified to be willing to consent to the instrument we have set our hands to.

"William Poker,
"William Sherwin by his X mark.

"Thus we see what shifting and shuffling there was with the first projectors, and then with these second. Now steps in a third under the wing of this Mr. Ayloffe and one John Gregory who was employed by him. That was Mr. William Wood, who, in his own hopes, stood fayre to carry all away. Soe that by forcing some by information, some few by threats, and these last by falsly certifying their submission, they got out this commission following :

"Charles by the Grace of God of England, Scotland, Ffrance, and Ireland, King, defender of the faith, and to our trusty and well beloved Sir Edward Mosley, Knt., our attorney general of our duchie of Lancaster, Sir Edward

Vernon, Knight, Symon Every, Esq., our attorney general of our said duchie, Walter Vernon, George Parker, and Thomas Ayloffe, Esqrs., and to divers of them greeting.

"Whereas we accordinge to an order made in our courte of duchie of Lancaster, the 28th day of May last, directed our commissioner unto the said Sir Edward Mosley, Sir Edward Vernon, Symon Every, Esq., and others our then commissioners to take the submissions and consents of the inhabitants and claymers of common in our ward called Uxater or Uttoxetor ward which had not answered our information preferred against them by our said attorney in our court of as our said duchee and also to treat with them for a proportion of the said ward or common to be set out for us, and to admeasure the said ward by a surveyor, and to divide and parte the said land whereupon the inhabitants and clayments of common (only fifteen out of at least two hundred and fifty commoners submitted and on condition they might have it themselves or some of them!) in general submitted to a division of the said ward. And upon the treatie made by virtue of our said commission by our said commissioners, the said inhabitants, claymants of common aforesaid the one halfe of the said ward or common to be set out and enclosed for us. And whereas it appeareth the common or ward hath anciently bin a wood belonging unto us and therefore could not be commonable with cattle, therefore our said court of duchie did declare that we should have the better thereof set out in severaltie for us, which our will and pleasure it should be forthwith done and effected. Know yee therefore that we trusting in your wisdoms and discretion, have assigned and appointed yee, and hereby doe give unto you our said commissioners or any two or more of yee full power and authority to call the said inhabitants, claymers of common within the said ward or common before yee, and to treat with them about the said division and according to their consent signified or certified to our said court to get out and divide and fence the said ward or common into two parts or halves as well by impannelling and swearing of one or more jury or juries upon oath, evidence, perambulation, examination of witnesses upon oath *(what need all this, being their own carvers!)*, as by all their *(Good!)* ways and means as to you our said commissioners or annie two or more of ye as aforesaid shall seame best and fittest for the division of the said ward or common being so divided as aforesaid to set out the best parte or halfe thereof for us by such notorious bounds, meers and marks as the same may be perfectly known and distinguished from the other part or halfe of the said ward or common, and from other lands adjoining or bordering upon the same. That thereupon such part of the said ward or common as shall be set out, divided and inclosed for us may by the decree of our said court or otherwise be settled and established for us, our heirs *(like to the last!)* and successors. And that the other part of the said ward or common which shall remayne and be left out unto the said inhabitants and claymers of common in the said ward as waste ground may be likewise continued settled *(kindly done!)* and for ever established unto them and their heirs by the said decree of our said court or by such other assurances and confirmation as by them or their councel learned shall reasonable desired or required, and as your acts, doings, and proceedings herein we will and require you or annie or any two or more of as aforesaid by your writings inclosed under your seals together with these our letters to certifie our chancellor and councel of our duchie of Lancaster in our duchie chamber at our palace at Westminster in Mense Pasche next coming. Not fayling hereof as we trust hereon at our said duchie of Lancaster the eleventh daye of May in the twelfth year of our reigne.

"H. GERRARD.

"May it please your honour.

"These are to certify your lordship that by vertue of a commission forth of his majestie's court of duchie chamber at Westminster, the seale of the said duchie bearing date the eleventh day of May in the twentieth year of his majestie's raigne, to us and other our fellow commissioners directed. We whose names are here underwritten have according to the effort thereof called before the inhabitants and claymers of common within the ward and common Uxather els Uttoxeter ward, one of the five wards of his said majestie's fforest or chase of Needwood, and treated with them concerning the dividing, setting forth of one halfe or moyitie of the said ward of his majesty, which said inhabitants and claymers of common on the most part and sufficientest of them *(spare them!)* being present on the twentieth and towards twentieth days of April last in the eighth year of his majestie's reigne according to their consents in general signified unto this honourable court. *(No other concent but what is before.)* We have set forth and divided for his majesty by which notorious bounds and meers as the same may be easily known from the other part or half thereof, and from lands adjoining thereunto, viz., three score and seven acres thereof or thereabouts commonly called or known by the name of Swethholme Knowle, being admeasured by a surveyor appointed by the inhabitants. *(appointed by William Spragg!)* clayments of common there which parcel of ground is situated and lying at the end of the said ward adjoining Mr. Fflyer's moors commonly called Uttoxeter moors northward and meered and bounded out by us as following: From Mr. Spragg's barn and straight forward on the right hand of an old tree upon the common westward to the length ass found four perches, and from thence straight down Mr. Fflyer's rayles against the moors northward about two roodes from an elme tree standing in length about one hundred and five perches as it is meered out by small trenches and from thence all along Mr. Fflyer's ring hedge to the barn aforesaid. And from thence by Mr. Hart's ground and hedge to the barn aforesaid. And the other parcel of the same halfe for his majestie we have set forth at the end of the ward lying southward, beginning at the corner of Ball's dimble along by a pit or ditch to timber lane. And from thence alonge the ringe hedge on the other side of the land to a gate leading to the widow Milward's ground and from thence to a lane called Hart's lane leading towards Bromley. And from thence towards a lane leading towards Lichfield: and from thence to a lane called Mistorfield's lane, which way leadeth to Marchington. And from thence to Mr. Hart's ringe hedge belonging to ould Hart ground to an hollin tree in Hand's fflatt: and from thence straight over to the aforesaid corner of Ball's dimble, which last parcel we have divided from the rest of the common by a ditch banke, and conceive both these parcels set out for his majestie as aforesaid to be halfe and somewhat better *(with a witness!)* part of the said common or ward which we humbly leave to the judgment of this court.

"EDWARD MOSLEY,
"SYMON EVERY,
"SERGE PARKER,
"WALTER VERNON,
"THOMAS AYLOFFE.

"After this it was taken in accordingly, and some of the ruder sort pulled down some of the fence which caused the information following:—

"22 May, 1637. Whereas the court was this day moved by those of counsell for his majestie that by virtue of a commission returned into this court (Monte Pasche) declaring that the setting forth for his majestie one parte or halfe of the waste ground or ward called Uxater or Uttoxeter ward, one of the five wards of his majestie's forests or chase of Needwood by the commissioners therein mentioned. That it would please this honourable court to establish and settle the said part or halfe so set forth for his majestie to his majestie his heirs and successors by order and decree of this courte and the other parte to the commoners. And whereas it was further moved that for the present some one might be appointed to set, let, and dispose for his majestie till Allhallantide next that so this summer's profit might not be lost. And likewise whereas the court was informed that divers disorderly persons and idle women have riotiously cast down a banke which was made for the separating of his majestie's side, parte, or halfe, from the parte or halfe set out for the commoners, it was prayed that an information might be granted to restrain the commoners from taking of all manner of common upon the said warde or waste grounde whatsoever and wheresoever till such tyme as his majestie's parte or so much thereof as should be thought fitt forthwith to be enclosed and fenced should be done. Accordingly it is therefore this day ordered that a decree shall forthwith be drawn up for the setting of his majestie's said part or half to his majestie's said heirs and successors, and the other halfe to be commoners. And Thomas Ayloffe, Esq., who hath bin employed hitherto in this service for his majestie, and now nominated by Simon Every, Esq., receiver general of his majestie's Duchie of Lancaster who was desired by the court to take care for his majestie in this business, shall have full power and authority hereby to let, set, and dispose of his majestie's said halfe, parte for his majestie's use and best benefit till Allhallontide next. 'And likewise that an injuction be forthwith awarded against all persons who clayme common on his majestie's said waste for the restraining of the said commoners from taking annie benefit of common by their cattle of what sort soever till his majestie's said parte or halfe be inclosed and fenced out from the rest of the common or soe much thereof as shall be thought fit to be forthwith enclosed to the end that the summer's profit of his majestie's said parted halfe may not be lost."

(This commission was from Sir Edward Mosley to Lawrance Dawson and John Dynes, the inhabitants of Uttoxeter!!!)

[The portions in brackets and underlined are special remarks by Mr. Lightfoot made at the side of his writing.]

UTTOXETER DURING THE CIVIL WAR AND REBELLION, &c., &c.

Although the opening of the civil war of the seventeenth century served so well the inhabitants of Uttoxeter in saving them from ruinous proceedings in the dreaded Star Chamber, in respect to their common rights, yet it came upon them otherwise with extreme severity, which continued a number of years. Uttoxeter being situated betwixt various places which were garrisoned for the King —as Alton Castle, Wootton Lodge, Barton Blount, and Tutbury Castle—the inhabitants were not only harassed by a continual apprehension of a siege, but they also suffered excessively by the exactions of the contending parties as temporary success placed either one or the other in the most advantageous position in the war. The accounts of the constables of Uttoxeter during that stirring time are still extant, and they afford a vivid picture of the amount of oppression the people of the town were called upon to endure. Raising large sums of money and furnishing provender and provisions for Tutbury, Lichfield, Alton, Wootton Lodge and Stafford, but chiefly for Tutbury, was almost a daily occurrence. The King passed through the town no fewer than three times; distinguished military individuals and soldiers were quartered upon it, as they passed and repassed from place to place, at no slight expense; bulwarks and barricades were made; trenches were dug and watches were set; and when an army could not be had for the safety of the town, the inhabitants were obliged to arm themselves and call in the countrymen from the surrounding villages to aid in defence of their property and homes.

King Charles I. paid his first visit to Uttoxeter in 1642, in the course of movements occasioned by the unsettled political state of the country, when he stayed at Mr. Wood's hall, which was swept for the august occasion, and was then the principal genteel residence in Uttoxeter. It was in this year that the King, failing to give satisfaction to his parliament by his concessions whilst he refused his assent to the militia bill, resolved to appeal to the sword for the maintenance of his rights, and commanded the High Sheriff of the County of Stafford to garrison Tutbury Castle, and levy contributions upon the county for all requirements. From Uttoxeter the King marched to Stafford, for it appears that the sum of £1 14s. 6d. was paid for trained soldiers accompanying him to Uttoxeter, and from there to Stafford to wait upon him.

A paper which was printed during the civil war affords more information than is derivable from the constable's accounts, respecting this or some other visit of the King in the same year to Uttoxeter. The date of the visit was on the 19th of September, 1642, and the paper was printed the fifth day after, viz., on September 23rd, 1642. The document leads us to infer that his majesty stayed some days, or over a week at Uttoxeter, although it states he purposed remaining only one night for its concluding remarks are these, and seem to imply as much :—" His majestie intends to leave Uxeter very suddenly and to go to Shrewsbury, but what his intent is we cannot descern." The paper including its title and imprint is as follows :—

"THE KING'S

Majestie's demands and propositions, propounded to the lords, knights, and gentlemen of Staffordshire and near adjoining counties of South Wales, at Uxeter in Staffordshire, on Monday, 19th of September.

" With the Judicious answers to the said propositions.

" Also a true Information of his majestie's proceedings since his arrival in those parts.

" London : Printed for Hen Rydiar, September 23, 1642.

"The propositions of his Majestie propounded to the lords, knights and gentlemen of Staffordshire and near adjoining counties of South Wales, &c.

"His majestie having made his residence a long time at Nottingham, found that his time and expences there had availed him little, where he resolved to remove from thence to Darby; from Darby into Staffordshire at Vxeter: to the end that he might be further from the Earl of Essex, and near to Wales, from whence he expected most of his troops should come.

"Where being arrived he found an unexpected welcome, for instead of multitudes of people assembled to entertain him with applause, he found a little army of knights and gentlemen called in warlike posture rather to oppose than welcome him. Wherefore he sent a herald to demand the cause of their appearance in such a form of opposition, who, being arrived, he received this answer: That they appeared rather petitioners than opposers, neither was it their intent any way to oppose his majestie whom they were bound to protect, but to defend his majestie and themselves from the oppression, Rapin and plunder of those bloodthirstie papists and others who had assembled themselves together under a pretence of standing for his majestie, when indeed their practices and endeavours are only to ruin both him and his kingdome. This being apparently known and seriously wheighed, they found themselves bound in loyaltie to his majestie and in case of their own safety (now while they had power in their hands) to provide both for the protection of his majestie and the peace of the kingdom.

Likewise they delivered to the said herald a short schedule wherein was contained a declaration of their affection both to the King and Parliament, with their resolutions, concerning certain propositions which they had received from his majestie by Lord Strange, the effect of which propositions was as followeth:—

"1. That when as a present rebellion and actual warr was levied in the South under a pretence of standing for his majestie and for the protection of his sacred person, when indeed it was done by some factious persons who only *aspire* at the subversion of the law of the land and the known religion of the church of England, absolutely include the prerogative of the King and the property of the subject, wherefore his majesty finding himself bound in conscience to defend all his loving subjects from being made subject to an arbitrary power, and whereas it was not in his power to defend them or himself without their large assistance, he was forced to demand their aid for the suppressing the present rebellion and insurrection.

" 2. That whereas a warre of such consequence and danger cannot be managed and maintained without money, which he was destitute of, by reason that his revenue was detained and all his means of subsisting taken from him, his goods seized on, and his forts and ships kept by violence from him; wherefore he was forced (they being obliged thereto; their own security and future freedom lying at stake) to demand their utmost assistance both of men and armies and money; which granted he doubted not but that by God's protection he should reduce those insurrectionary people to their future obedience, and make it a happy return to all those that had or should stand close to him in a time of such danger and distractions."

These propositions they returned his answer :

" That whereas his majestie was pleased to terme that a rebellion in the South which was done only to his own security and of whose loyal affections to his majestie they had received a large testimony; they humbly desired his majestie to recall that scandel which he had thrown upon them, it being only the fruit of the evil councellors about his majestie, who for the furtherance of their own desperate and bloody designs strove to make the true protestants of this kingdom (under the notion of Puritans) to appear odious to his majestie, so that by that means they might gain strength to themselves and weaken his majestie; by withdrawing the affection of his subjects from him. As touching his majestie's desires that they should assist him, they promised their best aid against the malignant party of Papists, Prelates, Protectors, under whom they so long groaned, and by whom his majestie had so long been seduced to make war against his loyal subjects, only to support them in their lordly pride and domineering prelacie. As for his majestie's securitie they provided during his abode there, that what forces he should think requisite for his guard should be at his command, and what other supplies should be necessary for princely support and might be agreeable to their dutie. But for any forces or assistance of men or money to be employed against the Parliament both their loyalties to his majestie nor their care of the peace of the kingdom could no way consent to.

"Likewise they humbly desired his majestie to abandon those evil councellors that laboured his destruction, and that he would withdraw his protection from those delinquents and deliver them up to the justice of the law that their punishment might deter others from offending in the like nature.

"Likewise they humbly desired his majestie to throw down his arms and embrace his royal subjects in the arms of his love, which was the only and most effectual means to increase a better obedience and a firmer obligation of love and peace than any forces could ever obtain; this, if they might obtain, they would be aiding and assisting and during life daily pray, &c.

"At the receipt of this his majestie seemed but little discontented, but with an affable behaviour marcht up to Uxeter, where having made his residence that night, on the morrow Prince Robert (Rupert) with his troops endeavoured to force men to serve and to seize their arms for the King's use, and such as refused he burnt their houses, inasmuch that the country was forced to rise and fall upon the troops. So that Prince Robert was forced to flie to Uxeter to his own securitie. Very few come in to the King: only some raged uncertain Welsh. His majestie intends to leave Uxeter very suddenly and to go to Shrewsbury; but what his intent is we cannot discern. FINIS."

Uttoxeter has generally been spoken of as a royal town, and it would appear that at some period of this unsettled time there might have been a predominant leaning to the Stuart dynasty. At the beginning of the war, however, whatever opposite compulsion might have been imposed upon them, it is evident the people of Uttoxeter inclined to the side of the parliament. The paper now given shows that the people of the neighbourhood were neither willing to serve with the royalist army nor to assist it by contributions of arms, and the whole of the document indicates that all Uttoxeter was disposed to do for his majesty was to show him civility and afford him protection while he remained in the town. We are not told that there was any welcome to the King pealed from the church bells when he stayed at Uttoxeter Hall, and the ruin threatened to the town in the Star Chamber was in remembrance against his being favourably received. This is also further evident. When Stafford became possessed by the royalists, the moorlanders, amongst whom the people of Uttoxeter and neighbourhood were included, applied to Sir John Gell, then at Derby, for his assistance.* According to the parliamentary narrative, "Sir John Gell asked what assistance they would have: they said two hundred musquetters and one saccer, not doubting but that they had men enough with that assistance to regaine the town—doubtless that of Stafford— and save themselves. Hee commanded his major Mollanus immediately with two hundred foot and one saccer to march towards their appointed rendezvous att Uttoxeter. His major being there two or three dayes, and nobody coming to assist him, and hearing that the enemy increased, was forced to retreat in the night to Derby." Sir John Gell, himself, joining his force with that of Sir William Brereton, soon after marched upon Stafford, and at Hopton Heath, near that town, on the east, came up with the enemy. "Whereupon hee sett his ffoot in order of battalis, and Sir William his horse, the enemy advancing in a full

---

* Hobson's History of Ashbourne.

body with above one thousand two hundred horse, whereof the Earl of Northampton was general, and soe setting upon their horse, Sir William's horse presently ran away, and left Sir John Gell alone with the foot. The enemy drew his horse into a body againe, and charged his ffoot, but hee gave them such a salute, that the enemy in a disordered manner drew off and marched away towards Stafford, but left many dead bodies behind them, whereof my lord Northampton was one, Captayne Middleton and many other brave commanders of horse, and at least one hundred dragoones ; and on the other side three carters and two souldyers were slayne ; we lost two casks of drakes, which the dragoons had drawne a greate distance from the ffoote, under the hedges to save themselves, and soe Colonel Gell retreated towards Uttoxeter, with his fforces, and Sir William Brereton with his forces towards Cheshire. And att Uttoxeter Colonel Gell remayned three dayes, and set Staffordshire in as good posture as he could ; within the said three dayes there came a trumpeter to him from my younge Lord of Northampton, for his father's dead body, whereupon hee answered, if he would send him the drakes which they had gotten from their dragoons and pay the chirurgeons for embalming it, hee should have it ; but he (the Earl of Northampton) returned him an answer, that hee would do neither th' one nor th' other, and soe Colonel Gell caused him to be carried in his company to Derby, and buried him in the Earl of Devonshire's sepulcher, in All Hallow's Church."

About this stage of civil commotion, Uttoxeter presented all the features of a place in a state of siege. Various defensive works were raised about the town, especially on its west and south sides. One man named John Sherret led clods for a period of five days to the bulwarks ; other day labourers and carpenters were paid the sum of £5 13s. 2d. for their services in the erection of similar works, in the construction of which timber and other articles were required costing the sum of £1 6s. 8d. No doubt the anxious inhabitants of the town made, also, voluntary contributions of materials and personal help for the same objects. But besides the expense of these works, which were intended for a vigorous defence, there were also coal, and the warlike materials of powder and bullets for the town was provided amounting to about £4 in value. In apprehension of an advance from Stafford way, trenches were dug in the Picknals, at which men from Loxley and other places were employed. That the town at this period was actually attacked there is not the slightest doubt. Wortley, with a force of men, came against it, but they were repulsed and a number of them taken prisoners. On this occasion the town was assisted by men who had been previously called in from most of the villages and hamlets about—as Tean, Loxley, Marchington, Crakemarsh, and Creighton. Lord Stanhope and his son were also this year in custody at the Crown, one of the two inns of that name then in the market place, and were kept there under the strictest watch of a guard.

In 1643, King Charles I. was at Uttoxeter again, but where he was passing to does not appear. This time he was honoured with a peal from the church bells. The bulwarks were this year pulled down, although there was still great cause for apprehension of another attack upon the town, as a strict watch had to be kept up on the neighbourhood from the church tower, which commands a view of most of the approaches to the town, for the safety of which other precautions were taken by the employment of guards and sentinels. One of the bulwarks, thus taken away, had been at the church gates, and the fact clearly intimates that the church would have been occupied as a defensive position, and perhaps as a last resort for the defenders of the town in case of their being much pressed by any body of besiegers. During this year Colonel Gell took Wootton Lodge, making, no doubt, prisoners of the garrison, to the defenders of which Uttoxeter sent a cart load of bread. The expenses occasioned to Uttoxeter by the war during these two years amounted to about £68, but they afterwards became excessive year by year for twenty years, and it is really a wonder how the town survived so fearful a crisis.

The levies upon Uttoxeter, in provisions and money, amounted, in the succeeding year, 1644, to no less a sum than £608 13s. 2d., whilst the hamlet of Loxley, for the same period, furnished the sum of £85 8s. 6d. There was considerable warmth of feeling amongst the two political parties in Uttoxeter at this period, and there can be little surprise if there was a ringing clash of wordy controversy, and sometimes of violent rancorous contention, and it must have been owing to some strife in the differences between the parties that one John Scott, who belonged to a family of respectability and property in Uttoxeter * was killed. The man who was guilty of committing the deed was soon discovered and seized, and the manner in which he was dealt with was amazingly summary, for a rope and cords, costing a shilling, were speedily procured, and with them he was pinioned and hanged, and then hastily interred in the churchyard, and the sum of eighteenpence was paid for taking him there. The place at which he was executed was, doubtless, the pillory, which stood at Bear Hill, and independent of authentic information of the fact in the constables accounts, tradition has kept in memory till the present time the same circumstances in the saying I have oft heard "that a man was once hung at the pillory near the Red Lion Inn." Probably the condemnation of the man was issued at a Court Leet, which was early granted to Uttoxeter, and which, as Riston informs us, was one of the most ancient kinds of criminal courts in England, for it is tolerably certain that his execution could not have taken place without some sufficient authority either military or vested in a local body which held its meetings at the court house of the town. Mr. William Fish, one of the constables, was also taken prisoner this year by Lord Goring, who lay in the town with his foot guards on the 4th of May. This worthy man, probably under the influence of his political leanings, either neglected or positively refused to supply provisions to Lord Goring,

---

* Lightfoot's Survey.

I

which was evidently held as a sufficient excuse for his imprisonment. The matter is referred to in the following entry by his brother official in the constables accounts, "Charges and martial fees expended by my fellow constable being kept prisoner three weeks concerning provisions, £1 6s. 4d."

On the 24th of May, 1645, it being Whitsun Day, the King arrived for the third and last time at Uttoxeter, from Stone. He was accompanied by Prince Rupert, son of Frederic V., elector of Palatine, by Elizabeth, daughter of James I., a rash and impetuous individual, but possessed of varied abilities, and well skilled in most pursuits, from engraving a picture to conducting an army. The King and Prince were at the head of a large force of horse numbering about 5,520.* On the succeeding day they proceeded to Tutbury, and from thence to Ashby-de-la-Zouch and Leicester, the latter of which place they took by storm on the 14th of June.

On the King arriving at Uttoxeter on May 24th, his Majesty was again saluted with peals from the church bells, and the records of the town fully confirm the traditionary account that he slept at Sir Thomas Milward's, judge, at Eaton. A hogshead of beer, which cost Uttoxeter £1 6s. 8d., was conveyed to Eaton for his Majesty's use by one Thomas Ball. A family of that name appear to have had some property in Uttoxeter, but the only source which could have shown what public house he occupied, fails to do so. † The account of King Charles sleeping at Eaton is also confirmed by a notice in Captain Symond's diary published by the Camden Society. There is in the possession of Mr. Milward, of Wolverhampton, an interesting Eaton heirloom in the form of a glass cup—a stirrup cup—which belonged to Sir Thomas Milward, of Eaton, and which bears an inscription which, it is stated, has the intention that the cup should be used to keep up the memory of King Charles having been at Eaton. The cup is of

---

* Shaw's History of Staffordshire.
† Lightfoot's Survey.

graceful form with two fluted handles, and on the reverse side is engraved a representation of the vine and two ears of barley. The front side bears the following inscription, engraved :—

M
T * M
KEEP IT UP,

and underneath it, with the bare ends crossing each other, two fronds of fern with apparently a lily at the centre of intersection. Prince Rupert and another Prince, whose name is not given, lay at Uttoxeter, and their quarters, for one night only, cost the town £5 12s., whilst the cook of Prince Rupert claimed and had paid to him a fee of 5s. The town was not capable of accommodating the whole of the King's troops, and consequently some of them were billetted on the villages about. The Earl of Lichfield and others were quartered upon Marstone, near which place a soldier, for ravishing two women, was tied with his shoulders and breast naked to a tree, and every carter of the train and carriages was to lash him in passing. On the army leaving Uttoxeter on the 25th, a waggon and several horses were required to accompany it, for the conveyance of luggage. Neither the horses nor luggage were, however, returned, the army being doubtless unwilling to part with them; and as the engagement for them had been made with their owners by the town officials, a demand was made upon the town for their value, which was paid and entered in the town accounts. During the time the army stayed at Uttoxeter, a man was slain at the house of Edward Ball, who was sent with the beer to Eaton. Under what circumstances the deed was committed is left entirely to conjecture. It seems that the town had no power to interfere with the man who was guilty of the act, as if it had, and had put it in operation as in a previous case, there would have been entries in the town accounts, specifying the amount of expenses attending his trial and punishment. But there are not any. It may therefore be presumed he was one of the soldiers belonging to the army who encountered a man of an opposite political bias, and both being probably in liquor, an affray most likely took place in which the man lost his life. The man who met with his death belonged to Draycot-in-the-Clay, and the sum of 6s. was given for the conveyance of his body to that village. During the remaining part of the year, bodies of soldiers were either constantly in the town for its protection, or quartered upon it in the course of their movements. In June, soldiers were drawn up in Balance Close, which is land, then known by that name, overlooking the town at the south-east side of the New Bridge, at the Hockley. A number of soldiers were also quartered at Blount's Hall, where they were supplied with provisions from Uttoxeter. A cannon ball has been dug out of the moat of the old hall, and it is now in my possession. Again, on the 20th of July, soldiers were drawn up in some place called "in the field," and before the close of the month the men of Colonels Ashenhurst and Watson, appear to have been encamped in the Broad Meadow, where they were supplied with provisions. Uttoxeter is specially mentioned as being guarded in August, when the Parliamentary forces went against Tutbury Castle for three nights, on each of which nights scouts were sent out from the town with guides, probably to Tutbury, to take account of the proceedings of the enemy, or perhaps more likely to report any danger apprehended to the town itself. At all events, Uttoxeter was in considerable trepidation, and a messenger was despatched to Alton for Colonel Bowyer, at the same time that Colonel Jackson's soldiers had their rendezvous on Uttoxeter Heath, having previously had their quarters at Somersall. In September, Sir William Vaughan had a guard at Uttoxeter, and for a fortnight in October General Poynes had Uttoxeter in his protection. The town ends, meaning the entrances to the town, and the street ends were barricaded and blocked up by the soldiers, who were in the town under him. All this seems to have presaged something more serious, and it did in reality happen that a soldier was slain in the public streets. The incident is somewhat difficult to account for, but as barricades were made and the town ends were blocked up, evidently in full expectation of an attack upon it, it may very reasonably be supposed that a detachment of the enemy actually succeeded in breaking through the impediments, although doubtless defended, and so a conflict ensued in the midst of the town, in which the individual referred to was cut down. Indeed, if he had been killed in the same unwarrantable manner as John Scott, the murderer would have met with the same summary retribution from the Court Leet which we have just described. The body of the unfortunate soldier was wrapped in a winding sheet, and for making the grave, for the purchase of beer, and for burying the body in so slim a protection from the crushing earth, a sum of 4s. was expended. The accounts for the year ending in October, as disbursed by Uttoxeter for the war, although not passed till February 5th following, amounted to the sum of £975 7s. 1d.

The battle of Naseby decided in effect the fate of the unfortunate monarch; but even then, despairing as the royal cause had become, the beleagured and trusty garrison at Tutbury boldly held out in his favour. But the difficulty of retaining it after this crisis was, of course, proportionably increased. The disposal of the troops of the Parliamentarians contracted the already limited district from which the garrison of Tutbury had to draw its subsistence,* and rendered it impossible for provisions to be conveyed to the castle without a strong escort to protect those who furnished them. But even then, as might be expected, repeated encounters took place with the Parliamentarian horse, and two occurred so near to Uttoxeter as Uttoxeter High Wood;—Uttoxeter furnishing a great portion of the provisions to the Castle. An account of two of these is preserved in the "Gesta Britaniorum," by Sir George Warton, in the following notice :—" Feby. 15th, 1645, a sharp encounter between a party of the King's

---

* History of Tutbury, by Sir Oswald Mosley.

troops from Tutbury Castle, and a party of the Parliament's from Barton House in Derbyshire." On February 18th he also says, "A party of the Parliament's forces routed by the King's forces near Uttoxeter." These occurrences are not mentioned in the constables accounts, but on the 22nd of the same month it appears that two soldiers, who had been maimed by Tutbury soldiers on the High Wood, were conveyed to Carswall, otherwise Caverswall, at an expense of 2s. 6d., which leaves no doubt of their having been in the engagement, and of having belonged to the Parliament forces. As evidence of fighting having taken place on the High Wood, it may be mentioned that a cannon ball has been found there, and also one at Ruff Cliff. By the accounts mentioned it does not appear whether any of either of the parties were slain, although Sir Oswald Mosley seems to think that such was the case, and a list of the slain which was printed in 1660, mentions that a Captain Sayers was slain at Uttoxeter at some period during the war. There were, doubtless, many other similar incidents occurring near Uttoxeter, and one in March of a less serious kind was that of the cavaliers carrying off a bay mare and a quantity of oats which were going from Uttoxeter to Tutbury. It appears probable, also, that Mr. Gilbert Gerrard lost six horses in a similar way, for at the same time he was paid the sum of £21 in lieu of that number and their furniture. The pressure of the times was very much felt in Uttoxeter; arrears due to the army through Commissary Ward, were only obtained by the force of a warrant. It is possible, at the same time, that the tide of affairs had also something to do with it, by disinclining the town to support the hopeless cause of an already fallen monarch.

If up to this time Uttoxeter had supplied chiefly the requirements of the Royalists, and now especially the besieged Royalists at Tutbury Castle who were in great want, the claims, also, of the Parliamentarians were required to be entertained and promptly met now that in full vigour they were investing the castle, determined upon its surrender, and producing thereby the utmost interest in its vicinity. On the 30th of March, 1646, stores were sent from Uttoxeter to the "Leaguer," as he is called in the parochial statements, meaning Sir William Brereton, costing £7 4s. 6d., and also again on the 8th of April, to the value of £11 2s. 9d.; and the occupiers of the castle, who had made repeated sallies with varied success, capitulated to the honourable terms proposed on the 20th of April of the same year. On the 21st a number of Leek soldiers, who had aided either in taking or defending Tutbury Castle, though the former is the more probable, arrived at Uttoxeter, on their return, and were entertained with "bread, cheese, and drink," and just coming excited and hot from the scene of conflict, smeared with the blood, and aching with the tussel of war, they had no doubt a great deal to tell to eager listeners of what they had done and seen. From Tutbury the "Leaguer," Sir William Brereton, marched to Lichfield, where on the 29th of April he was supplied by Uttoxeter with sixty strikes of oats, and for having gained Tutbury Castle, and for going against Dudley, he was paid by demand on the 5th of May, the sum of £16 by the town. On April 21st and 29th, and again on May 17th and 20th, many of the great guns which had been employed with success against the Castle at Tutbury, and very likely others which had been used in defending it, arrived at Uttoxeter on their way of transport to Eccleshall and Lichfield. A wall gun, from the walls of Tutbury Castle, was in the possession of the late John F. Lucas, Esq., of Bentley Hall, and was sold after his death. It is also to be observed that the quartering of General Fairfaxe's soldiers in October upon the town cost it £20, and on the 13th Colonel Cromwell's soldiers involved it in an expense of £20 more. The latter took a number of horses with them when leaving for Tamworth, but two were killed. The other remaining noticeable matter at the close of 1646 is that of Colonel Oakley's men having their quarters upon Uttoxeter at a cost of £13 6s. 2d. The Colonel himself stayed at the Crown in the Market Place, and his expenses amounted to the moderate sum of 3s. 6d. The accounts for the year ending October, 1646, which, however, were not examined till the 28th of April, 1651, amounted to the large sum of £796 2s., the whole of which was the fruit of the war with the exception of a few pounds.

The disbursements by the Constables of Uttoxeter from October, 1646, to May, 1647, amounted to £97 17s. 5d. At the beginning of 1647 Uttoxeter paid £2 10s. 4d. to fifteen men, to aid in pulling down Tutbury Castle, it having previously, in the month of May, 1646, contributed £3 to a Captain Cloyd for pulling down the bulwarks at Tutbury. After this period Uttoxeter was greatly relieved from the oppressive demands made upon it whilst Tutbury Castle was occupied: still the sums required by the British, or Parliamentary army, to which payments had commenced some time before, were of considerable amount and frequency. By the town accounts it does not seem whether Uttoxeter was now in a defensive position; but in the church book of Mavesyn Ridware of August 27, three or four months after the seige at Tutbury, it is noticed that the sum of 10s. 10d. was paid to twenty soldiers who had come from Uttoxeter from the siege. It should not be passed over, that in 1647 forty-six Egyptians (doubtless gypsies) with a pass from Parliament to travel for the space of six successive months for relief, arrived at Uttoxeter, and were given the sum of 4s. Their number and appearance must have excited considerable interest. Grants to Egyptians, or gypsies, for permission to travel and receive relief are mentioned in one of the volumes of the published papers of the Record Office for either 1858 or 1859. The constables' accounts of Checkly for the year 1666 mention a disbursement to a great company of gypsies.

At the commencement of 1648 the constables of Uttoxeter lost £1 1s. 7d. by exchanging £3 4s. 4d of clipped money for £2 2s. 9d. in good money, but in what way the constables of the parish received the clipped coin no record is left to show; still it may be presumed it was received for rates. It will be interesting, however, to notice what this money was and the circumstances attending its production. During the latter half of that century the clipping of coin was very frequent, and threatened to produce a financial crisis. For ages the coins had simply been stamped by hammering; the rims were consequently not marked, and they were seldom exactly round, and they also varied in size and weight even when they were intended to be of the same value. This state of the coinage almost tempted fraud; nothing was easier than to clip a little silver from the irregular edge, and by this process enormous fortunes were realized. The most severe punishments were inflicted, but the temptation was too strong. New coins with milled edges were melted down, and the old ones became smaller by daily chippings. What was a shilling, was sometimes not worth more than fourpence, and the Uttoxeter clipped coin was diminished in value about one-third. The country was filled with distress and complaints, until parliament issued a new coinage with milled edges, and called in all the old money, which involved a loss of more than a million of money which had to be met by extra taxation. *

In May, 1648, there was great fear of an insurrection in the town, and two men were placed in the church steeple, secretly, it is likely, to watch any risings of it. This seems to intimate how strongly and dangerously party feeling and opinion manifested themselves, although it does not appear that any more alarming evidence of it took place. At this time, and for several years, the town paid every three months to the British, that is the Parliamentary army, £13 and upwards. In June. 1648, the demolition of Tutbury Castle was still proceeded with, and a demand was made upon Uttoxeter for men to assist in the barbarous work, but there was great reluctance in the town to agree to it, and to free it from so undesirable an alternative the sum of £4 was given, and the work of spoliation left to hands less reluctant. In August, 1648, the Duke of Hamilton, who had an army of 20,000, sustained a

---

* Leisure Hour, 1870, and Prececocum by Bishop Fleetwood.

severe defeat near Preston by a small force under Cromwell of 8,000, and after escaping from the route, surrendered with his army on the 25th of that month to General Lambert at Uttoxeter. * The soldiers, who were Scotch, were lodged as prisoners in the parish church during their detention in Uttoxeter, and they desecrated the sacred edifice in a way many other churches were at that time, whilst they were similarly occupied by prisoners. These were a violent set of men, and a proper guard could not have been had over them. They broke up the planks of the church floor, smashed many of the windows, and left the sacred edifice in a state of perfect filth. The windows cost nearly £1 in repairing, and so detestable a state was the church in that the cleaning of it amounted to nearly half as much. The Duke of Hamilton was afterwards executed and his estates confiscated. The accounts were next passed on October 20th, 1648, but the amount is not given, and items entered, which make about £44, do not contain the whole of the payments made by the constables. Only the more remarkable items, on account of which payments were made, appear to be preserved.

In 1649 the accounts were taken on the 7th of November, and were £225 11s. 5d., chiefly in pay to "the army," but from then till the time of passing the accounts again on March 3rd, 1651, there is little to notice except that in August, 1650, there was a thanksgiving day when a person named Percival was paid for "warding," which was an old Saxon custom, like watching, kept up in Uttoxeter from an early date. At the same time there was a guard of sixteen soldiers at the Cock Inn, which was kept by and belonged to Mr. Thomas Gilbert, and which remained in existence till 1872, when it was destroyed to make room for the brewery offices in the Tudor style which were designed by Mr. Fradgley, architect, of Uttoxeter. The last occupier of the public

---

* Spectator Newspaper, November 18th, 1864.

house was named Wigley. The three months pay to the army, which had increased to £20, ceased in August, 1650. The accounts, when passed, appear to have been about £44.

The opening of 1651 found Uttoxeter in a state of internal danger, but the constables were determined to suppress any popular manifestation, and a warrant was carried into effect for searching for and seizing " Papists' and delinquents' arms." It seems that in April monthly pay to the army was renewed, when £20 was paid to it, and in June another monthly payment was made to it of upwards of £30. In August the magazine of the army was at Uttoxeter, and a number of teams were required, some of which were obtained by warrant in the night from Doveridge, intimating the necessity of great dispatch in the case, to convey them to Tamworth. One of the teams belonged to Mr. Peter Lightfoot, who was paid £1 4s. for its use. In August a number of Uttoxeter men were pressed for the militia, their names being John Clark, Fran. Allen, Phil. Needham, Richard Wilkinson, and Thomas Vernon. They were each provided with a horse and saddle and 7s. 6d., and about this time a pair of bandoleers were made to order by a Mr. Heaton, who was a saddler in the town, and the price paid for them by the constables was 8s. They were intended to contain some ten charges of powder and bullets, and were fastened round the waist or suspended over the shoulders by a strap. The general disuse, however, of such articles took place some years before these bandoleers were made. The militia horse were called in again in September, but in November they were resummoned, with some foot soldiers, to proceed for some purpose to Cheadle, where they remained for three days. Several lots of Scotch prisoners were at Uttoxeter during the year, in custody, one lot of whom was being taken from Chesterfield to Stafford. The accounts were not audited till May 3rd, 1651, and they amounted to £304 3s. 2d., and must comprise many more items than those which have been preserved.

By this time the entries in the town accounts had become much rarer, and only a few items of interest appear in the course of several years. Several of them are, however, of real interest. In 1652 one entry is very curious, especially as there are no circumstances recorded as attending it to afford any clue to its meaning. It is a notice of a public warning in Uttoxeter to set water at the door of every house in the town. On April 14th, one Robert Adin was prosecuted as a traitor; and in February, 1653, some excited individual disturbed the congregation in the church and was conveyed to Stafford for trial. At this time the town paid year by year to the army the sum of £67 10s. The proclamation of the Lord Protector was duly observed, and on May 29th, 1660, a similar demonstration was made on the advent to the Throne of King Charles II. On his coronation day the spirit of royalty had thoroughly regained its ascendancy in the town, and whilst only 1s. was expended over the proclamation of Cromwell, the sum of 5s. was given for ringing on the proclamation of the King, and 8s. when he was crowned; besides which the town went to the expense of "painting the royal arms and four tribes," now preserved in the church. The expenses occasioned by the political necessities of the times had now dwindled down to comparatively small amounts, except in 1667, when two amounts of £44 1s. 1d. each, one of £14 13s. 8½d., and another of £29 7s. 5d. were required to be paid for royal aid—no trifle, it may be thought, to be levied upon the town during the first three months of the year.

From the year 1653 to 1660 or 1661, most of the leaves are torn out of the constables' accounts. At a fair calculation, however, it may be inferred that during those seven or eight years the expenses caused to Uttoxeter by the times could not have been less than £250 a year, making something like a total for the whole period of at least £2,000. The town was in an excited condition in 1659 Derby at that period was in a state of revolt, and whilst a number of militia which had been sent for out of Staffordshire to quell it were halting at Uttoxeter, the inhabitants, evidently participating in the spirit of revolt which had broken out at Derby, closed their shops, seized the militia horse, and even one of the militia, a Captain Daughty, espoused their side. The affair, however, passed over without any worse consequences ensuing.

In June, 1688, Uttoxeter presented a scene of rejoicing such as, perhaps, had not before occurred in it. It was occasioned by the release and acquittal of the seven bishops whom King James II. had cast into the Tower of London, and brought to trial on an alleged false and seditious libel, pretended to be grounded on a petition which they had made to the King for not reading in the churches the Declaration of Indulgences to all Dissenters from the Church. The following graphic picture of the close of the trial is from the pen of Dr. Vaughan in his "History of England under the Tudors." It will serve to illustrate and confirm the old accounts of the constables at Uttoxeter, whilst the accounts themselves will lend corroborative evidence of the effect of the verdict of the jury upon the country in a way no other local records probably do. "The trial commenced at nine o'clock in the morning and lasted until seven in the evening. The Jury then retired to consider their verdict. Some hours passed, and they did not return. At midnight, and at three o'clock, persons who stood in anxious suspense near the door of the retiring room heard them in loud debate. This delay was occasioned by the opposition of a man named Arnold who was brewer to the King's household. His obstinacy, however, was at length subdued by the firmness of the rest, and at six o'clock in the morning the Judges were apprised that the jury were agreed. At nine o'clock the Court assembled; the benches were covered with the nobility and gentry; the people crowded every avenue, filling, in immense concourse, the great hall adjoining, and pressing in multitudes towards its entrance from the public streets. The foreman of the Jury, Sir Robert Langley, on the question being put whether the accused were guilty or not guilty, pronounced the verdict "Not guilty." These words were no sooner uttered, than the deep silence of the Court was followed by a loud shout of triumph, in which persons of every rank seemed to join to the uttermost ; the verdict was echoed from the Court within to the adjoining hall, and fled with rapidity from man to man in the streets beyond. The acclamation from the populace was described at the time as a " rebellion in noise," and compared to a falling of the massy and widespread roof of the structure from which it proceeded. In a few minutes the news and shouting reached to the Temple, and in no long time spread to the Royal camp at Hounslow, ten miles distance. James, on hearing the acclamations of the soldiery, inquired what it meant : and being told by Feversham that it was nothing but the men shouting because news had come that the Bishops were acquitted, his countenance instantly fell, and in the confusion of his thoughts and emotions, he replied "Call you that nothing? but never mind, it will be so much the worse for them." When the Jury left the Court they were hailed with the most enthusiastic cheers, as the defenders of Protestantism and the deliverers of their country ; while upon Bishop Cartwright, and Williams, the Solicitor-General, the crowd heaped every expression of reproach and derision. In the City all business was suspended for some hours, and men seemed to exist but to congratulate each other with tears of delight on what had happened. In the evening the bells were rung, and bonfires kindled in all parts of the metropolis. Before the windows of the Royal Palace the Pope was burnt in effigy, and the toast everywhere went round—Health to the Bishops and the Jury, and confusion to the Papists. The principal towns through the country vied with the capital in these expressions of feeling ; the proudest Churchmen and every class of Dissenters seemed to be of one mind ; and the parties who had done most towards urging the King to prosecute his obnoxious measures began to express their utter despair of seeing a people whose heresy partook of so much ' rancour and malignity ' ever brought within the fold of the Church."

In Uttoxeter bonfires were lit in High Street, at the

Churchyard, and at the Market Cross; drummers were employed to swell the acclamation, which, as we have seen, was national; the watchmen and populace of Uttoxeter were treated with ale, and the more influential inhabitants of the town both on that and the previous day (which was one of thanksgiving for the Prince of Wales) indulged in ale and wine at the "Crown," to the cost of £2 2s.

At the close of the old accounts in December, 1688, another interesting item appears, in which 'an alarm" is mentioned. Coals were collected for fires, and a quantity for the same purpose was paid for by a Mr. Shallcross. The excitement in the place was considerable; strangers were brought into it by the frightening notifications, the fear occasioned by which they and the towns people did their best to allay by copious draughts—about a guinea's worth —of the ale of Mrs. Norton who kept the Crown at the north side of the Market Place. The alarm was that produced by the men employed by the Prince of Orange, or his friends, to run or ride through every town in England in one day crying "fire and sword! the French are coming!" and which filled the minds of people with the utmost consternation and terror.

Uttoxeter does not furnish any particulars for the attention of the local historian from the interesting period just passed through until the rebellion of 1745, when Prince Charles Edward, called the Pretender, sought to recover the fallen fortunes of the Stuart dynasty by an appeal to arms. Previous to this his father had made two unsuccessful attempts upon Scotland, and he being encouraged by the zealous partizans of his house in England, and flattered by France with a promise of powerful assistance, resolved to make one more attempt for the throne of England. The nucleus of his army consisted of one hundred men, formed by a French officer, and it was pretended that they were for the East India Company's services, and they were put on board a small frigate carrying eighteen guns, which was joined by a French Man-of-War with sixty guns, arms for several thousand men, and about £400,000 sterling. He succeeded in landing in Scotland in August, where he was joined by about two thousand men. The number being shortly after increased to five thousand, he ventured with them towards the South, and after having gained several minor successes, including the memorable battle of Prestonpans, he continued his course to Carlisle, and so on to Manchester, and Macclesfied, and through Leek and Ashbourne to Derby.

The army of the Duke of Cumberland was at this time, November 28th, forming in Staffordshire. His troops lay in a line betwixt Tamworth and Stafford, with a line of cavalry in front. They consisted of 7,500 veteran soldiers, 3,000 newly raised soldiers, 1,400 veteran horse, and 800 newly raised horse, the whole being 12,700 men.* The Duke had taken up his position expecting that the Chevalier would have attempted to have proceeded by Birmingham to London. On receiving information that the insurgent army were at Derby the Duke despatched there a gentleman of the name of Birch to ascertain their strength. This person, the better to conceal his purpose, bought a pint of peas at a shop in that town, and put them into one of his pockets; taking, however, a quantity in one hand, he dropped a single pea into an empty pocket for each file of the Pretender's army as it passed. On the whole army having filed off he directly returned at an almost inconceivable speed for those days, and communicated the intelligence of the number of the enemy to the Duke.† The Duke thereupon started to Uttoxeter, having in the meantime sent to Parliament to enquire if he must proceed to Derby to attack the enemy there. He came through Abbots Bromley, and there were recently those living who knew well an old woman named Ann Buxton, *alias* Nan Brown, who used to talk of having seen them, and of displaying her best manners before the Duke and receiving a shilling

---

* A History of England published soon after.
† This information was told to the late Dr. Taylor by a descendant of Mr. Birch.

from his hands. The Duke of Cumberland remained at Uttoxeter two nights, waiting a reply to his message, and he was hospitably entertained by an ancestor of Sir Allan Gardner, at Uttoxeter House (now incorrectly called the Manor House), for many years occupied by the late Herbert Taylor, Esq., M.D., a deputy lieutenant of the county, where he slept in a room hung with fine tapestry. The single troop of horse he had with him were drawn up for review in the croft at the back of the same residence, of which a fuller account will be given further on.

It should be here remarked that it is traditionally stated that in consideration of this hospitality the Duke of Cumberland granted to Uttoxeter an immunity from having soldiers billetted upon it. A lady, the only sister of Mrs. Howitt, kindly informs me that her father used to relate the circumstance with every confidence of its truthfulness. I have, however, specially searched all the chests in the vestry to discover any document relating to the matter, but in vain. The words of the lady to whose communication I have referred are as follows:—"My father added, in relating this, that the Duke was so much pleased with the loyal hospitality he received, that he granted the town immunity from the burden of soldiers and prisoners of war. Can this be ratified by any parish record? This fact I remember that through the long war from the French revolution to the peace of 1814, no soldiers were quartered in the town nor French prisoners either." It is also said that Mr. Byrd, of the Wellington Inn, which he owned and occupied, also received a special grant by the Duke of Cumberland of the freedom of Uttoxeter markets, for having on the same occasion entertained a portion of His Grace's troop of soldiers.

It was on the 4th of December that the young chevalier arrived at Derby with his followers, numbering about 7,000 men, with fifteen field pieces and fifty covered carts with ammunition. Their first act was to hold a council of war, but the only resolution passed was to make a levy upon the inhabitants of about £3,000, besides making a successful demand upon the Post Office for

J

£100, and committing various ravages upon the town and neighbourhood. They remained at Derby two days, when they retreated from it with confused precipitation, through fear of surprise from the Duke of Cumberland's army, leaving behind them swords, pistols, targets, shot, powder, and other articles. Their loss of these was, however, made up by the plundering and robberies which they committed on their way back to the north. Gentlemen's houses were entered and robbed far and near; horses were forcibly taken away, and at Hanging Bridge one Humphrey Brown was shot dead for refusing to comply with their demand for his horse. Various gentlemen's houses in Ashbourne did not escape their ruthless visitation.* The late Mr. Crosley, of the Old Turnpike, Uttoxeter, who died in 1835 at the age of 100 years and eight months, was then a youth at Brailsford, of about eleven years, and he, with a horse and cart, were pressed into the service of the Pretender as he returned.† Indeed the Pretender's followers on their retreat spread themselves as far as Foston, and the people in the neighbourhood for miles round were terrified, and drove off their horses and cattle. Even at Knypersley, near Uttoxeter, the then owner of the place, Mr. Mynors, drove his horses and cattle into Flyer's coppice, and for safety buried various household valuables. A jar of guinies was really found hereabouts, some years back, buried in the earth in a hedge bottom, and the labouring men, who made the discovery whilst ditching, took them to Birmingham to sell. There was also found in the earth in 1872, at Gorsty Hill, close to Knypersley, a jar containing a large quantity of silver coin of reigns prior to the occurrences being noticed.

Some further interesting reminiscences of these exciting times I have the pleasure of giving from a communication of the late Mr. F. Cope, of Uttoxeter, and previously of Gellion's Hall, Bromley Hurst, of which place he was the

---

* Hutton's History of Derby, and Mr. Hobson's History of Ashbourne.

† Communicated by the late Rev. John Cook, of whose congregation he was a member.

owner.* This gentleman was born at an ancestral home in the Woodlands, in 1778, and his family had melancholy recollections of this stirring period. The traditions of the neighbourhood were the frequent theme of a large household at night, as they sat round a blazing wood fire, of a large old-fashioned house, when his father, surrounded by his family, and aroused by what he felt so much interest in, would recount the traditions of his predecessors as far back as Henry VIII., when they held only from the Crown; how at the great rebellion they suffered for their loyalty, when six brothers, each standing six feet high and upwards, a stature nearly attained by all Mr. Cope's sons, joined King Charles I. at York, and all perished except one from whom he descended; how the Bagots established the *Blue Coat Hunt* and Bowlinggreens at the Hartshorn Inn, at Lichfield, the Talbot Inn, Rugeley, and the White Hart, Uttoxeter, to keep up the loyal feeling towards the Stuarts; how they were betrayed and a King's messenger sent to secure their papers, and take the chairman, secretary, and other leading men into custody; how these parts were so loyal to the Stuarts that he (the messenger) was *detained* at Lichfield for post-horses, and finally forced to go forward with his jaded beasts to Ridware, when he applied to C. Robinson, Esq., who gave him an excellent dinner, a bait and a rest for his horses and two guides—one to show him or his assistant the way to Rugeley, and the other the way to Uttoxeter, where Mr. Robinson *knew* that the whole hunt were dining. However, whilst thus entertaining the officer, he dispatched his son on foot to Calton and Rugeley, and a faithful servant on his horse to Uttoxeter. Leaving Ridware the messenger in time got to the White Hart, found the room there crowded with bacchanalians, rosy, and as the Scotch say, *fou:* making his way with one Copestake, a lapidary, who was a constable, to the head of the room, he seized Sir Walter Bagot and Mr. Daniel,

---

* Mr. Cope started the first newspaper in Macclesfield, and during the time of the celebrated Mr. Rintoul he was a "reader" on the *Spectator* newspaper. He was a man of remarkable intelligence, ability and shrewdness.

the vicar of Bromley, who was secretary. The papers, however, on the table, expressed nothing but a scrawled programme of the dinner, a rather sneering toast to King George and the Queen, with lots of other lewd toasts and sentiments, and snatches of song, *purporting* to have been sung, &c. But unfortunately the fire-place told tales ; evidently much paper had been recently burnt ; so the messenger seized several of the party—Sir W. B. and parson Daniel being the principal—and believing that Mr. Daniel might probably have papers at home, he dispatched Copestake, who, knowing a private road by Uttoxeter High Wood and through Bagot's park, proceeded that way to Bromley to search his house. Again, however, they were foiled, for one of the young Mynors was at the dinner, and had already apprised both the Mynors, of Knypersley, and the Cope family ; so the grandfather of my informant and the Mynors were on the alert, but *apparently* drinking and enjoying themselves only at Mr. Cope's, in front of whose house the road went. Copestake was soon seen approaching, and as they saw him turn towards the door here they waited for him jug in hand. Thus he stopped to drink, and one jug succeeded another till Copestake was incapable of proceeding. Meanwhile my informant's father, then a young man, had been sent to Bromley, and getting there called on old Waltham, the thirdborough ; together they went to the churchwarden, a John Wetton (father of Mr. Wetton, printer in Uttoxeter), all old loyalists—and proceeded together from his back door to the vicarage—getting over the rails and crossing the garden. They searched the vicarage house, and finding the vicar's desk, took the back out of it, and, abstracting the papers it contained, bundled them up and took them away. Meanwhile the messenger and his prisoners had left Uttoxeter for Calton and Rugeley ; but the former recollecting that he had come that road in his way to Uttoxeter, calculated that it must go either through or by Abbot's-Bromley ; so he began to think that he had been wilfully misled, and insisted on being first taken to Bromley. Thus the chaise stopped absolutely at the front

door of the parsonage house, as Mr. Cope's father, with
the thirdborough, and the churchwarden were returning
over the pailings out of the parsonage garden with the
papers. So the affair ended. Copestake was taken up
and slightly punished for drunkenness. He afterwards
rejoiced that he had not been the means of any one being
sacrificed through his inattention to duty, and he left his
halbert at the house in token thereof, where it remained
many years. Wetton and Waltham had each a grant of
land on a long lease, which is more than half expired,
from Sir Walter Bagot. Mr. Cope's father, who was
always looked upon as the head tenant of this part of the
estate, had done his duty, and was, to his death, looked
upon with great favour.

After this the feeling in favour of the Stuarts became
much cooled; small bands of pretended or licentious
partizans ravaged the country; and the treachery and
mistrust which existed caused the stocks and pillory at
Uttoxeter to be in frequent requisition. The patience of
those who were faithful begun to wear out, so that when
the Scots entered Derby a general mistrust of them
pervaded the whole country, and serving men and
labourers hid themselves for fear of being pressed into
the King's service. Thus, for instance, the late Mr. Cope's
grandfather was, at the time of the occupation of Derby,
left for days together with one of his sons, a servant boy,
and an old man. Maids and women there were in
abundance, but the men had fled. It being in so wooded
and secluded a situation, every one who could claim
acquaintance fled to Knypersley, or the Forest Banks, to
be out of harm's way. Many an hour, Mr. Cope stated,
he has wandered, when a boy, through the deep ravines
which penetrate the Forest Banks, the cliffs of Bagot's
Park, or Buttermilk and Dixon's Hills, sauntering in a
moody way among the places where horses had been
picketed day by day, and where silver and pewter ware,
and other utensils, then considered valuable, had been
deposited. Thus in a narrow ravine which runs up into
the park called Franc Coppice Bank, Mr. Cope's father

and the old servant man stood sentinel every day alternately, and watched at night while the cattle grazed in the fields, and which were taken up again before daylight—his grandfather and the women attending to the cows and dairy, and occasionally making excursions across the Dove to Sudbury and Scropton to hear the news. And so, according to an old song, it was narrated that the rebels penetrated as far as Scropton; and were frightened away by the woodland lasses, who, peering over Draycot Bridge, were told to return, as the Highlanders were plundering the houses. This song, as far as it can be recollected, was very rude, and not particularly delicate in its allusions. It was, as such rude productions frequently are, coarsely but keenly satirical, and it enumerated the names of owners whose houses were ravaged, and many of whose families remained to Mr. Cope's time, and some—as Steel, Greatorex, Smith, Manlove, and Tavener—even to the present. Thus:

> " Manlove was a cudgel player,
> Of courage and renown,
> Who beat the Gilly from his house,
> And fairly cracked his crown."

Again the old women of the woodlands volunteered to look what was doing at Scropton, and, it raining, they pulled off their red flannel petticoats, putting them as cloaks over their shoulders, and, skulking under the hedges in large numbers, so alarmed the Scots that a panic seized them, and they fled with their booty. The chorus had for its substance the following particulars. From one house they took a pig (which the owners had killed to hide conveniently) and put it across a horse. They remained, however, to run the links of the pig puddings, just made and hot, upon a pole, that they might carry them away more safely. In the mean time some of the red petticoats neared the village, whom the Scots, who remained perceiving, took for soldiers of the Royal army, and they fled, struck with alarm. The song leads us to believe that the pig pudding stealers escaped through the back door of a cow-house, and, jumping from a heap of manure, fell up to the neck in a cesspool. The lines are something like this :—*

> "With the puddings strung upon a pole,
> They jumped from the muck-hill into the muck-hole."

Some reminiscences of a visit some of the insurgent army paid to a small farm house at the Panthans in the dale, north of and in the parish of Ellastone, have been communicated to me. The occupants of the farm were named Roger and Martha Smith. They appear to have been fully apprised of what was taking place all through the neighbourhood, and under the effects of the alarming anticipations naturally entertained they had their mules taken to the top of a hill above the house, and picketed in a deep hollow there out of sight. They buried their pewter and valuables in the ground, and sewed up all their clothing in the beds. A straggling part of the army entered the house and demanded something to eat, and on seeing some reeling pegs, used in spinning, on the floor, they accused the Smiths of having firearms in the house, supposing the pegs were pistol charges, and to convince them of their mistake the women of the house were compelled to show them the use of the articles by doing some reeling. A large pewter dish that was buried was in preservation some years ago by the late Mr. Richardson, of Rocester, who was great grandson to Roger and Martha Smith, and himself an old man when he gave these particulars to me. The dish which I saw, had on it their initials, the initial of the surname being before the initials of the christian names, as here :—

S.
R. M.

But one of the most amusing incidents arising out of the visit of the Pretender to these parts is the ensuing, which I copy from the "Reliquary" :—" A Relic of

---

* A copy of this song is recollected to have been pasted upon the inside shutter of Knypersley House. I should be glad to receive a copy of it if any body has one.

'1745.'—I have now before me an old stone bottle, some eight inches high, light in colour, and bearing upon it the words 'SACK, 1640.' Insignificant as it is it possesses some little interest, and claims connection with the stirring times of the 'Rebellion of '45.' On the rumoured approach of the insurgents at that memorable period, a worthy farmer, then living near Leek, deemed it prudent to conceal his valuables, and had for that purpose raised a flagstone in the stable. At the suggestion, however, of an old woman who was standing by, he changed his plan, and buried his treasure in a heap of manure in the farm yard. Among other articles so buried were forty-eight 'sack bottles' full of home-brewed ale; and when the storm was blown over the owner coming to examine his deposit, found the liquor exceedingly ripe and good. Bottle after bottle, on being handed out, met the admiring gaze of an aged (and perhaps expectant) looker on, who, being astonished at their apparently great number, exclaimed to the farmer, 'Mester, dun you think they'ne bred i'-th'-hole?' One of these is the bottle before alluded to, which is still possessed by the descendant of the worthy yeoman of 1745." *

The Duke of Cumberland receiving, whilst at Uttoxeter, an intimation not to proceed to Derby, and doubtless learning that the insurgents had hastily left that town, departed from Uttoxeter and rejoined his army.

From Ashbourne Prince Charles continued his retreat through Yorkshire to Carlisle, his progress to the heart of the kingdom and back with about 7,000 men having been effected in the presence of two regular armies under Marshal Wade and the Duke of Cumberland, in the depth of winter. After crossing into Scotland he attempted the siege of Stirling Castle, and Lord Murray gained a complete victory over General Hawley at Falkirk. The siege of Stirling Castle was raised, and on the 15th of April Prince Charles resolved to make a night attack upon the Duke's army, which had followed him; but it being two

---

* Many incidents of these times are given in the History of Leek by John Sleigh, Esq., and also in a lecture on "The '45," published in 1868.

o'clock in the morning when they had yet three miles to march to where the Duke lay, and being weary and dispirited, they retraced their steps to Culloden, where they had previously been drawn up in order of battle. The Duke of Cumberland had heard of the attempt. About eight o'clock his forces were observed on their march, and about one o'clock the King's troops opened a heavy cannonade, which was but feebly returned. The Highlanders suffered severely and became impatient; the Mackintosh regiment broke from the line and drove back the King's troops sword in hand, but they were brought to the ground by a terrible fire. The Macdonald and other Highland regiments, being thus deprived of the post of honour which they had possessed from time immemorial, retired, and it was in vain any attempts were made to rally them. The Prince himself became hesitating when urged to make a final attempt or die like one worthy of a crown; and Lord Elcho, who had sacrificed everything for him, left him with execrations, and swore never to see his face again. Prince Charles had a reward of £30,000 set upon his person, and for many weeks he wandered about in fatigue and hunger; and finally, after many escapes and much trouble, he arrived safely in France. After all hopes of recovering the crown of Britain were lost, he assumed the title of Count Albany, and died at Rome January 31st, 1788.

Until recently there was in existence a cup which was used by Prince Charles's adherents when they met at the White Hart Hotel, and at one time it was in the possession of the late Mr. Thomas Norris, stationer of this town. I also believe that the secret correspondence or collection of papers, which had so narrow an escape of being seized at the time, and which had reference to plans which were devised for the Prince's elevation to the throne of England, are all still in preservation in Staffordshire. T. C. S. Kynnersley, Esq., Stipendiary Magistrate of Birmingham, has a miniature likeness of him, given to a member of his family by the Prince, as a mark of gratitude for hospitality shown to him.

After a lapse of thirty-nine years, Uttoxeter became the scene of an incident all the more remarkable because it is associated with so distinguished a name and person as the celebrated Dr. Samuel Johnson. The occurrence was the act of penance by the Doctor which he self-inflicted for refusing to obey a request of his father's when he was a boy at home. It forms a striking feature in his biography, and has been referred to more, perhaps, than any other circumstance in his life. It is quite certain he never meant the act to be a satisfaction to Divine justice, for it is his own plain assertion that he did not hold commutation of offences by voluntary penance, and that he thought it an error to endeavour at pleasing God by taking the rod of reproof out of his own hands. Amongst modern writers who have expressed interest in this remarkable event are the late Mr. Thomas Carlyle, the late Mr. Nathaniel Hawthorn, and Mr. Walter Thornbury, and no less celebrated an artist than Mr. Eyre Crowe, A.R.A., so eminent for his technical knowledge and solid work, has made a rendering of the remarkable scene in a highly commended painting on canvas, entitled "Dr. Johnson doing penance in Uttoxeter Market Place." The same event has also been conceived in a different way and transferred to canvas by Mr. Adrain Stokes, of Kensington. Mr. Carlyle says, "The picture of Samuel Johnson standing bareheaded in the Market Place there is one of the grandest and saddest we can paint." As it is a matter of so much interest, it will only be proper to present the fullest account of it possible.

The father of Dr. Samuel Johnson was Michael Johnson, a native of Cubley in Derbyshire, a place not many miles from Uttoxeter. Although so much has been done to illustrate scenes, incidents, and characters in connection with the life of Dr. Johnson and his father, the birthplace of the latter has not hitherto been pointed out, nor has enquiries respecting it been made; much less has it till now been sketched and engraved. Most likely it has been thought that all knowledge of the humble abode had passed away. Fortunately, however, a recollection of the identical cottage has been preserved in the family of the late Mr. Bull, of Leek, whose ancestors resided on a farm adjoining the house for the long period of four hundred years. When the family left Cubley in 1853, to live at Dieu la Cress Abbey, a brother-in-law to Mr. Bull, who was at an advanced age, accompanied them, and he used to speak of this cottage as that of the father of Michael Johnson. The place is far on Cubley Common, say nine miles from Uttoxeter, at the right hand side of the road to Ashbourne. It had been occupied about forty years in 1868 by a John Coates, when its appearance was entirely altered by improvements. Before, however, the features it bore when it was occupied by the Johnsons were removed, I made a pedestrian journey to the place to sketch it, and from the sketch then taken the accompanying engraving has been prepared.

VIEW OF THE COTTAGE.

After some vicissitudes Michael Johnson became established at Lichfield as a bookseller, and, as such, he was in the habit of attending Uttoxeter on market days with books for sale. Doctor Johnson, his son, then

Samuel Johnson, spent two years when verging upon his twentieth year, in learning his father's business; and a few years back there were books in existence in Lichfield which were said to have been bound by his own hands. It was during this period, when his father, being unwell, requested him to go to Uttoxeter to attend the book-stall. He, however, in a fit of pride, probably, refused to comply with a desire which, one would think, any right-minded young man would, especially under such circumstances, have felt it to have been a pleasure as well as a duty to have regarded. But his better sense afterwards asserted its sway, and in contrition for the act of disobedience, he, towards the close of his life, in 1784, repaired to the spot where the book-stall had stood in Uttoxeter Market Place, and there remained for a considerable time bareheaded in the rain by way of expiatory penance, * or rather as a punishment for a gross act of disobedience to his father when he was a boy.

At the time this took place Dr. Johnson was on a visit at Miss Seward's and his other friends at Lichfield. During his stay he was missed one morning from the breakfast table, and on enquiry being made of the servants, they stated that they understood that he had set off from Lichfield at a very early hour without mentioning to any of the family whither he was going. The day passed without the return of the illustrious guest, and the party began to be very uneasy on his account, when, just before supper hour, the door opened and the Doctor stalked into the room. A solemn silence ensued of a few minutes, nobody daring to inquire the cause of his absence, which was at length relieved by Johnson addressing the lady of the house in the following manner:—" Madam, I beg your pardon for the abruptness of my departure from your house this morning, but I was constrained to it by my conscience. *Fifty years ago,* madam, *on this day,* 1 committed a breach of filial piety which has ever since lain heavy on my mind, and has not till this day been expiated.

---

* A short account of Lichfield, 1819.

My father, you recollect, was a bookseller, and had long been in the habit of attending Uttoxeter market, and opening a stall of his books during that day. Confined to his bed by indisposition he requested me, this time fifty years ago, to visit the market and attend the bookstall in his place. But, madam, my pride prevented me from doing my duty, and I give my father a refusal. To do away the sin of this disobedience, I this day went in a postchaise to Uttoxeter, and going into the market at the time of high business, uncovered my head, and stood with it bare an hour before a stall which my father formerly used, exposed to the sneers of the standers by, and the inclemency of the weather—a penance by which I trust I have propitiated heaven for this only instance of my contumely to my father."* A confession and an expression of contrition more touching never fell from the lips of a great and venerable man.

Is it then any wonder that distinguished writers should so frequently notice the circumstances; or that any one should even visit Uttoxeter to try to see the spot consecrated by Johnson's tears? Scarcely, however, would one think that a gentleman who lived three thousand miles away, although happening to be in England, would come to Uttoxeter for such a purpose. Yet, so it has been. No less noted a man than Nathaniel Hawthorn, of America, author of "Twice told Tales," "Transformation," and other works, visited Uttoxeter in 1857, to see the spot where this remarkable incident took place. It appears that nearly all concern, locally, about the place had passed out of people's minds, until this eminent foreigner, after visiting Uttoxeter with the intention stated, wrote a description of his visit for one of the annuals, which was copied into one of the local papers and perused with great eagerness. The production, as might be expected, was the occasion of several letters appearing in a local paper, having the intention, if possible, of finding out the place where the Doctor stood.

---

* Jonsoniana and Warner's tour through the Northern Counties of England.

The paper is so pleasing in its style, and so interesting as proceeding from such an author, and relating in the manner it does to such a subject, that anything but an apology is required for giving it in this place. Mr. Hawthorn writes:—"At Lichfield, in St. Mary's Square, I saw a statue of Dr. Johnson, elevated some ten or twelve feet high. The statue is colossal, though not more so than the mountainous Doctor, who sits in a chair with a pile of big books underneath it, looking down upon the spectators with a broad, heavy, benignant countenance, very like Johnson's portraits. The figure is immensely massive, a vast ponderosity of stone, not finely spiritualized, nor indeed fully humanized, but rather resembling a great boulder than a man. On the pedestal are three bas-reliefs. In the first Johnson is represented as a mere baby, seated on an old man's shoulders, resting his chin on the bald head which he embraces with his arms, listening to Doctor Sacheverel. In the second table he is seen riding to school on the backs of two of his comrades, while a third boy supports him in the rear. *The third bas-relief possesses to my mind a good deal of pathos.* It shows Johnson in the Market Place of Uttoxeter doing penance for an act of disobedience to his father fifty years before. He stands bareheaded, very sad and woe-begone, with the wind and rain driving against him, whilst some market people and children gaze awe-stricken into his face, and an aged man and woman with clasped hands are praying for him. These latter personages, I fancy (though in close proximity there are living ducks and dead poultry) represent the spirit of Johnson's father and mother lending what aid they can to lighten his half century's burden of remorse. I never heard of this statue. It seems to have no reputation as a work of art, and very possibly may deserve none. Yet I found it somewhat touching and effective, perhaps because my interest in the sturdiest of Englishmen has always been peculiarly strong; and especially the above-described bas-relief freshened my sense of a *wonderful beauty and pathos in the incident it commemorates.* So the next day I left Lichfield for Uttoxeter on a purely sentimental pilgrimage (by railway, however) to see the spot where Johnson performed his penance. Boswell, I think, speaks of the town as being about nine miles from Lichfield, but the map would indicate a much greater distance, and by rail, passing from one to another, as much as seventeen or eighteen miles.

"I have always had an idea of old Michael Johnson's journey thither on foot on the morning of the market days, selling books through the busy hours, and returning at night. This cannot well have been.

"Arriving at Uttoxeter station, the first thing I saw in a convenient vicinity was the tower and tall grey spire of a church. It is but a very short walk from the station up to the town. It had been my previous impression that the Market Place of Uttoxeter lay immediately round about the church; and if I remember the narrative aright, Johnson describes his father's book-stall as standing in the Market Place, close beside the sacred edifice. But the church has merely a street of ordinary width passing round it, whilst the Market Place, though near at hand, is not really contiguous, nor would its throng and bustle be apt to overflow their bounds and surge against the churchyard and old grey tower. Nevertheless, a walk of a minute or two would bring a person from the centre of the Market Place to the church door, and Michael Johnson might very well have placed his stall, and laid out his literary ware, in the corner of the tower's base; better there perhaps than in the busy centre of an agricultural market. But the picturesque and full impressiveness of the story require that Johnson doing his penance should have been the very nucleus of the crowd—the midmost man of the Market Place—the centre figure of memory and remorse—contrasting with, and overawing the sultry materialism around him. I am resolved, therefore, that the true site of his penance was in the Market Place. This is a pretty spacious and irregular vicinity, surrounded by houses and shops, some of them old, with red tiled roofs; others wearing a pretence of newness, but probably as old as the rest.

"The only other thing that impressed me in Uttoxeter was the abundance of public houses—one at every step or two—'Red Lions,' 'White Harts,' 'Bulls Heads,' 'Blue Bells,' and others. These are probably for the accommodation of the agricultural visitors on market days. At any rate, I appeared to be the only guest in Uttoxeter on the day of my visit, and had but an infinitessimal portion of patronage to distribute amongst so many inns.

"I stepped into one of those rustic hostelries and got my dinner—bacon and greens, a chop, and a gooseberry pudding, enough for six yeomen, besides ale, all for a shilling and sixpence. This hospitable inn, mis-called the 'Nag's Head,' and standing beside the Market Place, * was as likely as any other to have contained old Michael Johnson in the days when he used to come thither to sell books. He perhaps had eaten his bacon and greens, and drank his ale, and smoked his pipe in the very room where I now sat—a low, ancient room, with a red brick floor and white-washed ceiling, traversed by rough beams, the whole in the rudest fashion, but extremely neat. Neither did the room lack ornament, the walls being hung with engravings of prize oxen and other pretty prints, and the mantel piece adorned with earthenware figures of shepherdesses. But still as I sipped my ale I glanced through the window into the sunny Market Place, and wished I could honestly fix on one spot more than another as likely to have been the spot where Johnson stood to do his penance. How strange and stupid it is that tradition should not have marked and kept in mind the very place! How shameful!—nothing less than that— that there should be no local memorial of this incident, as beautiful and as touching a passage as can be cited out of any human life —no inscription of it, as sacred as a verse of Scripture, on the walls of the church! no statue of the venerable and illustrious penitent in the Market Place to throw a wholesome awe over its traffic, its earthliness, its selfishness.

---

* Since Mr. Hawthorn's visit to Uttoxeter the "Nag's Head" has been once partially rebuilt, and since, in 1878, entirely rebuilt. The sign has also been altered from the "Nag's Head" to "The Vine Inn."

Such a statue, if the piety of man did not raise it, might almost have been expected to grow up out of the pavement of its own accord on the spot that had been watered by Johnson's remorseful tears, and by the rain that dropped from him.

"Well, my pilgrimage had not turned out a very successful one. There being no train till late in the afternoon, I spent, I do not know how many hours in Uttoxeter, and to say the truth, was heartily tired of it, my penance being a great deal longer than Dr. Johnson's. Moreover, I forgot, until it was too late, to snatch the opportunity to repent of some sins. Whilst waiting at the station I asked a boy who sat near me—a school boy of some twelve or thirteen years old, whom I should take to be a clergyman's son—I asked him whether he had ever heard the story of Doctor Johnson; how he stood an hour doing penance beside that church, whose spire rose before us? The boy stared and answered 'No!' I enquired if no such story was known or talked about in Uttoxeter? 'No!' said the boy, 'that I ever heard of.' Just think of the absurd little town knowing nothing of its one memorable incident which sanctifies it to the heart of a stranger from three thousand miles over the sea! Just think of the fathers and mothers of Uttoxeter never telling their children the sad and lovely story which might have such a blessed influence on their young days, and spare them many a pang hereafter."

This sketch by a foreigner about Johnson's penance is very touching and beautiful. It has been mentioned that it gave rise to enquiring at the time, about the place where the Doctor did penance, but without it being discovered. I made inquiries myself amongst old people then, which resulted in about two years afterwards in some reliable evidence as to the identity of the place being afforded. Amongst others whom I asked was a then well known old man named Joseph Twigg. He had then no recollection of any such occurrence; but about a year and a half, or two years, afterwards, when he was no longer able to get out of the house, on going to see him

K

(he being at that time in his eighty-sixth year) asked me "if I had not once enquired of him whether some one, when he was a lad, had not done penance in the Market Place?" I told him I most probably had, and that a very great man had once done penance thereabouts. He then related that he had a recollection of something of the kind. He said that, when he was a lad, his father, one *market day*, came into the house late to dinner, and his mother asked him why he had not come sooner! To this enquiry he answered, *that he had been looking at a man standing in the Market Place, at the pillory, without his hat, doing penance.*" The pillory, to which the stocks were then connected, stood, he informed me, in the centre of Bear Hill, the open space at the east end of the Market Place. This is a considerable distance from the conduit and weighing machine, where the stocks stood in recent years, and where it was supposed the Doctor imposed upon himself the penance. Twigg also told me that what his father stated so struck him for its singularity, that either that day or early the next morning he went to Bear Hill himself, and although he did not see the renowned penitent, he saw the rubbish and stones which, in derision, had been cast at him by children. My informant was then about eight years of age, and was therefore quite old enough to have the recollection of so strange an affair—and particularly as he visited the spot himself where it took place—impressed upon his memory.

That the circumstance thus related by the old man, who fixes the site where it occurred at Bear Hill, is identical with the so-called act of penance by Doctor Johnson, there is scarcely a doubt. If the artist who designed the cartoon for Dr. Johnson's monument visited Uttoxeter prior to its execution, he would take the conception of the pig represented at the bottom from Bear Hill, for on one part of that space the pig market was held for more than three hundred years till the Smithfield was opened. Fixing, then, Bear Hill towards its northern side as the place of its singular incident, there is no necessity any longer to contend with the paradox of it happening at the conduit, where the view of the church is obstructed, and yet in sight of the church at the same time. At Bear Hill the church is quite conspicuous, and both are no great distance from each other, and it was also then an invariable feature of the market that it extended a considerable way into each street, and in reality quite "surged round" the old church yard wall. It was also round Bear Hill on the causeways where corn used to be set down in bags and opened for sale. But there is further evidence of the correctness of this view of the site where the penance was done. A Mr. Brandon, of Marchington, who has been deceased many years, used also to speak of having seen Doctor Johnson doing penance at Bear Hill. He personally related particulars of the circumstance to Mr. Clark, confectioner, of Uttoxeter. Mr. Clark was Mr. Brandon's grandson, and he told me that the stir in the town occasioned by the strange event, and the sight itself at Bear Hill, kept him so backward in doing his business, and consequently caused him to be so late home at night, that he found it necessary to relate the circumstances which had detained him to his wife and family. When he related them subsequently at any time in after years he invariably associated them with Bear Hill. Adding, therefore, this straightforward account to what is related by Joseph Twigg, as to the actual locality where Doctor Johnson relieved his mind of the torture of his sense of disobedience to his father, all further doubt respecting it may, I think, be reasonably ended. At all events I am unable to procure any better information on the subject. I know that Mr. Hawthorn in his collected papers entitled "Our Old Home," which comprises the paper about his visit to Uttoxeter, disputes what is said in the first edition of this book on this point; but the very indifferent way in which he made inquiries about the object of his special visit to the town, clearly shows that whilst we may be attracted by the charm of his writing and the beauty of his sentiments, little reliance can be placed upon what he has merely imagined respecting the identity of the site of Doctor Johnson's penance.

The supposed circumstances and features of the market day when the penance was performed, have been made the subject, with Johnson as the principal figure, of the following amongst other pathetic verses by the late Walter Thornbury, author of numerous works and an extensive contributor to periodical literature :—

"Here's th' April Fool!" a farmer cries,
   Holding his swollen side ;
Another clacks his wip, a third
   Begins to rail and chide,
While salesmen cried their prices out,
   And with each other vied.
Yet when he silent stood, nor moved
   For one long hour at least,
The market women leering said
   "This is some crazy priest
Doing his penance—pelt him boys—
   Pump on the Popish thief."
Some, counting money, turned to sneer ;
   One with raised hammer there
Kept it still poised, to see the man ;
   The buyers paused to stare ;
The farmer had to hold his dog,
   Longing to bite and tare.
As the old clock beats out the time,
   The stranger strides away,
Past deafening groups of flocks and carts
   And many a drunken fray ;
The sin of fifty years agone,
   That penance purged away.
Call it not superstition, friends,
   Or foolish weak regret ;
He was a great good man, whose eyes
   With tears that day were wet ;
It was a brave act to crush his pride—
   Worthy of memory yet.

Mr. Norris, formerly printer and stationer of this town, possessed a pen and ink sketch of two figures affirmed to represent Captain Astle, subsequently the Rev. Daniel Astle, curate of Bramshall, and Doctor Samuel Johnson. They are engraved in the "Life of the Doctor," in four volumes in the "Illustrated London Library," published at the office of the *Illustrated London News*, and they are stated to be sketches of Dr. Johnson in the act of penance, with Captain Astle in conversation with him. One figure indisputably represents Captain Astle, for his own autograph appears underneath it, at least so I judge, for it very much resembles his autograph, latinized, in a copy of Æschylus, in two volumes, now amongst my books. But it is quite evident that the other was not intended for Doctor Johnson. It does not in the least resemble him in his well known massive, thoughtful, and almost surly physiognomy, and arched nose, nor yet in statue; but it in every respect answers to descriptions of Samuel Bentley, the Uttoxeter poet, who was low in figure, bulged in his abdomen, had a hooked, not a Roman nose, with his chin turned up, and possessing a very prominent forehead, whilst he carried a staff, and dressed, as hereafter will be described, in the fashion of the age. I am, consequently, disposed to regard it beyond all doubt as a sketch of Samuel Bentley, and to look upon both as having been executed by him, especially as he was a skilful artist, and as Mr. Bentley's own servant intimated to me, a friend of Captain Astle. Such a discovery will be interesting, especially as no portrait of Samuel Bentley is known to exist.

As to the Inn where Michael Johnson stayed when he came to Uttoxeter, I think it is more likely to have been the Red Lion Inn, rather than the Nag's Head, especially as it is related that there used to be drawers and shelves for books preserved there, and reputed to have belonged to him. Besides, if the Nag's Head had then an existence, which is doubtful, it had no accommodation for market people, with horses and conveyances, notwithstanding the great but mere fancy entertained for it by Mr. Hawthorn in assigning it as the hostelry where he insists Michael Johnson used to stay.

When Doctor Johnson did his penance there was another Inn at Bear Hill, close to the Red Lion, and as it was a posting house, it is not at all improbable that the chaise which brought him to Uttoxeter in 1784 was drawn up there, though one would suppose the Red Lion was not destitute of similar accommodation. The following copy of a card, printed in 1793 by the late Mr. Richards, announces the amalgamation of the two inns :—

"Red Lion Inn (opposite the church). W. Garle takes the liberty of acquainting his friends and the public, that, having taken and laid to his house the assembly room, stables, and other conveniences lately belonging to the 'New Star Inn,' and made various other alterations and enlargements, he has very complete and desirable accommodation for gentlemen, travellers, and others who will honour him with their company. He begs leave to observe that he has laid in an ample stock of the very best port and other wines, and also spirits of the best quality. ☞ Mr. Garle continues the malting business as usual. May 14th, 1793." The Red Lion has just been partly rebuilt and is now called the "Lion Inn."

In bringing the story of Doctor Johnson's penance to a conclusion, it must not be omitted to name that a memorial thereof has at length been fixed in Uttoxeter Market Place in the north side of the conduit where it is visible to all who pass that way. It is a facsimile, in Portland cement, of the cartoon on the north side of Johnson's monument at Lichfield, and was executed by

Mr. P. Squagtræ, of Birmingham. The undertaking originated with the Rev. H. Abud, vicar and rural dean, and the monies were collected by Mr. F. T. Fearn.

It does not appear that there was any other bookseller in Uttoxeter at the period when Michael Johnson brought books for sale, and not for sometime afterwards. He must consequently be regarded not only as an early medium through whom books got disseminated in the neighbourhood, but also as one of the earliest pioneers in modern intellectual and moral improvement of whom Uttoxeter can boast, and of whose name, therefore, it ought to be proud. Not till at least sixty years after Michael Johnson, is there any account of Uttoxeter possessing a second bookseller as remembered by one of the oldest inhabitants when I first began to collect information for this volume. About that distance of time after, one Mr. Sanders, of Derby, opened a shop in the Market Place, at the north side, for the sale of books and stationery. Railway travelling not then being thought of, this worthy and plodding tradesmen brought his books and other miscellaneous goods to Uttoxeter in a couple of saddle bags over a horse.

The ensuing may have reference to the coronation of George III. in 1760. Still I should be more strongly disposed to attribute it to the time of the coronation of King William and Queen Mary on April 11th, 1689. The account was written April 13th, of a year not mentioned. The style of the composition makes me think it embodies an account of a celebration of the latter event.

" Uttoxeter, in Staffordshire, April 13th, ...

"'The day of their majesties' coronation was observed here with all imaginable demonstrations of joy. After divine service 100 young men, completely armed, marched to a common adjoining to the town, where they exercised for several hours, which done they returned to the Market Cross and there drank their majesties' healths, and several volleys of shot and loud acclamations. In the evening there were bonfires in the streets, and at each fire a table covered with plenty of variety of meat and liquors for the entertainment of the people."

There are no further notable events presenting themselves for record arising out of the last century, so far as research hitherto has availed, except that the fast of February 25th, 1795, was solemnly observed in the town, and for which Mr. Alkin composed an anthem; and we step into this century by noticing that the treaty of peace entered into in the year 1802 between England, France, Spain and Holland, was celebrated in the town with accompanying festivities. The town was illuminated, and Mr. Samuel Bentley, the poet, then in his eightieth year, appeared as the personification of Peace at his house door with a laurel wreath on his head, and he also gave memory to the event by the following poetic invocation, each line of which begins with the letters of the alphabet.

INVOCATION TO PEACE,

By Mr. Samuel Bentley, of Uttoxeter, March 30th, 1802.

All hail, sweet peace! hail, thou treasure!
Brightest source of real pleasure;
Come, lovely peace, triumphant come,
Deign to fix here thy lasting dome.
England shall then loud peans sing;
Fortessemo the bells shall ring;
Goddess, descend, nor make delay;
Hither, O! hither, wing thy way.
Infants shall lisp thy pleasing name;
Joyous all ranks thy worth proclaim;
Kings, Lords, and Commons, all shall join,
Loud to proclaim thee, Peace, divine:
Music shall all its graces lend,
No note of discord shall offend;
Organs shall swell each solemn sound;
Priests, poet's chorus hymning round;
Quite round our isle, on every shore,
Rejoicing, deathless cannons roar;
Shepherds shall pipe on open reeds;
Tight nymphs and swains dance round our meads,
Unblest war's ravages, no more
Virgins and matrons shall deplore;
Wise Kings, adored, O peace! thy grace;
Xerxes ne'er viewed thy smiling face;
Yearly to thee we'll homage pay,
Zealous to guard thee night and day.

CHORUS—
Tyrants of old usurped the laurel bough,
Laurels with olive wreathed, shall grace thy brow;
Peace, plenty, liberty, we will adore
Eternally—till time shall be no more.
Richards, Printer."

It will not be thought uninteresting and unworthy of notice that the Queen of these realms passed through Uttoxeter at the time she was a young Princess, when, as might be expected, a crowd of people filled the streets to have a glance at one so high in society as to have the prospect of the British Crown before her, which, since her succession to it, she has so worthily worn. In July, 1840, the Queen Dowager also passed through Uttoxeter to Alton Towers. A halt was made at the White Hart Hotel, Carter Street, where the Yeomanry Cavalry were drawn up to protect with military formality her carriage, and escort her to Alton, from whence she proceeded to Matlock. She was met by, amongst others, Lord and Lady Waterpark, Sir Thomas and Lady Cotton Sheppard, Sir E. M. Buller, T. B. Philips, Esq., and John Bill, Esq. ✻

About this period there was a matter before the inhabitants of Uttoxeter in which they were deeply interested. Reference is made to the circumstances attending the birth of William John Fox, Esq., which, with the attainment of his majority and marriage, have an historical importance in the estimation of the local chronicler. These circumstances were attendant upon a course of litigation which was instituted about 1835, and continued through several years, having issue to the question, who was the legal inheritor of considerable landed estates and other property which had belonged to Mr. Fox, an old and exceedingly wealthy inhabitant of Uttoxeter, then recently deceased. Amongst the legal proceedings arising out of this question, was the consignment of Mrs. Fox, who had been married to the deceased gentleman a very short time before his death, to the care of a jury of

---

✻ See Excursions and other papers by the late John Bill, Esq., 1850.

matrons, of Uttoxeter, until the birth of a posthumous child of which she declared herself pregnant, and who, it was contended, on her behalf, would be the heir or heiress to Mr. Fox's estates. The novelty of this proceeding, taken by direction of the Court, excited considerable interest at the time, and has since been referred to in several works on medical jurisprudence. In due time the child (Mr. W. J. Fox) was born, and when, after protracted litigation, involving trials at *nisi prius* at Stafford, Chester, and Gloucester Court of Appeal, the joy of the people of Uttoxeter, who all along had been faithful to the cause of the widow and fatherless, found expression in every conceivable way.* Mrs. Fox died in 1868. The solicitors who conducted the case on behalf of Mrs. Fox were the late Messrs. Bedson and Rushton, of Uttoxeter, to whose business Messrs. Cooper and Chawner are the successors.

It was to be expected that the attainment of his majority by a young gentleman, the circumstances of whose birth were so peculiar, would not be permitted to pass unnoticed. On this event, which took place on Thursday, October 14th, 1856, he was invited to a public dinner by the gentlemen of the town and neighbourhood, and which was held under the presidency of the late Joseph Bladon, Esq., of Old Field, in the Town Hall, Uttoxeter. A very full assembly did honour to the occasion. On the same day Mr. Fox himself gave to the poor of Uttoxeter a substantial quantity of coal and beef, and during the excessively severe winter of 1860-61, he again generously bestowed upon the poor of the parish almost thirty-five tons of coal.

The marriage of W. J. Fox, Esq., with Ellen, eldest daughter of the late Thomas Bladon, Esq., of Old Field House, which he erected as it now appears, took place on the 7th October, 1858. The marriage ceremony was solemnized by the late Mr. Dashwood, grandfather of the bride. Mr. Fox died at his residence at Woodvilla, near

---

* *Staffordshire Advertiser.*

Uttoxeter, in February, 1875, and was interred in a vault in the cemetery, and the death of Mrs. Fox occurred in January, 1881.

Preceding the birthday festivities of Mr. Fox by two years, the peace rejoicings in Uttoxeter following upon the proclamation of peace between the Allied Powers and Russia, were of a character to be remembered. After such an holucaust of victims to the lust of despotism and war as that which had been made in the Crimea, causing bleeding hearts and desolated homes in almost every town and village throughout several nations of Europe, it was sufficient to cause rejoicing in any town when a message of peace was sent forth. The rejoicings in Uttoxeter took place in the usual form, resulting chiefly in good doings to the poor, on the 1st of June, 1856. The sum of £75 was collected in the town in the short space of two or three days, and was expended in providing for the festivity, 1,200 lbs. of the best cuts of beef, 110 stones of flour for bread, and in the purchase of numerous barrels of ale. The distribution was made in the centre of the Market Place, where arrangements for it had been previously made, to about 450 families by ticket. The National Anthem, however, was first sung, and three cheers given for the Queen. The committee of management consisted of Messrs. R. Bagshaw (solicitor), J. B. Johnson (chemist), J. Dunncliff (draper), Joseph Wood (grocer), Charles Turner, Joseph Clarke (confectioner), and James Cook (of the Red Lion Hotel).

There was also a whole sheep roasted at Tinker's Lane, otherwise Stone Road end, under the side of a house, and distributed amongst the people in that part of the town. There were besides numerous public tea meetings in the town in the afternoon. In Carter Street there were three; in Balance Street one; in Smithy Lane one; and in Silver Street one; and likewise one in the Market Place, at which 300 persons gathered. The whole of the tea meetings were held in the public streets. The teetotallers also had one, and the people of the workhouse were handsomely provided for in a similar manner.

The streets were profusely decorated during the day with evergreens, wreaths, garlands and mottoes, and at night a display of fireworks and an illumination by gas were made in the Market Place. The day passed off pleasantly, and everything showed that if the terms of peace were not all that could be desired, the inhabitants of Uttoxeter yet valued peace as a blessing, and a fact worth rejoicing for.

"Were half the power that fills the world with terror;
 Were half the wealth bestowed on camps and courts
Given to redeem the human mind from error,
 There were no need of arsenals and forts."

LONGFELLOW.

CHAPTER III.

THE SHREWSBURY PEERAGE CASE.

We have only to pass along a few more years, in the interim of which nothing occurred in Uttoxeter to merit particular notice, to be brought to the most important local event of the century—one in which Uttoxeter and neighbourhood took a particular and lively interest. Indeed the part which Uttoxeter took on the occasion makes it almost historically its own. It need scarcely be said that it is the occasion of the Earl of Shrewsbury and Talbot taking possession of Alton Towers and the other Shrewsbury estates. Such an outburst of good feeling and popular enthusiasm could not, however, have been owing merely to a great legal achievement in the right of property. Nothing short of the noble qualities inherent in his lordship, than whom there "was no more brave, generous, and open-hearted Englishman amongst the subjects of Queen Victoria," and the estimable Lady Shrewsbury herself, in connection with the just decision, after a most trying struggle, in his Lordship's favour, could have produced such a spontaneous demonstration, unequalled probably in any similar case, as that which took place at Uttoxeter on the 13th April, 1860. As, however, the history of the Shrewsbury peerage, and an

account of the struggle which terminated in favour of the
Earl of Shrewsbury, seem to be an important preliminary
to a description of the festivities at Uttoxeter, which were
held to inaugurate the taking formal possession of Alton
Towers and Estates, the following accurate summary will
prove not uninteresting :— *

"We learn from 'Burke's Peerage,' and other equally
reliable sources of information, that the eminent family of
Talebote is one of ancient celebrity and almost unequalled
historic interest. It deduces its descent from a period
antecedent to the Conquest; but Richard de Talbot, who
came over to England with William I., may be considered
its founder. From him the Shrewsbury branch in England,
and the Talbots of Malahide, in Ireland, as well as the
untitled but elder branch of Talbots of Bashall, Yorkshire
(now extinct in the direct male line), can trace their pedigree through nearly eight centuries by direct descent to
the present day. From the second son Hugh, Governor
of the Castle of Plessy, in Essex, who afterwards assumed
the monastic habit, like so many warriors of his time, six
generations bring us down to Sir George Talbot, Lord
Chamberlain to King Edward III., by whom he was
summoned to Parliament as a baron in A.D. 1331. His
son, Sir Richard, Lord of Goderich Castle, and second
baron, distinguished himself in the French wars of Edward
III., and became great grandfather of Sir John Talbot,
sixth baron, summoned to Parliament in 1409, as Lord
de Furnivall. In 1412 the latter illustrious warrior was
appointed Lord Justice of Ireland, of which he became
Lord Lieutenant in A.D. 1414. He subsequently rendered
good service to his country in the French wars of Henry
V., but his highest renown was gained under Henry VI.,
upon the same field under the Regent Plantagenet Duke
of Bedford. It is said that his character became far and
wide so formidable to the French, owing to the constant
success which attended his expeditions, that mothers used
to hush their children into silence by pronouncing the

---

* A full account of the Talbot family appears under the head of "Ruling families of England" in the *Spectator* for 1863.

name of the 'Great Dogge Talbot.' He was attacked, however, by Joan of Arc, the maid of Orleans, at Patay, 1429, when his army was routed and he himself was taken prisoner. Being subsequently exchanged, and having gained for himself fresh laurels, he was created Earl of Shrewsbury by King Henry VI., in 1442. Again resuming the Lord Lieutenancy of Ireland, which at that day was rather a military than a civil post, and having been appointed Lord High Steward of that country, he was raised to the Earldom of Wexford and Waterford in A.D. 1446, and thus became Premier Earl in the Irish as well as in the English peerage. Again engaging in foreign warfare, though in the eightieth year of his age, the Earl advanced with a British force to the relief of the Castle of Chatillon, in France, beneath the walls of which he was mortally wounded, and died July 20th, 1453, with the reputation of having been victorious in•above forty different battles. His younger son, Lord Lisle, fell dead upon the same field. John, the second Earl of Shrewsbury, K.G., Lord Treasurer, first of Ireland and afterwards of England, was killed at the battle of Northampton in A.D. 1460, while fighting under the Red Rose. He was succeeded by his eldest son, from whom the title descended regularly to the fifth earl, the most constant statesman of Queen Mary's reign, and the only nobleman except Viscount Montague, who, on Elizabeth's accession, opposed the repeal of the act of submission of the House of Lords and Commons to the authority to the See of Rome, which had been carried into effect in the preceding reign. Though thus strongly attached to the religion of his forefathers, Queen Elizabeth retained him in her service, and even admitted him to her Privy Council. His son, the Scotch Earl, is known to history as the most wealthy and powerful peer of the realm, and the guardian to whose custody the person of Queen Mary of Scots was entrusted by Elizabeth. On the death of the eighth earl in 1617 the title reverted to a distant cousin, Mr. George Talbot, of Grafton, Worcestershire, as great grandson of the second earl; and from him it descended regularly to

Charles, twelfth earl, who, having conformed to the Established Church, became a prominent statesman in the reigns of William III., Mary, Anne, and George I., under whom he held the highest offices, and by whom he was rewarded with the Dukedom of Shrewsbury, the Marquisate of Alton, and the Knighthood of the Garter. At his death in 1717 the dukedom and marquisate expired for want of male issue, and it is not a little singular that from that day to this the earldom has never passed directly from father to son. The thirteenth earl, being a Jesuit priest, of course did not assume the title, which accordingly passed to the son of his brother George, as fourteenth earl, and the last of his male descendants is now deceased. It would be alike tedious and profitless to trace the exact pedigree for the last century, which merely exhibits a series of nephews and cousins inheriting in succession: we will therefore only mention that the son and the nephew of John, sixteenth earl, having died during his minority, Bertram Arthur Talbot, in 1846, became heir presumptive to the Shrewsbury title and estates, to which he succeeded as seventeenth earl towards the close of the year 1852. His lordship was the only son of the late Lieutenant-Colonel Charles Thomas Talbot, nephew of Charles, fifteenth earl, by Julia, third daughter of Sir Henry Tichborne, Bart. He was born December 11th, 1832, and died without issue at Lisbon, August 10th, 1856.

"The kindred of the Earl of Shrewsbury consists in his lineal descent from the famous Sir Gilbert Talbot, of Grafton (third son of the second earl of Shrewsbury), who was a High Sheriff in the time of King Edward III., but a staunch adherent of the Earl of Richmond, the right wing of whose army he commanded at the battle of Bosworth. The victorious prince showed his gratitude by bestowing upon Gilbert the honour of Knighthood, with the grant of the manor of Grafton, in Worcestershire, and other lands. Two years afterwards Sir Gilbert had command at the battle of Stoke, when the Earl of Lincoln and Lambert Simnel were defeated, and for this service he was made a Knight-banneret. The most noble member of this branch of the Talbot family was Charles Talbot, who was bred to the bar, attained to the summit of his profession, and established the highest legal reputation. On the 31st of May, 1717, Mr. Talbot was appointed Solicitor-General to the Prince of Wales, which office he continued to hold until 1733, when he was constituted Lord High Chancellor of England, sworn of the Privy Council, and elevated to the Peerage December 5th, by the title of Baron Talbot, of Hensol, Glamorganshire. His lordship married Cecil, daughter and heiress of Charles Mathews, Esq., of Castle-Menich, Glamorganshire, and was at his death (February 14th, 1736-7) succeeded by his eldest son William, who was appointed Lord Steward of the Household, sworn of the Privy Council in 1761, and advanced to the earldom as Earl Talbot, March 10th in the same year. His lordship dying without male issue the earldom expired, the barony of Dynevor (which title had been conferred upon him with special remainder to his daughter and her male issue) descended as limited, and the barony of Talbot of Hensol reverted to his nephew, John Chetwynd Talbot, who was advanced to the viscountcy and earldom July 3rd, 1784, by the title of Viscount Ingestre and Earl Talbot. He died May 19th, 1793, and was succeeded by his son Charles Chetwynd Chetwynd-Talbot, who was constituted Viceroy of Ireland on the retirement of the late Duke of Richmond, and executed the duties of that important government until the appointment of the Marquis Wellesley in 1821. His lordship was also Lord-Lieutenant of the County of Stafford. At his death, which occurred on the 10th January, 1849, he was succeeded by his second son, the present Earl of Shrewsbury and Talbot (1860).

"The present representative of the two great branches of this famous house has not, however, without a protracted struggle, succeeded in uniting in his own person the time-honoured titles. Within a few days of the death of the late Earl of Shrewsbury, an earnest was given of the serious intentions of the Ingestre branch to assert the claim of Earl Talbot to that title, for on the 18th of August, 1856, Viscount Ingestre (on behalf of his father, who was abroad), accompanied by Mr. Hand, his solicitor, formerly demanded at Alton Towers possession of that mansion, and the estates of the late earl, alleging that Earl Talbot was the legal heir. Lord Ingestre was informed that the trustees under the will of the deceased earl had taken possession, and he was refused admission into the house. Earl Talbot at once resolved upon appealing to the highest tribunal in the land to decide the question of the title to the premier earldom of England; but partly in consequence of the autumnal and winter recesses, and partly from the dissolution of Parliament in the Spring of 1857, it was the 11th of May that year before Earl Talbot's claim was formally brought before the House of Lords. On that day the petition of his Lordship to Her Majesty, praying Her Majesty that the title, dignity, and peerage, or honors of the Earl of Shrewsbury might be declared and adjudged to belong to him, together with Her Majesty's reference thereof to the House, and the report of the Attorney-General thereof was presented, by command of the House. The petition, reference, and report were read, and were subsequently referred to the Committee of Privileges to consider and report thereupon. The opponents to his lordship's claims were three in number—first, the Duke of Norfolk, as guardian of the interests of his infant son, to whom the late earl bequeathed his magnificent property at Alton Towers; secondly, the Princess Doria Pamphili (Lady Mary Talbot) of Rome (who, it is stated, was supposed to have been poisoned), as only surviving child of John, sixteenth earl; and thirdly, Major Talbot, of Talbot, county of Wexford, who traced his pedigree up to William, fourth son of George, fourth earl, who was made a Knight of the Garter for his brilliant conduct at the battle of Stoke, June 16th, 1487. The Committee of Privileges met for the first time on the 13th of the following July, when Sir Frederick Thesiger opened the case on behalf of Earl Talbot, and on the same day Mr. Sergeant Byles, who represented Lord Edward Howard, admitted that the determination of the claim to the title determined the title to the estates. On the 27th of the same month Mr. Sergeant Byles opened the case for Lord Edward Howard, and several subsequent days were occupied with the production of evidence against Earl Talbot's claim. On the 14th of the following month the Attorney-General replied on behalf of the Crown, and said that he proposed instituting further enquiries before asking the Committee to come to any resolution on the question at issue. The Committee unanimously approved of this course being pursued, and they then adjourned *sine die*. It is not until the 20th of April in the following year that we again find the Committee of Privileges engaged in this important investigation. The Attorney-General then stated the nature of the additional evidence which he intended to produce. This was chiefly of a documentary character, but its reception occupied their lordships during two days. On the 4th of May Sir R. Bethell addressed the Committee on behalf of Earl Talbot's opponents. Two or three days were then devoted to the production of evidence on this side, after which Mr. Roundell Palmer pleaded on behalf of the appellants against the claim, and the Attorney-General, during the greater part of three days, summed up Earl Talbot's case. The Solicitor-General was then appealed to for his opinion on behalf of the Crown, and he stated his conviction to be 'that the noble claimant had made out his case, and was entitled to the Earldom of Shrewsbury.' On the 1st of June the final sitting of the Committee was held, and their Lordships proceeded to give judgment. Lord Cranworth, addressing his Committee, and after going over the leading points of the case submitted on behalf of Earl Talbot, concluded by moving, 'that their lordships report that the claimant has made out his title.' Lord St. Leonards, 'having come to the clear and satisfactory conclusion that the claimant's title admitted of no doubt,' seconded the motion. Lords Wensleydale and Brougham also expressed themselves to the same effect, after which Lord Redesdale, chairman of the committee, put the question, whether the claimant had made out his title, and it was unanimously carried in the affirmative. We read in the journals of the day that the galleries of the house were crowded whenever their lordships met, and that the Earl and Countess of Shrewsbury and Talbot were warmly congratulated by a large number of their friends immediately after their lordships had come to the above resolution.

"Those who anticipated (if any such there were) from the admission made by Mr. Sergeant Byles at the opening of the proceedings in the House of Lords with respect to the title, that the right to the estates of the deceased earl would be quietly conceded to the successful claimant for the title, were undeceived at the earliest possible opportunity. On the 6th of December, 1858, in the Court of Common Pleas, before Mr. Chief Justice Cockburn and a special jury, the cause of the Earl of Shrewsbury v. Hope Scott and others first came on for hearing. The action was brought to recover the mansion-house of Alton Towers and the annexed estates, and defendants, who represented the infant son of the Duke of Norfolk, defended as to all property claimed. The Attorney-General opened the plaintiff's case, and produced certain documentary evidence. On the same day Mr. Sergeant Shee addressed the jury for the defendants, and evidence on the same side having been produced, it was agreed that a verdict should be entered for the plaintiff, subject to leave to the defendants to move to enter a verdict for them, or subject to a special case if the parties should so agree. On the 21st of January in the following year, in the Court of Common Pleas, Mr. Sergeant Shee obtained a rule upon all the points of law raised by him on behalf of his clients, and on the 31st of May the cause was again called on. The Attorney-General, on behalf of the noble plaintiff, appeared to show cause against the rule, and Mr. Rolt, Q.C., Mr. Mainstay, Q.C., and Mr. Sergeant Shee and Sir R. Bethell replied on behalf of the defendants, and on the 8th of June the Lord Chief Justice, and his brethren, Mr. Justice Williams,

Mr. Justice Willis, and Mr. Justice Byles, unanimously gave judgment to the effect that the rule to set aside the verdict for the plaintiff must be discharged. Undeterred by this defeat the defendants at once resolved upon carrying the case to the Court of Error. Little progress was, however, made during the next term, but on the 1st of February in the present year (1860) the writ of error was brought from the court below, and came on for hearing, both sides being represented by counsel of the highest eminence. The proceedings having lasted three days, the Lord Chief Baron said the Court had considered the very learned, elaborate, and ingenious arguments urged by the Attorney-General (Sir R. Bethell) on behalf of the defendants, but desired to give them still further consideration before delivering judgment. The Court would not then call upon the other side to reply, but would announce their conclusion as early as possible. This was naturally enough considered as virtually a victory on the part of the plaintiff, and all doubt was removed on the 18th of February, when the Court gave judgment against the defendants. Notice of appeal to the House of Lords was given to the other side, but, doubtless, believing that they had no chance of obtaining a reversal of the decision of the Court of Exchequer, the defendants from this time abandoned all idea of carrying on the litigation, and on the 25th of the same month the Earl of Shrewsbury and Talbot took possession of Alton Towers.

"As a record we may mention that the Counsel who appeared in the causes were—for the peerage, Lord Chelmsford (then Sir F. Thesiger), Sir Fitzroy Kelly, Mr. T. F. Ellis (Recorder of Leeds), and Mr. J. Hannen, of the Home Circuit. Mr. R. Nicholson, Earl Shrewsbury's London Solicitor, had charge of the proceedings. In the action of ejectment—Sir Fitzroy Kelly, Mr. Rolt, Q.C., Mr. Mainsty, Q.C., Mr. T. F. Ellis, and Mr. Hannen.

"The premier earldom of England having been thus adjudged to belong by right to Earl Talbot, his lordship delayed not in asserting his claim to those vast estates, which even his antagonists had admitted would legitimately pass to the successful competitor for the title of the deceased earl. These estates, the annual value of which is upwards of £40,000, lie in the counties of Stafford, Salop, Chester, Oxford, Berks, and Worcester. The Oxfordshire estate comprises the site and ruins of a magnificent seat called Heythorp, which was burnt down in the time of Earl John; and the Worcestershire estate an old family manor-house, at Grafton, also burnt down, the remains of a mansion which is supposed to have been one of more than ordinary size and magnificence in the time of Sir Gilbert Talbot, K.G., (Knighted for his valour in the field) in 1517. The estates are all old family properties; the Oxfordshire, Berkshire, and Worcestershire belonged to Sir Gilbert, while the Cheshire estates came into the family on the marriage of Mr. John Talbot, of Albrighton, son of Sir Gilbert, with Miss Troutbeck, a Cheshire heiress. The Cheshire estate comprises very nearly the whole township of Oxton, near Birkenhead. The greatest interest attaches, however, to the Staffordshire estates, chiefly on account of the magnificent mansion which the fifteenth earl erected at Alton, and which has from that time been the principal seat of the house of Talbot." *

As already stated the day for taking formal possession was Friday, the 14th of April, 1860, for which such great preparation had been made in Uttoxeter. Earl Talbot's tenantry, friends, and the Staffordshire Yeomanry Cavalry resolved to attend his Lordship to Alton. The procession was formed at Blount's Green, about three parts of a mile to the west of Uttoxeter, where, by ten o'clock, the Queen's Own Yeomanry Cavalry, under Captain Levett, the Uttoxeter and Blythfield troop, under the command of Captain Meynell Ingram, the Cheadle and Alton troop under Lieutenant, now Sir Percival Heywood, Bart, and the Leek troop under Captain Sneyd, took up their respective positions in the field at the junction of the Stafford and Lichfield roads. The number was between

---

* *Staffordshire Advertiser*, April 14th, 1860.

two or three hundred men and officers. At eleven o'clock the approach from Ingestre Hall was announced by outriders, and was met by a burst of cheers from the vast multitude of persons assembled.

The procession was followed by the Talbot tenantry on horseback, three abreast, numbering about sixty, being preceded by the Stafford troop of Yeomanry. Next followed the Leek troop, and after them the Alton tenantry on horseback, three abreast, and fully equal in number to those of the Talbot estates. The Uttoxeter troop of Yeomanry succeeded them. Then came the standards of the Yeomanry, with the trumpeters and outriders, Chief Superintendent of Police Sweeting, and Superintendents Cole and Povey, the High Sheriff's (R. H. Heywood) and five other carriages, including one containing Viscount and Viscountess Ingestre. Following these was the carriage of the Earl of Shrewsbury, containing—

Earl Shrewsbury, Lady Adelade Talbot,
Countess Shrewsbury, Hon. Walter Talbot,
Lady Gertrude Talbot, Hon. Reginald Talbot.

As the procession left Blount's Green the merry peals of Uttoxeter Church bells were heard, the flags on the battlements of the church were plainly seen in the distance, and the lively strains of the band proclaimed the hearty welcome awaiting the procession. The aspect of the town was of a very animating and exciting description. The townspeople and hundreds of strangers took up positions at every available place—at doors, windows, and on the causeways—along the line of route through Uttoxeter. Almost every house had some kind of decoration; and in High Street the sky was almost hid by numberless wreaths of evergreens, and by banners, garlands, flags, and devices so profusely displayed.

A triumphal arch of evergreens, surmounted by a flag, was erected at the entrance of Carter Street against the Far Talbot Inn, with the inscription in the centre, "Welcome, Premier Earl," it being the work of the late Mr. Edward Smith. The principal decoration, however, was a triumphal arch in the front of the Town Hall, designed by Mr. Fradgley, architect. The piers consisted of two spruce firs, transplanted from the Alton estates, the branches of which were cut off, except at the top, the trunks being thickly surrounded by sprays of fir, yew, and other evergreens tied on and festooned by ribbons. The arch was made in a similar way. On the right hand column was a shield charged with the ancient arms which the family bore when it came over with William the Conqueror, bendy of six *argent* and *gules* under which was placed the word Talebote, the original way of spelling the family name. At the crown of the arch were the present arms of Talbot, *gules*, a lion rampant, with an engrailed bordure, *or* (being the arms the family took on the marriage of a Talbot with Gwendylline ap Rhese, a Princess of Wales), over which stood an earl's coronet, and underneath the motto " Prest d' accomplis." On the left hand pier of the arch were the arms of the Earl's eldest son, Lord Ingestre, which were distinguished by a label for difference

At the front of the Town Hall a platform was erected, where a deputation, consisting of the Rev. H. Abud, M.A., vicar; Herbert Taylor, Esq., M.D.; Rev. R. Howard, Mr. W. J. Fox, Mr. Thomas Bladon, Mr. A. A. Flint, and Mr. R. Bagshaw, waited to present the Earl Shrewsbury and Talbot with an address. On arriving at the platform Viscount and Viscountess Ingestre halted a moment, and W. J. Fox, Esq., presented a splendid bouquet to the Viscountess, and shortly afterwards, on the arrival of the carriage containing the Earl and Countess of Shrewsbury, Dr. Taylor presented the Countess of Shrewsbury with a beautiful bouquet. Thomas Bladon, Esq., then presented an address to the Earl of Shrewsbury from the inhabitants of Uttoxeter. The address was written on parchment, having a deep gold border, and enclosed in a walnut wood box with mediæval mountings, and lined with silk. The following is a copy :—

" *To the Right Honourable the Earl of Shrewsbury and Talbot, Premier Earl of England.*

" May it please your Lordship, We, the inhabitants of

the town of Uttoxeter, in the immediate neighbourhood of the princely estate of Alton Towers, beg to offer your lordship our public respect and congratulations on the auspicious occasion of your progress through our ancient town, to take formal possession of a property and title now happily settled upon your lordship's branch of the house of Talbot, by the decision of the highest authority of these realms.

"We heartily congratulate your lordship on the successful issue of an anxious series of costly and arduous litigations, by which this influential estate has been finally, and, we trust, for ever, vested in a Protestant line of inheritance.

"Connected with your lordship as one of the Lords of the Manor of Uttoxeter, we the inhabitants, cordially welcome the event of your lordship's occupation of Alton Towers; and we beg most sincerely and respectfully to sympathise with your lordship's triumph over the formidable difficulties so gallantly encountered by your lordship and family, so skilfully disentangled by your lordship's eminent counsel, and at length, by the Divine blessing, so happily surmounted by the legal recognition of your lordship's title to the patrimony of the house of Talbot.

"We hail as a happy omen the coincidence of your lordship's first acts of public impropriation of the estate with the anniversary of the birthday of Viscount Ingestre, your lordship's eldest son, and heir to the united earldoms of Shrewsbury and Talbot.

"We cannot better express our felicitations to the Viscount Ingestre, than by the earnest prayer that he may prove as justly popular and esteemed a successor to the earldom of Shrewsbury and Talbot as his lordship's father inherited, without impairing the honours of the noble earl, the late Lord Lieutenant of this county.

"The example of the late Earl Talbot's administration of the vice regal government of Ireland, so as to secure the satisfaction of all parties in that difficult position, will encourage your lordship's Alton tenantry of every shade of sentiment to repose confidence in the successor of a nobleman so universally revered as your lordship's father. We are assured no well advised suggestions of the late noble proprietor of Alton Towers, for the social and benevolent interests in the neighbourhood, will fail of your lordship's cordial consideration.

"Most heartily and respectfully entreating the noble lady, the Countess of Shrewsbury and Talbot, and the other members of your lordship's family, to permit us to include them in our fervant prayer for the long life, health, and uninterrupted peace and happiness of your lordship, and all the noble family, we respectfully present to the Premier Earl of England, and to the now united house of Shrewsbury and Talbot, the public and unanimous congratulations of Uttoxeter."

The Noble Earl, on receiving the address, said:—

"Gentlemen, I beg leave to thank you most warmly and most cordially for the honour you have done me in so kindly presenting me with this excellent address. You will forgive me for not saying more now than to thank you, which I do from the bottom of my heart." His lordship having thus briefly acknowledged the address, the carriage moved away amid loud cheers, which continued for some time. High Street, just then, was crowded with people from end to end.

Before reaching Alton the procession must have increased to more than a mile in length. The scene at Alton, only that it was bloodless, reminded one of the days of chivalry, when some powerful lord was taking possession of some feudal castle, and at the blast of trumpet and with flashing sword was leading his knights and hosts of mounted retainers triumphant through its no longer defended entrances. It was calculated that some 35,000 or 40,000 persons assembled on the ground to witness the proceedings, or rather from their deep sympathy with the Earl and Countess of Shrewsbury and family on the occasion. Addresses were presented at Alton to the Earl of Shrewsbury from his Alton and Ingestre tenantry, by the late Rev. W. Fraser, and the late Mr. Hartshorne, as well as from his tenantry in Wales. About 4,000 persons were entertained at the Towers at the expense of his lordship. The Earl of Shrewsbury and family returned through Uttoxeter to Ingestre at night.

At Uttoxeter during the afternoon of the day the poor were made to enjoy the occasion by having given amongst 500 families of them, numbering several thousand persons, about 600 lbs. of beef, 600 loaves, and upwards of 300 gallons of ale. A band played at the Town Hall during the same period, and a cannon, planted on the new Cemetery ground, was occasionally discharged.

Richard Howard Heywood, Esq., High Sheriff of the County, at a dinner which he gave shortly afterwards at the Swan Hotel, Stafford, on proposing the health of the Earl of Shrewsbury, expressed a hope that the future historians of the county would not fail to record the circumstances that his first act after receiving the appointment to the shrievalty, was to give his lordship possession of Alton Towers, a duty of which he felt proud. As one of those historians it gives me much pleasure to record the circumstance for the first time in connection with a portion of the county's history.

The Earl of Shrewsbury, after a short illness, died at the seat of his son-in-law, the Marquis of Lothian, at Newbattle, near Dalkeath, on Friday, June 6th, 1868, at the age of 64. The deceased noble earl had the command of the Philomel in which he took part in the battle of Navarino. On safely conveying home the dispatches announcing the victory, he was advanced to the post of captain. In 1832 he was a member of Parliament for Hereford; subsequently he sat for Dublin, and afterwards from 1837 to 1849 he held a seat in South Staffordshire, when, on the death of his brother, Viscount Ingestre, he succeeded to the earldom of Talbot. He united in his person, after 1869, the three earldoms of Shrewsbury, Waterford, and Talbot, and was Grand Seneschal of Ireland, the functions of which had not been exercised since the Reformation (all the Talbots of Shrewsbury being Catholics) until the noble earl accompanied the

Prince and Princess of Wales, with the Duke of Cambridge, to Ireland in April, 1868, on a visit to the Earl of Mayo. He was succeeded by Viscount Ingestre, who assumed the duties of his influential position in a way which all admired, but his death occurred suddenly (and was deeply and widely felt), at London in May, 1877.

The most interesting event worthy of being kept in memory is the share Uttoxeter took in the national rejoicings on the occasion of the marriage of the Prince of Wales with the Princess Alexandra of Denmark, on March 10th, 1863. Business was entirely suspended in the town; the church bells were merrily rung all day; the principal houses were decorated with flags; the band played in the front of the Town Hall; a cannon was planted in the Smithfield, and frequently discharged, and every one heartily joined in the rejoicings. A committee of gentlemen was formed, and about £60 collected and expended in bread, beef and ale for the families of the poor; for the schools for tea; for the bell-ringers and for the band. At twelve o'clock at noon, or soon after, the Rev. H. Abud, vicar, amid an assemblage of persons and bursts of cheers, proposed the health of the newly-wedded Prince and Princess. A procession, consisting of a band of music, school children of all religious denominations, and a large number of people, paraded the principal streets, and added much to the appearance of the town. In the forenoon, however, an event took place which had no precedent in Uttoxeter, so loyal was everybody, and so utterley forgotten were all sectarian prejudices. This was the assembling in the Parish Church for a rehearsal of pieces to be sung in the Market Place in the afternoon by children of all denominations—Church, Wesleyan, Congregational, and Primitive Methodist. In the afternoon, after perambulating the streets, headed by the band, the children, numbering 700, were assembled with their teachers in the Market Place, being formed in a circle of some seven deep, the space round outside them being crowded with people, and the windows of the houses round being filled with ladies. Numerous pieces were sung, including the National Anthem, and loud cheers rose for the Prince and Princess of Wales and for the Queen. Illuminations and transparencies took place at night, and closed a day long to be remembered in the town.

The rejoicings on this happy occasion were not confined to the town of Uttoxeter only, but were general throughout the neighbouring villages, which seemed to vie with each other in the hearty demonstrations of joy on the auspicious events.

Not the least important and interesting public occurrence in Uttoxeter following the one just described, at the distance of some years, was the celebration of the centenary of Sunday Schools. The friends of St. Mary's Church Sunday School did not, unfortunately, arrange to have their children take part in this public demonstration, but only recognised it by sermons and collections in the church, and the public demonstration was an event which owed its occurrence to the zeal and energy of the Wesleyans, Congregationalists and Primitive Methodists in the town. On Sunday, August 1st, 1880, religious services were held in each chapel in connection with the celebration, and in the afternoon a children's service took place in the Town Hall, and was conducted by the Rev. R. Odery, of Spilsby, who gave an address. W. Y. Craig, Esq., M.P., and C. T. Cavendish, Esq., J.P., were present, and the former gentleman, the subsequent day, spoke truly of Mr. Odery's address in the following terms :—" As an example of an effective method of addressing children, he never heard an address that exceeded the one given in the Town Hall the previous day." On Monday, the 2nd of August, a public breakfast and convention at nine o'clock, in the Town Hall, was attended by 300 persons under the presidency of W. Y. Craig, Esq., M.P., who delivered a very able and interesting address on the origin of Sunday Schools. Mr. John Payne Hall afterwards read a paper in which he dwelt minutely on the history of the same institution. Soon after twelve o'clock the children of the Sunday Schools mentioned, and of others from the country, assembled in the Market Place, the total number being about 1,500. They were there addressed by W. Y. Craig, Esq., M.P., and E. T. Earp, Esq., of Cape Town, and the children sang several hymns. After this they re-formed in procession, and headed by the Rocester Brass Band, each child carrying a bunch of flowers, and many waving flags, and all wearing bright commemorative medals, walked round the town, and afterwards proceeded to Crakemarsh Hall, the gardens and grounds of which, by the kindness of C. T. Cavendish, Esq., J.P., were thrown open for the day. The managers provided tea there for the children, who in good time, after much enjoyment, were conducted back to Uttoxeter Market Place, and after singing several hymns, they were dispersed to their homes with happy remembrances of a day the second hundredth celebration of which will be participated in by succeeding generations only, and which it is hoped will, through the religious instruction of Sunday Schools, be an improvement upon the present. The interesting proceedings of the day were brought to a close by an evening public meeting in the Town Hall, at which addresses were delivered by Mr. Earp, of Cape Town (a native of Uttoxeter), J. C. Copestake, Esq., M.D., of the town of Wyoming, near Chicago, the Rev. T. Cross, of London, the Rev. R. Odery, and G. B. Chapman, Esq., of London, deputation of the Sunday School Union. The expenses of the undertaking, which were considerable, were obtained by subscriptions and collections.

CHAPTER IV.

HISTORY OF CHRISTIANITY IN UTTOXETER.

CHURCH MATTERS, CHURCHES, ALTAR-TOMBS, INSCRIPTIONS, CHURCH REGISTER, &C., &C.

The early history of Christianity in Uttoxeter lies in complete obscurity. Doomsday Book does not inform us whether it had a church and priest at the time of the Conquest, and there is no hint upon the subject in Bede, the Saxon Chronicle, or in any of the other old Chroniclers. It is nevertheless probable that Uttoxeter had a church even in Anglo-Saxon times, from the fact of the gate forming the south entrance to the church yard being still called, as already mentioned, "Light Gate," an expression, the former part of which is corrupted from the Saxon word "Lich," meaning a dead body. Lichgate therefore signified (amongst the Saxons) the entrance through which corpses were conveyed to their burial place. This, of course, could only have been after Christianity had been received amongst them, as before then they had practised the heathenish mode of interment in barrows. Uttoxeter is mentioned as having a church in 1251, which is about 171 years after Doomsday Book was written, and its rector at that time was Thomas, one of the witnesses to the charter of William de Ferrars. In 1297 it was held, however, by one Nicholas Butler, when its advowson was £66 13s. 4d., at that period a large sum of money,* and by a gift of Earl Robert Ferrars it formed part of the endowment of Derby Abbey.† About thirty-four years afterwards, viz., in 1331,‡ an ordination of the vicarage of Uttoxeter was made by Roger Northburgh, at Islington, and it was confirmed by the chapter of Coventry to the vicar of Uttoxeter in 1333. The document, of which a transcript follows, is curious and interesting as most that research is fortunate in bringing to light.

"Roger by the Divine permission Bishop of Lichfield and Covantrie wisheth health in the savour of all to the sons of the mother church that shall looke upon these present letters with you at the visitation which were lately authorised actually within the deanery of the Archdeacon of Alveton and Leek within the countrie of Stafford. It was found out that the viceridge of the Church of Uttoxeter of the said deanery was not in certain portions ordained by us or our predecessors, and under that pretense often matter of altercation and dissension did arise between the parson and the vicar of the said church. We hereupon in that particular the parson and the vicar became humble petitioners unto us that about the promises which concerned our pastoral charge we would have a care to do, determine, and order. We willing that either of them should be kept within certaine and due limits and that none or neither should break out to the wrong of the other a processe being had which is required in the matter to the petition of the said parson and vicar submitting themselves wholie in the matter to our order concerning the same vicaridge and reapening of the fruits of the same vicar and all he and wee thinke good thus to ordaine, viz., that the vicar of the said church for the time of his being shall have the mansion house which the vicar of the said church now dwelleth in with all the appurtaince and easements belonging to it. The vicar alsoe shall keap the

---

* History of Tutbury by Sir Oswald Mosley.
† Pilkington's Derbyshire.
‡ Lightfoot's Survey of Uttoxeter, 1658.

leat tythes, as the white tithes, the tithcalf, the colt, honey, wax of bees, the graine of marachants, the penny confession, and the tenth ofe labourers for the manor. He shall receive the tithe off egges, apples, pairs, flax, and hemp, except the tenth cominge ofe the flax growing in the Lord's lands, the Lord of the towne which hitherto the parsons of the said church have bin accustomed to receive. The vicar also may receive the tithe ofe fruits growing in the gardens, and also the penny's plough according to the custom heretofore used. He may alsoe receive the tythe of grase, pigs and pigeons, and also the tythe of hay growing in two meadows of Henry Owen and in a certain meadow at Crakemarsh of which the tythe the vicar of the church hath ben accustomed to receive. He may alsoe receive all oblations at annie tyme made in that church, but the tythe of lambs' wooll and milnes through the whole parish, and all mortuarys, together with other things at any tyme belonging to the said church, being not assigned below to the vicar (as is promised), wee assign to the parson of the church for the tyme of his then being. We order moreover that the vicar for the tyme of his then being in divine obsequies and offices at his own cost as heretofore he hath bin accustomed, shall see the church fitly to be served and the parishoners thereofe. He shall find also bread and and wine for mass celebrated in the said church, and the holy bread given to the parishoners of the church at the dayes of easter. He shall alsoe pay procuration money and exhibition money usually paid to the archdeacon. He shall find, moreover, ffrankencense in the said church and a wax candle at easter. As for other burdens together ordinary and extraordinary being not before expressed, lying, however, upon the church, let the parson for the time being undergoe and acknowledge. In testimoney whereof we have thought good that this our seal be put to. Dated at Islington the mones of Februarye, in the year of our Lord 1331, and the tenth of our consecration."

  A grant of Rent-charge on Lands in Uttoxeter by

John Harpdale, of Uttoxeter, to Walter Fitz Herbert, of Somersale, on Wednesday in Easter week 1366—1373, and in the possession of Sir William Fitz Herbert, Bart., of Tissington, has, as one of the witnesses to it, the name Robert de Sanston, vicar of the church of Uttoxeter, which is not, perhaps, preserved anywhere else.

It was at this period, during the decorated style of architecture, extending from 1272 to 1377 that the late church, of which the tower and spire connected with the present one are remains, was erected. If the church which was superseded by the one which was built in the time of Edward III. had stood nearly as long as it, the date of its erection would not be later than the eighth century when the old wooden churches were destroyed and churches were built in stone in their place. But, of course, if there is any validity in this inference, it rests upon the supposition that the earliest church in Uttoxeter was erected of equally durable materials, a supposition not unreasonable when we consider the substantial character of Saxon church architecture. However, when preparations were being made for the construction of the nave of the present church, remains of some description were found which fixed the existence of a church at Uttoxeter more than a thousand years before that date, or about the year 828. And this is confirmed by the fact that there was a rector, Thomas, at Uttoxeter in 1251, nearly thirty years before the decorated style of architecture was inaugurated. The church at Uttoxeter is mentioned by Leland, who wrote in the sixteenth century, in the words :—" Uttoxkcester has one paroch chirch."

The ordination by Bishop Northburg of the vicarage of Uttoxeter church was evidently occasioned by some very palpable dissatisfaction betwixt the vicar and parson of the church—the priest or parson owning the living and the vicar who performed the duties—respecting emoluments arising from a great variety of tythes and for the performance of certain duties, and the responsibility of making provision for certain services in the church. The bishop decreed that the vicar should have the vicarage

UTTOXETER OLD CHURCH.

house and its appurtenances, and also receive Lamb tithes, White tithes, Tithe calf, Tithe on colts, honey, wax of bees, the grain of merchants, of eggs, apples, pairs, flax and hemp (except the tenth of the flax growing on the lord's land—the lord of the town which hitherto the parsons of the said church had been accustomed to receive), the tenth of the labourers of the manor, the penny confession, the penny plough, the tithe of fruit growing in the gardens, the tithe of pigs and pigeons, of grass and of hay which growed in a meadow at Crakemarsh, and in two meadows of Henry Owen, and also all oblations made in the church. He ordained that the parson should receive the tenth of the flax growing in the lords land, and of lambs' wool and milnes (probably mills—meaning tithe on the quantity of flour and meal ground at them), of mortuarys and other things (not specified) not assigned to the vicar. But it was decided that the vicar should exclusively find bread and wine for mass, and the holy bread given to the parishoners of the church at the days of Easter, and also frankencense for the church and a wax candle at Easter, and in addition likewise pay procuration money and exhibition money usually paid to the archdeacon. This analysis of the ordination places in a small space all the interesting particulars of the ancient document and may in many cases render the perusal of it more intelligible. As showing possibly the value of some of the tithes enumerated, I am enabled to quote the following from a Survey of Uttoxeter made in 1775. It relates to the Great Moor estimated at 1401a. 22p., and reads, "Pay a modus of 13s. 4d. for the Tithes of Hay, Herbage, Lamb and Wool, covering many others." The "many others" altogether amount to a considerable quantity of land. With respect to a farm of 55a., the following is the observation as to the tithe upon it :—"This farm had a modus of 2s. per annum for the tithe of hay, herbage, wool and lamb." I cannot, however, assert that these extracts are of any value in any way in their bearing upon any items specified in the ordination.

There is a long hiatus after the ordination of Bishop

Northburgh before anything else, so far as I can ascertain, transpires of any moment in connection with Uttoxeter church, when we find an interesting inventory is taken of church goods at Uttoxeter in the time of Edward VI., 1552-3, as here given :—

INVENTORY OF CHURCH GOODS AT UTTOXETER IN THE TIME OF KING EDWARD THE SIXTH (1552-3).

Fyrste, on challes of silver & gilte with a patent, on crose of coper & gilte, iij vestements, a cope, a pall of redd & blew velvet.

Itm. on corporas case of blewe velvett, iij albeses, iij ames, iij stolles.

Itm. iij fannes, a pix of coper with a case of redd silke.

Itm. ij shuttes of old vestements, iiij old copes of silke.

Itm. iij alterclothes, on veil, iij howseling towelles.

Itm. on holliwater stoke of brasse, on cruett of tynne.

Itm. iiij tunacles of old silke, a crosse staffe with a fotte of copper.

Itm. a peare of organs, iiij grett belles, on of them a clocke bell, on sanctus bell, & iiij pillowes of silke.

MD. on crosse of silver, parcell gilte weing xlij ounces, vas solde by Thomas Harte, Thomas More, Richard Starten, Robte Russell, William Harte, John Taylor, Thomas Chamberlen, William Midelton, Raffe Bagnold, and Robert Taylor, parishonars there, for iiijs. viijd, an ounce, to William Mastergent and Richarde Fliar, without thassent of other the parishoners, which comes to ixli. xvjs., whiche some of ixli. xvjs. was delyvered to Thomas Harte and others above named.

MD. ij sensors of silver, sold by John Tayllor & Lewes Walker, for ixli. xvjs. which was delyvered to Thomas Chamberlen and Thomas Dudley, then Churchwardens.

MD. on challes of silver parcell gilt, sold by Thomas Harte and Richard Starten, of the church still for Ls.

Itm. ij brason candelstikes, sold by Thomas Harte and Thomas Dudley, for how muche they cannot tell.

MD. on shippe, supposed to be silver, stolne, as they say, but bi home they knowe nott.

MD. delyvered by the right honorable Walter Vicounte Hereforde, Lorde Ferers and of Chartley, Thomas Fitzharbert, Knight, Edwarde Lyttelton, esquier, Commissionars for Churche goodes within the Counti of Stafford, to Humffrey Kinston, Lewes Walker, and John Tayllor, Churchewardens there, on Chales of Silver with a Patent, iiij Lynen Clothes for the Holli Comunyon Table, on Surples for the Curat, and iiij grette belles in the Stepull, safely to be kept untill the Kinges Majesties pleasure be therein furder knowen. In witness whereof as well we the sayd Commissionars as the sayd Churchwardens to thes presents interchaungeabli have putto our handes the viijth of May, Anno regni Edwardi Sexti Septimo.

Luys Wallkar.

But we soon enter upon times of persecution in the town. In the reign of Mary, daughter of Henry VIII., the antagonism of Protestants and Papists in Uttoxeter appears to have been carried to a violent extreme, ending in the death of a gentleman and protestant of the town. The outrage occurred at the time of those sanguinary persecutions of the adherents of the reformed faith, about 1555, when 280 victims, including Hooper, Bishop of Gloucester; Farrar, of St. David's; Latimer, of Worcester; Ridly, of London; and Cranmer, Archbishop of Canterbury, perished at the stake. The victim at Uttoxeter was a Thomas Flier, belonging to an ancient family of property in the town who was slain by a desperate Papist.* The persecutions in the See of Lichfield which led to this tragedy were instigated by Dr. Bayne, bishop of the diocese. Besides the compulsion of many in the See to do penance, several others had to pay with their lives the penalty of their adherence to the reformed doctrines, one of whom was Joane Waste, who was burnt at Derby in 1555. Dr. Bayne was successor to Richard Sampson, in the See of Lichfield, and his character will be seen by the following notice:—He was a Doctor of Divinity of St. John's College, Cambridge, and was a great proficient in the Hebrew tongue, which he taught some years at Paris. He returned to England in 1554, about the time of Bishop Sampson's death, and was promoted to the See of Coventry and Lichfield the same year. His persecutions grew out of his endeavour to restore the See to its popish condition before the Reformation, and in trying to recover its possessions. He did not hold the bishopric long. Being appointed by Act of Parliament to give the holy communion to Queen Elizabeth, he refused to administer it to her, and was *ipso facto* deprived of the See. He returned to Islington, and died and was buried there in 1559.

The celebrated and pious Bishop Hacket, who restored Lichfield Cathedral after the damage it had sustained during the Civil War by the Parliamentarians, preached in Uttoxeter Church, and held a confirmation

---

* Martyroligia, by Samuel Clarke, 3rd edition, folio, 1677.

in 1664. A brief memorandum of the fact is preserved on the inside of the cover of the early register of Uttoxeter Church, and is this—" Bishop Hacket came to this town the second day of July and preacht and confirmed the third, 1664." It is not improbable it was on this occasion that this venerated bishop visited Stanton, in the parish of Ellastone, north of Uttoxeter (a place difficult of access), to view the birth-place of Archbishop Sheldon, when, from a great regard for the memory of the archbishop, he wrote the following lines, which appear on a thick ash board clamped to the wall in a bedroom of the old house :—

> "Sheldonus *illæ* prœsulum *primis Pater.*
> Hos *inter ortus aspicit lucem* Lares,
> *O ter beatam* Stantonis *villæ casam!*
> *Cui canita possunt invidere Marmora.*"

The father of Archbishop Sheldon was in the service as a labourer of the then Earl of Shrewsbury, who, having become the godfather of the embryo archbishop, also educated him, and so he became prepared for the Church and advanced until he became Archbishop of Canterbury. The house remains as it was at his birth, except that a tile roof has recently been substituted for a thatched one.

ARCHBISHOP SHELDON'S HOUSE.

An augmentation to the Church was obtained in the year 1646, and Peter Lightfoot was delegated by the parish of Uttoxeter to apply for the same; and his journey to London for the purpose, at the instance of the parish, cost about £5, according to the parochial account. After this the bounty of Queen Anne was also obtained at Uttoxeter by the Rev. Mr. Ledgould. With this sum a piece of land was purchased, called Monk's Field, belonging now to the vicar, and the following case, which unquestionably had respect to it, and in which is shown what monastic lands were freed from the payment of tithes, was heard in the Exchequer Chamber sometime before 1685. That eminent lawyer, Sir Symon Degg, in " Parsons' Councellor," page 271, part second, published in 1685, remarks—" Now the reader must observe once for all, that all monestries under £200 a year were to have been dissolved by the Statute of 27, Henry VIII., and are usually called the Smaller Abbeys; and those of £200 a year and upwards were not dissolved till 31st year of Henry VIII., and are commonly called the Greater Abbeys. And upon these two statutes the case lately happened in the Exchequer Chamber between Walklate, farmer of the rectory of Uttoxeter, in the County of Stafford, to the Dean of Windsor, and Wiltshaw, owner of the farm in that parish, that was part of the possessions of the Abbey of Croxden, in the same county, and was one of the Cistercian Order, which order was freed from the payment of tithes, as shall been shown hereafter; and this abbey was discovered by the defendant Wiltshaw, to be continued by letters patent under the Great Seal of England, and so not dissolved till the statute of 31st Henry VIII., whereupon the defendant was dismissed, and the Court clearly held the lands discharged of payment of tithes by the statute 31st of Henry VIII."

The land, the tithe of which was the subject of dispute, was held by Ralph Wiltshaw, and is thus described in Lightfoot's Survey:—" One tenement and two closes of pasture and arable land adjoining to the bounds of the manor of Marchington Woodlands, called Nether Munk's Field, 26a. 2r. op., and one acre in Great Broad Meadow called Munk's Acre." In a survey made in 1775, the Munk's land is mentioned as being in several lots making 24a. or. 34p., and belonging to the vicar of Uttoxeter, and claiming to be *free from all tithe*. Another lot is called Munk's land, then held by J. Smith, at Netherland Green, amounting to 29a. 2r. 16p., and as stated as belonging to Croxden Abbey, and claimed being free from paying tithe of all sorts, paying 1s. per annum to the vicar of Uttoxeter, but not known for what.

In the old accounts at Checkley of the 17th century, there are several entries mentioning visitations at Uttoxeter in 1630, when 2s. 4d. was paid. In 1631 another visitation cost 2s. 4d., and the same again in 1633.

About the year 1649, during the ministry of the Rev. Thomas Lightfoot, who was then at a venerable age, a theological controversy was rife in Uttoxeter, and threatened very much the peace of the church. It originated in attacks upon the ordinances of the church by a Mr. Heming, who appears to have occupied a pulpit in Uttoxeter, although it is not stated to what religious persuasion he belonged, though probably he was an Anabaptist. He had indiscreetly, in the pulpit, called the sacrament as administered in the church, "a communion of dogs and devils; a rotton twopenny communion," and bragging to prove to all men "that Judas did not receive the sacrament;" and telling the congregation "that if they did believe that if Judas did receive the sacrament they might do as Judas did; that is, go and receive, and then go and hang themselves." This kind of irreverent teaching naturally appeared exceedingly repugnant to some, if not to all the church people, and particularly so to Mr. Peter Lightfoot, physician, whose father's ministry in the church was so thoroughly evangelical, and whose life was so truly modelled on that of Christ, and he drew up notes upon the points for his own and the satisfaction of a few friends; and although it was not intended they should, they fell in their manuscript form into the hands of Mr.

Heming. The latter thereupon put his declarations into print in a pamphlet entitled, "Judas Excommunicated; or a Vindication of the Communion of Saints," in which he made Mr. Lightfoot the especial object of his abuse. Whether he makes out his point as to Judas not receiving the sacrament, or as to whether it is not scripture for persons indifferently to receive it in the church without any regard being had to their being godly or ungodly, it would not do any particular good here to go through his arguments to show. But some of the passages of abuse are so strongly expressed, particularly against Mr. Lightfoot, that it can be little wondered at if they produced a strong and resentful sensation in the Rev. Thomas Lightfoot's congregation, and indeed through the town. Some of them are thus given:—" Mr. Lightfoot and his unholy communicants;" " Mr. Lightfoot and his unholy crew;" " his profane fellow-members;" " I should superabundantly wrong him if I should not rank him with the vilest in the kingdom; for with them he will have communion as a member of the same external, visible body, by virtue of which relation they are all his bretheren and sisters; so that he hath his brother drunkard, brother thief, brother murderer, brother liar, &c., sister whore, sister witch, &c.; yea, all that have been hanged at Tyburn, and all other gallows in England, ever since he was born and baptized into that fellowship he pleads for, have been his bretheren and sisters, and this I dare say I can prove against all the devils in hell."

Peter Lightfoot replied to the pamphlet of Mr. Joseph Heming in a lengthy and curious tract of fifty-two pages, entitled, "A Battle with a Wasp's Nest," London, 1649. He accuses his opponent of spleen, virulence, and scandal, and points out that such arguments as he had used he had cooked from a Mr. Gillespie, in "Aaron's Rod Blossoming." Mr. Lightfoot goes through his antagonist's strokes of vile insinuations, and caustically exposes their baseness, and indicates the punishment he was deemed worthy to merit.

Mr. Heming appears to have looked upon Uttoxeter

as a place of Babylonish darkness, stating that "what he had done was for their souls who came out of Babylon, out of Egypt, the other day." Mr. Lightfoot regarded this expression as a reflection upon the ministry of his father, and in a dignified appeal respecting it, he writes— "The reader, if he were of Mr. Heming's charity, and no higher, might be induced to think that poor Uttoxeter is the veriest Sodom and Gomorrah upon earth ; and that till he came hither, it had been led and lived in the deepest superstition and darkness that ever Babylon and Egypt did. It is not for me to speak what ministry this town hath had ever since before Mr. Heming was born. The relation I stand in to him that hath been their minister so long does stop my mouth. But let all in the countries hereabout Cheshire, Shropshire, Staffordshire, Derbyshire, &c., let any in England that ever heard of old Mr. Lightfoot, minister of Uttoxeter, what he hath been, what his ministry and conversation hath been ; nay, let Mr. Heming's own saints be witnesses what his pains, doctrine, life, and ministry hath been among them for above these thirty years. If they have not dissembled, the day hath been when some of them have acknowledged and taken upon them to think this town, in a happy ministry, hath gone in equal pace and degree with most towns in England. And the case is so altered that till Mr. Heming came amongst them, poor Uttoxeter is said to be in darkness, and in Babylon and Egypt, and he proved a Moses and a Zorobabel to bring it out."

Mr. Peter Lightfoot gives the following picture of the condition of Uttoxeter produced by Mr. Heming:—" It seems Mr. Heming hath a singular faculty of reconciling dead men ; and I wish he would let the evangelists alone, who are at sacred peace among themselves, and that he would reconcile poor Uttoxeter, which is torn in pieces with dissensions since he came among us. I know not whether Tenderden Steeple was the cause of the stopping up of the haven two or three miles of it ; this I know, that till Uttoxeter knew Mr. Heming, peace, amity, and charity dwelt amongst us, in few towns more ; but now nothing but dissention, biting, and backbiting, in no town the like." This is a hint taken from a sermon on cause and effect by Hugh Latimer, and contained in the following extract : —"And before that Tenderden Steeple was in building, there was no manner of speaking of any flats or sands that stopped the haven, and therefore I think that Tenderden Steeple is the cause of the destroying and decay of Sandwich haven. And so to my purpose, preaching of God's word is the cause of rebellion as Tenderden Steeple was the cause that Sandwich haven is decayed." This is, no doubt, a tolerably fair representation of the case, and it would be the natural result of Mr. Heming's violent language and grossly exaggerated teaching. Mr. Lightfoot finishes with his opponent thus: —"A wisp or a cuckstool, the reward of scolds, had been a fitter return for your railing than patience and reason, but you see I have waited upon you with salt and spoons," &c.

Mr. Heming appears also to have been the author of another work, entitled, "Queries touching the rise and observation of Christmas Day," which Mr. Lightfoot accuses him of having filched out of Mr. Prynne's "Histriomastic," and the "Scripture Almanack." This was answered, according to a bibliographical work, in 1655, and the answers were printed in Fresher's "Christian Covenant."

In the year 1814 the spire of Uttoxeter Church sustained a serious accident by lightning. On the 6th of February of that year or as another account states in December it was struck by the electric fluid, by which a stone about half way down was forced out. It passed through the belfry, and finally penetrated the wall of the chancel, on the north side of the window. The damage which the spire sustained by the shock, made it necessary for a part of it to be taken down. When it was rebuilt, and the gilt cross, globe, and vane, had been placed at its apex, two incidents occurred, which, as they show the daring spirit of two females, deserve to be perpetuated in their remembrance, as well as on account of their intrepid nature. When, as stated, the whole was finished, Mary Allport, a chambermaid at the Red Lion Hotel, ascended, stood upon the ornamental stone-work under the globe, and kissed a young man named Henry Smith, of Uttoxeter Heath, who was one of the masons, and who stood on the opposite side. Sarah Adams, a fellow servant of Mary Allport, also accomplished the same feat, to win a kiss from another workman whose name was Henry Adams. A crowd of spectators, some of whom were living in 1864, and a smaller number now (1881), thronged round the church at the time. Both the female adventurers descended safely, and subsequently became the wives of the young men. Henry Smith, with Mary Allport for his wife, settled down at Wetley Rocks, as parish clerk, but what became of the others is not to be learnt. The circumstance has occasioned the following amusing rhyme :—

"Maggy the maid, in a moment of bliss,
Ventured her neck for a sweetheart's kiss ;
Higher and higher she ascended the spire,
Till she reached the top stone and attained her desire."

The old church, the period of whose erection has been mentioned as that of the decorated gothic, was built of stone, and has been described as (when in existence) being very much out of repair on the exterior parts. The churchyard was then enclosed by an ancient stone wall. The church consisted of a nave, two side aisles, and a chancel, and it was roofed with lead. Where the present vestry-room is, at the south side of the present church, the family of Mynors, formerly of great distinction at Uttoxeter, had a chapel where a mass priest was appointed to say mass for the family.* It was also their burying place. This chapel was one of those private religious foundations called a chantry, of which it is stated the family of Kynnersley also had one. There has been as much as 46a. 1r. 16p. of chantry land in Uttoxeter parish ;† but it does not appear by whom the land was left, or whether by one or more persons.

* Gentlemen's Magazine, 1788.
† Lightfoot's Survey.

Chantries were established for the purpose of keeping up a perpetual succession of prayers for some particular family whilst living, and for the repose of their souls when dead, particularly of the founder, and other persons specially named in the deed of foundation. Chantries were first founded in the twelfth century, on the decline of the taste for monasteries. They were usually founded in churches already existing, all that was required being an altar with an area before it, and a few appendages; and places were easily found in churches of even small dimensions, in which such an altar could be raised without interfering inconveniently with the more public and general purposes for which the churches were erected. An attentive observation of the fabrics of the parish churches of England will often detect where these chantries have been, sometimes in remains of the altar which was removed perhaps at the Reformation, but more frequently in one of those ornamental niches called piscinas, which were always placed in proximity to the altars. Sometimes there are remains of painted glass which it is easy to see has once been the ornament of one of those private foundations, and more frequently one of those arched recesses in the wall which are called " Founder's Tombs," and which in many instances, no doubt, were actually the tombs of persons to whose memory chantries were instituted. When the fabric of a church afforded of itself no more space for the introduction of chantries, it was usual for the founders to attach little chapels to the edifice. It is these chantry chapels, the use and occasion of which are now so generally forgotten, which occasions so much of the irregularity of design which is apparent in the parish churches of England. Erected as they generally were in the style of architecture which prevailed at the time, and not in accommodation to the style in which the original fabric was built, they are a principal cause of that want of congruity which is perceived in the architecture of different parts of the parish churches. *

※ Penny Cyclopedia, Vol. 6.

The same family of Mynors had likewise a private gallery at the south side of the interior of the old church, and it was reached by stone steps from the outside. The steps are represented in the engraving of the old church almost at the junction of the nave of the church and the chapel of that family built at the south side of the chancel. Within the chantry chapel of the family of Mynors an incised slab formerly existed of the fifteenth century, representing probably John Mynors, of Uttoxeter, and Johanna his wife, daughter of John Fitz Herbert, of Somershall, and at their feet six daughters and five sons. The lady was represented in the reticulated head dress of the period, and her husband as a knight. The daughters appeared wearing hoods and the sons uncovered. The whole had their hands upraised. Centrally the upper part of the slab showed their armorial bearings ; over each principal figure appeared three crosses Pommé, and over them was represented a scolloped canopy with an outer border bearing the wheatear ornament. The slab was in a broken state, and when the church was rebuilt the representative of the family allowed it to be taken away to Birmingham.

Passing from these matters appertaining to the old church, those features belonging to it architecturally may be attempted to be pointed out. There are no means of saying whether the window in the west end of the tower is a restoration of the previous one, but as it now is it is of the style of 1275, of which there is a similar example in the church of Dorchester, Oxfordshire. The windows of the north aisle and the clerestory windows on the same side were decorated and had three lights each, and above the windows in the north aisle just under the eaves there were four square-headed windows of two lights each. There were four decorated clerestory windows in the south side The south side aisle had three lancet windows of two lights each, and there was a decorated window of several lights on the west side of the south doorway. This doorway was very fine and richly moulded. The east end of the nave had a circular or rose window, and in the end of the chancel there was a window of the perpendicular period. From appearances on the side of the tower the roof had been high pitched, and in the tower there remains a noble built up arch which was open to the nave. The engraving of the old church shows on the south side other external details, especially in respect to other windows. A view of the north side, not engraved here, I have copied from an old fruit dish on which it was specially executed for a gentleman, and the dish is in the possession of Mr. J. B. Johnson, M.P.S., and chemist of this town.

Previous to his entering upon the laborious undertaking of compiling a history of Staffordshire, the Rev. Simeon Shaw first visited most of the places in the county, both for church inscriptions, sketches of churches, sepulchral monuments and family records. In a communication, giving an account of his success, to the "*Gentleman's Magazine*," in 1794, he mentions that the fine old spire of Uttoxeter Church afforded him a good subject for a drawing, and the inside some curious monuments of the Mynors, an ancient family in the parish, and of the Kynnersleys, of Loxley, very ancient. All the monuments of the former family have disappeared, two other monuments remain, but they have been placed within iron rails under the stairs leading to the gallery in the north west entrance. These monuments are in alabaster and of the altar-tomb description, a kind which was introduced about the thirteenth or fourteenth century, having on them effigies in alabaster, or incised slabs with engraved outlines of persons and arms, or engraved plates of brass, the latter of which were particularly prevalent towards the close of the fifteenth century. Both the altar-tombs have been much mutilated. One is to Thomas Kynnersley, de Loxley, whose name is legible in the letters of the period, although but little more can be made out of the inscription to him, and its period is of about 1500. On the top is an engraved figure of the deceased, as a Knight with his head evidently on an helmet, but the border to it next to the wall consisting of pillasters, has been cut off the whole length, and the surface of the remainder is so much disfigured with dates, initials, and other senseless markings, that many parts of the figure and border ornamented with pillasters, are effaced. The engraving has been filled with pitch or some other bituminous substance. The remaining side of this monument—for the opposite side next to the wall has evidently been cut away with the border to the incised figure at the top—contains shields of arms, and several figures of persons in bas-relief, with intervening foliated pillasters, supporting three canopies. The central figure represents Christ on the Cross; the figure with armorial bearings on it is most likely a female child of the deceased; the others are probably nuns represented in the reticulated headdress of the time, and the folds of their robes appear to be very gracefully and naturally given by the artist.

The other altar-tomb has a more recently sculptured effigy reposing upon it, in the habit of a *religieuse*, and Gorden H. Hills, Esq., who examined it very particularly, states that it is in memory of a lady of the Stanley family. It had previously been supposed to be a memorial to a lady of the Kynnersley family who came into the possession of Loxley by marriage with the noble family of Ferrars. One end of the tomb has been sawn off, including the feet of the effigy, to make it fit in the place where it is. The inscription is nearly all obliterated.

There is an interesting legend respecting this effigy, to which rise has probably been given by some lingering tradition of what possibly occurred at the dispersion of the nuns at Hanbury by the Danes. It is said, and also firmly believed by many, that the effigy represents an abbess who had been lost in the woods below the town many centuries ago—an idea which has been embodied in "Wood Leighton" with the addition of such imaginary circumstances as give the story an air of truthfulness. The following is the account of the discovery of the effigy, made at the time the church was destroyed, as related to me by an eye witness. At that time the altar-tombs and effigies had been walled, or boarded over for a period of

ALTAR-TOMB OF A LADY OF THE STANLEY FAMILY AND THOMAS KYNNERSLEY.

sixty years, for the purpose of making pew room, and when the pews were being removed at the time the nave of the old church was being taken down, the covering which hid the effigy and altar-tomb, fell, none of the workmen present being aware that there was behind it such an exquisite piece of art. When the altar-tombs and effigy so suddenly and unexpectedly appeared, the people present started back in fright, thinking the effigy, which was quite black with dust, was the corpse of some one long hidden there. Recovering themselves, they approached it, and on brushing off the dust, lo! a most beautiful alabaster female figure revealed itself. She had a fine Roman nose; a chain hung round her neck that reached down to her abdomen; she had a handsome stomacher; there were four crests of arms round the figure, with an inscription, and the date 1555. So it was represented.

A knowledge of this discovery soon spread through the town, and numbers of persons crowded to see the interesting objects. Amongst them were the late Mrs. Hart, and an aged female of the name of Reeves. The latter, on going to the effigy, was at once excited with remembrances of former days—days that blended with her youth—and giving vent to her feelings, clapped her hands and exclaimed, "Oh! it is my Lady Tansley; I am glad to see her again." "Oh! Mrs. Reeves," said Mrs. Hart, "what do you mean; did you know her? Tell us all about it." "Why, madam," replied Mrs. Reeves with great simplicity, "I used to play round it when I was a girl. She was a lady abbess, and being driven away with a single attendant from Tutbury, she came for Uttoxeter, and was lost at night in Uttoxeter woods; but hearing the curfew bell ring she was enabled to direct her course to Uttoxeter by its sound. She was very much wearied by anxiety and rambling about, and when she reached the town she left a bell full of money for the bell to be perpetually rung." "And did you see the bell full of money?" interrogated Mrs. Hart. "Oh! no," she replied, "it is so long since, *but it used to be said so.*" So far was the tradition believed that, till a new sexton was appointed about twenty-nine years ago this 1881, three tangs for the lady abbess were invariably given before the curfew bell was rung night and morning; and it is said that a daring individual on once willingly omitting to give the tangs was alarmed by the sudden appearance of the abbess in person, who ascended the bell rope and vanished out of sight of the terrified individual. I have, perhaps imperfectly, turned the legend into rhyme,* and the ensuing lines embody the last named incident:—

> "Three tangs the curfew always led
> For the good abbess ages dead,
> Till, as is held as strangely true,
> A daring sexton careless grew,
> And ceased the tangs to gently chime
> Late within living memory's time,
> When the pained abbess, all in white,
> Suddenly rose before his sight,
> High in the grey and silent tower
> At the dim, wild, and spirit hour;
> Then with sad look she passed away,
> Leaving him bent in awe to pray."

Besides the altar-tombs and the incised slab belonging to the family of Mynors, the former church had a skeleton effigy of the sixteenth century, which is yet preserved out of sight over the door of the west entrance in the window bottom. Such effigies are supposed to represent the buried corpse of a person of high ecclesiastical rank, contrasting with the gorgeous effigy of the deceased in his robes in such a manner as to convey a wholesome lesson of the transitory nature of human greatness to persons destitute of learning, and to whose feelings a highly coloured representation of the fate of all flesh would appeal in a startling manner.†

The nave and chancel of Uttoxeter church were rebuilt in the year 1828, in the style called "Decorated English." The roof is supported by two rows of six arches, betwixt the side and middle aisles. The cost of rebuilding

---

* See "Dove Valley Rhymes," by F. Redfern. Bemrose, Derby and London, 1875.
† Vestiges of the Antiquities of Derbyshire, by Mr. Bateman

UTTOXETER CHURCH.

this part was £6,061 1s. 11d., of which £1,632 was raised by subscription, £1,779 by rate, £2,249 by the sale of pews, and £400 by the society for building churches. The pews are of oak, and the number of sittings about 1,414. Of these 422 are free. During the rebuilding of the church the worship of the members of the Church of England in the town was conducted in the Wesleyan Chapel, with the approbation of the bishop of the diocese, and in the books of the churchwardens at the time are entries of payments to a woman for cleaning the chapel. I transcribe fuller particulars of the accounts attending the erection of the church from the same books.

	£	s.	d.
Total Subscriptions	1,632	0	0
Sale of Seats	1,067	0	0
Loans	1,500	0	0
Removal of seats per Mr. Clewley	609	15	0
The Societies Grant for free sittings	400	0	0
Drawback of duty on materials	303	7	5
Church Brief	169	9	7
Collection at opening of church	100	5	0

18 Levies granted Aug. 1827—£27 9s. 10d £494 17s. 0d.
Returned to Mr. Orton, £14 8s. 9d.

	£	s.	d.			
Arrears £16 14s. 11d.	31	3	8	463	13	4
For Loxley and Crakemarsh £11 11s. 5½d.	208	6	3			
Deduct arrears	4	8	10½	203	17	4½
Old Bricks sold				14	0	
				£6,450	1	8½

The following were amongst the largest contributors to the subscription list :—Mr. T. Hart, £105 and £25 ; Sir Thomas Cotton Sheppard, £105, and Lady Cotton Sheppard, £21 ; The Deans and Canons of Windsor, £200 ; The King, £100 ; Mr. Tyrrel, £100 ; Thomas Bladon, £50 ; Joseph Bladon, £50 ; Thomas Sneyd Kynnersley, £50 ; Herbert Taylor, M.D., £50 ; F. Flint, £80 ; Sir Thomas Cotton Sheppard and Thomas Hart, Esq., also gave respectively £50 each towards altering and ornamenting the church windows.

Mr. Robert Henderson was paid £126 3s. 0d., for

stained glass, and Messrs. Trubshaw and Johnson were paid at sundry payments for building the church the sum of £5,597 17s. 9d.

Since the enlargement of the church the spire has been re-pointed in 1849, by W. Critchlow, and the dangerous task was accomplished without an accident. More recently, in 1858, a new finial stone was put on and the nave regilt and replaced by men in the employment of Mr. Evans, of Ellastone, cousin of "George Elliot," many people venturing to the top when the work was finished, although the spire rises to the height of 179 feet.

The living of Uttoxeter is a discharged vicarage, in the Archdeaconry of Stafford, and in the patronage of the Deans and Canons of Windsor. The tithes were commuted in 1839, and produced to the late lay impropriator, about £725 annually. The ecclesiastical commissioners made a grant in 1884, of £120 a year to the vicarage of Uttoxeter towards the maintenance of an assistant curate. The Rev. H. Abud, M.A., is the present vicar and rural dean, and he resides in the ancient parsonage house near the church, and recently the tithes have reverted to him by efflux of time.

In 1877, the chancel of the church was extended five yards and received an addition of two windows, and at the same time an organ loft was erected at the junction of the nave and chancel over the Mynors' chapel or vestry. A reredos, the gift of Mrs. Sneyd Kynnersley, was also made a beautiful and costly addition, it being executed in alabaster, marble, and mural tile decoration. The central portion of the work consists of a cross in white marble, upon a polished panel of exquisitely beautiful dark Derbyshire marble. A deep cornice in alabaster is supported on four polished shafts of Derbyshire marble, having elaborately carved capitals, two being at each side of the central panel bearing the cross. Each side of the design in marble and alabaster is filled in with Minton's tiles, which bear a series of designs intended to show the various incidents in the betrayal of Christ. The floor of the chancel is relaid with Minton's tiles of a costly character and rich design at the expense of the late C. M. Campbell, Esq. The costs of the alterations amounted to about £1,100

At the time these improvements were made one or two interesting tiles of the old church were found.

The collection of church rates for the support of the church was discontinued in 1868, owing to a strong and unexpected opposition to levying the rate at a vestry meeting convened by the then churchwardens Mr. G. Cooper and Mr John Caulson on the 19th December, 1867. However on a rate being lost, a poll was demanded, and it took place in the Town Hall on Monday the 30th, of the same month. The votes taken for the rate at the poll were 337, against 85 negative votes, giving a majority of 252 votes for the rate. But it was generally understood that if the rate was granted in this instance, no attempt would afterwards be made to enforce it. The amount required was £75. At a vestry meeting held on December 18th, 1868, it was decided to obtain the sum required annually in the future by an assessment on the pews, and in this way the average amount realized has been for several years about £105.

The church contains a large number of mural tablets, all of beautiful design, in marked alabaster, and some of a really elaborate character and high artistic workmanship. In the chancel, besides the costly stained window in glass in the east end, the gift of the late Thos. Hart, Esq., and Sir Thos. Cotton Sheppard, Bart., representing the apostles of Christ, there are two memorial windows to Thomas Sneyd Kynnersley, Esq., who died in 1844, aged 70 years. The oldest memorial tablet in the church is in the chancel, and is to the memory of the Rev. George Malbon, the friend of Samuel Bentley, who has perpetuated his memory in his poem on the river Dove:—

"The cell where the bank slow doth bend
Was Malbon's, the learned and the sage;
My teacher, Mecænas and friend,
With pleasantry tempered with age.

> Flow tears the dear urn to bedew ;
> Flow elegy mournfully tuned ;
> Oh ! could I those chords wake anew,
> When Milton his Lycidas mourned."

The inscription to Mr. Malbon, which is in Latin, is as follows :—

D. O. M.

GEORGIUS MALBON, A.M.

Hujus Parochiæ Vicarius,
Ex Vico de Bradley, in Argo
Cestrensi,
Antiqua Stirpe Oriundus.
In matrimonium duxit
Mariam,
Johannis Alleyne, de Greseley,
In Com. Derb, Armig.,
Filiam Natu Maximam
Hoc Monumentum
Optimæ Conjugi Ponen—
dum Mandavit
Et Sibi
1768.

Some of the other memorials are as follows :—

"In memory of Joseph Mallaby, Esq., of Loxley Park, a Justice of the Peace of this County, who died at Lugano, Switzerland, September 15th, 1855, aged 50 years."

"Sacred to the memory of Jonathan Stubbs, M.A., who died November 27th. 1810, aged 57 years. In grateful testimony of his faithful and laborious exertions while curate of this parish, the inhabitants, by voluntary contribution, have caused this stone to be erected, and on an open volume are the words, ' Be thou faithful unto death and I will give thee a crown of life.'"

The Rev. Mr. Stubbs was greatly beloved in the parish, and his death, from the circumstances under which it occurred, was most acutely felt and deplored. On the 13th of November, 1810, he had an overturn in a carriage, occasioning a compound fracture of a leg, which eventually produced a delirious fever, and terminated his life on the 27th of the same month. The beautiful passage of Scripture on his tablet formed the words of his text in Uttoxeter Church on the Sunday before his accident. He only preached on the first part, and promised to preach on the latter portion, "and thou shalt receive a crown of life," on the succeeding Sunday, but as is observable, he was called away to enjoy what he was not permitted to describe to his congregation. His remains were deposited in the chancel of the Parish Church of Tutbury, near which place the accident transpired. Mr. Stubbs was the son of the Rev. Jonathan Stubbs, Rector of Overton Longueville, Buckinghamshire. He received the early part of his education at Hitchin, in Herefordshire, under the Rev. Thomas Evans, and was successively a Scholar of Winchester College, Pensioner of Emmanuel College, Cambridge, and was afterwards elected on the foundation of New College, Oxford, and in course of time succeeded to a fellowship of that College. In 1789 he became curate of St. Alkmund's Parish, Derby, in which he continued till 1803, when he had the care of the churches of Scropton and Broughton, in Derbyshire. He undertook the curacy of Uttoxeter in 1804, and in 1807 married Miss Kirk, of Derby. He left one son of the age of sixteen months. There is an inscription also to his wife, Mrs. Stubbs, who died March 12th, 1846, in the 73rd year of her age. The following most appropriate lines were written respecting some of the virtues of Mr. Stubbs by a Mr. Ferneyough, but they have hitherto remained unpublished:—

"To the memory of the late Rev. J. Stubbs, of Uttoxeter, a truly amiable and benevolent character.

  Bright and unsullied was this good man's fame;
  His numerous virtues generous tribute claim;
  And tho' these virtues were their own reward,
  From high and low they must command regard.
  Then cease not ye who chant sublimer lay,
  Now at his tomb a last respect to pay.
  In him transcendent piety to find,
  Unwearied kindness occupied his mind.

> Charity show'd she there bore powerful sway,
> For sweet pursuits fill'd up his constant day ;
> No vain delusive pleasures could remove
> His thoughts from labours of true Christian love.
> He sought the hut where mis'ry laid her load ;
> Viewing the scene he cheer'd the dark abode ;
> Stretched out his hand to mitigate each pain
> Poverty felt,—to all her weeping train
> His bounty flow'd and widely did extend ;
> He proved their guardian, father and their friend."
>
> WM. FERNEYHOUGH, A.B.

Another memorial is to Lieutenant-Colonel John Herring, C.B., (son of the late Rev. A. Herring, Vicar of Uttoxeter) who died at Hyderkhail, September 3rd, 1839, in his 50th year, when he was in command of the 37th regiment, Bengal, No. 7, on his march with the army of the Indus. He was interred in the Armenian burial ground at Cabul. He had been with the regiment thirty-four years.

Another memorial bears the following inscription :—

"Sacred to the memory of Joseph Bladon, of Oldfield House, who departed this life January 12th, 1862, aged 75.

This marble is erected by Thomas Kynnersley, Esq., in memory of his beloved wife, Barbara Kynnersley, eldest daughter of Sir Gilbert Clark, in the County of Derby, Knight.

She was virtuous without ostentation,
Cheerful without levity, the delight of the neighbourhood, and the pleasure of her family.

Her maternal and conjugal duties she acquitted with tenderness, affection and honour.

In her religious capacity she was sincere without austerity ; she was justly esteemed by all that knew her, and more particularly so by those that knew her best.

As her conversation was innocent and amiable, so her patience and behaviour in her last tedious sickness was pious and admirable.

She left two sons, Craven and Thomas, and three daughters, Barbara, Mary and Dorothy. She departed this life, ye 6th of July, 1717."

"Sacred to the memory of Dame Margaret, second wife of Sir Thomas Cotton Sheppard, of Thornton Hall, in the County of Buckingham, Bart., who departed this life on the 26th of December, MDCCCXIII., in the LXIII. year of her age. Her remains were deposited near this place."

"Near this place lieth interred the body of Miss Dorothy Kynnersley, daughter of Thomas Kynnersley, Esq., of Loxley, who departed this life June the 23rd, 1759, aged 52 years."

On the west end of the church are the following inscriptions :—

"Sacred to the memory of Humphrey Oldfield, Esq., of the Marines, who died, whilst on service in America, A.D. 1776, ætat 54. John Nicholas Oldfield, Esq., late of the Marines, who died at Portsmouth, April 9th, A.D. 1793, ætat 41. Thomas Oldfield, Esq., Major in the Marines, who fell during the memorable defence of St. Jean D'Acre, in Syria, by Sir Sydney Smith, against General Bournaparte and the army of Egypt, whilst leading a sortie made by the garrison, on the 7th of April, 1799, for the purpose of destroying the enemies' approaches; ætat 45. And Elizabeth, daughter of William Hammond, Esq., Lieutenant in the Royal Navy, and widow of J. N. Oldfield, Esq., obiit November 30th, A.D. 1808, ætat 51."

The above are all on one oval tablet of black marble —a group of names of Uttoxeter men whose lives were spent in the service of their country. But for known and tested bravery the name of Thomas Oldfield, Major in the Marines, stands out conspicuous from the rest for our admiration for leading the sortie against General Bournaparte and the army of Egypt at St. Jean D'Acre under Sir Sidney Smith. I do not find any one of the name of Oldfield as either owners or occupiers of property in Uttoxeter in 1775, but in the first half of the previous century a Humphrey Oldfield had a little land, and an Edward Oldfield was the owner of about 23a. 3r. 6p. of land in the parish, and I have no doubt Oldfields, a villa residence near the town, on the site of which a fine mansion now supersedes the old one, took its name from that family who were doubtless owners of the place, and have in consequence such a group of names associated with Uttoxeter on one tablet in the church.

A very beautiful tablet in alabaster on this wall is to the memory of Edward John Smith, late of the Borough of Stafford, son of Edward Smith, and Sarah his wife, who died 4th July, 1753, aged 20 years. He had a sister Sarah, and two brothers, John and Paul, who died in their minority.

On a neat tablet, erected by his widow, is an inscription to Thomas Gardner, architect, who departed this life October the 8th, 1804, aged 67. Near to this is another tablet, to the memory of his widow, erected by their son, William George Maxwell. She died September 1st, 1806.

On this wall also is fixed the interesting old black letter memorial, in Latin, to the Rev. Thomas Lightfoot, father of Dr. John Lightfoot, the distinguished Hebrew scholar and biblical commentator. It was written by his son, Peter Lightfoot, of Uttoxeter, physician :—

M. S.

Huc Oculus et Lachrymas, O viator
Qui veteri studes veritati, pietati, charitati,
Huc : ubi teipsum es olim celaturus,

THOMAS LIGHTFOOTE,

Verbi Divini per Annos 56 fidelissimus minister.
Ecclesiæ hujus per Annos 36 vigilantissimus pastor
Vir antiquorum, et primævæ sanctitatis,
Coruscantis zeli, doctrinæ, virtutis, exempli,
Vir verum excribens virum ; Pastor pastorum :
Sudore semper squalidus, et formosus pastorali :
Salutem suam inhelares semper et aliorum,
Glorium magni pastoris ambiendo indefessus,
Annis Satur tandem et bonis operibus,
Confectus studendo, docendo, faciendo, patiendo,
Onustus spolii de Satana triumphatis,
Idemque improborum odiis bene oneratus,
    Hic suaviter in Christo obdormit
    Abstersis lachrymis et sudoribus,
        Vivacissimus resurrecturus,

Unaque ELIZABETHA tori consors et pietatis,
Digno Conjuge Conjux digna.
Obiit ille Julii 2, 1653, Ætat 81.
Obiit illa Januarii 24, 1636, Ætat 71.

The following is a translation of this beautiful and touching inscription :—

On this bestow a glance and tears, O passer by ;
Who car'st for ancient truth, for piety and love,
On this : for here thou soon thyself shalt buried be.

THOMAS LIGHTFOOTE,

For 56 years a most faithful minister of God's Word ;
For 36 years a most watchful pastor of this church ;
A man of antiquated habits and primitive sanctity,
Of distinguished zeal, learning, virtue, example ;
A very pattern of a true man, pastor of pastors,
Always bedewed with sweat and exemplary in the discharge of his duties,
Always anxious for his own salvation and that of others,
Unwearied in seeking the glory of a true pastor ;
At length, full of years and good works,
Worn out with study, teaching, labour and patience ;
Loaded with spoils recovered from Satan,
And also well laden with the hatreds of the wicked,
He placidly sleeps in Christ,
Tears and sweat being wiped away,
To rise again to life.

And also Elizabeth, his spouse and pious consort ;
A worthy husband and a worthy wife.

He died July 2, 1653, aged 81.
She died January 24, 1636, aged 71.

From this memorial it appears that the Rev. Thomas Lightfoot was vicar of Uttoxeter for the long period of 36 years, and that he lived to the advanced age of 81 years.

According to the Church Register, one Richard Taylor was clerk to Mr. Lightfoot, during the whole period of his ministry—

" Richard Taylor, who served 44 years clerk of this church in Uttoxeter, and died at the age of 88, and was buried on the 24th, of January, 1656."

The entry of the burial of the Rev. Thomas Lightfoot is as follows:—

"Thomas Lightfoot, Vicar of Uttoxeter, was buried the 2nd day of July, 1663."*

Another tablet on the same side of the church records the death of the Rev. Thomas Keeling, who died February 20th, 1804, aged 75 years, and Mary, his wife, who died the 17th of January, 1799, aged 62 years; and John their son, aged 2 years.

Also there is a mural tablet to Miss Grace Copestake, second daughter of Henry Copestake, and Mary his wife. She died January the 3rd, 1808, aged 56. Miss Copestake is mentioned in "My Own Story."

There is also a memorial with this inscription:—

"Sacred to the memory of John Hawthorn, Surgeon, late of this town, who died March 14th, 1843, aged 71 years. And Mary Ann Hawthorn, wife of the above, who died September 4th, 1861, aged 79 years."

Likewise on the south wall of the church, the family of Kynnersley have several tablets, with inscriptions as follows:—

"In memory of Clement John Sneyd Kynnersley, eldest son of Thomas Sneyd Kynnersley, of Loxley Park, who died at the age of 4 years. Also to Harriet Berthe, who died December 5th, 1839, aged 9 months. To Mary, wife of the Rev. Henry Sneyd, curate of Stone, who died March 13th, 1838, aged 23 years. And to John Clement Kynnersley, who died February 12th, 1836, aged 28 years."

In the west entrance to the church are two long monuments bearing inscriptions in old English letters. That at the right hand or south side has a Latin inscription and verses to Sir William Milward, of Eaton, with his shield, bearing *ermine* on a fess *gules* three plates, for Milward, impailing his wife's arms party her pale nebutée *or* and *table*, six martlets, countercharged. His age, the

---

* It is curious that the death and burial of Mr. Lightfoot should be recorded as occurring on the same day.

date of his death, and other particulars have been erased, and the places painted over again with black paint. It is of the 17th century, Sir William dying in 1630. It was written by Peter Lightfoot.

Carmnud in commemoratione reverendi
VIRI GULIELMI MILWARDE DE ETON,
In Comitatu Derbiæ Armigi,
nuper defuncti.

Uteeter antiqui memor esto insignis amici,
  Qui tibi vicinus pervenerandus erat,
Nomine Milwardus Gulielmus sit sibi junctus,
  Eton quem coluit villa propingua tibi,
Armiger inque gradu quoque tei venerabilis inde,
  Ac semper patriæ pater amausque suæ,
Ut spargit rivus vicinis partibus undas,
  Vicinis Milwarde sparsit opesque amorum,
Quæ pars in patria non ejus sensit amorum,
  Pauper enim quisnam non sapuisset eum,
Non apud humanos erat his generosior heros,
  Promtior auxiliis gratior autve suis.
Quo sibi dum vexit meruit sic laudis honorem,
  Ut sua posteritas laudet abinde deum,
Hei mihi quot vivunt vixisset mortuus ardent,
  Nestoris ætatem tei magis atque suam.
Sed fera dum rapidæ tenuere hunc vincula mortis,
  Mors ipsum laqueis vinciit atra suis
Quo quæ mortis erant solvit cupidissimus inde
  Atque deum petiit qui fuit ante dei.
Ossa sepulta manent quia sic rata terra reposcit
  Spiritus in cælo est luce perenne vigens.
Heu mors infelix patriæ cur tollis amentem ;
  Vulturiosque viros vivere posse sinis.
Vivit edax vultur ducitque per aera gyros
  Milvius ac phiviæ graculus author aquæ.
Vivit et armiferæ comes invisa Minervæ,
  Illa quidem seclis vix moritura novem.
Dulcis avis philomela suis citius cadit odis
  Quo felix avium gloria nempe jacet.
Six apud humanum genus est mado cursus in orbem
  Vivit ut indignus dignior ipse cadit
Sed tamen haud doleat quisquam quod terra recondit
  Quem deus in tabulam scripserat ante suam.

This inscription may be thus translated—

Strains to the memory of that worshipful man,
WILLIAM MILWARD, OF ETON,
in the County of Derby,
lately deceased.

Be mindful, Utceter, of an old friend renowned
Who was to thee a neighbour and with right worship crowned;
Sir William Milwarde to thyself associate,
Whom Eton reared, a village near to thee;
A Knight he was, and in degree a truly noble man,
And ever to his country a father and a friend.
As spreads a stream fertility o'er plains that skirt her bounds,
So Milwarde's wealth was lavished on all who dwelt around.
No portion of his country but experienced his love,
And never poor man failed relief from him to move.
Throughout the human race was worthier hero none,
More ready to assist, or more benignant to his friends,
By which the whiles he lived he earned his meed of praise,
So great they'd fain exaggerate the honour due to man.
Ah me! how many living men would welcome back the dead
That three long lives of Nestor he here below might live.
But since, alas! fierce chains of rapid death do bind,
Him gloomy death hath vanquished with its snares.
His bones lie buried underground; earth hath her perquisite;
His spirit breathes free air in realms of everlasting light.
How sad that death should carry off a patriot so sincere,
And men less well disposed permit to live on year by year.
The rude, rapacious vulture lives and wheels in circling flight;
The jackdaw which does bring the rain in torrents down; the kite;
The crow whom wise Minerva doth in deep abhorence hold;
The sweet, melodious bird, doth fall more quickly than its songs;
A greater glory hence to it than other birds belongs.
So fares it with the human race, and man in his career;
What though in life unhonoured, in death men him revere.
Yet may we cease to mourn for them, their sorrows overlook,
Whose names a just Divinity hath written in his book.

The other ancient monument is against the wall at the left hand, or north side of the west entrance to the church, and is to the memory of John Archbold. It is in old English letter, a good deal faded, and was also written by Peter Lightfoot. It informs us that after his eightieth year he studied earnestly and acquired a knowledge of the liberal arts as then known, and wrote and published a book treating of the rules of the priests, the regard due to them, and adoration to God. At each side of the long inscription are two representations of death, one significantly holding a dart and spade, and the other a pick and spade, showing that it is the function of death to take away life and also to inter its victims from the sight of the living. Beneath these figures in the centre of the board, are depicted an altar-tomb with a mourner kneeling at each end clad in sable cloaks and having a great expression of grief in their appearance. At the bottom the crest and arms of Archbold are represented. He died in 1629, aged 103.

Epitaphium JO. ARCHEBOLDI,
generi philomeli in sepulchrum suum.

Hic jacit Archboldus generosus dummodo vixit,
  Redditus in cineres, qui fuit ante cinis.
Hunc fere quem rapidæ retinent sud vincula mortis
  Mors ipsum laqueis vinciit atra suis.
Bis tamen ipre decem lustris prius autæ vixit
  Bis quoque, sex annis plus erat orbe manens.
Opsimathes didicit (res nota est pluribus) artes
  Octoginta annis præte ritisque prius
Edidit ipse librum quem fert sua musa libellum
  Dedita sacricolis, qui sua jura canit.
Laus datur inde deo et reverentia scā ministris
  Quos deus obsequiis jusserit esse suis.
Plura senex senio seruoque studendo peregit
  Credite, quam vix est tot pepigisse senex.
    Carmina quoad mortem.
Aspice mortalis quam formam mors tibi format.
  Quamque jubit nullo sit varianda modo,
Maudat ipsa locum tibi quem dedit esse tedendum,
  Dum deus ipse domum vult tibi ferre novam.
    Carmina de insignibus authoris
Author ab antiquis tulit hic insignia avorum,
  Arma per antiquum munera nata sibi.
Si genus excutias satis hoc ab origine longâ
  Usque per innumeros invenietur avos.
Nos non degeneres proavis succedimus illis,
  Terra maneus genitis, nomine cumque meo.
Scono pri antiquos vatum vestigia gressus,
  Ac feror hinc uti quod cecinere patres.
Fecit hoc Ovidius permulti aliique poetæ,
  Cur imitans veteres hoc tulit author opus.

The following is a translation of this curious and interesting inscription :—

Epitaph on JOHN ARCHBOLD, on his tomb, by his poetical son-in-law.

Here lies Archbold, in life a liberal man,
Ashes before, returned to ashes now.
Him whom fierce chains of rapid death do bind,
Death, gloomy death, hath conquered with its snares.
But full the space of five score years he lived,
And well-nigh six years more he lingered still.
Late on in life (the legend's widely known)
He learnt the arts when past his eightieth year.
He published a book, which his muse calls small,
Dedicated to the priests and treating of their rules.
Their praise to God is given and reverence to the ministers
Whom God has commanded to engage in his service.
The old man, full of years, by study hath done much,
Believe me, how hard it is at such an age so much to achieve.
  Strains on occasion of his death—
Look, O mortal, what form death leaves to thee,
And how she wills it should be varied in no wise.
She choses out a place and gives it thee to keep
Whilst God himself prepares a new abode for thee.
  On the author's armorial bearings—
This author brought his armorial bearings from the ancients,
His arms from antiquity at his birth bestowed on him.
If you trace out your pedegree from sufficiently remote origin
It will be found continuously through innumerable ancestors.
We, not degenerate, our fathers do succeed,
Our land remaining to our children with our name.
The poets I have followed and in their steps I've trod,
Which has led me to refer to the tales my fathers told ;
Ovid has done the same, and many poets more,
So imitating them the author published this. ✻

THE CHURCH BELLS.

Notice must not be omitted of the church bells—those reminders of so many joyous and also of so many sad events to us all ; whose tones so constantly welcome and announce the gladsome Sabbath morn ; celebrate the nuptuals of early love ; and peal forth the tidings of great national events.

✻ The whole of these epitaphs have been copied into Messrs. Black's Guide to Alton without any acknowledgment.

Bells, we are told, were first used to drive away evil spirits, and keep away storms, and were formerly tolled to call upon the good to pray for souls taking their departure to another world. Until recently Uttoxeter church had a peal of six bells which were cast in 1729. Each bell bears an inscription, which I here give in the order of their scale—

1st Bell.—Abr. Rudhall, of Gloucester, cast us all. 1729.
2nd Bell.—" Prosperity to this town and Parish." A.R., 1729.
3rd Bell.—" Peace and good neighbourhood." A.R., 1729.
4th Bell.—Henry Cotton, Vicar. A.R., 1729.
5th Bell.—Edward Ball and Thomas Marret, Church-wardens, 1729.
6th Bell.—" I to the Church the living call,
And to the grave do summon all." 1729.

It does not appear whether this set was cast from the metal of the old bells or from new metal. In the previous century, however, four of the bells were recast, each at a different date, and most probably all at Nottingham, and I am in possession of information about them. In 1640 the great bell was recast at Nottingham and cost £10 13s. The fourth bell was cast at the same place in 1641, and with overweight of both bells cost £17 4s. 9d. In 1648 another bell was recast and had twenty-eight pounds of metal added to it, which incurred a charge of, the account states, of £1 8s. In 1671 the great bell was cast a second time at Nottingham and cost doing £19. At the beginning of that century the great bell founders at Nottingham were Oldfields who cast the great bell at Lincoln. In 1874 Geo. Kirk, Esq., of Uttoxeter and Etruria, gave a tenor bell to the church, at a cost of £137 10s. and at the same time the two churchwardens, conjointly, gave a treble bell at a cost of £50. A new set of chimes was also erected at a cost of about £130, by Messrs. Smith and Son, of Derby. The following are the tunes played by them :—Sunday, 108 psalm, to the tune of "Hanover;" Monday, "My Lodging is on the cold ground;" Tuesday,

"The last Rose of Summer;" Wednesday, "The Minstrel Boy;" Thursday, "The Postman's Knock;" Friday, "The Blue Bells of Scotland;" Saturday, "Home, Sweet Home."

Uttoxeter is one of the few places where the curfew bell is still rung every night at eight o'clock. This custom was in existence at the Conquest, but as it was observed in other countries before his reign, it is not certain that it was introduced by William the first. The object of it being rung was to warn people to put out their fires and lights at eight o'clock in the evening, as a precaution against fires, which were frequent and fatal owing to many houses being built of wood.

CHURCHYARD INSCRIPTIONS.

Uttoxeter churchyard does not possess any very early memorials for the notice of the antiquary, it being entirely devoid of mediæval remains. There are several old tombs perhaps of the seventeenth and eighteenth century, and one of the oldest which was sketched by Mr. Ferneyough, and whose sketch is preserved in the Salt Library, at Stafford, and of an earlier date, is believed to be the tomb of the ancient family of Degg, and has much the appearance of Celtic and Indian Dolmen. Perhaps this one as well as many others, with probably earlier and more interesting remains, were broken up and laid in the foundation of the present church when it was rebuilt. The principal epitaph in the churchyard is, perhaps, that on the tomb of Colonel Gardener—" In memory of Colonel Gardener, late of his Majesty's Eleventh Regiment of Dragoons, in which he served with honour from a cornet, and died lamented, August 1st, 1762, aged 91 years. The widow, for the sincere affection for him, caused this stone to be erected."

According to Mr. Samuel Bentley, who was his contemporary, "Colonel Gardner, who at the same time that he was the polite and agreeable gentleman, was the truly worthy veteran. He was of signal service to his country at the battle of Culloden, and served several campaigns abroad in the last war with honour to himself and his king. He sold out of the army a little before his death, but had for some time before settled his family at Uttoxeter."*

There is a slab over the remains of a lady about whom an interesting story is told, but it has no inscription upon it, further than the initials of the lady's name. She had arrived, as was well remembered by several aged persons from whom I obtained particulars respecting her, in a post-chaise at the White Hart Hotel, in a dangerous state of illness, accompanied by a gentleman. Medical aid was procured for her, but it proved unavailing, and she died the next day. The gentleman was greatly distressed on account of the unpropitious issue of her case, and he interred her in a most costly manner, but refused, it is stated, to tell who either himself or the deceased lady were, and he had no communication with any persons except the clergyman and undertaker. All was mystery. The stone is said to be a little below the church on the right hand side of the walk, and laid on bricks. The Rev. Clement Madely preached an affecting funeral sermon in improvement of her death, and the discourse was handed about the town afterwards in manuscript.† The rev. gentleman would doubtless receive satisfactory information respecting the lady, although public curiosity might not have been gratified by being made acquainted with the details.

The following few tomb stone inscriptions in the church yard will, perhaps, be found curious and interesting enough in their several varieties for preservation :—

To three brothers of the name of Crosby, of Stramshall—Thomas, who died in 1808, aged 43 ; Phillip, who died in 1816, aged 54 ; and George, who died in 1815, aged 48, a bachelor, are these lines :—

> Three loving brothers doth lie sleeping here,
> That lov'd each other from their cradle dear,

---

* This refers to a period previous to 1774.
† See also, " My Own Story," by Mary Howitt.

But found this world a city full of crooked streets,
And death a market-place where all men meets;
If life was merchandise that men could buy,
The rich would live for ever, and the poor must die.

The next is in memory of Joseph Slater, a clock and watch maker, of Uttoxeter, who died November 21st, 1822, aged 49.

Here lies one who strove to equal time,
A task too hard, each power too sublime ;
Time stopped his motion, o'erthrew his balance wheel,
Wore off his pivots tho' made of hardened steel ;
Broke all his springs, the verge of life decayed,
And now he is as though he'd ne'er been made.

* * * * *

Such frail machine till time's no more shall rust,
And the archangel wakes our sleeping dust ;
Then with assembled worlds in glory join,
And sing—"the hand that made us is divine."

Where the vacant space appears in the middle of the epitaph, which is on a brass plate, there were at first two other lines, but as they were objectionable to the clergyman of the parish he required them to be obliterated. The missing lines, however, were well remembered, and are these :—

Not for the want of oiling ; that he tried ;
If that had done, why then he'd ne'er have died.

They referred, I believe, to his habits of drinking too much intoxicating liquor.

Many interesting incidents are related respecting the conspicuous monument, surmounted by a resemblance of flame, typical of love, which stands at the south of the church, and is surrounded by massive iron railings—how deep and enduring in its sorrow after their death was the affection of the mother whose two children had been entombed underneath—how bitterly she wept at the tomb long after their death, and kissed its very stones, consecrated as they were by holding the ashes of those she so deeply loved—how frequently she had the sepulchre opened to see the mere but sacred dust of all that she esteemed precious in this world, and so showing how hard it is to part with dear ones even when God calls them to a better sphere. Let such love be an example to mothers, and a rebuke to those callous people who can say when a child dies, "it is only a child." If Christ loved children so much, and if the inhabitants of heaven are like unto them, how much, with so much that is tender, innocent, and loving in them should they be loved by a mother, and by others. One of these was a son, and the other a daughter, and the following are the inscriptions to each respectfully :—

"Sacred to John Fox Corker, son of John and Mary Corker, of Newcastle, born May 10th, 1801, died July 12th, 1807.

> Sweet interesting boy, how ardent
> Thy wish to live, veiling thy sufferings
> In cheerful smiles, and as nature ebb'd
> In melody of song the bright ethereal spark evanescent."

"Sacred to Elizabeth Fox Corker, daughter of John and Mary Corker, of Newcastle, born January 28th, 1806, died July 12th, 1822.

> Most beauteous she was, and gifted
> With every charm the muses could inspire;
> In song, in music, and in eloquence
> She formed a star; and when she fled
> Within her tomb, nature made her bower
> To shed the sorrowing tear."

The family of Corker owned property in Uttoxeter Market Place, now in the possession of Mr. Fearn.

The following interesting memorials and epitaph are copied from a gravestone erected to the family of Chamberlain which was of remote date in Uttoxeter, and of much respectability, owning in 1658, much landed and some household property in the parish, the owners being Christopher, Edmund, Richard, Edward and Thomas. Mr. Chamberlain, who is here commemorated, kept the White Hart Hotel, and he appears to have survived not only his wife but also the whole of their thirteen children. It is an affecting record. It is stated that one of the sons was killed by a wild beast in India, that another fell at the battle of Waterloo, and that a third died of neglect occasioned by the appointed officer in the lock-up at Ashbourne, in which he had been placed on some trifling account. The epitaph is one of the most poetical in the church yard.

"In memory of Penelope, wife of Richard Chamberlain, of this town, and also eight of their children. She died April 27th, 1806, aged 44 years. Richard Chamberlain, late of this town, and also five other of their children. He died February 25th, 1816, aged 65 years.

> So where this stone in silence weeps,
> A friend, a wife, a mother sleeps,
> Abreast within whose sacred cell
> The peaceful virtues love to dwell,
> Affection warm, and faith sincere,
> And soft humanity were there
> In agony—in death resigned,
> Yet felt the wound she left behind.
> Her infant image here below
> Sits smiling on her father's woe,
> Whom what awaits, while yet he strays
> Along the lonely vale of days;
> A pang to secret sorrow dear,
> A sigh, an unavailing tear,
> Till time shall every grief remove
> With life, with memory and with love."

"To Thomas Ryder, who died August 5th, 1833.

> In hopes of future bliss content I lie;
> Tho' pleased to live, yet not displeased to die.
> Life has its comforts, and its sorrows too;
> For both to Allwise Heaven our thanks are due,
> How far my hopes and views are founded well
> God only knows, but the last day will tell."

"In memory of the children of Richard and Anne Keates. One died 29th March, 1825; the other February 13th, 1825.

> Bold infidelity turn pale and die,
> Under this stone the infant's ashes lie.
>   Say are they lost or saved?
> If death's by sin, they sinned, for they lie here;
> If Heaven's by works, in heaven they can't appear.
>   Ah! reason! how depraved;
> Revere the Bible's sacred page, for there
>   The knot's untied;
> They died for Adam's sin; they lived for Jesus died."

"To Sarah wife of Robert Moor, who died in 1804.

My fleeting moments swift did pass,
My glass did quickly run ;
My life decayed like tender grass,
When cut before the sun.
My husband and relations dear,
I in my grave did leave,
And died in faith and hope sincere
That Christ would me receive."

There is a headstone to Elizabeth Powell, who died January 1st, 1812, aged 132 years. Such was the inscription when I first copied it, but it has been so weathered since as to have become scarcely readable. It is in the lower part of the churchyard on the south side.

There is a most elaborate scroll decorated headstone in slate near the houses at the south side of the churchyard of the date 1763, to James Bradbury. It is truly beautiful, and as fresh as if it had only been recently carved.

The following are inscriptions on headstones to persons who have died at great ages :—

"Sacred to the memory of William Orpe, of Combridge, who died December 23rd, 1849, aged 104 years.

Also to Elizabeth, his wife, who died August 19th, 1851, aged 88 years."

There is also a tombstone recording that John Crosley, of the Old Turnpike, died in 1833, aged 100 years and eight months.

On the south side of the old church, close by the old chancel wall, there was formerly a vault and tomb of the Musgrove, or perhaps rather a family of the name of Musgrove and Adams, and it is said that when the last of the family was placed therein, the key of the oaken door admitting into the vault was thrown into Dovehole. The name, Musgrave, appears in the survey of 1774 in connection with the ownership of a small quantity of land, but it does not occur in the survey of 1658. The tomb was destroyed when the old church was taken down, when seventeen leaden coffins, which it contained, were cut in halves and sold. The buyer, however, who was a plumber of the town, could not rest with his purchase ; and it is affirmed that a supernatural being haunted him until he took them back to the churchyard. He was glad to get rid of them again in that way, to obtain ease of mind, although it was by sacrificing their value.

THE PARISH REGISTER.

The register of Uttoxeter Church commences in the year 1596, from which date it is complete to the present time. A remark on the cover of the oldest book proves, however, two things—that the Register of Uttoxeter Church extended further back; and that Mr. Barns was minister prior to 1596. It is "Thomas Barns hath been vicar of this parish —— years." The register is very voluminous, and fills a large iron safe in the robing room. From a close examination of its contents, it does not appear that the vicars have been in the habit of making many remarks with their entries, so that the register does not contain much by which the public can be interested. I was disappointed at not finding the christening of Sir Symon Degg, nor the burial of John Archbold, who died in 1629, aged 103 years; nor the burial of Mr. John Scott, who was slain in Uttoxeter streets in 1644. The name of Degg, at an early date, is however of frequent occurrence. The signature of the first vicar whose name occurs in the register, is that of Thomas Barns. It runs through the first book, and far on in the second, beginning in 1596, and continuing over a period of twenty-one years till 1617. He had born to him and christened in Uttoxeter seven children—four sons and three daughters. Their names were as follows:—John, Thomas, James, William, Jones, Mary, and Anne. I do not find the burial of this vicar in the register, so that he very probably resigned. He was succeeded by the Rev. Thomas Lightfoot, who was a vicar from 1617 until 1653. The next register's name is William Roiston, whose autograph is very fine in letters not resembling those of the period. Lawrance Dawson was minister in 1657, and the Rev. Michael Edge, a correspondent of the Rev. Thomas Lightfoot, became vicar in 1658, and in 1677 he was succeeded by Richard Jackson whose signatnre continues till 1689, although in 1688 that of Joshua Robinson occurs. A few extracts are used in connection with persons or subjects referred to in this volume. The following may be introduced here, and will show that there was poverty, crime, and pity in Uttoxeter more than two hundred years ago. 1624— John Degg, son of Thomas Degg, and Dorothy, his wife, was buried the 4th day of November. Thomas and Dorothy, here mentioned, appear in Degg's pedigree. Although there is not an entry of the burial of John Scott, in 1644, there is this of a christening—John, son of Thomas Scott, and —— wife, christened the 2nd day of June. The question may be asked, should not this have been for the death of John Scott, instead of the birth of a child of the same name? 1644—Robert Clark Barker (or Barber) Surgeon, buried the 23rd day of April. He must have been an assistant, or in lodgings, for his name does not appear in the survey. 1645—*Mr. Walter Mynors* was buried the 3rd day of August. Eliza Burton, a poor, low woman, buried the 5th of March. William Spragg, whose name figures so unfavourably in connection with the enclosure of Uttoxeter ward or common, is recorded to have been buried at Lichfield the 2nd day of May. Henry Porter, a poor man, buried the 10th day of November. 1650—Edward Oudfield and Joane Taylor were married ye 6th d Sept. An Edward Oudfield subsequently married a Katherine Aston. 1656—John Blount was buried 18th day of January. Richard Taylor, who served forty-four years clerk of this church in Uttoxeter, and died at the age of 88. 1658—John Barlow, a soldier, buried the 23rd July. 1660—John Wood and Ellen Lightfoot were married the 2nd day of August. 1671— Mr. Peter Lightfoot buried ye 18th day of Auguste, but although he wrote so many fine epitaphs for others, no one appears to have commemorated his name in so worthy a manner, unless such memorial of him may have perished. John Harding, a poor boy, buried ye 9th day of October.

Lawrance Dawson, immediately after the above date, became minister of Bromshall, unless he had previously officiated there as well as at Uttoxeter. His will was drawn up by Mr. Peter Lightfoot apparently in 1674. He was connected with the family of Warner, of Bromshall, by whom the will has been preserved to the present time, it having been in the possession of the late Mr. T. Frost, late relieving officer of this Poor Law Union.

WILL OF LAWRANCE DAWSON, CLERK, BROMSHALL, 1674.

" In the name of God, amen, the nine and twentieth day of June, Anno Domini 1674, and in the five and twentieth year * of the reign of our Sovereign Lord Charles the second by the grace of God of England, Scotland, France, and Ireland, King, defender of the faith. I Lawrance Dawson, of Bromshall, in the county of Stafford, clerk, weake in body but perfecte in minde (praised be God) doe make and ordain this my last will and testament in manner and form following. Ffirst and personally, I bequeath my soul into the hands of Almighty God my Creator and Redeemer hoping and assuredly trusting that through the merits of my Saviour Jesus Christ I shall obtaiyne everlasting salvation. And I bequeath my body to the earth, to be decently buried when and where it shall please God to appoint. Ffor my worldly goods I dispose of them as followeth : I give and bequeath to my daughter Hester Townsend five pounds, and to John and Thomas her two sons twenty shillings apeice. Item. I give my grandchildren, Thomas Beech and Mary Beech twenty shillings apeice. Item. I give to Lawrance and George, children of George Warner, twenty shillings apeice.

---

* There is evidently a great blunder in the dates in this will, for at the time it was made, according to the date given, King Charles 2nd had only reigned fourteen years, and the writer of it, Mr. Peter Lightfoot, had been dead nearly four years. Otherwise the will is genuine, as it is written in the curious style of the period which but few persons would be able to imitate.

Item. I give to my two servants John Startin and Elizabeth Clark. ten shillings apeice. Item. I give to the poor at my funeral three pounds, six shillings and eightpence. All the rest of my goods, cattall, chattels, household stuff, husbandry, cart, and yimplements, my debts, legacys and funeral charges being all discharged, I give and bequeath to my son William Dawson, whom I make executor of this my last will and testement, hoping he will see the same truly performed as my last trust is in him reposed. And I doe hereby renounce all other wills whatever by me formerly made, for witness whereunto I have hereunto put my hand and seal the day and year first above written. Sealed, signed, and witnessed in the presence of

PETER LIGHTFOOT.
FRANCIS THOMLINSON."

Shall the old muniment chest in the vestry filled with indentures and other similar papers, but not containing any writings of the least historical value, be left unnoticed? Perhaps it may give a clue at least to the names of the churchwardens of the time. It bears a date and initials on the front as follows :—

1598.   E. C.   R. W.   Wardens.

The only persons living then or soon after in Uttoxeter having names with those initials were Edward Chamberlain and Richard Warton, and their names are most likely intended.

COMMUNION PLATE.

On the Paten, or receptacle for the consecrated bread, is the following inscription :—"The gift of Lettice Pratt, daughter of Thomas Degg, Gent., of Stronshall." On one of the chalices, or cups, is engraved, "In 1637, Mr. Wm. and Mrs. Ann Hart gave a cup, ten ounces and a quarter. In 1716 added to it p E., a private person, forty." On the base of the flagon there is inscribed, "The gift of Mrs. Sarah Smith to the Parish Church of Uttoxeter, 1752," emblazoned with the monogram I. H. S., Jesus Homium Salvator (Jesus the Saviour of Mankind).

CEMETERY.

Owing to urgent requirements a new cemetery was provided for Uttoxeter in 1861. The ground selected is a few hundred yards west of the town by the side of the Stafford road. The chapels and the elegant spire are in the Ornamental Gothic Style, from designs by Mr. B. Wilson, architect, Derby. The extent of the ground is three acres and thirteen perches, and cost £671 17s. 2d. The contract for the chapels and entrance lodge was £1333. The sum of £3000 was lent for the whole purpose from the Public Works Loan Commissioners. The Lord Bishop of the diocese consecrated the cemetery on June 25th, 1861. For some reason the spire was taken down and re-erected the succeeding year. The severe gale of the 13th and 14th of October, 1881, blew down a number of pinnacles and crockets which have not been restored.

CHAPTER V.

HISTORY OF DISSENT IN UTTOXETER.

The religious body known as the Society of Friends had an existence in Uttoxeter previous to any other form of dissent so far as it is known with any certainty, for we have no particulars of the religious sect, nor the time of their introduction into the town over whom Mr. Heming, the controversialist, exercised the functions of a minister. The earliest mention of the Society of Friends in connection with the town occurs in the old parish records of 1662 or 63, when a warrant for the apprehension of a number of Quakers cost the constables 1s. The item plainly indicates that the act of persecution proceeded from the civil authorities in Uttoxeter, but it leaves to conjecture the cause which induced the warrant for their arrest being issued. It is likely, however, that as they were, on moral and criminal grounds, unexceptionable in the sight of the law, it was for the simple attempt at promulgating their peculiar religious opinions and on account of their mode of worship. Such proceedings were about that time very common in many parts of the Kingdom, where the magistracy were not very liberal and tolerant. According to an old Quakers' book preserved at Stafford, there were, at this time, Quakers at Doveridge, Tean, Chartley, and Stramshall, as well as at Uttoxeter, and it is recorded that the following persons contributed sums of money towards the erection of a meeting-house at Stafford in 1674: "Walter Pixley, of Uttoxeter, £2; George Godridge, of Doveridge, £1 10s.; Humphrey Ball, of the same place, £1 10s.; and William Hixon, Tean, £1 10s. Walter Pixley was honoured in 1673 by the Friends in being delegated to the general annual meeting at London, and he attended the quarterly meeting at Stafford in 1700. In 1671 a Quakers' burying ground was granted to them at Stramshall, and the following is the indenture of it :—

"One indenture dated the 3rd of the month called December, 1671, wherein William Heath, of Kingsley, in the county of Stafford, grants unto Humphrey Wall, Thomas Duce, of Dowbridge, John Scott, of Stramshall, and Walter Pixley, of Uttoxeter, one parcel of land lying in Stramshall aforesaid containing in length twenty yards and in breadth twelve yards lying at one end of a croft for a burying place in trust for the use of the people called Quakers." The site of this burying place is at the south west angle of the field in which Stramshall church stands, and is known, though on what account tenants of the land are in ignorance, as "The Quakers' Bit." The ground there is much higher than the road, and some years ago a commencement was made to get marl at the side of it, and as the men worked on into the place of interment they dislodged two lead coffins which they cut up and sold, and for many years no more marl has been carted away from the place. There is a slight ridge showing the boundaries of the little cemetery, and independently of the Society of Friends having evidently a right in the bit of land, it is a pity it is not in some way enclosed or marked as a site sacred to the dead not to be further encroached upon by marldiggers.

The meeting-house of the Society of Friends at Uttoxeter stands secluded in Carter street, down a yard, at the south side. It was erected after 1700, and the ensuing is a copy of the deed of gift of the property of the body as preserved in the old Quaker's book previously **referred to.**

"One copy of a deed of gift wherein Robert Heath of Nether Tean conveys unto ye people called Quakers one messuage house lying and being in Uttoxeter in a street called Carter street, for certain uses therein expressed; that is to say the house aforesaid to be for a public meeting-house for ye worship of God and that part of the land thereto belonging to be set apart for a burying place for ye aforesaid people, and also that there shall be paid out of ye profits arising from the said premises yearly and every year by the said people the sum of one pound eleven shillings for ye use of Biblique friends in ye ministry for provision both for man and horse when they come to ye meeting—Nominating and appointing Walter Pixley, John Alsop, Richard Bowman, and Thomas Shipley, trustees to take care that all things contained in that grant be fulfilled to ye time, intent, and meaning thereof.

Dated ye 27 of the month called March 12th, R. W. 1700."

The attendance at the chapel comprises now but one family, that of Mr. Godbehere, other families of that persuasion having either died out or left the town. The predecessors of Mary Howitt, for two generations, of the name of Botham, were worshippers there, and that lady herself was, when in Uttoxeter in her younger days, of the same persuasion. The burying place is on the south side of the chapel, and it contains "many a mouldering heap, each in his narrow cell forgotten laid," there being in the whole enclosure but one little memorial slab laid over a grave of the date 1872. Walter Pixley, above named, who was an ancestor of Mary Howitt, suffered imprisonment for his principles, and, to escape from his persecutions, he went over with his family to America with the founder of Pennsylvania, and became noted amongst the most worthy and influential settlers there. *

---

* "Martha and Mary," a true narrative by Mary Howitt. Stafford, J. Halden.

ANCIENT PRESBYTERIAN CHURCH IN UTTOXETER.

I am informed by T. L. Peake, Esq., B.A., of No. 123, Edgware road, Hyde Park, that there formerly existed a Presbyterian church in Uttoxeter, that they had a meeting-house in the town, and that he finds the following names of pastors of the congregation :—The Rev. John Merret, from 16... to 1704, when he was removed to Coventry. The Rev. — Sparry, July, 1705 to 1708, at which time he left Uttoxeter to become pastor of a congregation at Burton-on-Trent. He was succeeded at Uttoxeter in the same year by the Rev. Daniel Maddock, who sustained the pastorate till the memorable year 1745, thus being the minister of this church thirty-seven years, and the interesting fact is recorded that in 1715 he had two hundred persons forming his congregation. After this no mention of this ancient church occurs, and Mr. Peake supposes that after the death of Mr. Maddock it was immersed and lost in the new independent interest in the town in consequence of the great liberality of religious sentiment amongst the Presbyterians. It can scarcely, however, be admitted that so prosperous a congregation would allow themselves to lose their identity as a church so suddenly on the death or necessary retirement of their pastor, and it may rather be suggested whether they did not select another minister, and that in time the church dwindled away or lost its separate existence ultimately in the manner indicated.

Congregationalism was introduced into Uttoxeter in the year 1788. The first ministers who preached in the town in connection with the body were the Rev. James Boden, of Hanley, and the Rev. Mr. Whitridge, of Newcastle. The first meeting house of the Congregationalists in Uttoxeter was at the west end of Carter Street, in a building which was subsequently a hoopmaker's shop, and since converted into cottages, just past Lathrop's Almshouses. They worshiped at this place about four years, when they erected a more suitable building for the purpose at Bear Hill, in 1792. The same premises were afterwards purchased by the late Messrs. Bladon and Son (now Messrs. Lasbrey) for a carpet store room, notwithstanding that interments had been made in them. This meeting-house or chapel was opened by the Rev. Jonathan Scott, minister of a chapel at Matlock Bath, which had been purchased by Lady Glenorchy for the use of the Independents and Presbyterians. The opening of it was attended by a degree and kind of persecution to make the occasion memorable. A number of riotous persons met in the street, near the meeting-house, who, besides disturbing the congregation, made a bonfire at the pillory (a centre of offensive occasions as well as a place for the punishment of crime), in which they fixed the effigy of a minister, which they afterwards committed to the flames. At night the rioters threw firebrands at the people as they returned from the meeting, but fortunately no one was materially injured. *

The first pastor over the congregation at Bear Hill was the Rev. Mr. Cole, who was intended to be represented by the figure which was burnt at the pillory. Mr. Cole was succeeded in 1796 by the Rev. Stephen Chester, at which time there were but six church members and twenty others for a congregation, and who I find was still minister in 1818. Mr. Chester was followed by the Rev. J. Johnson, who afterwards joined the Church of England, and became the travelling secretary of the Church of England Missionary Society, and died in 1867. He, however, remained but a short time. The Rev. John Cooke, who was educated at Lancashire College, entered upon his ministerial labours at the same place in 1825. The congregation increased under the ministry of Mr. Cooke and a more suitable building than the meeting-

---

* Evangelical Magazine.

house became requisite, so that in 1827 the large chapel in Carter Street was erected. The foundation stone of the edifice was laid by the Rev. John Cooke, who also delivered an address during the ceremony. The chapel was finished by, and opened on, the 15th of April, 1828, the sermons being preached by the late Dr. Raffles, of Liverpool. The school-rooms adjoining the chapel were built in 1842, and the sermons on the occasion of opening them were preached by the late Rev. John Angel James, of Birmingham, and the Rev. James Galloway. The minister's house was erected in 1848, and was the gift of the late John Vernon, Esq., founder of free Sunday schools in Uttoxeter, who died in 1856.

The Rev. John Cooke was held in the highest esteem by persons of all christian denominations in Uttoxeter; his co-operation was always freely given when required for the promotion of the religious, educational, and social welfare of the town generally. On completing the thirty-second year of his ministry, on February 3rd, 1857, he was presented by the members of his church with a handsome token of esteem. The gift consisted of a silver salver, and a purse containing eighty sovereigns, the salver bearing a suitable inscription. The presentation was made at a social meeting by Mr. John Vernon, junior (deceased in 1880). The rev. gentleman, in acknowledging the gift, read the names of those members of his church who had died during his ministry, and the reading of the list produced considerable emotion in the assembly. After this Mr. Cooke continued his ministry until he had completed the fortieth year of it, and he died in 1871, and was buried in the Cemetery on the 17th of February.

The Rev. John Cooke was succeeded by the Rev. J. M. Hodgson, B.A., now Professor Hodgson, of Lancashire Independent College, and Glasgow University, and he was ordained over the church in 1866, the charge being delivered by Professor Newth. Mr. Hodgson resigned his pastorate in 1875, and ultimately the Rev. Dorrel Lee, in 1876, was chosen the pastor of the Congregational Church. He left in 1883, and was succeeded by the Rev. Mr. Barker, who is the present minister.

Methodism became known in Uttoxeter during the life of its founder, the Rev. John Wesley. The first preaching house of the Wesleyans in the town stood at the lower part of the Sheep Market exactly opposite to Balance Street, and in it they worshiped from 1775 till 1790. It has since been a butcher's shop, and recently the premises have been again transformed into a plumber's shop and a grocer's shop. The itinerent preachers at that time, in whose district Uttoxeter lay, were the Rev. Samuel Bardsley, a man of great popularity; the Rev. Robert Costerdine; the Rev. Robert Swan, and the Rev. Joseph Taylor. The house was occupied by a family attached to Methodism; and an apprentice they had to the shoemaking business was in the habit of cleaning the preachers' shoes—a not very pleasant employment, from the amount of dirty walking the preachers had to perform at that time—and for which he, no doubt, expected to be recompensed. On one occasion one of the preachers appears to have possessed either a not very generous disposition, or a purse not too full of money—the latter then being a circumstance not unfrequent amongst Wesleyan preachers—or of a forgetful mind, for he omitted to give the lad anything for cleaning his shoes. The neglect became known to one of the other preachers, the Rev. Joseph Taylor, who, in trying his wit to correct the fault of his brother preacher, perpetrated the following rhyme upon paper, and stuck it upon the chimney-piece of the room in which they slept:—

> Pray give Jack a penny for cleaning your leather;
> Your boots are so long, so dirty the weather;
> You know that the lad has a sad nasty job,
> And if he cleans them for nothing he must be a hob.

Joseph Taylor preached in the chapel in High Street after he had been in the ministry forty years. *

At an early date the Rev. Mr. Davenport, curate of Uttoxeter Church, opened his house for the public prayer-meetings of the Wesleyans; and his house was also

---

* For some of this information I am indebted to the late Mr. W. Bunting, Uttoxeter.

opened for the preachers after he was promoted to the vicarage of Radcliffe.* The time when this liberal-minded clergyman countenanced the small and probably despised society of Methodists in Uttoxeter, was certainly before 1780, and very likely previous to 1775. He was an intimate friend of John Wesley, and their correspondence appears in the "Armenian Magazine."

It used to be related by a person living at this period, that he remembered John Wesley once preaching in Uttoxeter Market Place. It is also confidently stated that he passed through Uttoxeter on another occasion, and whilst staying at the White Hart and Old Star Inn in the Market Place, some of the premises of which, as we have seen, became united to the Red Lion Hotel, for a change of post-horses. he was met by the members of the Society in the town. At another time, when there was a dispute amongst them, he addressed a letter to them which had the desired effect of producing a reconciliation.

It appears that when the Wesleyans discontinued preaching at the house in the Sheep Market, a house was opened for them on Uttoxeter Heath, which was shortly afterwards exchanged for the building in Carter Street, previously used by the Independents. This they occupied till the close of the last century. The Rev. John Hampson, a preacher of some eminence, once preached in this humble meeting-house, when he received no little annoyance from a number of young men who had assembled to persecute and disturb the congregation. The preacher was a powerful man, and was no doubt pretty well used to riotous proceedings when preaching, and had no fear of them. The way in which he treated one of the number reminds one of the rough handling David Cartwright, of American backwoods celebrity, sometimes gave to his wanton tormentors when travelling from place to place preaching the gospel. Without any ceremony he took him by a leg and an arm and flung him into a cess-pool in the back yard, a very salutary though unpleasant

---

* History of Methodism in the Leek Circuit.

and unexpected recompense for annoying the assembly. The preacher with great composure, and I should think with no little satisfaction, resumed his duties and went through the service without any further molestation. A son of Mr. Hampson wrote a life of Mr. Wesley which was comprised in three volumes.

At the beginning of the present century Methodism in Uttoxeter had become almost extinct; preaching was discontinued, and only one or two persons remained clinging to the Wesleyan form of worship. A person of the name of Cartwright, and a family of the name of Seckerson—whose ancestors existed in Uttoxeter two centuries before—were all the Methodists that remained in the town, and these went weekly to Doveridge Wesleyan chapel, which was then attended by the family of the late Michael Thomas Saddler, M.P. for Leeds. The family of Cartwright appears to have been in a very respectable position, for I find in the survey of 1774, that Mr. Cartwright owned in his own right 6a. 1r. 1p. of land, and had a share with a Miss Bull in 56a. 1r. 30p., and in 9a. 3r. 29p. About 1805 a house was opened at the Wharf, and was thronged; but it appears the congregation was not allowed to worship there without annoyance. There were rude persons who sought to tease them by blowing the fumes of asafœtida through the keyhole in the door; and on one occasion when the people were assembled, a number of the rabble forced open the door and pushed a donkey into the house. Yet Methodism extended itself in Uttoxeter, and at length a large room at the Old Star Inn was taken, which, however, was no protection against the violence of disorderly visitants. The windows were frequently broken by them and the congregation was disturbed. The chapel in High Street was built in 1812, and opened by the Rev. Jabez Bunting, afterwards the Rev. Jabez Bunting, D.D. The chapel has a spacious gallery. So far a great step was taken in the history of Methodism in Uttoxeter, and ministers were appointed to it, but it would appear for long after that the comforts of the preachers was not sufficiently attended to. A single case illustrating this is given in the Wesleyan Magazine for June, 1875, where it is stated that "on the 11th of August, 1817, Miss Brocas was married at St. Mary's Church, Shrewsbury, to the Rev. Thomas Harris, whom she shortly accompanied to Uttoxeter, where she found, in exchange for the comfortable home she had left, *inconvenient* and *poorly furnished lodgings* provided for the preacher and his wife. The preachers were then away from home days together." The chapel contains an excellent organ. In rear of the chapel there is a commodious schoolroom. It may be recorded as an interesting occurrence that J. B. Gould, Esq., M.A., the American Consul, then at Birmingham, preached two able sermons in the Wesleyan Chapel on Sunday, September 22nd, 1872. The Wesleyans started a Sunday school in Uttoxeter in 1814, for which they engaged the large room at the Old Star. I possess a copy of the first rules, the introduction to which is a model of good writing. In 1882, Mr. Thomas Gresley, of Uttoxeter, purchased a house in Bradey Street for a minister's residence and made a gift of it to the Wesleyan Society. This gentleman and John Sketch, Esq., also gave £50 each to be expended in the improvement of the property. The sum of £500 was also left to the Wesleyan Society in the town by the late Mrs. Hawkins, and that with £200 more raised by a bazaar in 1885, was expended in altering the interior of the chapel and in helping to complete the improvement of the house and furnishing it. Of the latter sum only about £30 was left towards the chapel improvement.

The Primitive Methodists have a chapel in Carter Street, which was erected in 1842, and greatly enlarged in 1875. Previous to this they had a meeting-house at the top of the Hockley. Beyond these facts there is nothing more that I am able to gather respecting the history of this body in Uttoxeter.

The Roman Catholic Chapel, which was erected in 1839, stands in Balance Street, and is in the early English style of almost the thirteenth century; the architects were the elder and younger Pugin. It was greatly enlarged and improved in 1879, the Rev. — McGarahan is the priest. Previous to this they had a preaching-room in the Blue Bell Yard.

The taxation of Pope Nicholas at Uttoxeter in the time of Edward I., in 1291, was the sum of £12, according to the item relating to it—"Uttokeshatre pter pens XVIII. marc —— XXIVS." This tax was levied on all families possessed of thirty pence yearly rent in land, out of which they paid a penny. Peter's pence was presented from England by Ina, King of the West Saxons, towards the endowment of an English college at Rome, A.D. 725, and was so called because agreed to be paid on the feast of St. Peter. It was confirmed by Offa, 777, and claimed by the Popes till suppressed by Henry VIII.* Amongst the Roman Catholic non-jurors who refused to take the oaths in 1745, was one Henry Alport, a yeoman, of Uttoxeter, who for refusing was fined the sum of 40s.†

The Plymouth Brethren have a small society in Uttoxeter, and they worship in the saloon of the Town Hall, which they rent.

Uttoxeter has two cottage churches of the Church of England, one on the Heath being re-built with £500 given by the late Mrs. Hawkins, of Uttoxeter and Burton-on-Trent.

---

* Camden's Britannia.
† Book entitled "Non-Conjurors."

CHAPTER VI.

LIVES OF DISTINGUISHED PERSONS, EITHER NATIVES OF OR HAVING BEEN RESIDENTS IN UTTOXETER.

THOMAS ALLEN.

This learned and distinguished mathematician and philosopher was born at Uttoxeter on the 21st December, 1542, and according to Camden was a descendent, through six generations, of Henry Allen of Bucknel. He was admitted a scholar of Trinity College, Oxford, in 1551, became a fellow in 1565, and took his Master's Degree in 1567. He pursued his studies in this college for three years afterwards; but in consequence of his disinclination to enter holy orders, as required by the statutes, he resigned his fellowship and went to Gloucester Hall (now Worcester College) in the year 1570. Here he pursued the study of mathematics with great attention and success, and in consequence of his attainments, acquired a high reputation for his superior knowledge in his favourite branch of learning.

Mr. Allen was now patronized by a nobleman much devoted to mathematical science, Henry, Earl of Northumberland, who invited him to his house, and introduced him to those celebrated mathematicians, Thomas Harrison,

THOMAS ALLEN.

Walter Warner, and Nathaniel Thorperly. Mr. Allen enjoyed in their society the greatest gratification by the discussion of topics most congenial to his habit of thinking; and his friends were no less pleased and instructed in their intercourse with a young philosopher, whose demonstrations of science were so complete and conclusive.

Amongst other distinguished persons who respected the talents of Mr. Allen was Robert, Earl of Leicester, who was emulous to patronise him, and offered to confer a bishopric upon him. He, however, declined the clerical preferment, and continued in that retirement which was so agreeable to his unostentatious character, and the simple and temperate habits of his life. Devoted to the studious pursuits of science, Mr. Allen continued in the University, and availing himself of the advantages of his situation, he collected many valuable manuscripts relating to antiquities, history, philosophy, mathematics, and astronomy, a catalogue of which collection is preserved in the Ashmolean Museum. Mr. Allen published in Latin the second and third books of Ptolemy, concerning the judgment of the stars, with an exposition. He also wrote notes on many of Lilly's books, and some of the works of Bates, entitled "De Scripturibus Mag Britannia," and was doubtless misled by the belief in judicial astrology so prevalent in that age. His skill as a mathematician induced the vulgar to suspect him of practicing the art of magic; and the author of a book entitled "Leicester's Commonwealth," accused him of exercising his necromatic art to promote the Earl of Leicester's ambitious schemes, and effect a match between that nobleman and Queen Elizabeth. This absurd assertion doubtless originated in the well known confidence which existed between Mr. Allen and his patron, between whom a constant correspondence was kept up, inasmuch that nothing important respecting the State was transacted without the cognizance of the philosopher, who, in return, informed the Earl of what passed in the University.

From the uniformity of a collegian's life few interesting incidents are to be expected; and Mr. Allen was content with the esteem of a few select friends, in preference to emolument and fame. He was highly respected by several celebrated contemporaries, particularly by Mr. Camden, Sir Robert Bodley, Sir Henry Saville (whose rare collection of MSS. and books were sold in 1864), Sir Robert Cotton, Sir Henry Spelman, and Mr. Sheldon.

Mr. Allen died at Gloucester Hall September 30th, 1632, in the 90th year of his age, and he was interred with great solemnity. Mr. Burton, who delivered his funeral oration, called him not only "The Coryphæus but the very soul and sun of all the mathematicians of his time;" and Mr. Sheldon, who was his intimate friend, mentioned him "as a person of most extensive learning and consummate judgment, the brightest ornament of the University of Oxford." Camden says, " He was skilled in most of the best arts and sciences." These high panegyrics from such distinguished men are most certainly honourable memorials of the learning of Mr. Allen, yet he does not seem to have been ambitious of transmitting his name to posterity by any literary production which might have promoted the progress of science. In fact, it has long been the practice of the learned to compliment each other hyperbolically; and in the ardour of their admiration and wish to shine as encomiasts, they over-praise the abilities and attainments of men of real worth.

The following sketch of Mr. Allen is from a manuscript in the library of Trinity College, Oxford :—" He studied polite literature with great application; he was strictly tenacious of academical discipline; always highly esteemed, both by foreigners and by all of the highest stations in the Church of England and the University of Oxford." Yet with all this boasted knowledge, it is to be regretted by the world that Mr. Allen was so secret a lover of the muses; for we have not a single scrap to illustrate his taste for polite literature, and very few articles indeed from his pen respecting even his own favourite story of mathematics.

This eminent mathematician has hitherto been identified with the founder of Uttoxeter Grammar School, which is a great mistake. The founder of the Grammar school is a different person. The mathematician was of Trinity College, Oxford, and Thomas Alleyne was a fellow of Trinity College, Cambridge, and was the oldest by probably forty or fifty years, inasmuch as he made his will when the philosopher was but in his 14th year, and who never entered holy orders, which the founder of the school did. Nicholson, in his history of Leicestershire, informs us that he was the son of Sir John Allen, Lord Mayor of London, and in that case he must have been born in London. Burke's Extinct Peerage and Baronetage, however, make no mention of him in the pedigree of Sir John Allen.

SIR SYMON DEGGE, KNIGHT, JUDGE AND ANTIQUARY.

Sir Symon Degge, Knight, was descended from Hugh Degge, gent., of Stramshall, who lived in the time of Richard II. Sir Symon Degge was born at Uttoxeter, January 15th, 1612, and was educated for the law in which he was much distinguished, and practiced in Doctor's Commons as a civilian. The fact of Sir Symon's birth at Uttoxeter is attested in the handwriting of his son, Doctor Symon Degge, in the copy of Dr. Plott's " Natural History of Staffordshire," in Cambridge University library. He says on the margin of page 313, that Sir Symon Degge died in the 92nd year of his age, and that he was born at Uttoxeter, a town remarkable for the great age of its inhabitants."

Owing to his eminent legal attainments, King Charles II. appointed Sir Symon Degge judge of West Wales, a position which he retained for a period of fourteen years; after resigning this post he became counsel in the war of Wales during the space of twelve years, an appointment to which he was also preferred by the same King. He received his discharge from this office on his own petition, when he entered the commission of the peace for the counties of Derby and Stafford, and became at the same time recorder of Derby. He was in the commission of the peace twelve years, but the recordership of Derby he held thirty-nine years. In 1675 he was High Sheriff for the county of Derby. At the same time he was in great practice as a barrister, and which he is said to have served in a barrister's gown with a sword by his side. In the churchwardens' accounts of the parish of St. Werburgh, Derby, this entry occurs in reference to Sir Symon Degge :—" Paid for a warrant and copy of it to remove Sarah Moore 1s. 6d. pd Symon Degg's man for sealing it 6d." "Account of what money we laid forth at the session when the dispute was with Mark Heaton about Sarah Moore as followeth given Sir Simon Degge for his fee 5s. od." At that time he probably occupied Babbington House. Sir Symon was the author of two distinct legal treatises, entitled, "The Parson's Counsellor," and "The Law of Tithes and Tithing," dedicated to his son-in-law, the Rev. Anthony Trollope, rector of Norbury. His legal opinions are quoted by Coke, in his Ecclesiastical Law. These works have been re-published under the editorship of Mr. Ellis.

Sir Symon Degge is, however, principally known as an eminent antiquary. He wrote copious manuscript notes to his own copy of Plott's "Natural History of Staffordshire," which is now in the library of Trinity College, Cambridge, and to Erdeswick's "Survey of Staffordshire," about the year 1660, in which appeared his remarkable letter on Abbey Lands, and with some of these notes I have been kindly favoured for use in this volume.

Sir Symon Degge was twice married. His first wife was a daughter of Richard Brandon, Esq., of Shenstone Hall. She died July 2nd, 1652, aged 42 years. His second wife, whom he married December 7th, 1652, was Alice, daughter of Anthony Oldfield, Esq., of Spalding, widow of James Trollope, Esq. Sir Symon Degge resided at some period in the old fortified house at Fenny Bentley, and died at Blythe Bridge Hall, at the age of 92 years, and his remains were buried in the chapel on the north side of Kingstone Church, which was taken down in 1861. In 1655, Sir Symon was living at Callowhill, when he compounded for his estate, for £007 00s. 00d.

SIR SYMON DEGGE'S FORTIFIED HOUSE.

The accompanying engraving represents the interesting fortified house of the thirteenth century of Sir Symon Degge, at Bentley The name of Sir Symon is cut on the lead on the top of the tower, in which there is a curious spiral flight of steps conducting nearly to the top.

His son, Dr. Symon Degge, was a physician at Derby, living in the parish of Allhallows, and like his father, he possessed a taste for antiquarian pursuits. He was the discoverer of Roman antiquities at Fenny Bentley. in Derbyshire, as well as of antiquities in other parts of that county. He was the purchaser of the manor of Marchington and Agardsley from Charles Egerton, Esq, and the Earl of Bridgewater. * Although the last male descendant of Sir Symon Degge is stated to have died in

---

* Harwood's Erdeswick.

1812, there are now persons of the name in Uttoxeter claiming male descent from him. There are also descendants in America, one being on the Surgeon General's Staff at Washington.

The above is the fullest and most correct account of any yet given of this distinguished man.

The following are inscriptions to Sir Symon Degge and his wives which I carefully copied from three tablets which were in the old church at Kingstone, but all of which have since become obliterated by exposure to the atmosphere:—

"Here lyeth the body of Sir Symon Degge, Knt., who was judge of West Wales, to Civri the 2nd XIV years, and of the same King, Counsel in the War of Wales 12 years, and then upon his petition (his) discharge he was in the commission of peace for the counties of Derby and Stafford, and Recorder of Derby above thirty-five years. Was born Jany. vth, MDCIXII. Dyed February X, MDCICII."

On the right side of the slab bearing the above is another slab, with an inscription to the second wife of Sir Symon Degge.

"Here lies the body of Dame Alice Degge, daughter of Anthony Oldfield, of Spalding, Lincolnshire, Esq., and second wife of Sir Symon Degge. Was born and christened June xxvth, MDCIXIV. Died March xxxth, MDCIXCVI."

The following inscription to Sir Symon Degge's first wife, and other persons, was on a stone which was fixed in the north side of a chapel projecting from the nave and said to have been built by Sir Symon Degge:—

"Against this place, in the body of the church, was buried the bodies of William Whitehall, gent., who died 12 March, 1615, aged 83, and Elizth, his wife, formerly the wife of Thos Degg, of Stramshall, gent., great grandmother of Sir Symon Degg, ys built this chapel. She died 10 June, 1620, aged 94, and Symon Whitehall, their son, gent., who died 17 May, 1630, aged 63 ; and Letice, his wife, who died Octbr 20, 1649, aged 97 ; and Dame, first wife of the said Sir Symon Degg, who died 2 July, 1652, aged 42 years."

The arms of Degge are, *Or* on a bent, *azure* three falcons mounting. *Argent*, fesses and beles of the field. Crest. On a ducal coronet, a falcon reclaimed, *arg.* *

All the above inscriptions have perished since I copied them.

SAMUEL BENTLEY.

Mr. Samuel Bentley, "The Uttoxeter Poet," was born at Uttoxeter, according to his own statement, on the 9th of May, 1722. He must, however, have possessed an erroneous memorandum or recollection of this event, for in the church register there is this entry of his baptism : —"Samuel, son of Richard and Elizabeth Bentley, Baptized the 3rd of May, 1722." It is much more likely, therefore, that his birth took place early in April—perhaps on the 9th. The house in which he was born was the then third or fourth house in the Market Place from the corner of Church Street, almost opposite to the conduit. His grandfather and father had lived there before him, and although they were otherwise in good circumstances they carried on the business of barbers.

Mr. Bentley was well educated. His lingual acquirements embraced Latin, Greek, Italian, and some knowledge of the Hebrew language ; and amongst his other accomplishments he had an acquaintance with music, drawing, and painting. His bass-viol, bearing his initials, is still in existence, and for many years it was used by a subsequent owner, Mr. Henry Hudson, in the choir at the Wesleyan Chapel, Uttoxeter. It has recently been sold, and its value is estimated at £30. The early school acquisitions of Mr. Bentley were probably made at Alleyne's Grammar School ; but as he mentions the

---

* See Lyson's Derbyshire.

Rev. Mr. Malbon, vicar, as his "Macænas, teacher, and friend," which implies something more than religious teacher and literary patron, it is not improbable that he was indebted to Mr. Malbon for some of his classical knowledge.

Mr. Bentley's first literary attempt was a rhyming description on the River Dove, entitled "The River Dove, a Pastoral Lyric," a portion of which, through the entreaties of his friends, made its appearance in 1768, in a thin quarto of twenty-eight verses, occupying fourteen pages, and was "printed and published for the author by Elizabeth Stephens, at the Bible and Crown, over against Stationers' Hall, London." His collection of poems was published at the same office in a goodly octavo volume in 1774. The "River Dove" appears in it, in an extended form of seventy-four verses. Some of the other principal poems are entitled "An Essay on Painting," "The Bowling Green," "The Haymakers, a Pastoral;" a poem on "The Coming of Age of William, Duke of Devonshire," with some other miscellaneous poems and translations. Mr. Bentley had subscribers for two hundred and thirty-four copies of his collection, amongst whom were most of the nobility about the neighbourhood, and many living at a great distance from it. He also wrote a poem entitled "Napoleon," a copy of which I am unable to meet with. As well as being a moderately good poet he had a taste for antiquities and was a contributor to the "Gentleman's Magazine." One of these contributions, which describes a remarkable natural phenomenon, which was local, I transcribe. He writes:—

"Mr. Urban,—As I have been a constant friend to your Magazine ever since I was a boy, I cannot resist the inclination to send you a slight sketch of a phenomenon seen here on the 13th of April last, at ten minutes before five o'clock in the afternoon, and which lasted about fifteen minutes. There were three rainbows, or slates, appeared together; but, what was contrary to the common appearance of rainbows, which are frequently seen from the opposite horizon from the sun, they were all seen betwixt the spectators and the sun. The sky was rather cloudy, but without rain; and the place of the sun could but just be discerned. The first bow, which exhibited nearly half a circle about the sun, had all the prismatic colours extremely vivid and bright. The second bow was inverted with the back of the bow joining the first, and a portion of the large circle and the colours fainter. The moon, then about a quarter old, could just be seen. The whole made a most beautiful appearance I ever beheld, and a great number of people here saw it with myself. I am apt to think that this phenomenon was quite local, as I have not seen any mention of it.— S. BENTLEY."

Unlike many poets, Mr. Bentley was in independent circumstances. His happy abundance is alluded to in one of his poems not in the collection, but given at the end of this notice. Indeed he had a little property at Uttoxeter, and a farm at Veaveley. He bestowed the sum of £10 upon a namesake poetess at Norwich, named Elizabeth Bentley. She was self-educated and in very humble circumstances. Her second volume of poems were very favourably reviewed in the "Gentleman's Magazine" of 1822, as had been her first volume in 1790. This volume consisted of sixty-nine pages, with a portrait, and nearly 2,000 subscribers' names were secured to it, including many in this neighbourhood, its price being about 3s. 6d. The second volume of her poems, which was published in 1821, in paper boards, of 168 pages, at 6s. a volume, received 700 subscribers' names, but her kind friend, Mr. Samuel Bentley, having been long dead, no Uttoxeter names appear amongst the list of subscribers to it.

Mr. Bentley was very much respected, and was on terms of intimacy with Lord Gardner, who invariably called upon him, when professional duties allowed him to visit his native place. On one of these occasions, when Mr. Bentley was almost totally blind, Lord Gardner, on calling to see him, went the back way to his house, which he unceremoniously entered. On Mr. Bentley hearing Lord

Gardner's voice he at once recognized it, and exclaimed, "Lord Gardner, I presume." Lord Gardner's reply showed how little he esteemed mere titles of dignity for eminent services, without something more substantial, and he said, " Don't call me Lord Gardner; they have given me titles and honours, but they have not rewarded me according to my merits." Of the accuracy of the statement, I have not the least doubt, for it was related to me by the late Mrs. Baxter, who was his servant at the time, and remembered it well.

The blindness of Mr. Bentley was owing to a flash of lightning, which struck him in the face as he stood in the front room of his house, being at the time in his 75th year. Simultaneous with the flash, a large oak tree, which was standing at Dove Bank, was split to pieces. By this accident he became unable to read, and Mrs. Baxter, his servant (whose maiden name was Jones) recollected reading to him Homer, Virgil, and Don Quixote.

Mr. Bentley died in the year 1803, at the age of 81 years. His death was sudden. He was taken ill on the night of the 27th of February, and his servant sent for Dr. Madeley, physician, to see him. He got up the next morning, dressed his hair, and went about the house during the day. In the afternoon he expressed his wish for tea, which was accordingly prepared for him, and when he had taken one bite of bread and butter, he significantly shook his head, bowed forward and died. This account of his servant is corroborated by a scrap which I copied at the Salt Library. It states, " Samuel Bentley. Suddenly, as he was drinking his coffee in the evening, Mr. Samuel Bentley, of Uttoxeter, a gentleman well known by his many poetical productions."

Mr. Bentley never married; but three maiden sisters, whose names were Hannah, Elizabeth, and Sally, resided with him, and they all died in the space of the five last years of his life. He had an intelligent appearance, although afflicted with squinting; he was of low stature; he dressed in the fashion of the day— hair curled, pigtail behind, cock and pinched hat, and walked with a long

SAMUEL BENTLEY'S HOUSE.

cane staff. He left his servant, Mrs. Baxter, who lived with him the last five years of his life, and saw the death of himself and sisters, a legacy of £90. Besides her regular wages he gave her a guinea every Christmas, for her great attention to him; and the last he gave her he accompanied with the remark, "You have been an excellent servant, Elizabeth, and I hope you may never want for one,"--a hope that was more than fulfilled, for she died the owner of a freehold house and garden on Uttoxeter Heath, for which she was probably indebted to the legacy of her kind master. The remains of Mr. Bentley lie beneath a flat defaced stone on bricks, a little below the church on the right hand side or south of the walk.

The following pathetic autobiographical lines by Mr. Bentley are from the original copy in my possession. When he wrote them it will be perceived that he was blind:—

LINES

Written on my birthday, the 9th of May, 1799, when I had completed my 77th year of age.

Oh! what avails it that in early prime
    In innocence and ease I passed my hours?
My lesson o'er, all sportive was my time;
    My life seemed then bespread with blooming flowers.

Oh! what avails it when in perfect health,
    Blessed with kind relatives and friends in store?
A few paternal acres was my wealth:
    I was content—what could I wish for more?

Oh! what avails it that my mind was fraught
    With moral precepts from the sacred page;
From many authors ancient lore was taught,
    And was well read in many a Grecian sage?

Oh! what avails it, that with taste and skill,
    From ivory keys full harmony I drew;
And with melodious strains my flute could fill,
    And from the viol strings form concord new?

Oh! what avails it that I joined the dance,
    Cheered by the fiddle's animating strains;
Taught in right steps to follow and advance;
    Mixed and involved amidst the nymphs and swains?

Oh! what avails it that in light and shade
  I could expression to bright painting give;
And in good laws and attitudes displayed,
  Bid all the imaginary group to live?

Oh! what avails it, favoured by the muse,
  In flights poetic that I penned the lay?
Glee both in youth and age, formed to infuse—
  No Satire from my pen ere winged its way.

But oh! the sad reverse—one fatal day,*
  The thunder rolling with tremendous crash;
The vivid lightning winged it's rapid way,
  Blasting my eyes with instantaneous flash.

My eyesight now bids not my pen to write;
  Poring I guide irregular my pen;
Nor words to words can properly unite;
  Nor when once formed can scarce my writing ken.

Veiled almost to me's the sacred page;
  No more am charmed with the Horacian lyre;
Virgil's sweet numbers now no more engage,
  Nor lofty Homer with his muse of fire.

And now, alas! no more my flute I fill;
  Melodious strains I now must breathe no more;
My instrumental keys and viol still;
  All harmony is fled—is ever o'er.

I now no more must join in festive dance,
  Or with agility again must spring;
Nor with light steps through lengthened ranks advance;
  Nor hand conjoined with hand lead round the ring.

Nearly two years their destined course have run,
  While day by day my recreation fled;
No blue expanse gives joy, nor mid-day sun,
  Nor sparkling morn, nor glowing evening red.

My pencil now no more must lend its aid,
  The beauteous landscape glowing to display;
No more my colours mix for light and shade;
  And charms of beauty never more portray.

Not yet extinguished quite is yet my muse;
  Some small faint glimmerings with me still remain:
It cheers my mind—nor will its aid refuse—
  And is my antidote 'gainst grief and pain.

---

* August 1st, 1797.

Though now so full of heaviness my soul,
I put my trust in God—his mercy sure.
His goodness stretches forth from pole to pole,
Is ever present—ever will endure.

Bentley

ADMIRAL LORD GARDNER.

The distinguished Admiral, Lord Gardner, was born at Uttoxeter on the 12th of April, 1742, in the house in High Street, formerly called Uttoxeter House, but now "The Manor House," and till recently occupied by Dr. Taylor; but now by the Misses Hawthorn.

He was the eighth son of Lieutenant Colonel Gardner, of the 11th regiment of dragoons. Having at an early period shown a strong bias towards the naval service, he was rated, when fourteen years old, as a midshipman on board the "Medway," of sixty guns, under the immediate order of Captain Sir Peter Denis, an officer of distinguished merit. In this vessel Mr. Gardner remained two years, during which time he was present in an action, in which the "Duc D'Aquitaine," a French ship of the line, was taken. From the "Medway" he afterwards accompanied his captain, first on board the "Mamur," and afterwards into the "Dorsetshire." In the former he served under Admiral Hawke during the expedition against Rochfort; and while on board the latter, was present at the capture of "The Raisonable," on which occasion Captain Denis put in practice the plan adopted by the new school, of not firing a single ball until within a few yards of the enemy's ship. He likewise bore a share in the general engagement which took place off Bellesile, in 1769, between the British and French fleets, commanded by

Sir Edward Hawke and Marshal de Conflans. Mr. Gardner, having at this time been five years in constant service, was, at the customary examinations, appointed Lieutenant on board the "Bellona." In this station he distinguished himself at the capture of the "Courageusx," whereupon he was raised to the rank of Master and Commander, and appointed to the "Raven," of sixteen guns. After a lapse of four years he was made First in the "Preston," of fifty guns, which had been fitted out as the flag-ship of Rear-Admiral Parry, whom he accompanied to Port Royal, in Jamaica. During the whole time of his being stationed there Great Britain was at peace with all the nations of Europe; so that the only circumstance which occurred requiring notice in this sketch, was his marriage with Susannah Hyde, daughter of Francis Gale, Esq., a West India planter. This lady having brought him a numerous family, and being himself ambitious to rise in the service, he made every effort to obtain an appointment as soon as the American contest began. Accordingly he was nominated to the command of the "Maidstone" frigate, in which he sailed from the West Indies early in 1778, and in the course of that year was so fortunate as to make a rich capture on the coast of America. On the 4th of November he fell in with the "Lion," a French man-of-war, having on board fifteen hogsheads of tobacco; and after a severe action compelled her to surrender. With this prize he sailed for Antiqua, and was soon after promoted by Admiral Byron to the command of the "Sultan," of seventy-four guns. In the drawn battle which was fought some time subsequently with the French fleet under Count de'Estaing, off the Island of Grenada, Captain Gardner led the van, and greatly distinguished himself. His ship, however, suffered so much, that he was ordered to Jamaica, from whence he shortly sailed for England when the "Sultan' was discharged. He did not, however, remain long out of commission, having been appointed to the "Duke" in the course of a few months, with which ship he sailed to join the fleet in the West Indies, when under the orders of Sir George Rodney. He was fortunate

LORD GARDENER'S HOUSE.

enough to arrive in time to participate in the glorious victory of the 12th of April, 1782. On that memorable day his ship was the first to break through the enemy's line of battle, according to the new plan of attack then for the first time put in practice. At one period of this action the " Duke," in conjunction with the " Formidable " and " Mamur," had to sustain the force of eleven of the enemy's ships. Soon after this triumph the American war terminated, and peace continued for several years to shed her benignant influence over the several nations of Europe. For some time he acted as commander on the Jamaica station : and in 1790 was appointed a lord of the admiralty, when he likewise obtained a seat in Parliament. In the year 1793, having been raised to the rank of Rear-Admiral of the Blue, he hoisted his flag on board the " Queen," of ninety-eight guns, in which he sailed as Commander-in-Chief to the Leward Islands. Soon after this event, finding the disputes between the Republicans and Royalists in the Colony of Martinque to run very high, and being earnestly pressed by the latter to effect a descent on the island, Major-General Prince landed with three thousand men, but that officer judged it expedient to re-embark almost immediately, being satisfied that the Republican party was too strong to afford just hopes of success in the Royalist cause. Admiral Gardner now returned to England, and in the following year bore a part in the action of June 1st, under the gallant Earl Howe. On this occasion his conduct was conspicuous in the extreme, his ship having suffered more than any other in the fleet, with the exception of the " Brunswick." In consequence he was not only particularly thanked by the Commander-in-Chief, but was appointed Major-General of Marine, and created a Baronet of Great Britain. On the 22nd of June, 1795, Sir Allen Gardner was present at the action of the Port L'Orient, when the French fleet only saved itself from total destruction by timely flight. Two years after this event, when a dangerous mutiny had broken out at Portsmouth, he manifested a degree of firmness and resolution during that trying period worthy of his high character as a British naval officer. From this time he continued to serve in the Channel Fleet, till the close of the year 1799, when he was sent with sixteen sail of the line to reinforce the fleet off Cadiz, and in the Mediterranean. Perceiving, however, that little danger was to be apprehended in these quarters, he returned with nine sail of the line, accompanied by the envoy from Lisbon.

In 1800 he served in the Channel Fleet, but soon afterwards, being previously raised to the dignity of an Irish Peer, was appointed to succeed Admiral Kingsmill, the naval commander in Ireland. This command he continued to hold till the year 1807, when he hoisted his flag as Admiral of the Channel Fleet, which ill health, however, soon obliged him to relinquish. He died in 1810, and was buried in the Abbey Church of Bath, with the grandeur and solemnity due to his rank and merit.

Lord Gardner's political career was not distinguished by any circumstances of great moment. He sat in three successive parliaments. His first election took place in 1790, when he was returned for Plymouth. In 1796 he was colleague to Mr. Fox in the representation of Westminster. On this occasion he was opposed by Mr. John Horne Tooke, whose wit, satire, and eloquence were more alarming to the Admiral than a shower of cannon balls from the enemy's fleet. Notwithstanding, he once more offered himself for the same city, and was successful. At this time Mr. Fox, in addressing the electors, said, "A noble Admiral has been proposed to you. I certainly cannot boast of agreeing with him in political opinions; but whom could the electors pitch upon more worthy of their choice than the noble Lord—in his private character universally respected, and a man who has served his country with a zeal, a gallantry, a spirit, and a splendour, that will reflect upon him immortal honour."

MARY HOWITT.

In a copy of "My Own Story," which belonged to the late Thomas Hart, Esq., banker, of Uttoxeter, is this pleasing note in that gentleman's handwriting, occasioned by early remembrances called up by a perusal of that interesting little book—"I remember this Mary Howitt well, and think I see her now bringing home large bunches of flowers, which she was fond of gathering in the fields." Uttoxeter may be truly proud that it contains the early home of this lady, who ranks amongst the most distinguished and pleasing writers of the day. She was born early in the present century in Gloucestershire. Both her parents were descended from ancestors of honourable reputation, her father having been Samuel Botham, Esq., surveyor, and her mother of the family of Wood, the Irish patentee, about whose half-pence, minted under a contract of the Government of George II., Dean Swift raised such a disturbance with his "Draper's Letters," preventing the issue of the coinage, and saddling Mr. Wood with a loss of £600,000. Sir R. Walpole resisted all recompense for his loss, although Sir Isaac Newton, who was appointed to assay the coinage, pronounced it better than the contract required, and Mr. Wood, of course, justly entitled to remuneration. His son, Mr. Charles Wood, the grandfather of Mrs. Howitt, and who became assay master at Jamaica, was the first to introduce platina into Europe. Many of her ancestors, who were attached to the Society of Friends, have suffered for the assertion of their rights in religious matters.

Mrs. Howitt, who was brought up in the religious tenets of the Quakers, pursued her early studies under her father's roof in Balance street, in this town, in association with her eldest sister (now Mrs. Harrison), where they made proficiency in Latin, French, and Chemistry. At this period she also made stealthy draughts at those sources of literature which were looked upon as vain, and strictly forbidden by the rules of the religious society to which she belonged; and to satisfy the taste thus acquired, such books as were in the neighbourhood were laid under contribution. She was at this early period, too, an observer of nature, and an admirer of its varied beauties. Nor less so was her sister. How beautifully her love for flowers is spoken of by Mr. Hart, and I believe she has a little work in MSS. on the flora of this neighbourhood, where she delighted to botanize. She had also a love for poetry, which led her to make available for metrical illustrations such subjects as she deemed suitable; and these, which were handed about in manuscript, fell into the hands of Mr. Howitt, a young poet of kindred mind, and of the same persuasion in religion. This circumstance led to their early marriage, and in 1823 their first and joint production appeared, under the title of "The Forest Minstrel," and was warmly welcomed by the public. She continued to devote herself to literature, and in 1827 "The Desolation of Eyam," a touching subject, pathetically treated, was published, with a selection of Lyrics, also the joint production of Mr. and Mrs. Howitt. Mrs. Howitt next published "The Seven Temptations," in which she eschewed outward objects, and painted the struggle of the inner being. The three-volume novel was at that time, as it is still, in the ascendant, and she resolved in her succeeding literary effort to meet the taste of the day, and gave to the reading public, "Wood Leighton," in three volumes, which met with considerable success, and has several times been re-issued in a cheap form. This book has been much read in Uttoxeter, and there is a general impression that it is intended throughout as a description of persons, events and scenes, belonging to the neighbourhood of her early home, and altogether as real and distinct as any that are to be found in history. With respect to "Wood Leighton," and other fictitious works which this lady has written, she kindly writes, in a letter respecting them, as follows:—"Although Uttoxeter has been the groundwork of a good deal I have written, yet I have allowed myself the privilege of a writer of fiction, and not felt the necessity of adhering more closely to the details of facts than first suited my purpose. I have filled up any gap or *hiatus* according to my own fancy, and as best perfected my picture; so when strict accuracy is requisite I am not in such works wholly to be depended upon." This passage will enable many of the readers of "Wood

Leighton" to surmount some of their misapprehensions of many of the characters and localities described in the work.

In the year 1837 Mr. and Mrs. Howitt made a tour in the Scottish Highlands, where they gleaned information for subsequent literary use. During their journey they travelled over the space of more than five hundred miles. They afterwards made Esher, in Surrey, their place of abode, it being surrounded by scenery of a varied and most beautiful description. About this period Mrs. Howitt wrote a series of books for the people and their children, of which "My Own Story" is one, it being really an autobiography of her own childhood. They consist of thirteen distinct books, and it is not saying too much, that they possess a charm which can be found in no other works of a simillar kind. After their completion, Mr. and Mrs. Howitt went to Germany for the education of their children, and resided at Heidelberg for three years. From thence they visited every part of the German states, and made themselves acquainted with the literature and social life of the people.

The works of Miss Bremer having fallen into the hands of Mrs. Howitt about this time, she applied herself successfully to the acquisition of the Swedish language, to enable her to present them to English readers. The work of translation was admirably executed, and by this means the works of Miss Bremer have justly obtained a popularity co-extensive with the English language. She was equally fortunate with the Danish language, from which she translated the beautiful story of the "Improvisatore" of Hans Christian Anderson, and other fictions of less importance.

In 1847 Mrs. Howitt published a handsome edition of her ballads and other poems to which was prefixed an excellent likeness of the author. At a later period Mrs. Howitt assisted her husband in the compilation of a "History of the Literature of the North of Europe," in two volumes, including specimens in prose and verse, the latter metrically arranged. Previous to that, she, in 1844, edited the English translation by Anne Von Schoultz of Auders Fryxell's "History of Sweden." She also edited, for three years, the Drawing-room Scrap-book, and, illustrated by biographical vignettes, a series of portraits of the Queens of England. Besides having been an extensive contributor to periodical literature for upwards of twenty years, she has written "The Heir of West Wayland," "The Children's Year," "History of America," "Calendar of the Seasons," and other books, besides having translated Miss Bremer's "Letters on the Holy Land," and assisted her husband in a beautiful work on the "Abbeys and Castles of England," in which the language possesses all the freshness of these gifted writers. In 1864 Mrs. Howitt published "The Cost of Caergwyn," "the most carefully elaborated of all her prose-works of imagination."

Some of the principal works by William Howitt, who died in 1879 at Rome, at the age of 84, are "The Book of the Seasons," "Traditions of the most Ancient Times," "A popular History of Priestcraft," "Rural Life in England," "Colonization and Christianity," "Visits to Remarkable Places," "The Boy's Book of the Country," "Rural and Domestic Life in Germany," "German Experiences," "Homes and Haunts of the Poets," "The Year Book of the Country," "Popular History of England," in five large volumes, "The Mad War Planet," a poem, besides works on Australia, translations, fictitious works and contributions to Journalism. *

A daughter of Mr. and Mrs. Howitt, Miss Anne Mary Howitt, married to Mr. Watts, and deceased in 1884, has won success both as an author and artist. The "Art Student in Munich," of which a second edition appeared in or about 1880, is from the pen of this lady. She has embodied her conceptions in a pre-Raphaellite style in a painting entitled "Margaret returning from the Fountain," derived from this portion of Goethe's "Faust,"

–"Margaret having heard the harsh judgment of her companions at the city fountain, returns home tortured by

---

* Men of the Time ; *London Quarterly Review*, 1860, and *Leisure Hour*, Sept. 1877, &c.

self-accusation." A son of Mr. and Mrs. Howitt is Mr. Alfred William Howitt, who was at the head of the relief party sent out in 1861 by the Royal Society of Victoria, who discovered the remains of Burke and Wills, and also of King the sole survivor of the Australian exploring expedition. He is the author, it is supposed, of "A Boy's Adventure in Australia." Another enterprising son, Mr. Herbert Charlton Howitt, was drowned in June, 1863, on Lake Brunner, in the Western District of Canterbury, New Zealand, by the upsetting of a canoe.

The house in which Mrs. Howitt spent the early part of her life until her marriage, and of which an engraving is presented, is pleasantly situated in Balance street, its front having a south-westerly aspect. A flower garden slopes from it towards the valley, and the wooded hills and green fields beyond form a pleasant scene which is commanded by the house. A portion of the residence towards the street has undergone alterations within the last few years, and belongs now to H. Hawthorn, Esq., Surgeon. For several generations Mrs. Howitt's ancestors had property in Uttoxeter, of which this and an adjoining dwelling formed a part, together with the "Shrewsbury Arms" Inn, the cottages at the top of the Hockley, a large space of garden ground and the buildings near the Hockley Bridge, as well as land beyond. Mrs. Howitt now resides in a beautiful house, built by herself, and called Marienruhe, at the Mardine, or Meran, on the slopes of Obermae's, Switzerland, where she intends spending the remaining part of her life.

EDWARD RUDYERD.

This individual was a minister in Uttoxeter, but as I do not find his name in the church register, he must have been identified with some branch of Puritan persuasion in Uttoxeter. In 1615 he published a religious book entitled "The Thunderbolt of God's wrath against the hard-hearted and stiff-necked sinners." He was descended from an ancient Saxon family who settled at Rudyerd, temp., Canute the Dane, 1030. Of the same family was

Sir Benjamin Rudyerd, a noted wit, poet and statesman of the reign of Charles I. the friend of Lord Pembroke, Pym, and Hampden, and upon whom Ben. Johnson wrote several epigrams. John Rudyerd, the architect of the second Eddystone lighthonse in 1706, was also of the same family. *

J. TURNER, D.D.

An eminent divine named the Rev. John Turner, D.D., was born at Uttoxeter on the sixth day of November, 1660. The only person of the name in Uttoxeter at that time was a tenant under a Mr. Middleton, and he lived in one of the houses standing betwixt the Market place and the back lane, and he was no doubt the father of the divine here mentioned, who was educated at Trinity College, Cambridge, became master of a School at Blackheath, a faithful pastor at Greenwich, Canon of Lincoln, and also a Canon of the Metropolitan See of Canterbury. For piety, learning and sweetness of life he was remarkable. He died of a fever at Canterbury, on the 17th of December, 1720, aged 60 years.

CAPTAIN DANIEL ASTLE.

This person claims a brief notice as the author of a scarce little local book entitled ".A Prospect from Barrow Hill," dated Uttoxeter, June 25th, 1777, and printed by Pearson and Robinson, Birmingham. He was educated at Barton-under-Needwood. and was the son of Mr. Daniel Astle, keeper of Birkley Lodge, and brother of the learned antiquary, Thomas Astle, Esq., F.R.S., F.S.A., &c. He served in the army under General Howe, and was at the attack of the American forces at Bunker's Hill. He subsequently entered holy orders and became clergyman of Bromshall church for many years, and he resided in the

---

* History of Leek, by John Sleigh, Esq.

MARY HOWITT'S HOUSE.

house adjoining the National School and now part of the National School property. The figure of Captain Astle appears in an engraving on a previous page. He closes his book with these words: "With the woman one loves, with the friend of one's heart, and a good study of books, one might pass whole ages here and think it a day." He died in 1826, aged 83, and was buried at Uttoxeter. The library of the Rev. Daniel Astle was sold by auction, on Thursday, the 3rd of August, 1826, and following days, and the number of volumes comprised in the catalogue, a copy of which I have met with, is 911, with sundry lots not enumerated. As it might be useful and interesting to mention some of the more important works contained in the library of a local clergyman at that period, I will add the following:—"Spencer's Fairy Queen, printed by Lownds, 1611;" "Bacon's works by Mallet, four vols., folio, 1740;" "Davenant's works, folio, 1673," "Chaucer's works, folio, 1687;" "Machiavel's works, folio, 1695;" "Hooker's Ecclesiastical Polity, folio, 1682;" "Leigh's Natural History of Lancashire, Cheshire, and part of Derbyshire, with plates;" "Taylor's Great Exemplar, 1649;" "Jeremy Taylor's Sermons, 1673;" "History of Women, by Alexander;" "Rousseau's works, four vols., with plates;" "Bewick's History of Quadrupeds, with cuts;" "The works of Jonathan Swift, fourteen vols.;" "The Spectator, eight vols.;" "Bishop Burnett's History of his own times, six vols.;" "Bishop Burnett's Reformation, three vols.;" "Anacharsis's Travels, seven vols., with book of plates, *to be bought in at £2*;" "History of the Holy War, by Fuller, 1639;" "De-Saint Pierre's Studies of Nature, five vols.;" "Buffoon's Natural History, ten vols.;" "Nature Displayed, seven vols.;" "The Rambler, six vols., *for Mrs....for £1*." The Catalogue abounds in collections of Sermons; many of the works of the last century on Christian Evidence; some Miscellaneous, Historical and Political works, and works on natural and metaphysical and moral science; not many Biblical works, and is very poor (for a scholar's library) in classical works, some three or four being all. One of these I possess, it being the fine tragedies of Æschylus in two volumes, translated by Dr. Potter.

JAMES BLADON.

The late Mr. James Bladon, of Albion House, Pontypool, Wales, was a native of Uttoxeter, and one of the family of Bladon of this town. The acknowledged founder of the family was Thomas Bladon, of Bear Hill, who died in 1819, and Thomas Bladon, son of the above, and who died in 1841, was uncle of the subject of this notice. The mother of Mr. Bladon died in 1811, and in 1813 his father removed to Ashbourne. Previous to, or about that date, Mr. Bladon acquired a taste for artistic pursuits as well as for science and literature in general, and in practical geometry, mensuration and dialling. His attention was subsequently directed more especially to natural history. In 1821, Mr. Bladon was living in Birmingham, from which place he removed to Pontypool, where he married in 1825. Being successful in business and having no family he retired from his trade in 1847 and undertook the parochial offices of collector of taxes and poors rate amounting together to about £13,000 per annum.

In the course of his literary and scientific studies he has contributed to the Entomological Magazine, Charlesworth's Natural History Magazine, Newman's Entomologist and Zoologist, the Phytologist (both series), the Athenæum, Notes and Queries, and some other journals. He was a member of the Wernerian Club which was established for the purpose of editing and republishing old standard works on natural history, and as such he was the joint editor of an edition of "Ray's Wisdom of God in Creation," the notes to which he contributed were intended to disprove the doctrine of Spontaneous Generation. He was also a member of the Entomological Society of London, and of the Botanical Society, and in 1837 he published in the Entomological Magazine an article in opposition to the views upon spontaneous generation as put forth by the celebrated Burmeister of Berlin, and which was republished by Erichson in his "Bericht," Berlin, in 1838, and by Wregmann in his "Archives," in 1839, which gave him a wide notoriety in Germany. Mr. Bladon pursued the same subject in the Magazine of Natural History in 1840, against another German doctor, Wiessemborn. The opinions of the continental naturalists thus combated by Mr. Bladon were the forerunners of those of the Darwinians, which are a mere resuscitation of the theories of Lamark.

Mr. Bladon had the good fortune of having a wife who could appreciate literary and scientific pursuits in common with himself. It was chiefly owing to her treasured store of traditionary lore that Mr. Bladon was enabled to contribute an extensive series of papers on the "History of Pontypool, Past and Present," to the Pontypool *Free Press*.

Mr. Bladon, with his wife, in 1836, planned an exploratory tour in the interior of South America, but the consideration of the health of Mrs. Bladon made it necessary that the project should be abandoned.

Mr. Bladon accumulated a library of 7,000 vols., which he informed me he intended should, after his death, be presented to Pontypool. He had previously presented 1,000 vols. to the library and reading-room at the Town Hall of that place.

Mr. Bladon, it is believed, had an extensive knowledge of history, and was a good linguist. He died in 1874, and was interred at Pontypool.

ARTISTS.

John and William Sparks, engravers, were born in Uttoxeter, and the family lived in a house in Balance Street. John enlisted in the army, and was sent with a regiment to Van Dieman's Land, for the purpose of guarding convicts. Whilst in that settlement he made numerous sketches of some of its most attractive scenery, and these, after his return to England, he engraved and sold to a manufacturer at Hanley, to be transferred to porcelain. He resided at Hanley at the time. His brother William was also an engraver, and lived in London, and was contemporary with Greatbach and Robinson, the former of whom engraved the "Wellington Banquet." Mr. Outram, an eminent engraver, lived many years in Uttoxeter, where he engraved several valuable pictures on steel, one of which belonged to the late Prince Albert. The Rev. — Phillips, formerly a clergyman at Longford, near Derby, was an artist during the early part of his life, and was sent for from London to Derby to paint on china. He married a wealthy lady, who induced him to enter Holy Orders. Late in life he purchased a property at Roper's Hill, near Uttoxeter, where he died. The farm was left to a son, who, although a steady man, got through it, and lived many years in Uttoxeter as a labouring man in great indigence. As showing his singular character, he took his father's books in a wheelbarrow to Lichfield and Birmingham, at several lots, for sale, from Roper's Hill, and he has several times fetched wheelbarrow loads of coal from Cheadle to Uttoxeter, a distance of ten miles, for disposal, both of which are feats having, perhaps, no equal.

Another artist of the neighbourhood remains to be mentioned, although he was neither born nor lived in Uttoxeter. The individual now referred to was John Lownds, engraver, of Withington. He was born at this village in 1790, and learnt the art of engraving in London. After completing his knowledge of business he returned home, where he executed work sent down to him from London, I believe, by Ackerman. I have not been able to obtain very particular information about him, or the work which he executed, but I have seen copies of small landscapes and emblematic devices which he engraved on copper, and also copies of portraits of Earl Camden, Cardinal Wolsey, Lord Hutchenson, and of Locke, which he engraved on copper, and the engraved plate of Locke and another engraved plate by him are in my possession. I am of opinion that these, with probably other portraits, were executed by him for an illustrated edition of Hume's

History of England. Judging from his work he appears to have been a good artist in his style—that of stencilling. The house in which he was born and in which he engraved, may be recognised by its half-timbered character, with a garden in front and with yew trees about, on the right hand on passing through Withington to Leigh. Through too close application to his pursuits he died at the age of 28 years, in 1818, and was buried in Leigh Churchyard.

CHAPTER VII.

THE EXTENT OF UTTOXETER;
ITS PRIMITIVE APPEARANCE; NOTED
BUILDINGS OF ANTIQUITY; COURT HOUSE
AND COURT LEET; FIRES WHICH HAVE
HAPPENED; POPULATION OF UTTOXETER;
INSTANCES OF LONGEVITY, &c.

EXTENT OF UTTOXETER.

Uttoxeter differs very little in extent at the present time from what it was in 1658. Leaving out the Heath and Balance Hill, the opinion may be ventured that there were as many houses in Uttoxeter at that period as there are now, even if we reckon in the new ones which have been recently built along the east side of Dove Bank and in the direction of the Wharf, or, as it is newly called, Park Place. On the Heath there were but ten cottages, and they were probably by the side of the turnpike road, on the left hand in going out of the town north, the rest being an open common, or heath, of about sixty-four acres and thirty-five perches. The Heath is now the size of a large village, and within the last few years (this 1881) some of the best houses it comprises have been erected. On Balance Hill there were eight cottages in 1658, but there are now about thirty-four, counting from those adjoining the railway crossing. Through the middle of the churchyard there was a row of houses, and one house at the church gates was called a cell.

Uttoxeter is remembered to have had a very quaint and antique appearance. Until almost within memory a great proportion of the houses were of the frame-timber class, with the spaces filled in with watlings of wood, covered with tempered clay having over it an outer coating of plaster or slap-dash. The chimnies were almost constructed in a similar manner. In many instances the gable ends came to the street ; and it is also remembered, that many of the houses had porches to them. The only one remaining till recently was that of the White Bear Inn, in Carter Street, which is here engraved. It will be perceived that there is a flight of steps against the house, as there also used to be at the door of the Bell Inn, High Street, intended probably as horse blocks for convenience when farmers' wives rode behind their husbands on a pannel to market. It is also remarkable that at the west end of Carter Street several houses came out to about the middle of the street. It is not less noticeable that when the roof of an old house in Carter Street, exactly opposite the one in which I reside, was taken off, so that a frame-timbered wall might be replaced by a brick one, it was found to have been originally thatched with ling.

Modern requirements, however, have rendered it necessary that many antique houses in, and much of the primitive appearance of Uttoxeter, should undergo a change and be swept away. A very picturesque frame-timbered place stood at the beginning of this century where the Town Hall is, and one part formed the ale stores of Messrs. Earp and Sanders (now the old Uttoxeter Brewery Company), prior to a large house and cheese warehouse being erected on its site. I recollect a fine old house of the same class standing nearly forty years ago at Dove Bank, the black wood work contrasting so with the whitewashed parts and rendering it so conspicuous and noticeable. It was taken down to make way for the residence originally erected by Mr. Bedson, solicitor. It will be well, however, to point out such portions of similar architecture as remain, and in the course of this chapter some relics of the kind will be found mentioned of much interest, and to require rather lengthy descriptions. The house and shop of Messrs. Johnson and Wolrich, chemists, High Street, is a capital half-timbered building, covered with stucco. At the junction of Stone road with Carter Street a number of cottages of the frame-timbered description, but evidently of two periods, remain entire.

The house in which I live in the same street is of the same class, built evidently early in the seventeenth century of timber from a vastly earlier destroyed timber residence. Portions of the Old Talbot Inn, in the Market Place, in the same style, are of great antiquity and interest. The end along the side of the yard appears to remain as it was built, and at the angle a fine corbel in oak continues perfect—or what may be called a bracket and pillar combined—and its style indicates it to be probably of the fourteenth century. The late Post Office and adjoining house in High Street, with street gables, are in oak, and the Buffalo's Head and the house of Mr. Bamford in the Market Place, were of the same material, but in corbel, and of the fourteenth century. The Cross Keys, in High Street, is an earlier building in brick than might be supposed, it being of the seventeenth century. On the string-course in stone the date of its erection and the name of the builder are carved as follows:—" 1697, Edward Hadley, builder." An interesting article in copper, about the width of a shilling and in thickness about a quarter of an inch, was found some years ago, in the course of some alterations, underneath this inn, it being engraved on one side

WHITE BEAR INN.

and probably a seal. On the left side of the motto is a cross *formé*, the builder's mark, and the remaining surrounding space is occupied by six astragals. There cannot be any doubt of the mark and motto being those of Mr. Hadley, the initial in the centre having been cut as the initial of his surname. The vicarage house, which is in brick, appears to be of the early part of the seventeenth century, and is very curious in having a funnel-shaped roof. One extraordinary interior feature of many old half-timbered houses is the space occupied by the chimnies projecting into the rooms. In the case of the house I have occupied over thirty years, the lower part of the chimney starts with a width of more than nine feet by three feet six inches which only rapidly diminishes towards the top of the room above.

It is possible to point out several places of public interest of antiquity, although some of them have undergone great alterations. The ancient Chief or Manor House has continued almost intact nearly three hundred years, except that the wooden frame-work has been covered with *slap-dash*. This, however, was removed in 1881 to be renewed, when I was enabled to represent the wood-work in a sketch of the house as shown on page 297. It stands in Carter Street a little west of the Congregational Chapel. It has two gables towards the street and one looking west, and a number of very old half-timbered houses till within the last thirty years extended from it by the front of the White Hart Hotel to opposite my house. The building of the ancient Court House is only partially in existence, a portion having been converted into houses and shops, and the rest part having been entirely rebuilt. Mr. Parker, clothier, is the owner of some of this property, and in 1869 Mr. Phillips, painter, took the remainder down, and on the site built himself a new house and shop. This interesting place adjoins the Old Talbot, in the Market Place. It is traditionally said to have been the building where the soldiers, who had the defence of Uttoxeter during the civil war, had their rendezvous and depôt of ammunition and arms. The Court Leet of

Uttoxeter was held there; and it appears that the common oven, in which the inhabitants of the town by feudal prescription in the ancient charters of the lords of the manor baked their bread, was in connection with the manor court, and in, or perhaps previous rather to, 1658, it was held by Laurance Bradshaw, and the following is a description of it in Lightfoot's Survey:—"The furnace, or common bakehouse, with the highest room over it (the middle room being reserved to the use of the town for a Common Hall), and the bakehouse connected to a dwelling-house, with a shop and cellar, at the rent of XI. IJ. yearly." This cellar is probably the underground kitchen of a baker's shop. Another entry relating to the same interesting place refers doubtless to an earlier date still:— "Walter Mynors, Esq., houldeth the furnace and common bakehouse with the chamber over it at the rent of XI. VJ."

The Court Leet, just mentioned, is of very great antiquity, and has the same meaning as "View of Frankpledge," which was granted by Earl Ferrars to Uttoxeter in the thirteenth century, although it is probable this was only a confirmation of a right then already existing. The word "leet" is derived from the Anglo-Saxon *lathian* or *gelathian*, to assemble, both *lath* and *leet* indicating, under different modifications, a district in which the free male resiants (residents), or indwellers, assembled at stated times, as well for preparation for military defence, as for purposes of police and criminal jurisdiction. The borrow-holders, or borhes-alder, or seniors of the pledges, who were responsible for the good conduct of each of their co-pledges, who appear to have had authority analogous to that still exercised by the resiants, for the preservation of the peace, are thus mentioned in "Lightfoot's Survey," "The Thirdborrow Fine or Frith-Silver paid at the leet by two borrowholders chosen by jury, being yearly XVIJS."

Behind the Common Hall and Town Oven there was a building in which the malt mill for the town then was; and till recently there were some outer places there which were, judging from the appearance they had, portions of malthouses. There are also or were two small mill gritstones

MANOR HOUSE.

in existence in a farm yard on the High Wood, which were said to have belonged to a mill situated at the same place, and in the Black Swan yard, close to, a small millstone forms the door flag of a cottage.

Another interesting place was "Mr. Wood's Hall," which was "swept for King Charles when at Uttoxeter, in 1642," not any portion of which, however, is in existence. Its site is at the highest part of the field at Dove Bank nearly opposite to the house of the principal of Alleyne's Grammar School, and new houses have been built recently upon the site. The interest attaching to it is increased by the fact of its having been the ancient residence in Uttoxeter of the family of Mynors, and it is, no doubt, the same as that referred to by Erdeswick in his Survey of Staffordshire, in these words:—"In Uttoxeter is a house of the Mynors'; very ancient gentlemen are they," and not Hollingbury Hall, as has been supposed. The antique residence was sold in the seventeenth century, as will be more particularly noticed hereafter, to Mr. James Wood, son of a citizen and salter of London, one of the last of whom in Uttoxeter was a solicitor. It was a half-timbered building of very great antiquity, and of considerable dimensions, and contained altogether about forty rooms, some very lofty and spacious and one a large gallery. There were two gables towards the street, with a wide retiring space betwixt them having it is said an embattled parapet; and there was a coach yard in front. It was several stories high, and the roofs had numerous dormer windows along their sides, the roof of the central part being, it is stated, flat. It contained secret hiding places at a chimney back and elsewhere, the deception being aided by the rooms being wainscoated with oak; and it is traditionally stated that King Charles was on one occasion hid in one of these places, but whether it was when the Hall was swept for his reception or some other time when he was at Uttoxeter the tradition does not say. The residence has many strange stories associated with it; but of curious things of this nature it will be sufficient to preserve some amatory lines remembered to have been inscribed upon one of the old green glass windows, and an account kindly communicated to me by Mrs. Harrison, sister of Mrs. Howitt. The lines seem to imply that the young lady, possibly a daughter of Mr. Wood who purchased the Hall, was in deep distress on account of the indifference and absence of her neglectful swain, and her pathetic and imploring strains shall be preserved :—

"I bleeding at your feet do lie,
Unless you yield ; or else I die,
Harmless Anne Wood.
Soul and body murdered here,
I shall never rest till I see my dear."

The lady whom I have named and who well knew the old hall kindly writes :—"Some time about the years 1816-7 after the Copestakes had left the Old Hall, it was occupied by a Mrs. Parker, an excellent and accomplished lady, as a boarding school. She was an officer's widow with two young daughters. She frequently visited at my father's, and for some time my sister and myself were her pupils, but not while she resided at the Old Hall. We both retain a grateful remembrance of her wise and intelligent instruction and influence. Once I remember she spoke of her life in this interesting and antique house which left on my mind a mysterious awe, 'that said as plainly as a whisper in the ear that the place is haunted.'" Mrs. Parker told of strange sounds like sighs and troubled breathings ; said footsteps were heard pacing the gallery or landings and staircases, when no form could be seen, though diligent search was made ; at length the fears of her daughters and the pupils became so great, she was compelled to leave and remove to Doveridge. This good woman, in addition to untiring industry as a teacher of youth, wrote for them several stories full of moral truths. The title of one I remember was the "Midsummer Recess." I have received similar and even more extraordinary accounts from others who lived in the Hall.

A notion of the most improbable circumstance was also in existence and widely credited, that a secret subterranean passage connected this ancient residence with Tutbury Castle.

We will leave this old hall for a while, and follow the ancient Survey of Uttoxeter by Lightfoot a little way outside the town to Dove Bridge where he informs us there was formerly an hermitage. A little consideration, however, will lead to the conclusion that so conspicuous and public a situation could not have been one to tempt the attention and inclinations of secluded religionists, whose "business is prayer and pleasure praise," and it rather insinuates that the hermitage, in this case, was the roadside cell of the turnpike keepers, who, instead of having been retired and reserved, had a good share of assurance and sauciness, and were intent on levying tolls. *

Considering the character of the houses in Uttoxeter in past times, it is not surprising that at different periods fires of an alarming description have happened to some of them; but it is far more surprising, for the same reason, that more have not taken place. One of the most destructive fires in Uttoxeter took place in the sixteenth century, and Erdeswick mentions it in his "Survey" rather pathetically, saying, "That it (Uttoxeter) was reasonably well built, but pity it hath suffered of late great losses by fire." In the Church Register is also preserved an interesting note relating, no doubt, to the same fire:—" The towne was burnte the xxist, of Auguste ano domini, 1596. The vicarage house was burnte then, and almost all his goods, to his greate hurte .. years paste." There was considerable sympathy with the town in this great calamity, which is evidenced by the following borough document, the original of which is preserved at Newcastle :—

Fire at Uttoxeter.

1 Dec., 1599, 41st, Elizabeth. Uttoxeter.

At a meeting of the Corporation, present John Smith, mayor of Newcastle-under-Lyme, INTER ALIA.

It is also agreed by ye assembly aforesaid that there shall be given to ye use of ye towne of Uttoxeter being decayed by fire for a gratitude and towards ye speedy-

---

* Such is the opinion of the *Athenæum*, July 9th, 1859, in a Review of the "Hamlet of Knight's Bridge."

fiing of the same' towne ye sum of £X.
And in the margin :—Given to Uttoxeter £X.

R.F.

The name of the minister was apparently William Barns, for that name as minister of the parish, with the names of his children, appear on the same cover of the register as the entry about the fire. The register is of vellum or parchment, and is very much burnt, an injury it most probably received at the same time. Another serious fire broke out in 1672, in the rear of a Mr. Cludd's house, * and it did not stop till it had extended over most of the lower part of the town. The entry giving this piece of disastrous information is this :—" 1672, July 30th, a great fire happened on the back side of the house of Richard Cludd which consumed most of the lower part of the town." According to Mr. Lightfoot's Survey, which was taken previously, Mr. Cludd resided in a house about where the Black Swan Inn is, so that it extended from this public house to the lower corner of the Sheep Market and along Balance street, which agrees with the account of its consuming the "lower part of the town." Whether from wilfulness or carelessness over the origin of the fire, or some dispute amongst the owners of so much destroyed property, does not transpire, but Sir Edward Bagot and Mr. Kynnersley came to Uttoxeter about it, at a cost to the constables of 15s., and Mr. Edge (the Rev. Mr. Edge) and Mr. Chamberlain were sent to Stafford to the judge with a petition respecting the unfortunate occurrence at a cost to the parish of 12s. 6d. The fire spared the tall half-timbered house standing in the Sheep Market adjoining the Black Swan yard, for it is a building of an earlier date than the origin of the fire, although it cannot now be recognised in its primitive condition, owing to its owner, Mr. Harvey, greengrocer, having hid its antique features by caseing over the whole front, including the dormer windows, with a thick wall. Whether this Mr. Cludd was a relative of Edward Cludd, a remarkable man of the

---

* Constables' accounts at the time.

same period, of Norwood Park, near Southwell, who gave the name to Cludd's Oak, and with his servant, "ruled all Nottinghamshire," I am unable to say. But Edward Cludd was decended from a family of that name in Shropshire. Since the fire occurred several others have happened. One about sixty years (this 1881) ago broke out in Tinker's lane, and burnt down two houses. Mr. Bewley's Iron Foundry (now malthouses belonging to Mr. Stretch at Brook Furlong) has, except the brick walls, been burnt twice. In the old houses which stood opposite to the White Hart Hotel, when taken down in 1860, it was found that some of the beams were half burnt through; and such was also found to be the case at the White Bear Inn, in Carter street, when improvements were being effected in the house in the following year.

In passing on with this narrative of events and things, it cannot be deemed inappropriate to give a glance at the public houses in Uttoxeter, which, as elsewhere, have not only been places of great public convenience, and resorts for social intercourse, but in some instances, of considerable interest in other respects. The number of Inns in the town two hundred and fifty years back was not so great; indeed there were few, comparatively, to those in existence at this day. There was the "Crown" at the north side of the Market Place, belonging to the heirs of Townsend, and in the tenure of Mary Moreton, widow of Henry Moreton; the "Old Crown" at the corner of the Sheep Market, which consisted of two burgages and-a-half at IJs. VId., and being now Mr. Bamford's house and two others, all of which belonged to Mrs. Sneyed, and previously to John Archbald, gent, (whose curious memorial is in Uttoxeter Church) and in the occupation of John Startin; the "Old Swan," where the premises of Mr. Atkin, butcher, are in the Market Place; the "Cock," which was in existence until a few years ago, it was absorbed into the Uttoxeter Old Brewery premises, after a duration of perhaps nearly three hundred years, as appears from documentary evidence, and it belonged to and was held by Thomas Gilbert; the "Greyhound," where the shop of Mr. Dams, jeweller, is at "Bell's Corner," which has also been remembered to have been in existence, and belonged to Thomas Kynnersley, Esq., and was in the tenure of widow Goodwin; and the "White Hart," which was at the corner of Carter Street and the Market Place. The "Old Swan" here mentioned, which was the crest of the Stafford family and to which the existence of many Swan Inns in Staffordshire is due, existed in the time of Queen Elizabeth, and an interesting character named Edward Toyke, who figures as a correspondent of Mary Queen of Scotland, stayed at it one night. He applied to the Queen by letter for one hundred ducats, on the ground that his father had some acquaintance with her—it is supposed through a negotiation for a marriage with her of Robert, Earl of Leicester. The letter fell into the hands of Sir Ralph Saddler, who suspected some secret matter lurked underneath it, and examined him to see if it was so. In his examination he mentions having slept at the "Old Swan," in Uttoxeter. It proceeds thus—"Firste, this examinate saithe that he came from the Forest of Fechan, and lay with one Shrewe there half a year, a tenant of his father's, and from thence he came to Wedsberie, Tewesday, where he lay all nighte at an alehouse not knowing his host's name. Wednesday he came to Uttoxeter, and there he lay all nighte at the sign of the Swanne. Thursday he came to Ashbourne," &c., &c. Signed, E. Tokey. * An interesting portion of the "Old Crown Inn" underwent alteration in 1867, and I was fortunate in being just in time, before it disappeared, in making a sketch of it, and the information I had previously gathered about it enabled me to pen the following account:—Time sweeps away the vestiges of former things, and therefore many objects, rendered interesting by old associations, disappear to make way for real or fancied improvements, themselves again being liable to give place in future generations to the dictates of convenience or the caprice of others. The latest destruction of the frontal appearance of old build-

---

* Notes and Queries, September, 1862.

ings in Uttoxeter has been that of the quaint old hostelry in the Sheep Market, known as the "Buffalo's Head Inn." This old inn really used to be a part of the primitive and venerable "Old Crown Inn," where Uttoxetertonians did their quaffing nearly three hundred years ago; indeed it had attained the distinction of being called the "Old Crown Inn" about two hundred and fifty years ago, when it was of decidedly larger dimensions than it now is, comprising, besides the present tenement, another burgagee tenement and a half more. How the sign has undergone the change from the "Old Crown" to the "Buffalo's Head" will be interesting to any deeply acquainted with the lore involved in the history of sign boards. There is reason to believe that the alteration took place owing to political partizanship in the town. The late Mr. Francis Cope, who was a man of much observation and reading, had a nearly four score years' knowledge of the place, and he gave me these memorials of the spot:—
"The inn was of very large size (which agrees with the account that it once consisted of several burgagee tenements), that the back premises were entered by two gateways, and that it extended to the very corner of the Sheep Market. Not only had the Crown been changed to the Buffalo's Head, in derision of the Hanoverian succession, and that afterwards, to make it less libellous, the head, typical of the German race, was placed in the golden circlet holding the Prince of Wales' plume, but it had connected with it the sign of the 'Old Star,' in reference to the old Stuart line, and in opposition to another inn at the other side of the Market Place named the 'New Star,' erected by the friends of the Hanoverian succession." Time has wiped the political feelings away, giving evidence formerly to these political public-house badges; and their interest having passed out of mind, the crown has been omitted by modern sign painters, and nothing but the bull's head has been retained.

This large building, now in three houses, proved itself, when being altered in 1869, to be of no little architectural interest. The central portion had probably been a hall, and most likely the entrance hall of the inn. A fine oaken Gothic arch with a boss at the point intended for the ash leaf ornament, and standing in the centre of a built up wall adjoining the Buffalo's Head Inn, where it still remains, was discovered, the whole of it being quite perfect from the ground. This was probably one of three arches supporting an open-timbered roof, its height being twenty-two feet. Part of a massive upright piece of oak, which I considered the lower part of an arch, or support from which it sprung, had a moulding up the centre of it three inches in thickness, or projecting from the main piece three inches. That there was a hall here, is also clear by window frames and forms of doorways with marks of the ends of two flights of stairs. At the corner of the house occupied by Mr. Bamford, formerly a part of the Old Crown, and just opposite, or nearly so to the Black Swan yard, a clustered pillar was found having two brackets springing from it, two sides of one being ornamented with Gothic paneling. A series of brackets supporting the corbel table which has a richly moulded cornice, was found to extend along the whole end of the house. Brackets with a similar cornice ran along the front of the building as may now be perceived at the side of the entry or passage against the Buffalo Inn. The boss representing the Vine, including leaves and fruit, at the point of a rather depressed arch which was found prostrate over the cellar, indicates perhaps sufficiently that this range of building was first erected for an inn, and as all the architectural features mentioned—the bosses and arches, the corbel work, and clustered pillar, and ornamental paneling are of the perpendicular or Tudor period, the first existence of the Old Crown hostelry may be referred back upwards of 500 years.

Some interest attaches to the building which was known as the Crown at the north side of the Market Place, and now occupied by Mr. French, grocer, and from what has been stated it would appear to have been an influential inn. The back of this building remains as it used to be, and retains its wooden framework.

BUFFALO'S HEAD.

More recent inns, although they were before my recollection, have been known as "The Tanner of Joppa," where the Albion, or Green Man now is; the sign of "The Three Dancing Ducks," where the "New Era" office is; "The Barley Mow," known also as the "Sot's Hole," in Spiceal Street; "The Split Raisin," on Balance Hill; "The White Swan," below the Black Swan, one formerly at the corner of Pinfold Street, the Oddfellow's Arms, and another in Carter Street; the Bowling Green, and another on the Heath.

Seeing that the extent of Uttoxeter, except on the Heath and Balance Hill, has not materially altered during the space of nearly two hundred and fifty years, it would be interesting to ascertain, if possible, the relative amount of population therein at that and the present time, and this, I think, it is possible pretty accurately to do. In 1662, six hundred and twenty two, if not five more fire hearths were made in Uttoxeter, * or a tax under that name was levied, upon that number of houses or families. Now the population of Ireland† has been attempted to be ascertained by multiplying the number of houses by $5\frac{1}{2}$. The same rule may just as appropriately be applied for arriving at the extent of population in Uttoxeter at the period mentioned, especially as it is adopted by government for such purposes, and found to give as correct results as can by any other means, short of actually taking the census of each house, be obtained. Multiplying, then, 627, the number of firehearths in Uttoxeter levied in 1662 by $5\frac{1}{2}$, we find as a total of inhabitants in Uttoxeter at that time about 3,348 persons of all classes, and this gives an excess over the population in 1801, when it was 2,779 only, of 669 inhabitants. That this is as correct a mode of obtaining the sum of the population, indiscrimatively, as can be adopted, viz., by multiplying a given number of houses or families by $5\frac{1}{2}$, is proveable by applying it to the census returns for Uttoxeter in 1811, the number of houses being 605, and the population 3,155. It will be seen to

---

* Constables' Accounts.

† "*Illustrated London News*," Sept. 1861.

give an excess over the exact population of 272, whilst multiplying by five only would give a deficiency of 130. But if, in reality—which is probably not the case, as an allowance must be made for circumstances varying with places—the population of any one locality bears with another, as a general rule, a relative proportion to the number of houses. According to this principle, then, it is demonstrable to the value of a fraction, that the proper multiplier is $5\frac{1}{4}$, and applied to the return of houses in Uttoxeter in 1811, gives the total population of the town within seven persons.

The population in 1831 was 4,864. In 1851 it was 4,990, and when the census was taken in 1861, the number of inhabitants, as given by the local register at the time, was 4,810, of whom 2,324 were males, and 2,486 females. The result shows a decrease since 1850 to the extent of 180 persons; but on the whole two hundred years, an increase of 1,372. But by what law a decrease of the population in the space of one hundred and fifty years, or thereabouts, has taken place to the extent of 357 persons, which was the case in 1801, and then have gone on in an opposite direction till a surplus is attained of 1,372 persons in, at that time, so settled a place as Uttoxeter, it is perhaps impossible to say. The decrease during the last eleven years may, however, be attempted to be accounted for, although, from there having been an accession of new houses, the fact may appear somewhat puzzling. In 1850 many navvies who were employed on the Churnet Valley Line and in making a branch to the cheese warehouse at the Wharf, but which has been taken up again, were in lodgings in Uttoxeter, which was not the case in 1861, a little before which date, as I remember with sorrow, many children were carried off by diphtheria; and then during the ten years many persons, not finding employment in Uttoxeter, left their native place to enlist their energies in more promising hives of industry—places which have been found to have swelled by such accretions during the same space of time to an enormous extent. It might even be added that the great improvements in the town, extending to localities which at one time were deemed almost repulsive, have excluded a great number to whom anything like respectability, decency, and daylight do not promise favourably for their avocations. The population in 1871 was 4,692, and in 1881 as much as 4,981, which shows an increase in the population of the parish of 289. This unusual increase in ten years may, to a great extent, be accounted for on three grounds. In that period there has been a material progress in several lines of business in the town, and it has attracted many respectable people to it on account of its general healthiness; and then, I believe, the death rate has not on the whole been nearly so high. Also at the time the census was taken a large body of navvies and other workmen were employed in making the new line and all other works for the new railway junction.

Although diphtheria is mentioned as having visited Uttoxeter in common with other places, yet the town appears to have had an immunity from most other epidemics, which, when they happen any where, often decimate the population. Indeed, as has been noticed, Uttoxeter is noted for its salubrity. When in August and September of 1646 the plague was blighting to an alarming extent several towns about—as Lichfield, Stafford, and Ashbourne, as well as the adjoining place, Clifton— Uttoxeter appears to have escaped; and, although so much oppressed by the exactions occasioned by the Civil Wars, was in a position to afford relief in sums of money to each place. To Ashbourne it sent a contribution of £3, to Clifton 5s., to Lichfield and Stafford £2 9s., being a part of £300 for those infected places, and £2 to Stafford again, all collected in the town with the exception of 6s. 8d. given from the parish rates.

It is asserted, however, in a Staffordshire Directory, that the plague did visit the town; but there is nothing in the constable's accounts to bear it out. A stray soldier or two pestered with it got into the town, and it must have been respecting them that warrants were taken out. That it was confined to these men is the more probable from the determination to isolate them from the inhabitants, by placing them in cabins which were erected for the purpose, at doubtless, outside the town. The entries are 1646, June 1, " For three warrants concerning the plague 7s."

" To soldiers pestered with the plague 2s."

" To carpenters who builded a cabin 8s."

All this precaution proves how great an alarm was produced from its dreadful nature; but as there is no further mention of it it is almost certain that the inhabitants happily escaped. But during the time of the plague, which carried off from the end of 1664, to December, 1665, one-sixth of the population of London, and in the summer months five-sixth of the inhabitants of Eyam in Derbyshire, there would be a general alarm throughout the kingdom. From its extremely fearful character it can scarcely be considered astonishing if inscriptions relating to or occasioned by the plague are found even in Uttoxeter. The following inscription must have been caused in consequence of this horrid and desolating visitation:— "Daniel Spakeman, 1666, Sampson Allkin, mors mihi lucrum" (for me to die is gain). The inscription was written on a pane of glass in the house of the late Mr. Woolrich, chemist, High Street, and the pane is still preserved by Messrs. Johnson and Woolrich, his successors. There is a date with initials inlaid in a small door in a wall cupboard of the house in which I reside which also must be commemorative of the plague. They are P., 1664, W. E. The P. was, I am inclined to believe, intended to be the initial letter for plague, followed by the date of its earlier visitation, and the initials of William Heaton or Eaton, the then owner of the house. The inscription is accompanied with *fleur de lis*. Indeed the fear of the plague extended far and wide, and it was regarded for generations after, even to the time of my youth, as one of the worst judgments or punishments that could be inflicted, and hence people frequently, under provocation, exclaimed "the plague tack thee," as has been said to me, when a lad, many a time.

Uttoxeter certainly did not escape the fever of 1868, when it was so general throughout all the towns and villages in the kingdom. Still it was principally limited to certain localities in the town. Tinker's Lane suffered severely from it, and Bradley Street almost equally so. It visited every house in Tinker's Lane except two or three, and the number of deaths resulting from it in the lane was five, and the number of persons having it there at one time was twenty-eight. It made similar visitations in 1858 and also in 1861. The lane was in a bad sanitary condition, and the alarm produced in 1868 caused a culvert to be constructed up the lane, and a large one from the lane end to the Hockley to carry away the noxious accumulations which had previously no outlet. The result is that the lane is now in a good sanitary state. The following record of five deaths in a family at Spath, in the parish, of fever, of father and children, is almost as appalling as any similar occurrence during the plague. The newspaper entry is January 15th, 1879:—"On the 13th instant, at Spath Farm, Uttoxeter, Mr. James Ash Pace, aged 43 years.—On the same day, Charles Earnest, son of the above, aged 1 year and 5 months.—On the 7th instant, Annie Augusta, daughter of the above, aged 2 years and 8 months.—On the 27th ultimo, Emily Amelia Rebecca, daughter of the above, aged 3 years and 7 months.—On the 29th November, James Frederick Joseph, son of the above, aged 7 years and 11 months."

But on the whole Uttoxeter is a healthy town, in consequence of which it has obtained a distinction for the great age many of its inhabitants have attained. Dr. Symon Degge, son of Sir Symon, was the first person to record this circumstance specially in a letter preserved in Sir Symon Degge's copy of Dr. Plott's "Natural History of Staffordshire," at Cambridge. The letter is dated August 27th, 1726, and he says, "In the three weeks I have been at Uttoxeter there have been buried four men and two women, one woman aged ninety-four and the other eighty-three; one man eighty-one, and another eighty-seven, another eighty-two, and one young man sixty-

T

eight. Yesterday I talked with a man of ninety who has all his senses, and walks without a staff. About a month since he had a fever; he was speechless two days. His daughter is sixty, and about six months since he buried his wife, who had lived sixty-three years with him, and was aged eighty-five years. In this town are now three men and their wives, who have had fifty-three children, and each hath their children alive. They are all young men, the oldest being above sixty-... I will only tell you that in 1702 there died three women, their years as follows:—one hundred and three; second, one hundred and twenty-six; and the third eighty-seven." John Archbald, gent., died at the age of one hundred and three in 1619, as already seen by his epitaph. Sir Symon Degge himself was a remarkable instance of longevity, he having lived to the age of ninety-two years. With respect to his family on the subject of long life, he states in a note to his copy of Plott, page 313, sec. 8—"I had seven brothers and sisters, besides myself, all living together not long since, and the youngest sixty years of age." *

Similar observations might have applied to inhabitants of Uttoxeter many times since, and the following instances, of a recent date, have an interest not much less. Mary Blood, a native of Spath, and said to have been the last person baptized at Crakemarsh Church, died a few years since at Uttoxeter, at the age of one hundred and six. In 1814 Samuel Bell died at the age of eighty-six; John Hill at the age of ninety and Catherine his wife, in the same month, in her eighty-sixth year, and as previously noticed, there is a tombstone in the churchyard to a Mary Powell, who died at the age of one hundred and thirty-two, on the 1st January, 1812. A Mrs. Adin whom I knew died at the age of ninety-seven; and Mary Hodkinson died in Tinker's Lane, soon after, at the age of ninety-five. Mr. John Ault died in 1861, June 4th, aged ninety-six, and was an active man to the last. On the eleventh of the same month of June four persons died

---

* I am much indebted for these extracts to the Rev. F. Martin, Burser of Trinity College, Cambridge, who has kindly copied them from Plott for me.

whose united ages were three hundred and twenty-six. Their names and distinct ages were Mary Machin, eighty-three; Joseph Twigg, eighty-seven; Mary Kynnersley, eighty-one; Ann Banks, seventy-five. A tombstone informs us that Mr. John Crossby died at the age of one hundred years and eight months, on September 20th, 1836, and his wife at the age of eighty-five in 1812. To William Orpe there is a headstone recording that his age at his death was one hundred and four. In 1867, Miss Mary Smith, a lady residing in Bradley Street, died at the age of one hundred years; she having been born in 1767. An old Uttoxetertonian, named James Alkin, who died at Pendleton in 1878, and of whom a lengthy account appeared in the *Salford News* of March 9th of the same year, reached the age of one hundred and two years. Towards the close of the last century there lived a shoemaker in Carter Street, in an old house which has been removed to make way for the minister's house adjoining the Congregational Chapel, who worked at his trade after his one hundredth year, and he exhibited a pair of shoes in his window which he made after that age. This is a remarkable case, and will scarcely permit the mention of the late Mr. Willis who worked at the same trade at Dove Bank close to Silver Street at the age of eighty-six, in the same house in which he was born. In about the year 1877 the following interesting record appeared of two old townspeople, Mr. and Mrs. Stephen Udall, who died, one on the Saturday and the other on Monday. It says "The deceased, who was in his 91st year, was highly respected in the neighbourhood, and had been married to his wife seventy-two years, she also being in her 91st year. Both the old people had been ailing for some time, and it is remarkable that the lives passed together should have terminated on dates so near each other. Both bodies were conveyed to their last resting place in the same hearse, and placed side by side in the same grave."

CHAPTER VIII.

ANCIENT FAMILIES OF UTTOXETER AND FAMILIES OF DISTINCTION.

The family of Mynors is one of great distinction and antiquity in Uttoxeter. Their pedigree goes back to the time of King John, early in the twelfth century, the first of whom there is any account being Roger de Mynors, who had a son, Stephen, to whom and his heirs Robert de Ferrars granted lands at Barton-under-Needwood, and, by another charter, land lying near White Heath, for their homage and service with house-boot and hay-boot through the whole ward of Barton, and twenty hogs, quit of panage. The land granted by the second charter was afterwards called Blakenhall, of which Sir John Mynors, Knight (son of John Mynors, Steward of Tutbury, tenth, Edward II., by Sybel his wife, daughter of Sir William Bagot), was Lord, sixth, Edward II., and by Cicely his wife, daughter of Thomas Noel, of Newbold, county Leicester, left Thomas Mynors, Lord of this manor, fourteenth, Richard II., and Robert Mynors, his second son, from whom those of Uttoxeter, the Woodlands, and other places, were descended. In a collection of twenty-two ancient Somershall charters, now in the possession of Sir William Fitz Herbert, Bart., a John Mynors, of Uttoxeter, is mentioned in two of the date 1437, and again in one of the date 1460. A John Mynors (probably the same) married Johanna, daughter of John Fitz Herbert, of Somershall, fourteenth, Richard II.,* and Henry IV. * A grant was made to the Uttoxeter branch for the free fishery of the river Dove, from Dove Head to Dove Foot, and five miles up Bentley brook. The state calendar papers record that in 1607, a grant was made to Henry Mynors, sergeant of carriages of the benefit of the recusancy of Richard Brook, of Tapley, and John Mynors, of Uttoxeter, in the county of Stafford. Captain Richard Mynors, to whom Hollingbury belonged, flourished in the seventeenth century, and served with great bravery in the Dutch wars, and also against the Royalist insurgents at Colchester. Several others were eminent and prosperous navigators, particularly William Mynors, son of Richard Mynors, gent., of Hollingbury Hall, near Uttoxeter, who safely returned eleven times from the East Indies, before 1660. In the Salt library, at Stafford, a copy of a manuscript is preserved entitled, " Transcript from the Journal of Edward Mynors, of Uttoxeter, master of the E.I.C. ship, the Eagle, A.D. 1624-5." It has generally been supposed and asserted that the property of the family at Hollingbury Hall, which was on the High Wood, where a modern built farm house stands on its site, near Toot Hill, had been wasted in the seventeenth century; but the enterprising character of its owners strongly contradict it; and besides, in Mr. Lightfoot's Survey finished in the middle of that century, it does not appear that any of it had been sold, and indeed it is in the possession now of their descendants; and although Erdeswick says there was a house of the Mynors, it has been supposed to refer to that on the High Wood. The property which was dispersed was that at Uttoxeter; and it is singular this was not known to Mr. Samuel Bentley, who in the last century seems to have had no knowledge of there having been one of the family in the town, and mentions the wasted property as belonging to Hollingbury Hall, in the " Gentlemen's Magazine," in 1788. The ex-

---

* Fitz Herbert Charters, edited by the Rev. R. H. C. Fitz Herbert.

tent of each estate is exhibited in the Survey of Peter Lightfoot. The last owner in the town was Walter Mynors, Esq., who died in 1646, who is reputed amongst his descendants to have been a man given to convivial habits. His residence stood at the top of Dove Bank, and it is described as the capital messuage or mansion house at the north east end of the town, with garden, orchard, and yard, and one close adjoining called Horse Close. The homestead, with all the estate in land, amounting to 357a. 3r. 2p., was sold in 1642, three years before their owner's death The house or hall, where King Charles was entertained, was bought by Mr. Wood, together with 12. 3r. 10p. adjoining. Mr. Rowland Cotton, Mr. Dawson, Nicholas Mynors, Peter Lightfoot, John Millward, Esq., with others bought the rest. The little Park, or Mott Close (the site of a Roman Camp on which a new house stands) was purchased by Edward Villars, gent. This ancient and interesting residence with the adjoining land, passed by purchase to Mr. Cope, jeweller, and subsequently to Thomas Hart, Esq., who destroyed the house.

Hollingbury Hall and the land about it remains in the possession of the descendants of the family now resident at Bramshall. In 1658 this remarkably ancient place is described in the following way :—" Thomas Mynors, gent., houldeth divers lands and tenements, purchased of divers several persons, part copy, part freehold, at the yearly rent of xxxs., viijd., viz., " One capital messuage adjoining to the High Wood side, with the barns, stables, court-yard, called Mynors of the Hill, or Hollingbury Hall, and the close called kitchen croft, one close called barn yard, and one large close of pasture or meadow adjoining ;" then follow particulars of all the other land and the different situations of it, which it is unnecessary to give, the total being 70a. or. 8p. The land was let to a number of tenants but a great proportion of it was rented by a Nicholas Mynors, probably a son, who at the above date occupied the house. Thomas Mynors, who has just been mentioned, was a man of some note ; he was a member of parliament and a great benefactor to the city of Lichfield, where he was in business as a draper, and the following interesting particulars respecting him are taken from a Charity Commissioner's enquiry copied from the *Staffordshire Advertiser*:—

"Opposite the tower, and at the corner of Bore street, is a curious looking building, with an inscription :—'Tho. Minor's House,' now in the occupation of Mr. Batty, veterinary surgeon. This house has a somewhat curious history, having been specially left to Lichfield for the purposes of a school, but which school, by one of the Charity Commission schemes, has since been incorporated with the Free Grammar School. Thomas Minor belonged to an old family in the county of Stafford. He was a draper living in Sadler (now Market) street, in the city, and issued tokens in 1656, 1658, and 1660. He was elected M.P., 1654–56 and 1658–59, and died on the 7th September, 1677, aged sixty-eight, ten years after his first wife. A tablet to their memory is in the vestry of St. Mary's Church —where he was buried. By his will, proved the 12th of October, 1677, he bequeaths his property at Uttoxeter to his then wife, Dorothy, and others, in specified portions, and upon special conditions; he leaves £100 for his funeral mourning apparel, and 'for a gravestone and a small monument for me ;' to his niece he leaves the Unicorn in Lichfield ; he directed a sermon to be annually preached on St. Thomas's Day, in St. Mary's ; left £5 to the poor of the city ; and to certain trustees he left 'all that messuage, house, or tenement, which I lately buylded at my own proper costs and charges, standing at the upper end of Bore street,'—this was in 1660—and 'to employ the said messuage, as now they are employed, ffor a schoole house, wherein may be taught thirty poore boys to read in English bookes untill they can well read chapters in the Bible, whose parents are not able to keep their children at schoole at their own charge.' He left lands specially to support the institution, and to pay the master £10 a year, 13s. 4d. for annual repairs, and 6s. 8d. 'for one carte or wagon load of coals to be yearly laid downe about Symon and Jude's Day, at the said schoole, done for the use and benefit of the said poore boyes,' and 6s. 8d. 'to be laid out in wine and cakes yearly for a small treatment' when his feoffees paid their annual visit of inspection.

The present representitive of the family is the infant son (he being under age) of the late John Mynors, Esq., of Eaton, to whom descended the Knypersley estate in the Woodlands, the old house of which remains as here shown on a plate.

The late Mr. E. P. Mynors, of Uttoxeter, was the owner of a farm adjoining Hollingbury on the west.

The late John Mynors, Esq., of the Parks, who died unmarried about 1853, was an ardent collector of objects of antiquity, and at a former part of his life he had been in partnership with Michael Thomas Saddler, M.P. of Leeds, in the woollen business.

A branch of the ancient family of Floyer, Flier, or Flyer, of Hints, Devon, formerly resided at Uttoxeter, and owned and lived in Uttoxeter House, now called the Manor House, at the upper end of High street. One of the family in the town, named Thomas, was a mercer, and his son Richard bought Uttoxeter Moor, upon the sale of it from the Crown, it being on a lease for a long time. He was lord of the manor of Weston in the Moorlands. The family also possessed most of the demesne land in the parish amounting to 343a. 1r. 1p., besides various other lots and houses in Balance street. Richard Floyer, grandson of the lord of Weston, married Elizabeth, daughter of one of the Barons of the Exchequer. Sir John Floyer, an eminent physician, was settled in Staffordshire after 1649. Their old residence in Uttoxeter is described in these terms at the time they owned it, " One fair house at the upper end of High street." In the sixteenth century the house was owned by Francis Flier, and afterwards by Ralf and Richard. There was a Richard Flier in Uttoxeter in 1552. The occupier of the house in the time of Richard Flyer, was a Mr. Hurt, doubtless of the Derbyshire family of that name, and in 1774, a Miss Hurt was personal owner in the parish of 17a. of land, and joint owner of 9a. more. Thomas Flyer, who was a victim to the ire of a

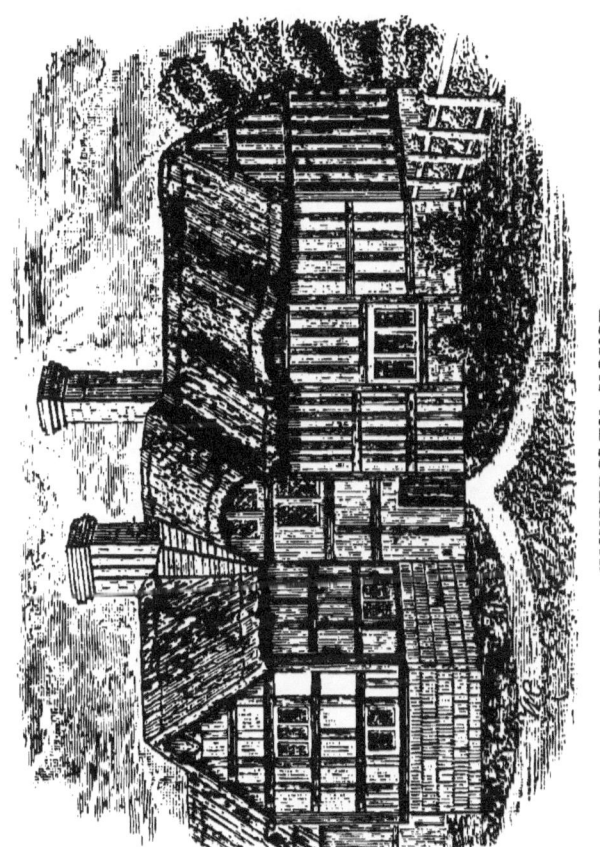

KNYPERSLEY HOUSE.

papist, was one of this family. The "Fair House," which was closed as far as possible from the scrutiny of the public during the life of Dr. Taylor, was regarded with feelings of almost superstitious awe, and after his death there was a rush of people to inspect it when it was open during a sale of some of its effects. Like others I was curious myself to examine its rooms and penetrate its awe, and the ensuing is a portion of a sketch which I wrote about it at the time, and which may be interesting, perhaps, to preserve:—"The house of the late Dr. Taylor, of this town, had acquired a considerable degree of mysterious interest during the course of many years, from various circumstances, and the people of the town and neighbourhood had long been anxious to examine the interior of the place and to come in contact with any of the mysterious influences which might have wrought their weird spell upon it. It was known to possess an historical interest, and tradition, with perfect truth, asserted that a lady of almost matchless beauty had committed suicide in one of the rooms, where it was stated the blood of the unfortunate self-immolated victim had so stained the floor that it could not be effaced by any means employed for the purpose. And besides, the retired peculiar habits and isolated life of the Doctor only aided to give a keenness to the desire of people to inspect a place only the precincts of which they had been permitted previously to tread upon. The demise of the Doctor offered the opportunity for doing so, and during two days' sale in March, 1877, the curiosity of the majority of people was to a certain extent gratified. The bulk of the belongings to the rooms—the furniture and the old paintings which were supposed to have decorated the walls—were to a great extent removed, and other people's superfluous goods helped to extend the sale. The removal of so many things tended to disenchant the place considerably, in people's anticipations, and to that extent limited their curiosity. The rooms of the residence were found to be numerous and tolerably spacious, but gloomy, and to require the attention of the painter. Some of the apartments are wainscotted, and one in the second storey of the house is hung with fine old tapestry, said to have been worked by the needle, and to have taken a long course of years, if not several generations to execute, by ladies of the family of Flyer. The scenes represented are four, worked on distinct pieces of canvas, with borders varying in design, and bearing evidence of successive periods. The *tableaux* on the earliest worked portion, which may be nearly four yards in extent, and which has its counterpart in size on an opposite wall, represents Elijah ascending to heaven in a chariot. The lower part of the view is crowded with magnificent trees, beneath which figures of the prophet's friends appear looking in amazement upwards at the ascending spectacle. The other portions of tapestry represent scenes which are said to be Indian and combine figures, magnificent trees, and massive buildings as the bold conceptions of ladies who must have been endowed with great artistic taste and skill, and exhaustless patience, to have executed such splendid work. In the room in which the tapestry hangs are two carved griffins projecting from the wall, and which, no doubt represent the crest of the Gardner family— Colonel and Sir Allen Gardner. It is singular however, that whilst they ought to be *azure* they are shown to be *or*. The mistake may be very modern, and may have been committed in ignorance to hide the original *azure* which might have become, through length of time, degraded and dirty in appearance. Indeed, the purport of the figures might not have been known. It was in the room so decorated that the Duke of Cumberland slept two nights when he was at Uttoxeter in the memorable year 1745, in pursuit of the army of the Pretender, which he came up with in the north and utterly routed. It was quite new information to be told that it was in tradition that King Charles on one of his visits to Uttoxeter was secreted in the house, and to have the exact place pointed out. The spot is difficult of access, the way to it being along the top of the residence close under the old naked rafters, and the person going to it must bend and take care he does not lame himself as he proceeds to the place. When it is reached it proves to be a triangular space into which an individual desirous of being hid must drop himself down to a depth of five or six feet, where there is a firm floor and a stone seat to sit upon. Such a hiding-place must have been thoroughly secure from the most zealous persecutors. There is a date and initials carved in wainscoting over a fireplace in an upper room, but it would be too presumptuous to assert that it indicates the time when the house was built. The letters are too rude to suppose that they were cut by the artist who so beautifully carved the floral devices on the panels. The inscription is as follows: —R. B. 1600. M. B. After the house had been occupied by the family of Smyth after the Gardners, it was taken by Mr. Bell, a banker of the town, who failed, when it was occupied by Mr. Taylor, and subsequently by his son the late Herbert Taylor, Esq., M.D., and deputy Lieut. of the county. For some years, it is said, there was no owner to the house, but that the doctor paid the rent regularly into the bank. After his death, however, it was sold by auction, Mr. Hawthorn being the purchaser, and the Misses Hawthorns have now an excellent school there for young ladies.

Another family of note in Uttoxeter was that of a branch of the Tixalls. A representative of Robert Tixall, in the time of Edward III., was Richard Tixall, butcher, of Uttoxeter. The heirs of Tixall had in the manor of Uttoxeter about eleven acres of land. A William Tixall became seized of Leese Hill by marriage with a daughter of the Normans, a branch of whom had property in Uttoxeter in the sixteenth century. Sir Walter Raleigh, the historian of the world, was descended from an Uttoxeter family of that name. The family of Hart was a very ancient and wealthy family in Uttoxeter, and John Hart, gent., temp., Charles I., had an estate in the parish of 285a. 3r. 36p. At that remote period it was described as, "anciently in the possession of the Harts," an expression which carries the mind back to a remote date from that time, and the name of Hart is distinctly mentioned in the inventory of church goods in the time of Edward VI., as

is that of Flyer. John Hart was succeeded in Uttoxeter Woodlands by his son William Hart in 1678, and another son, Samuel, settled at Hitchen, in the County of Hereford, A.D. 1679. The male line is extinct in Uttoxeter by the death of the late Thomas Hart, Esq., banker, whose only son died in his infancy. The only daughter of Mr. Hart, by his wife, who was sister of the late Lady Cotton Sheppard, was married to the Honourable Richard Cavendish, who, by his wife, succeeded to the estates, both of Sir Thomas Cotton Sheppard and Mr. Hart, and he died March 18th, 1876, aged 81 years, and his career appears to deserve the following fuller notice of him:—
"The Hon. Richard Cavendish, born December 23rd, 1794, was the second son of Richard, second Lord Waterpark, by Juliana, eldest daughter and co-heir of Mr. Thomas Cooper, of Mullynart Castle, County Kildare; he was uncle of the present Lord Waterpark, and also heir-presumptive to the title. In 1841 he was married to Elizabeth Maria Margaret, daughter and heiress of Thomas Hart, Esq., banker, Uttoxeter, formerly of Thornton Hall, and lineally descended from the ancient family of Tyrrells, who have been the owners of the Thornton Estate ever since the beginning of the 16th century. Mrs. Cavendish died at Thornton Hall in the year 1858. The lamented deceased leaves a family of nine children, viz., three sons and six daughters; the four eldest daughters and two eldest sons being all married. He was Deputy Lieutenant for the counties of Stafford and Bucks, having large estates in both counties. His estates devolve on his eldest son, William Thomas, born in 1843, and married, and who was late an officer in the 5th Dragoon Guards, and who held the commission of Captain in the Royal Bucks Yeomanry Cavalry, and died in 1878. The deceased, Hon. Richard Cavendish, had seen considerable service in India. In 1811 he proceeded to Calcutta in the Hon. Company's Civil Service; after studying the languages of India with great success, he was sent to Rajpootana as Political Agent. Very soon afterwards he was promoted to the Presidency of Gwalior, at a salary of

six thousand a year. For his services at Gwalior, Mr. Cavendish was promoted to the Presidency of Nagpore, salary seven thousand a year. After a splendid career he retired on a pension of £1,000 a year in 1848, after thirty-two years continuous service, during which long period he scarcely had a single day's illness, and never accepted furlough to England. Although in his eighty-second year, he retained full possession of all his faculties to the last, and was a remarkably active man and very methodical in all he did."

There were also in the seventeenth century in Uttoxeter branches of the family of Manlove, Berisford, Bowyer, Bakewell, and Oldfield, as before observed, all owners of land in the parish. The heirs of Richard Middleton had about one hundred and thirteen acres of land. John Shawcross, of an old family from North Derbyshire, of whom there are descendents living in divers places, owned fifty-three acres of land, and Thomas Mastergent, of a very old family, possessed upwards of twenty-two acres. Catherine Mastergent, who gave her barn in Carter Street for alms houses, was daughter of Thomas Bagnall, of Penkhull, Stoke-upon-Trent, and sister of Elizabeth, wife of the Rev. Thomas Lightfoot, vicar of Uttoxeter. The old survey states that the alms houses were built by Thomas Mastergent. The sole executor of the will of Elizabeth Mastergent was Ralph Bagnall, living in Uttoxeter, and being the owner of the Old Swan, and residing against the Crown Inn gate on the north side of the Market Place, at the entrance to there from Church Street. Ralph Bagnall was her brother. Her kinsman, Peter Lightfoot, John, son of Thomas Lightfoot, Josias Lightfoot, Samuel Lightfoot, Thomas Lightfoot the younger, John, son of Thomas Lightfoot the younger, and many others had legacies bequeathed to them by her. *

---

* Some of these facts have been kindly communicated to me by Colonel Bagnall, of Shenstone Moss.

THE MILWARD FAMILY.

In connection with the foregoing notices of old families of Uttoxeter, I have much pleasure in adding the following interesting details respecting the families of John Archbold, gent., of Uttoxeter, and of Sir William Milward, epitaphs to both of whom, of the seventeenth century, as they appear in Uttoxeter Church, have been copied, for the first time translated and transferred to these pages. Mr. E. J. Milward Barnard, of Greenwich, afterwards of Albany, Piccadilly, London, who is a descendent from both of these worthies, and who has expended much time and trouble in collecting the arms, pedigrees, and other matters relating to his ancestors and their various branches from the " Herald's Visitations," and from churches and private sources. Sir William Milward married Catherine, daughter of John Fleetwood, of Caldwich. He had three sisters; the first of whom, Elizabeth, married John Archbold, gent., of the Woodlands, Uttoxeter, and also of London. His descendant, Colonel Henry Archbold, was with Penn and Venables at the conquest of Jamaica in 1655, where he settled. By his wife, who was the daughter of Colonel Byndloss, he had many children, who are now represented by some of the families possessed of property in the island. His second sister married Thomas Chambers, and his third married Walter Mynors, of Uttoxeter. His father married Margery, daughter of William Dethick, of Newhall. His earliest recorded ancestor was Owen Mylward (so spelt in the " Heralds' Visitations "), who lived in the year 1392. Of his subsequent ancestors, one was married to Joane Pembridge, who was descended from an ancient Herefordshire family. Another was of the Kniveton family, of Kniveton, * near Ashbourne. Another married Felicia,

---

* "Kniveton hath given both name and seat to the famous family of Kniveton, of whom St. Leo Kniveton (an antiquary), to whose study and diligence I am so much indebted." Camden.

The first recorded Parliamentary representative for the county of Derby was Henry de Kniveton, who served that office in the twenty-third Parliament of Edward I.

who, through her mother, represented the ancient families of Daniel, Baguley, and Cheadle, and was daughter and co-heir of Sir John Savage, whose father had married Catherine, daughter of Sir Thomas Stanley, afterwards Lord Stanley, and who himself commanded the left wing at the Battle of Bosworth, and was very instrumental, with Lord Stanley, his uncle, afterwards made Earl of Derby, in promoting Henry VII. to the throne. Sir Thomas Milward, above mentioned, died in 1630; and his son, Sir Thomas Milward of Eaton, the celebrated Chief Justice of Chester, married Thomasine, co-heiress of Henry Berisford, of Alsop-in-the-Dale, County of Derby, her sister having married a member of the ancient family of Coke. John Milward, Esq., owned in Uttoxeter, 36a. of land.

Mr. Milward Barnard considers himself by descent on the side of his mother to be the rightful claimant to the estates of Eaton, which are now in Chancery, and he possesses the title deeds to them.

JOHN LIGHTFOOT, D.D., MASTER OF St. CATHERINE'S COLLEGE, CAMBRIDGE,

was the son of the Rev. Thomas Lightfoot, Vicar of Uttoxeter, in the County of Stafford, a man not to be named without a preface of honour and respect. He was born in the little village called Shelton, in the parish of Stoke-upon-Trent. He was a man of exemplary piety, and of indefatigable industry, and was one of the greatest examples of the last age for his constant care of those souls which were committed to his charge. This he showed by his constant preaching, and diligent instruction and catechising of the youth of his parish, from which his preaching did not excuse him. He was a burning and shining light, and showed his love to his Great Lord and Master by the unwearied care of his sheep. He was in Holy Orders six-and-fifty years, and thirty-six years Vicar of Uttoxeter, above named. He died July 2nd, A.D. 1658, and in the eighty-first year of his age.

The Rev. Thomas Lightfoot married Miss Elizabeth Bagnall, as already remarked, a gentlewoman of very good family in Staffordshire, three of whose family were made Knights by Queen Elizabeth, for their martial prowess and valour in the then wars in Ireland against the rebels. She was a woman of exemplary piety, and died January 24th, A.D. 1636, at the age of seventy-one years.

The inscription on the Rev. Thomas Lightfoot's monument in Uttoxeter Church was written by his son, Peter Lightfoot, the physician, as stated, and furnished to Strype by the Rev. Michael Edge, then Vicar of Uttoxeter, who printed it with the life of Dr. Lightfoot, in the folio edition of his works. The monument still exists in Uttoxeter Church. Strype also adds, as a *curioso*, an epitaph, which the same Rev. Thomas Lightfoot had prepared for himself, and which was found in his study after his decease. This I subjoin, to let the world see somewhat as well of the pious and heavenly breathing mind, as the scholarship of that man from whom our doctor was derived—

THOMAS LIGHTFOOT,

Olim superstes nunc defunctus alloquitor amicos suos, qui in vivis sunt.

En mea tam multis pupis quassata porcellis,
Nunc tendam, portum, practa quietis habet.
Nil scopulos ultra bibulas nil curat armas.
Istius aut mundi quæ mare monstra parit,
Namque mare est mundus puppis vaga corpus obumbrat,
Atque animam siquat navita quisque suam
Portum quem petimus calum est ; sed ea aura salutis,
Quæ navem impellit, spiritus ille Dei est,
Solvite felices igitur portum que tenete,
Post ærumnosi tuo biba demua maris.
Sed non ante datur portum contingere quam
Fracta per undosum vestra carina mare.

The Rev. Thomas Lightfoot had five sons—the eldest was Thomas, the only one of all his sons bred to a secular employment being a tradesman at Uttoxeter, though his burial is not to be found there. The second son, John, of whom we shall say more below. The third, Peter, a very ingenious man, and practical physician in Uttoxeter; and besides his art he was of great usefulness in that town, and often in commissions for ending differences. He had intended to write the life of his brother, Dr. John Lightfoot, but was prevented by death. He was the compiler of the "Survey of Uttoxeter," which has been useful in writing this work; and he also constructed a plan of the town. He appears from the Survey to have been a man of property, and his place of residence, which was burnt down in 1672, was in Balance Street. He was also the author of a tract called "A Battle with a Wasp's Nest." He was witness to many of the wills of those who left bequests to the town, and to indentures, great numbers of which are preserved in the old chest in the vestry room, and till I examined them had never been opened for 250 years, the blotting off in all cases having been done with sand. The next was Josiah, who succeeded his brother, Dr. John Lightfoot, in the charge of his living at Ashby, though he was never inducted to the living, but acted as curate to his brother, who gave him the profits of the benefice; and on the Doctor's death, in 1675, a son of his brother, also named Josiah, a graduate of the University of Cambridge, and member of St. Catherine's college, was inducted to the living, that "the old man (as Strype adds) might enjoy it during his life, and his son after him." But, alas! for all human plans and forethought, both father and son died in the year 1683, and were buried at Ashby, the father on August 24th, and the son on the 17th of November following; and descendants of the former were resident at Ashby till within the last few years. The last of the family buried there was Mr. John Lightfoot, who died in 1847. We are indebted for some particulars illustrating this notice to another member of the family, Mr. William Tomkinson Lightfoot.

The youngest son of the Rev. Thomas Lightfoot was Samuel, who was a member of Christ's College, Cambridge, and took the degree of B.A. in 1631, and M.A. in 1635, and entered into holy orders, but died young. His signature occurs in the Ashby register, as curate, in the year 1632; but where else he exercised his ministry, and the place and date of his death, have not been ascertained.

The arms of the family are barry on six, *or*, and *gules*, on a bend *argent* three escallops of the second.

Crest, a griffin's head erased, gorged about the neck with a collar charged with three escallops.

Evidence of these arms still exist in the seal of Dr. John Lightfoot, attached to letters of his to Dr. Edward Bernard, and preserved in the Bodleian library, Oxford; on the portrait of the Doctor engraved by White, of which a fine impression is in the print room of the British Museum; and on the seal of the Rev. John Duckfield, Rector of Aspeden, Herts, who married Joice, the eldest child of Dr. Lightfoot, attached to letters preserved in the manuscript department of the same Museum.

The family of Snape, of Uttoxeter, of whom only a female of the name remains in the town, * are descended from ancestors of much consideration, although they have only been known within recollection in humble circumstances. The arms of the family, which were rescued from oblivion by the late Mr. Heap, of Cheadle, whose widow, now, or lately resident in Rocester, is of the family of Snape, are described as the arms of the *ancient* family of Snape, in Oxfordshire, viz.. *Ermine*, on a chief, *azure* three portcullises, *or*, lined ringed of the last, a martlet *gules* (for a difference).

Crest, a buck's head per pale *or* and *vert*, attires counterchanged, viz., two colours. Motto, Stat fortuna domies, (In English), "The good fortune of our house continue." These are the only arms belonging to the name in the Kingdom.

The Snapes at an early period had property in Uttoxeter, and one in 1731, was designated "James Snape, Yeoman," and fuller particulars of their property will appear

---

* Since the above was written she has died.

in a notice of the late Mr. Condlyffe. They also appear as owners in ancient deeds in the possession of the representatives of the late Mr. Keeling, High Street, in which there is this extract, not relating, however, to the Snapes:— "To hold unto the said William Barnet, his exors., admors., and ags. for five-hundred years these next ensuing at a peppercorn rent." Some tenures as in this instance were merely nominal, such as a grain of cummin, or a red rose; others were of more or less value, such as a pair of white gloves, a tun of wine, a gold spur, or a silver salver; and others by such service as holding the lords stirrup, keeping a pack of hounds, &c. Some of the Snapes of the Uttoxeter branch lived in the vicinity of Alton, and in Bradley churchyard there is an ancient headstone to one of them with this inscription upon it:—" Here lyeth ye body of Anne Snape who died March ye 25th., anno dom, 1307."

ANNE SNAPE'S HEADSTONE.

This transisional stone is interesting as a singular development of the coffin stone, of which the greatest number of remaining examples belong to the same—the fourteenth century. The head is represented at the top; there are circles formed by mouldings to show the position of the arms, and also oval ones to indicate the position of the feet. At the back of this stone there is carved a broken lover's knot. There is an inscription accompanying it, but

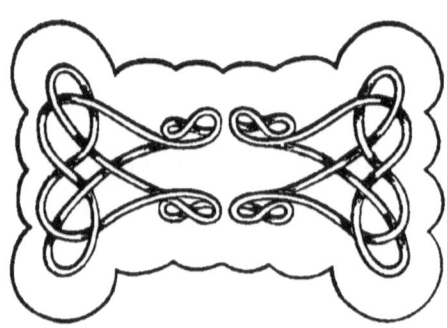

BROKEN LOVER'S KNOT.

only the following part remains visible:—" And so hath broke a true love's knot," which recalls lines in Tasso, but which have a joyous, instead of a melancholy interest, like the above fragment,—

"Still by his side a faithful guard went she,
One true love knot their lives together ties."

The last male resident in Uttoxeter was James Snape, who for upwards of sixty years was in the employment of the Trent and Mersey Canal and North Staffordshire Railway Company, and died in 1868 at the age of 78 years.

As family documents are much enquired after by compilers of local histories, and are of interest and importance, I give two extracts from such having relation to freehold property in Balance Street formerly in the possession of the late Mr. Condlyffe, of Leek, who was the freeholder in a lineal descent, commencing with his greatgrandfather, who was succeeded by his grandfather, and after passing through the two sons of the latter John and Joseph Condlyffe, came to himself as the only surviving son of Joseph Condlyffe; and it is presumed that not any freeholder on a small scale took a priority.

On the 20th of July, 1705, the present ancient house in Balance Street, Uttoxeter, now, and for many years past in the occupation of Mr. William Harvey, was purchased for £35, the description of the premises in the title deed being as follows :—

"All that messuage-house or tenement, situate, standing, and being in Uttoxeter aforesaid, in a certain street there, called Balance Street, adjoining to the land of Rowland Manlove, gentleman, * on the next, to the land of James Snape, of Uttoxeter, aforesaid, on the north, and the aforesaid street called Balance Street on the south. All which said premises now or late were in the tenure, holding, possession, or occupation of Mastyn Green, and the ground whereon the house stands was lately purchased by Richard Mottram, of Uttoxeter aforesaid, blacksmith, of and from William Green, of Uttoxeter aforesaid, brazier, but the house was built by the said Richard Mottram since his purchase of the said ground."†

By a subsequent purchase deed, dated 16th June, 1731, from James Snape, yeoman, James Horobin, of Uttoxeter, shoemaker, and Thomas Bentley, blacksmith, of the first part, and the greatgrandfather of Mr. Condlyffe, of the other part—

"All that piece, moiety, or parcel of ground consisting and being five yards and sixteen inches and a half in length and three yards six inches in breadth, having the land of the said James Snape on the north, and to the said house on the south, and to ye house now in possession of James Snape, party to these presents, the east, to the house in the tenure, holding, or occupation of Daniel Wood on the west." The purchase money was £3 13s. 6d.

A tolerably full account has already been presented of Sir Symon Degge; but some further particulars remain

---

* Rowland Manlove, was living in 1658, and he had various closes of land making 42a.

† The land was probably left unoccupied till then, subsequent to the fire which destroyed all that portion of the town, for before the fire the land had houses upon it.

to be added with respect to his descent and property. I have no access to information to enable me to unravel any difficulties bearing either upon the property or pedigree of the Degges, but I have met with a number of papers having reference to both subjects, and as they are of considerable interest I should not feel justified by withholding them from publication in this work. With regard to the descent of the family, the Rev. Mr. Lysons, the historian of Derbyshire, has the following remarks:—
"The present representative of the family of Degge, is Edward Sacheverall Wilmot, Esq., son of Dorothy, only daughter of Symon Degge by the co-heiress of Staunton, her two brothers having died without issue." The original papers to which I have referred, are in the possession of Mr. Thomas Degge, of Uttoxeter Heath, into whose hands they came on the death of Miss Lettice Degge,* an unmarried sister. Mr. Degge traces his descent immediately from those who seem to present so fair a claim to the property in question from their remote ancestor Sir Symon Degge. These are the documents:—

"PORTION OF THE DEGGE PEDIGREE.

"June, 1609. Robert Degg, son of Thomas Degg and Dorothy his wife, was baptised the 2nd.

"January, 1612. Sir Symon Degg, son of Thomas Degg and Dorothy his wife, was baptised the 10th.

"March, 1627. John Degg, son to Thomas Degg and Dorothy his wife, was baptised the 22nd.

"March, 1650. Robert Degg, son of John Degg and Ann his wife, was baptised the 21st.

"April, 1700. Robert, the son of John Degg and Mary his wife, was baptised the 28th." (In the middle of this century a Robert Degge had 1a. 1r. 3p. in the Woodlands.)

These extracts seem to be running into the descent of the family from Sir Symon's brother John, who would be entitled to the property, if it were hereditary, the direct male issue from Sir Symon having become extinct.

---

* How the Christian name "Lettice" has come down in the family from the seventeenth century.

"THE ESTATE OF THE DEGGS.

	£	s.	d.
In Staffordshire, Blythe Bridge, two farms	85	15	0
,, Booth, one farm	53	10	0
In Derbyshire, Fenny Bentley, five farms	203	14	0
,, Chapel-en-le-Frith, five farms	126	0	0
In Worcestershire, Kidderminster, several farms	25	19	0
,, Broadwaters	49	10	0
,, Allchurch and Bosley	93	10	0
Total Rental	£637	18	0

"This is the estate that my father sued for fee simple * as next heir-at-law, and it was kept in law for the space of three years. Then they told him that they would give him £25 a year, and pay all the law charges, viz., £150, and give him a bond of £200 for payment of the money. But since then there is an old deed found and Staffordshire estates are tied upon the male heir for ever, and counsel are of opinion that it should never be broke. I have seen the deed and heard it read. It was in Mr. Spencer's hand of Caulton, and Mr. Spencer told me that no man could hinder me of Staffordshire estates by that deed when my father was dead. So he brought an old deed quite contrary to what I had seen, and I should never see that no more, for he had done a wrong thing in letting me see it. There is some of the heads of the deed in the *papers* as I remembered and wrought out there in an older deed in London if the name of it can be found. What is the Court of Green Cloth? (Signed) Robert Degg."

"DEGG SENIOR AND DEGG JUNIOR, TO JOHN WARD, BOND, 11TH JUNE, 1768.

"Know all men by these presents, that we Robert Degg the elder and Robert Degg the younger, both of the Parish of Uttoxeter, in the County of Staffordshire, laborers, jointly and severally held and bound to John Ward, of Loxley, in the Parish of Uttoxeter aforesaid, yeoman, in the sum of £500, of good and lawful money of Great Britain, to be paid to the said John Ward or his

---

* An absolute estate which is given in these terms, "To him and his heirs for ever."

certain attorney, extors, admstrs, or assigns, for which payment well and truly to be made, we bind ourselves each of us by himself for the whole demand each of our heirs, exts, admstrs, and assigns and every of them firmly by these presents. Sealed by our seals, dated this eleventh day of June, 1768.

"Whereas the said Robert Degg, the elder, and Robert Degg, the younger, or one of them, have for some time past been satisfied that the said Robert Degg, the elder, is the right and lawful heir male of and to Sir Symon Degg, Knight, deceased, one of the Judges of West Wales to his Majesty King Charles II, and also the right and lawful heir male of and to Symon Degg, late of Blythe Bridge, in the said County of Stafford, Esq., deceased, and whereas the said John Ward hath assisted the said Robert Degg, the elder, with money, and has been at great trouble and expenses in other respects in assisting the said Robert Degg, the elder, in making enquiries after the estate, ✷ and which the said Symon Degg, of Blythe Bridge aforesaid, died possessed of, for which trouble and expenses which the said John Ward hath been at in and about the aforesaid enquiries, the said Robert Degg, the elder, and Robert Degg, the younger, have agreed and do hereby agree to pay and actually give unto the said John Ward for his good offices and assistance in the aforesaid affair one shilling out of every twenty shillings which they the said Robert Degg, the elder, and Robert Degg, the younger, or either of them, their heirs, exts, admstrs, or assigns, shall have or receive clear from all expenses, payments, and deductions whatsoever out of the real and personal estates of the said Symon Degg, of Blythe Bridge aforesaid, or Sir Symon Degg, on account of their being their next heir male.

"Now the condition of the before written obligation is such that if the said Robert Degg, the elder, or Robert Degg, the younger, or either of them, their or either of their heirs, exts, admsts, or assigns shall and so well and

---

✷ Propex premises.

truly pay or cause to be paid unto the said John Ward his executors, administrators, assigns, shall actually receive and recover clear of all expenses from the real or personal estates of the said Symon Degg, of Blythe Bridge aforesaid, immediately after they the said Robert Degg, the elder, and Robert Degg, the younger, or either of them or their heirs, exts, administrators, assigns, shall have recovered and actually received the monies from the estates of the said Symon Degg, of Blythe Bridge aforesaid, delivered an account of the said Robert Degg, the elder, being the proper and right heir male of and to the said Sir Symon Degg, of Blythe Bridge aforesaid, without any deduction or abatement whatever. These the before written obligations to be void or else to be and remain in full force and virtue.

"Sealed and delivered the before bond on Robert Degg, the elder, and Robert Degg, the younger, being first duly stamped in the presence of us.

"SAMUEL WILSON.   The x mark of Robert Degg, the elder.

"ELIZABETH SARGEANT.   Robert Degg, the younger."

Robert Degge, of Blunt's Green, was a surveyor. He was father of Francis Degge, of Uttoxeter Heath, who was grandfather of the present Mr. Thomas Degge, carpenter and wheelwright.

The following is counsel's opinion on the subject of the Degge pedigree. It is entitled—

"ABOUT THE PEDIGREE OF DEGGES.

"The pedigree shown to me is incomplete, inasmuch as it does not contain the dates of the baptisms, marriages, and burials, and is defective likewise in sometimes omitting the baptismal and sometimes the maiden name of the wife. These, however, may be easily supplied from the materials, and when this is done it will clearly appear that Robert is the next heir male to the estates in question. It is stated that the father of the claimant contended at law for these estates, but was induced to accept £25 a year for relinquishing his claim, and that he signed three or four releases. How far these releases might operate to the extension of his issue, it is impossible to say with certainty, but upon the supposition of these being a family estate, these releases should have no effect whatever after ye death of the person who gave them. It is expressly stated that an old deed has been found whereby the Staffordshire estates were settled upon the male heir for ever. This cannot be true to the full extent, for the law will not endure perpetuities; but it may be true so far as to satisfy a belief that there has been as strict a statement as the policy of law will allow, and, therefore, it is expedient that a search should be made in the fine and recovery offices in order to ascertain what attempts have been made to bar such estates, or alter the prescribed line of descent. When this is done I should advise a bill of discovery to be filed containing well pointed and judicious interrogations relative to facts necessary to be known, and praying a production of all deeds, writings, releases, papers, &c. Such a proceeding will neither be tedious nor expensive, and will elucidate the mysterious part of this business and give one a commanding view of the subject. Such a bill is frequently filed as a preparatory step to an ejectment, and can in no case be more necessary than in the present. Such a suit can be of no long duration, for it is determined by the coming in of the owner, supposing that answer to be full and explicit, and never goes before the Chancellor at all.

"J. MOSPITT,
"St. Paul's Square, Birmingham,
"9th June, 1801."

Whether the enquiry was prosecuted any further the Uttoxeter papers do not state. The applicant for counsel's opinion was the father of Mr. Thomas Degge, now living on Uttoxeter Heath as stated, and he was grandson of Robert Degge, the younger, and the granting to Robert Degge, the elder, an annuity of £25 to relinquish his claim and the paying legal expenses clearly shows, at least, that he was entitled to an interest in the Staffordshire estates of Sir Symon Degge, and most probably, as contended, was the heir at law male. A John Degge, most probably the brother to Sir Symon Degge, emigrated, with others of the family it is supposed, to America, where he patented two estates, one on September 26th, 1678, and the other in Lower Norfolk in April, 1683, and he took with him a portrait of Sir Symon, still in preservation, as the person represented is stated to be a Degge, of Callowhill and Derbyshire, which Sir Symon was. This information I have from W. H. Degge, Esq., in the Surgeon General's Office, Washington, America, who also states that after 1700 there were a Symon, Joseph, William and also an Anthony and Augustine, and that there is now an immense family of the Degg in the Southern and Western States of the Union who vary their names as Degges, and Deggs, &c.

The family of Warner, of Ratcliffe and Rowington, in the County of Warwick, and Bramshall, and Uttoxeter, in the County of Stafford.

The family of Warner, who have been owners of property in Uttoxeter till recently for more than two hundred years, are a very old Warwickshire family, residing formerly at Ratcliffe and Rowington in that county. The family were residing at Bramshall in 1583, for when Robert Glover, the Somersetshire Herald, made a visitation of the County of Staffordshire, he recorded a family of Warner, Stephen Warner, of Bramshall, marrying Margaret, daughter of Humphrey Cotton, of Bald, who had Henry (the eldest) and Thomas, Humfrey, Joane and Elizabeth. At this time they were settled at the old Manor House, called "The Stocks," at Bramshall, belonging to Lord Willoughby de Broke; and it continued occupied by the Warners, descending from father to son, till the year 1860. Many centuries ago, the Warners, besides possessing much freehold property in Warwickshire, were owners of considerable landed property in Staffordshire. In Dr. Harwood's edition of Erdeswick's "Staffordshire," page 246, is the following notice of a part of it: "Blythbury. The priory. Since the dissolution [*i.e.*, of the priory] it has passed through the hands of Watson, Leicester, and Warner, to John Chadwick, Esq., by purchase in 1789." At the time Erdeswick wrote the owner was, it is stated, Hugo Malvoeson Chadwick, Esq.

During the present century Roger Warner owned property at Ellastone, Hollington, Tean, and around the town of Uttoxeter, all of which has been gradually sold, the last and smallest portion being disposed of in 1860. A considerable part of this property was left to Thomas Warner, of Bramshall, who was born in 1736, and died in 1803, by his kinsman, Miss Elizabeth Hurt, daughter of Charles Hurt, Esq., of Alderwasley, by Catherine his wife, daughter of Rosell, of Ratcliffe. This lady, who died unmarried in 1789, was buried in the porch of Uttoxeter old church. Her father was sheriff of Derbyshire in 1712. Her brother Francis married Mary, daughter of Thomas Gell, Esq., of Wirksworth, and her nephew, Charles Hurt, married Susanna, daughter of Sir Richard Arkwright, which family is related by marriage to the Fitzherberts, of Tissington. The eldest son of Thomas Warner, above mentioned, was Roger Warner, the last at Bramshall. He was born in 1766, and died in 1825. His eldest and only surviving son, William, is living a widower, in America, without issue. The youngest male representative is a grandson, Thomas Roger Warner, of Loxley, son of George Edwin T. Warner, who died in 1864. Of the female issue, Lydia (deceased) was married to Henry Chawner, Esq., of Houndhill;* Clara or Clarisse to Thomas Fradgley, (architect and surveyor) of Uttoxeter; and Sarah Maria, who still occupies the residence of the family, at Bramshall, to Richard Lassitter, surgeon and farmer.

One of the family of Warner figured in the civil wars of the Commonwealth. He was a staunch Royalist and went by the name of "Crab Warner" amongst his brother

---

* The arms of this family, who were of Muselane, Co. Derby, are *Sa*, a Chev, between three cherubins' heads, *or.* Crest, a Sea Wolf's head, erased, ppr., Motto, Nil Desperandum.

soldiers, probably from his sour manner towards the Roundheads whom he thoroughly detested. In the Rev. Mr. Gresley's "Siege of Lichfield" mention is made of this very Crab Warner. R. F. Tomes, Esq., of Welford Hill, near Stratford-on-Avon, states that the Warners of Wormington were connected with the Staffordshire family of Lane, of Bentley Hall, where King Charles took shelter, and who, after leaving, was conducted to the house of John Tomes, of Long Marson, by Mistress Jane Lane, this same John Tomes being a son of Ann Warner, and left a king's ward on the death of his father.

The arms of the family of Warner, are *or*, a chev, between three boars' heads erased, *Sa* :—Crest, a horse's head erased, *Sa*, per fess *Ermine* and *Gules*; maned of the last. These arms of the Warners are taken from the volume in the British Museum containing the visitation of the Heralds to Warwickshire in 1619. They describe them as " belonging to Robert Warner, of Ratcliffe, Co. Warwickshire, Harl., MSS., 1100, folio 79."

Amongst individuals of distinction who held property in Uttoxeter in the seventeenth century in Uttoxeter were Lord Cromwell, Sir Thos. Wolsley, the Earl of Essex, Lord Ashton, Roland Cotton, Esq., Peter Lightfoot, Anne Lightfoot, Callingwood Lightfoot, and Elizabeth and Mary Lightfoot. In the middle of the eighteenth century Lord Bagot had a large property in land in Uttoxeter, which has been sold. Richard Stubbings had land at Uttoxeter. The arms of his wife, whose name was Mary, daughter of James Sargeant. of Uttoxeter, who had 29a. 3r. 25p. of land in the Bromshulf field, Uttoxeter, were *arg.*, a chevron between three dolphins. She was buried in Somershall church. In 1366—1375, John Harpedale, of Uttoxeter, granted a rent charge in lands there to Walter Fitz Herbert, of Somershall. ✻

In 1583, on the 8th day of August, for the hundred of Totmonslow, a visitation was made at Uttoxeter by Richard Glover, the herald, and many who beforetime had called

---

✻ Somershall charters.

themselves gentlemen were disclaimed, and amongst those at Uttoxeter and near were the following :—Richard Flyer, Uttoxeter; Thomas Madeley, of Denstone; and John Fearne, of Crakemarsh. *

The following are names of gentlemen who were summoned to receive Knighthood at the Coronation of King Charles I., with the amounts they were fined for non-attendance :—†

	£	s.	d.
Richard Middleton, of Uttoxeter, gent.	10	0	0
William Hart, of Uttoxeter, gent.	10	0	0
Luke Bushby, of Uttoxeter, gent.	10	0	0
Henry Gorrenge, of Kingstone, gent.	10	0	0
Francis Kinnersley, of Loxley, gent.	20	0	0
Roland Manlove, of Kingstone, gent.	10	0	0
William Fearn, of Crakemarsh, gent.	10	0	0
William Cotton, of Crakemarsh, gent.	12	0	0
Henry Gorrenge, of Croxden, gent.	10	0	0

In 1663-4, the following Uttoxeter gentlemen, who alleged their right to armorial bearings, were disclaimed at the public assize held at Stafford :—

Peter Lightfoot,
William Gilbert,
Daniel Spateman,
George Bowyer,
George Butler.‡

---

* See vol. 3 of collections for a "History of Staffordshire," edited by the William Salt Archæological Society, 1882.

† See vol. 2 of same work.

‡ Vol. 2, "Staffordshire collections," edited by the William Salt Archæological Society.

CHAPTER IX.

ANCIENT CUSTOMS.

MAY GARLANDS AND MAY-POLE; SACRED WELLS; OMENS AND SUPERSTITIONS; SPORTS AND PASTIMES; CIVIL USAGES.

One of the principal and most interesting of old customs still observed in Uttoxeter takes place on the 1st of May, and it is that of groups of children carrying garlands of flowers about the town. The garlands consist of two hoops, one passing half-way through the other, which gives the appearance of four half circles, and they are decorated with flowers and evergreens in much profusion, and surmounted with a bunch of flowers as a sort of crown, and in the centre of the hoops is a pendant orange and flowers. Mostly one or more of the children carry a pole or stick, with a collection of flowers tied together at one end, and carried vertically, and the children themselves are adorned with ribbons and flowers in a profuse manner. On the 1st of May, 1881, I saw only two children, being girls as they invariably are, with a garland, one holding it with the left and the other with the right hand, it being betwixt them. They each wore a clean muslin frock, a

v

muslin cap, white stockings and good boots, and they were decorated with but a few ribbons, and they appeared the nicest garlanders I had seen. Thus they go from house to house, which they are encouraged to do by the pence they obtain, and so, unsuspectingly, perpetuate a custom of the highest antiquity; for, like other May customs, it is a relic of heathenism, the Druids observing the first of May, in honour of the goddess Flora. More than a century back Mr. Bentley appears to have been pleased with the observance, which, were he living, would delight him as much as when he thus commemorated it—

> "How oft has thy rural parade,
> So famed on the first of sweet May,
> With garlands bedecking each maid,
> Delighted me through the long day.
> O May! with thy beautiful train,
> How joyous thy happy return;
> But wishing thy stay is in vain,
> And only thy swiftness we mourn."
>
> "The River Dove," a Lyric Pastoral.

Another observance at Uttoxeter was the festivity of the May-pole, or sacred pillar, being a personification of the producing power of nature, in that it received its name from Maid, the mother of Mercury, to which a space, about where the Wesleyan chapel stands, was assigned some two-hundred and fifty years back. But interesting as the custom was from its great antiquity, the observance of it has been discontinued in Uttoxeter a long time. In his days Samuel Bentley speaks of it as having then passed away—

> "No more the May-pole's verdant height around
> To val'rous games the ambitious youths advance;
> To merry bells and tabor's sprightly sound,
> Wake the loud carol and the sportive dance."

Various learned authors consider the festivities to be of Egyptian origin in honour of Osiris, an Egyptian deity. The festivals of phallus were instituted by the Greeks, and introduced in Europe by the Athenians, who made the procession of phallus part of the Dionysia, or festivals in honour of Bacchus, the god of wine. Those who carried the phallus at the end of a pole were called the Allaphoria.

They were smeared with the dregs of wine, covered with skins, and wore on their heads a crown of ivy.

There is much interest attaching to several ancient wells at Uttoxeter, one of which is Penny Croft Well, which exists just over the railway which is crossed by an arch constructed for the road to the fields from the entrance to Slade Lane. It has lately been turned into a common drinking place for cattle; but it is recollected to have been kept in neat order, when flowers, especially the march marigold *(caltha palustris)*, which appears early in the month of May, were strewn about it. This well was supposed to have possessed curative properties, especially for weak eyes, for which purpose it used to be much resorted to, and it is probable it derived its name of Penny Croft Well from the pence which the afflicted offered for the use of its healing virtues. The stone cistern into which the water flows out of a bank side, is worn slantingly inwards from the outer front edge to nearly the bottom, showing that there has been much wear in former times by lading water out with buckets or cans, and it is evidently of great antiquity. *

Another interesting well, which is situated close to the road side on the High Wood, a little south of Balance Hill tollgate, on the left hand side, has the name of Maiden's Well, Maiden's Wall Well, and Marian's Well. I have previously attempted, when speaking of Roman ways, to show how it may have acquired the name of Maiden's Well. At the same time the name may be a corruption from *Mai-din*, a British word applied to a fort. It appears to have been notorious in Saxon times, from the Saxons having given it the name of Wall Well from the Latin, vallum, a wall. The well is now enclosed in a field, but formerly it was evidently open to the road, and a wide space of the bank side of the land has been removed on its account, and although this escarpment round or along the back of the well is much worn and broken, it

---

* When I visited this well, after many years, on December 28, 1881, I found that a bog had been allowed to accumulate over it, hiding both the well and the trough.

may have formed the vallum or wall, from which *Wall Well* is derived. From the great celebrity of the well, the floral festivity of the Maid, Marian, the wife of Robin Hood, has probably been celebrated at it, from which circumstance it would readily and naturally receive the distinction of Marian's Well.

Road side wells were particularly appreciated in Saxon days. Travelling being difficult and tedious, and there existing no houses of refreshment, way-side wells were of great importance and convenience. This was so much the case that Edwin, King of Northumbria, A.D. 628, had stakes driven down at them and a brazen dish affixed thereto with a chain, so that the fatigued wayfarer might be enabled to refresh himself.

The waters of this well have always had a great reputation for their supposed healing virtues; and the grandfather of an aged female whom I knew, wished in his dying moments to have a bottle of water from it to drink, on account of its remarkable properties; so that its fame remained great until less than a hundred years back, although, perhaps, not six persons at this time, except by this account, know anything about it. But what is remarkable respecting it is, that it was believed to be haunted by the ghost of a handsome young lady, on account of which people were much afraid of going past it at night—a superstition originating, probably, in a former belief of the well having been inhabited by spirits, there being superstitious beliefs of this kind in Scotland at this day.

These, doubtless, were two of the Holy Wells of a remote age, and which were regarded sacred amongst the Britons; for at similar wells in Cornwell Borlaise says the Druids pretended to predict future events. On the subject of Holy Wells in Staffordshire, Dr. Plott has these interesting observations—" They have a custom in this country which I observed on Holy Thursday at Breewood and Bellbrook, of adorning their wells with bows and flowers. This, it seems, they do, too, at all gospel places, whether wells, trees, or hills, which being now only for decency's sake is innocent enough. Heretofore, too, it was usual to pay the respect to such wells as were eminent for curing distempers on the Saint's day whose name they bore, diverting themselves with cakes and ale, and a little music and dancing. But whenever they began to place sanctity in them—to bring alms and offerings, or make vows at them as the ancient Germans and Britons did, and the Saxons and English were too much inclined to, I do not find but they were forbid devotion in those times as well as now, this superstitious devotion being called well-worship, and was strictly prohibited by Angelican counsels as long as King Edgar, and in the reign of Canutas."

There is a striking resemblance betwixt the mode of adorning wells in this county, as described by Plott, and the manner in which the far-famed wells of Tissington were decorated about a hundred years ago. I learnt from an old man, deceased many years back, that when he was a boy green hawthorn bows were cut down in Dovedale, where, from the warmth of the situation, verdure would be earlier than in exposed places, and were conveyed to the village and stuck in the ground about the various wells, when flowers were simply strewn over them and tied to them in the form of garlands. This account is confirmed by a similar one of the mode of decorating wells at Tissington at even an earlier period, and it is contained in the "Gentleman's Magazine" for 1794, or about the time, perhaps, to which the recollections of the old man carried him back. It states, "In the village of Tissington, a place remarkable for fine springs of water, it has been a custom from time immemorial on every Holy Thursday, to decorate the wells with bows of trees, garlands of tulips, and other flowers placed in fancied devices; and after prayers for the day at church, for the parson and singers to pray and sing Psalms at the wells." The writer proceeds to enquire whether the custom is not handed down from the Druids? Indeed I think this fact fixes the practice of the interesting custom in the village before the introduction of any Christian ceremonies, and probably proves that it has been continued there almost uninterruptedly from British times.

There has been an interesting antique well near the Dove, and known in the last century as St. Cuthbert's Well. After much trouble I think I am enabled to identify the site of the well at a grove of trees enclosed by a slightly raised circular vallum of earth with an outer ditch on the side of the hill betwixt Doveridge Hall and Church, and almost overlooking the mill house. It answers to the description of it in Samuel Bentley's poem entitled "The River Dove," the only source of any account of it, and which is—

"And Cuthbert's Old Well 's in that Grove."

Now Doveridge Church is dedicated to St. Cuthbert, and the name of the well implies that it was a baptistry to the church in Saxon times, the Saxon Church requiring immersion, so that wells and springs often formed the Saxon Fonts. No trace of the well chapel remains, and the water of the well has been conveyed away by a drain; but the late Mr. Povey, Lord Waterpark's agent, who was unfortunately killed on the same acclivity by a tree which was being felled, informed me that when the drain was being laid down from the place, some stones were found which had the appearance of having been steps, and for which in such a situation he was not able to account. A cow-shed has recently been built upon this consecrated site.

Amongst omens in which many persons at Uttoxeter place credence, and which it is perhaps difficult for educated people to shake off, are the chirpings of the cricket, the creaking of furniture, the howling of dogs, and the falling of the weights of the clock, which have been so strictly observed by some that they declare that when they have happened a death in the family has invariably taken place.

It is also believed that if people will bow nine times to the new moon they will have a present; and the moon is likewise an object of superstition in deterring people from killing pigs when a change in the moon takes place.

Bad luck, it is also particularly declared, will follow those who marry or make any fresh undertaking on a Friday. Witchcraft has been no less prevalent, and from a pool somewhere not far from Dove Bridge having, some two hundred and fifty years ago, been called in ancient writings "Witches' Pool," it is likely this was the place where unfortunate witches were drowned, when the practice of witchcraft was punished with death.

During the deeper superstition of former times, it is stated that a ghost used to alarm people at some spot which it is alleged to have haunted betwixt the Moorehouse and the Sevenacres, and the late Thomas Milner, of this town, assured me that it is a fact that seven clergymen, including the late Rev. Mr. Keeling, of Dove Bank, a very credulous man of whom many singular accounts are still related, but withal possessing many admirable qualities, proceeded to the place to lay the unearthly visitant in the Red Sea, which, it is stated, they attempted to effect by the reading and performance of some service. Superstition, we are told, is very difficult to kill, and if not all the clergymen, yet some of them very probably entertained the popular belief in the existence of the ghost and the propriety of the means employed for its removal to the Red Sea.

But the imagination in superstitious times has not restricted itself to giving pictures of ghosts and impressing the idea of them on the popular mind, but generations back it peopled the formerly dense woods in the neighbourhood of Uttoxeter with vastly more frightfully imaginative beings, such as fiends; and hence there was a *Hob* or Fiend Hurst, and a Hob Lane, hob meaning fiend. There is also still in existence, a Gendall's Wood, which has most likely a similar import; for Gendall is probably a name derived from Grendall, which is a myth of Scandinavian and German mythology or superstition, and bears in meaning, according to Dr. Latham, in his "Ethnology of the British Isles," an analogy to our devil. If this is so, such an identity of early superstition is interesting. Grimmer, or Grimmer Lane, near Uttoxeter is evidently derived from Grim, a Goblin, or Ghost.

These names, which are still applied to places close to Uttoxeter, strikingly show in what dread the then dark surrounding woods were held. Indeed we learn from divers sources that in the forest lands which surrounded or existed near to dwelling places, there were woods so awful in the estimation of the Saxons, that the fear-stricken shepherd restrained his flocks from straying into them, whilst the traveller turned away in terror from their precincts. *

The tale of Beowulf is taken up in the first part with his adventures against a monster called Grendall, and also against a terrific worm or earth drake. Grendall is thus spoken of :—

"The grim stranger was Grendall hight
Mighty pacer of the marsh ; who held the moors,
Fen and fastnesses—Land of the Fifel-kin."

But we will turn from this weird and fascinating subject, to consider some civil and feudal customs which have a more palpable interest, and some occurrences and pastimes which, in various ways, engaged the attention of Uttoxeter people generations ago. For the punishment of people the civil authorities of the town had a pillory, an instrument of Saxon origin, standing at Bear Hill, and with it were associated a cuckstool and a stocks, and they were all in existence together there early in this century, and so far back as 1667. Anthony Blake, a joiner of the town, was paid 10s. 6d. by the constables for a thorough repair of them. Every one who has read the Acts of the Apostles knows that the stocks were a very early invention for making prisoners secure by the feet, but many might find it necessary to enquire what kind of implement of punishment were the pillory and the cuckstool. The pillory was intended to secure the prisoner in a conspicuous position by the head and arms, in nearly a similar manner to the feet being fastened in the stocks, whilst the cuck-

---

* *Athenæum*, 1858.

stool was an implement having a long beam with a seat at the end in which brawling and unruly women were made secure and dipped into a pool of water, with a branks, perhaps, on her head at the same time, and having an iron flat prong passing into her mouth over her tongue. In those days there was actually at Bear Hill near the pillory and cuckstool a pool of water for the purpose, with a railed fence round it, but mostly the cuckstool was attached to a framework on wheels, so that it could be taken to a pit of water or a river side, and there, much to the amusement of crowds of people, be employed in a mode of punishment to which modern ideas and feelings are, happily, not familiar with. It is in tradition, as already stated, that a man was hung at the pillory, it being, no doubt, the man who slew John Scott, in Uttoxeter, at the time of the civil war. The last person placed in the pillory was a blind man for nearly killing his wife with a large stone; and it is remembered that the town was in a state of great excitement on account of it during the day. But more horrid than these implements of punishment, was the gibbet, which was claimed very early for Uttoxeter, and which was situated, according to tradition, on the High Wood, at the Four Lane Ends. Not less abhorrent to proper feelings and good sense was the barbarous custom perpetrated upon the bodies of suicides of driving stakes through them after being interred, the places where such practices took place being the Four Lane Ends, in the vicinity of the Gibbet at Kiddlestick, where the branch road leads to the Heath, and in Timber Lane. The spot which was so used in this lane was an open space, now enclosed, just past the garden at the entrance of the lane.

The ugly pastime of bull-baiting was a particularly favourite sport in Uttoxeter in former times, but it was suppressed through the exertions of a number of gentlemen about 1824. The scene of the sport was in the Market Place, the ring being a few yards south-east of the conduit. A description of the rough and exciting scene, written by Mr. George Foster, of Endon, for the *Animal World*, who was a witness of one of the occasions when he was a youth, will be worth preservation. He says—"About the year 1819, arrangements were made for a bull-bait at Uttoxeter Wakes. We lived about three miles from the town, and my father very properly declined to take me, but eventually I obtained permission to go with a neighbour of the name of Sharratt. It was announced to take place at noon on the Wakes Monday in the Market Place. It was a fine September morning about ten o'clock, and when we got there we found a considerable crowd collected, waiting for the sport to begin. These were not days of railways, but vehicles of all sorts were bringing in their contingents of blackguards from Bromley, Tean, Lane End, and the surrounding hamlets. I had never seen such a concourse of people together before. My guardian selected our stand on the raised causeway, in front of Mrs. Wetton's shop (now Mr. George Bunting's). The 'ring' was near the 'Nag's Head' side. After waiting about an hour there arose a Babel of yells and shouting, and there was a terrible rush in the direction of the 'Red Lion.' 'They are coming!' resounded on all sides. The poor brute came quietly enough, led by a strong rope, surrounded by a host of roughs more brutal than himself. At the ring a dispute arose as to the length of tether the poor beast should have, and the stentorian voice of Joe Twigg the blacksmith—then in the prime of manhood—was distinctly heard; and I well remember John Wigley, and Bladon the shoemaker, giving their advice in language which, if not complimentary, was doubtless suited to the audience. While the bull was being secured, several gentlemen came up to protest against the disgraceful scene about to take place. The managers, however, took very little notice of them. Amongst the number whom I recognised, as they came near where we stood, were Dr. Taylor, Mr. Alsop, Mr. Smith (usually called Smith Wetton), Mr. Chapman, and Mr. Birch, the 'Methody,' names that in after years were held in great respect by the writer for their honourable act of humanity on this occasion. A ring was quickly formed around the bull, and the dogs, of the orthodox breed, let loose upon him; he seemed at first to hardly know what to do, but by-and-by he became furious from the punishment received, and one of the dogs was sent high up in the air by him, and on alighting was trod upon by the beast. Then there were shouts in the foulest language that he was 'finished.' The baiting went on for about twenty minutes, when the bull made a furious plunge at the dogs, broke loose, and dashed away through the crowd (who gave him a wide berth) towards Bridge street. There was a panic where we stood, all wishing to get out of the way as quickly as possible. I was lost to my conductor, and carried with the crowd up the entry next to Mr. French's present shop, into Church Lane, with others, into Mr. Hart's yard, the banker, and we closed the large doors. We stayed until the noise and tumult outside had ceased, and then with fear and trembling, I ventured out in quest of Mr. Sharratt, whom I finally found at Billy Mason's, of the 'Talbot.' We trudged off home together, and the sight of that quiet home had never before been to me so welcome."

The game of football used also to be an exciting play here on a Shrove Tuesday, but without any interference of authority it has become on that day and in the usual way almost disregarded. Trap and ball—a game which can be traced back to the fourteenth century—was, until recently, in much repute amongst the working classes, and appeared to have been so for time out of mind.

All Souls' day, which takes place on the 2nd of November, in commemoration of the departed faithful in Christ, is not yet forgotten in Uttoxeter and neighbourhood, but its mode of celebration has in two instances of late had a tendency to make it less profitable to those who might be disposed to keep up the custom. The cases are interesting and deserve being placed on permanent record. Both instances occurred within a year of each other. In 1862, Thomas Edge, of Gratwich, was, at an Uttoxeter Petty Sessions, charged with being out with a number of others during the night making a tour of the village of Leigh, singing at farm houses,

> "You gentlemen of England
> I'll have you to draw near,
> And mark the lines we're going to tell
> And quickly you shall hear,"

and begging for drink, it being All Souls' Day, on which occasion they called at the house of Mr. Marson, at Field, and finding that he was in bed and not to be roused, they commenced throwing stones at the house, pulling gates off their hinges, and committing other acts of malicious damage. In the succeeding year six labourers of Uttoxeter were charged with being at the house of Mr. Cope, at the Marlpits, for drink and other things generally obtained on All Souls' Day, and Mr. Cope being in bed and unwilling to get up, they threw off several gates and did other damage. Fines were inflicted in both cases. The same custom of All Souls' day is mentioned with additional features of interest in the unpublished diary of George Heath, of Gratton, the Moorland Poet, as follows:— "November 1st, 1867. How strangely ancient customs and superstitions are clung to by the humbler classes. To-day the 'Souls' Cakes' have been about, and to-night the children are all in a flutter of expectation, listening for the uncouth strains and bungling tramps of the geesers or guisers. And even I am expecting a little fun from their grotesque appearance and mummery." It is well recollected how the Plough Bullocks one year ploughed up the yard of Mr. Botham, in Balance Street, father of Mrs. Howitt, who refers to it in "The Pictorial Calendar" of the Seasons.

In theatrical amusements the town of Uttoxeter was well cared and catered for till the beginning of this century; for during the theatrical season it supported one and often two theatres—one at the Black Swan Inn, and another at the Red Lion Inn Assembly Room. The company of Mr. Stanton catered for the admirers of the drama in Uttoxeter for many years, and were well patronized by all classes in the neighbourhood. Mr. Samuel Bentley wrote several prologues for them in 1767. One of these was recited by Master S. Stanton, when a benefit was being given for the children of the company. Another of these compositions was spoken by Miss Stanton in 1770, when the Right Hon. Sir Henry Cavendish, Bart., the Right Hon. Lord and Lady Vernon, and many other persons of distinction, were present. But to a late period Mr. Bentley favoured the Stanton company with effusions of this class, and to the last was one of their patrons and friends.

It is said that it was at Uttoxeter, with this company, that the famous Miss Harriot Mellon first made her *debut* on the stage, although, it is stated, that she appeared first on the stage at Ulverston when a mere infant, as *Little Pickle* in the "Spoiled Child." When she first came to Uttoxeter she stayed at a house in Church Street, occupied by the friends of the late Mrs. Baxter, servant of Mr. Bentley, the poet, and she recollected carrying the luggage of Miss Mellon to the room of the Red Lion Inn, where the performances took place. Mrs. Baxter remembered this her first appearance very well, and spoke of her as not less amiable and kind in disposition, than handsome in appearance, being in every way the opposite of her mother, who was, as Mr. Sleigh says, "a vulgar virago." The celebrity of this lady is, however, more especially due to her becoming the wife of Thomas Coutts, Esq., the wealthy banker, and afterwards, on the death of Mr. Coutts, being married to the Duke of St. Albans. Mr. Coutts had been previously married, but he lost his first wife, by whom he had three daughters, all of whom were married to noblemen of the highest rank. Mr. Coutts was a munificient patron of the meritorious actors of the day, and it is supposed his intimacy with Miss Mellon originated from this circumstance. In marrying her he had his reward, for she proved to him the greatest blessing, and made him the happiest of men, and owing to that he left to her his immense wealth. At her death, however, at which time she was a duchess, she, having no children of her own, bequeathed her riches to Miss Angela Georgiana Burdett, daughter of Sir Francis Burdett, who had married Sophia, third daughter of Mr. Coutts, by his first wife, accompanying the inheritance with the condition that she should assume the name and arms of Coutts. This lady is the Baroness Burdett Coutts, who has such fabulous wealth, and whose munificence in doing good is so well known. *

Edward Knight, the comedian, also took part with a company at Uttoxeter. He was born in Birmingham, and was brought up as an artist, but made choice of the stage as a profession. At Uttoxeter he appeared in "Arno Silvester Draggerwood," and "Signo." Some of his personifications have been instanced as the most chaste and truly natural on the British stage. One day, at Uttoxeter, Mr. Knight received a note requesting his attendance at the inn adjoining the theatre, and intimating that he would receive information which would be of advantage to him. On hastening to the inn he found a gentleman of the name of Phillips, who recommended him to apply in his name to Mr. Tate Wilkinson, manager of the York Theatre, who was a person of very eccentric character. Mr. Knight immediately wrote a polite note, in the name of Mr. Phillips, to Mr. Wilkinson, and in a very short time he received a very laconic epistle, which utterly extinguished his glittering expectations. The note runs as follows:—

"Sir,—I am not acquainted with any Mr. Phillips, except a rigid Quaker, and he is the last person in the world to recommend a person to my theatre. I don't want you.

TATE WILKINSON."

Recovering from this uncivil and mortifying repulse, he wrote, in the bitterness of his anguish, a second letter to the manager, which is as follows:—

"Sir,—I should as soon think of applying to a Methodist preacher to preach for my benefit, as to a Quaker to commend me to Mr. Wilkinson. I don't want to come.

E. KNIGHT."

This letter was too much in Mr. Wilkinson's own peculiar style to meet with an unfavourable reception, but

---

* "*Gentleman's Magazine,*" 1822, and "*Men of the Time.*"

nothing resulted from it at the time. At the end of the year, however, during which time Mr. Knight remained with the Stafford Company, he was agreeably surprised with a second letter from his former correspondent. In brevity and elegance it was no wise inferior to his former epistle, but the matter of it sounded more sweetly to his ears. The following is a transcript of it :—

"Mr. Methodist Parson,—I have that produces 25s. a week. Will you hold forth?

TATE WILKINSON."

Mr. Knight, thus engaged, continued to perform at York, Leeds, and other places, and was afterwards promoted to Drury Lane, and to the Lyceum; so that what was played upon Mr. Knight as a jest, at Uttoxeter, ended in his permanent benefit. He died in 1826,* and he was interred in St. Pancras new church.

It is stated that in private life the manners of Mr. Knight were domesticated and methodical, that he disliked convivial parties, but possessed that kindness and benevolence of heart which reflect honour upon human nature.

A son of Mr. Knight, born in 1803, rose to great eminence as an artist. His name was Mr. John Prescott Knight, R.A. He was not only a Royal Academician, but also Secretary of the Royal Academy from 1848 until 1873, and he acted one year as deputy to Mr. Howard, R.A. He was professor of perspective in 1860, and for many years a trustee of the Royal Academy, and it is stated that he was the most influential of its officers, and practically had his own way. He painted in an able, clear and discriminating manner, and produced besides other works comprising combinations of figures, innumerable portraits, including those of many of the eminent men of his time, some of which have been engraved.†

Uttoxeter, too, although the times were, in comparison, more play-going, had, in the last century, a musical

---

* The *Mirror*.
† *Athenæum*, April 2nd, 1881.

society, existing under the classical, though somewhat high sounding name of "Uttoxeter Anacreontic Society." The leaders in this musical undertaking were Mr. Samuel Bentley, the Uttoxeter poet; Mr. Palmer, organist of Uttoxeter Church, and Mr. John Allkin. Mr. Samuel Bentley was advancing in years; Mr. Palmer was a young man, and all I can say of Mr. Allkin is that he was of an old and respectable family in the town and probably in middle age. The name "Anacreontic" was no doubt devised by the ingenuity of Mr. Bentley, for he was skilled in the Greek and Latin classics, and the "Odes of Anacreon" were familiar to him. The motive for giving this name to the society can only be surmised; it might be to keep before the minds of the members the lyric sweetness and rapture of the music they wished to cultivate. If instrumental music was practised at the concerts of the society, and if Mr. Bentley took a part in them, it is not difficult to say what instrument in his hands was made to discourse with charming effect; it was a fine bass viol, which proves at this day to be of great value. Mr. Bentley was an artist, a poet, a linguist and a musician, with ample leisure to sustain, as an amateur, all those distinctions, and I have rescued from oblivion a poem in which he paints himself in all those diversified aspects. As to his musical acquisitions he states:—

"From ivory keys full harmony I drew,
    And with melodious strains my flute could fill,
    And from the viol strings form concords new."

Besides the names already mentioned, the society was graced by the membership of at least one lady, a Miss Smith, who was so far a proficient as to take a part vocally in concerts. At what period the society was organized, and for what length of time it flourished, there are no means of showing. That it existed a number of years may be justly inferred by the numerous pieces of original music which were its offspring, and the fruit of a number of musical seasons, extending through the winter months. It was certainly in great popularity in 1794, for I have a copy of a programme with words of one of its concerts for

December 29th, of that year, the contents of it being excellent. But neither any portion of either the music or words of this programme were written by any local authors. At the same time a considerable number of songs and numerous pieces of music were produced both by Mr. Bentley and Mr. Allkin, the latter of whom also wrote a " Hymn for Christmas Day ;" an anthem, psalm vi., " Con Supplicanzione ;" as well as several other anthems, including one for the fast of February 25th, 1795. These facts show that he was a man of considerable musical culture and aspiration, which could not have been exerted upon the town without a refining and elevating effect upon a large portion of its inhabitants.

CHAPTER X.

MARKETS, TOLLS, FAIRS, AND TRADE OF UTTOXETER.

It does not appear at what time markets were first granted to Uttoxeter, but it is evident that one was held in the town by Robert de Ferrars, and it was subsequently confirmed, first to Edmund, Earl of Lancaster, 21st Edward I., 1292, and afterwards to Thomas, Earl of Lancaster, in the 2nd of Edward II. Before that time markets were held chiefly on Sundays and holidays, for the convenience of dealers and customers brought together for hearing divine service; and perhaps this may be one reason why groups of people are seen congregating in numbers in many churchyards at the present day before service commences. Uttoxeter market has long been noted as one of the best in the kingdom, and it is mentioned as such in the Harleian manuscripts. Before cheese fairs were established, cheese, as well as butter, was one of the commodities with which it was supplied.

Uttoxeter market has always been, and still is, particularly depended upon for a supply of good butter, which has been done up at different periods in various ways, to suit the taste and convenience of both the manufacturer and buyer. It is at present chiefly turned out of hand either in the shape of rolls, and consequently called "rolled butter," or from round butter prints having pleasing figures cut upon them, such as of a cow, a domestic fowl, a wheat-sheaf, a heart, a cluster of acorns, nuts or flowers, with suitable borders incised round the outer edge. Many years ago the butter prints were nearly eliptical in shape, or of a boat form, with lozenge shaped and other designs cut in, some of which had a great resemblance to the ornamentation upon busks which were in use many generations ago. Very different was the method of preparing butter for Uttoxeter Market two hundred and fifty years back in this neighbourhood, at which remote period it was put up and sold in "butter pots," which were coarse, cylindrical, unglazed vessels, the making of which then formed a considerable branch of the pottery trade in Staffordshire. An account of these curious vessels, as manufactured for Uttoxeter Market, and of some legal restrictions respecting them, is given in Dr. Plott's " Natural History of Staffordshire." " The butter they buy by the pot of a long cylindrical form, made at Burslem, in this county, of a certain size, so as not to weigh above six pounds at most, and yet to contain at least fourteen pounds of butter, according to an act of Parliament fourteen or sixteen years ago (about A.D. 1661, 13 and 14, Charles II., cap. 26), for regulating the abuse of this trade in the making of the pots, and false packing of the butter, which before was good for a little depth at top, and bad at the bottom ; and sometimes set in rolls, only touching at the top, and standing hollow below at a great distance from the sides of the pot. To prevent these little moorlandish cheats (than whom no people are esteemed more subtle), the factors keep a surveyor all the summer here, who, if he have any ground to suspect any of the pots tries them with an instrument of iron made like a cheese-taster."

The use of the butter pots was continued to nearly a hundred years ago. The observations of Dr. Plott are accompanied by the remark, that the London Cheesemongers, who had set up a factory at Uttoxeter, laid out on a market day as much as £500 in cheese and butter alone.

BUTTER POTS.

Butter pots, however, are mentioned in the parochial records of the town forty years before Dr. Plott wrote; for five pots of butter were sent from Uttoxeter to the garrison of Tutbury Castle, on the 7th of May, 1644, and had been bought at the sum of 12s. As this was seventeen years before the Act of Parliament for the regulation of the sale of butter in pots, it is difficult from this to judge of the exact price of butter per pound at Uttoxeter at that remote period. And yet it may be reasonably inferred that the pots of 1644 were of the size of those manufactured after 1661; for it appears the act was passed more for the prevention of any irregularity in the size of the pots, and the mode of packing butter in them, than for any actual alteration of the size the pots were understood to be. If so, butter then at Uttoxeter was worth but 2d. per pound, supposing the five pots of butter sent to Tutbury, costing 12s., contained fourteen pounds of butter each. About fifty years before butter was retailed throughout the kingdom at 7d. per pound;* but this was

---

* *Chronicum Preciosum*, by Bishop Fleetwood.

regarded as an enormous price, which, Stowe says, "was a judgment for their sins." It is highly probable, therefore, that the pots contained fourteen pounds of butter each, which consequently was 2d. per pound at Uttoxeter, when the five pots were bought, especially as it corresponds with the price of cheese at that time in the town, as to which the old parochial accounts have preserved very distinct information, the sum of £7 15s. 10d., having been paid for 8cwt, 2qrs. 7lbs., which was also for the besieged garrison at Tutbury Castle. Six chickens about the same time cost 2s., or 4d. each, for Lord Goring when he was at Uttoxeter with his soldiers. In 1812, as I gather from a household book, butter in Uttoxeter was 1s. 6d. per pound, cheese 8½d. per pound, flour 4s. 11d. and 5s. 1d. per stone, and salt 4½d. per pound, and in 1815, at the shop of Messrs. Porter and Keates, green tea was 7s. 6d. per pound, hyson 11s. per pound, starch 10½d. per pound, raisins 9d. per pound, and loaf sugar 1s. 5½d. per pound.

At this distant period (the seventeenth century) the tolls, fairs, and markets, with the borough court, were held by the heirs of John Gorenge, at the yearly rent of £4 13s. 4d.* They had been held before by Mr. Gorenge and by a Mr. Spragg, at £3 3s. 4d. yearly. The accounts of the Checkley constables for 1639, make this mention:— "My fellow churchwardens were given to pay the workmen on Uttoxeter fair-day £1 2s. 0d."

Corn, instead of being offered for sale by samples, was brought in large quantities in bags to the markets for sale by the farmers of the surrounding district, and for the lots so offered for sale a certain measure was taken in toll, and called toll-in-kind. Corn, thus taken, when the tolls were received by the lord of the manor, was stored in a room called the granary, which was over, or in connection with the court-house, and it was reached by a flight of steps at the outside of the building; and it is stated that it was ultimately ground to flour—such as was wheat—

---

* *Lightfoot's Survey.*

and sold to the poor at a very low price. Against this house a market-bell used to be rung at ten o'clock on the mornings of the market-day, by the collector of tolls, to prevent chapmen forestalling or buying marketable articles before the town was supplied, and an instance of an infraction of the right has been related to me which was followed by prosecution and a severe fine. *

Cheese was discontinued being brought to the markets for sale in the year 1818, when in the month of March, a meeting was convened, consisting of some of the principal gentlemen and agriculturists in the neighbourhood, with the late Lord Waterpark in the chair, to petition Lord Talbot, who held the manorial rights, to allow three cheese fairs to take place at Uttoxeter during the year, and to be toll pickage free, that is to be toll free.† The request as to the fairs was granted, although it does not appear that a legal charter was obtained for them from the crown (in which case, I presume, like markets established without charter, they cannot be legal, the parties setting them up being liable to be called upon to show by what warrant such a right is exercised), for in the same month of March, the first cheese fair ever held in Uttoxeter took place, and was successful. There being no documents accessible to the public containing any further information relating to the origin of cheese fairs in the town, and none perhaps in existence, except the one from which these particulars have been derived, nothing further can be said about them, except what has transpired in a course of litigation about the tolls. Till then, however, the proprietors or lessees of the tolls did not enforce the payment of toll upon cheese, pitched in the fair, upon parishioners, but only upon parties living beyond the boundaries of the parish. Of the origin and result of the law-suit it will not

---

* This I have, since the above was written, found confirmation of. In the *History of the towns and villages in Staffordshire*, *1818*, by Parson and Bradshaw, it is stated "The clerk of the market regulates the weights and measures, and endeavours to prevent forestalling by ringing a bell at half-past ten o'clock."

† See the *Staffordshire Advertiser* of the time.

be unimportant to give such a *resumé* as reports occurring at the time will enable me to furnish.

The dispute about the tolls originated in 1857, in the case of Moss v. Buckley, which was heard before the late R. G. Temple, Esq., Judge of the County Court, on Saturday, January 24th of that year. The defendant, as lessee of the tolls, had seized a basket of apples, which the plaintiff alleged he was carrying through the Market place on a market day, owing to a refusal to pay the demand of a penny for alleged toll. The money, however, was ultimately paid, and the apples restored to the owner, and the action was brought to recover the penny, with damages, or more correctly speaking, to test the legality of the claim. Judgment with costs was given for the plaintiff, on the evidence that the goods were not exposed in the Market Place for sale, but were merely being taken through to a person who had bought them, and that therefore the distress was illegal.

The case caused considerable excitement, and led to the insertion in one of the local papers* of March 11th, of a letter not likely to allay it. It called in question the validity, either by charter or act of parliament, of the right of toll on cheese set down in the Market Place for sale on the cheese fair days, and urged resistance to the demand for toll until it was proved that the claim was lawful.

The proprietors, however, remained firm in their demand, and issued placards announcing that the demand for toll for cheese would be strictly enforced at the fair on September 2nd, 1857, and, although there was much opposition to it, the requisition was generally complied with. But at the fair on November 12th ensuing, many farmers refused to pay, and the names of several were taken, with the view of suing them at law, and amongst them was Mr. Deoville, of Thorney Lane, who took the position of defendant, though with the prospect of being supported by his brother farmers in the case an action against them for refusal was brought. Subsequently

---

* *Uttoxeter New Era.*

several letters appeared in the same paper, apparently intended to produce an amicable arrangement betwixt the opposite parties, followed by one on the 9th of December, 1857, from a writer who contended that the document upon which the proprietors of the Town Hall and tolls rested their claim for toll was a feudal law of the time of John of Gaunt. The result was a public meeting in the Red Lion Room, on January 13th, 1858, to discuss measures by which the vexed question of cheese toll might be settled. Although this meeting did not terminate in any decisive issue, the parties concerned shortly afterwards arranged to have the question brought to arbitration. For this purpose an eminent legal gentleman, C. H. Scotland, Esq., was mutually fixed upon by the parties, and he attended at the Town Hall, Uttoxeter, on the 20th of May, 1858, and the day after, and the plaintiffs were represented by Mr. Crompton Hatton, and the defendants by Mr. Grey, of the Northern Circuit. The plaintiffs rested their claim on the ground that the soil and freehold of the Market Place where the cart of the defendant stood belonged to them, and Mr. Fradgley, architect, and Mr. E. S. Bagshaw were examined, as witnesses to repairs, cleaning, and the erection of the weighing machine in the Market Place by the plaintiffs. The plea put in for the defence rested upon two points—first, that although the Market Place belonged to the plaintiffs, the defendant exercised only right of road as one of the Queen's subjects; and second, that the Market Place belonged to the lords of the manor, for that by the court rolls, the lords of the manor amerced a person for breaking up the soil of Bear Hill, part of which is in the Market Place, and a number of witnesses were called upon to depose to having never paid toll.

No award was immediately given on this evidence, for several meetings were subsequently held in London, at which translations of documents of great antiquity were produced on the part of the defendant affecting the question, the principal point in dispute in which being, " whether or not the freehold and soil of the Market Place belonged to the plaintiffs," as already stated, and which they contended did, and were consequently entitled to the cheese-toll in question. The defendant strenuously disputed the ownership of the soil, and contended that the soil of the Market Place and the tolls were distinct, although it was admitted that the plaintiffs were the owners of the tolls, which they were empowered by their charter to levy on certain days, but not on articles not included in their charter, and on days never mentioned in it, and at fairs established subsequently to their charter, the tolls at which had always been disputed. The award was at length made, and it decided that no toll was payable by the defendant in respect of cheese exposed for sale at a fair held in the Market Place, not on a Wednesday, and that the Market Place was not the property of the plaintiff.

Notwithstanding this decision, a demand for toll was made at the cheese fair on November 11th, 1858, and complied with, except in a very few cases.

The Market Place, from that year till 1861, remained unrepaired and uncleaned, when a complaint was made against the proprietors of the market tolls for none repair. Mr. Dunnett, on their behalf, at the Petty Sessions of June 12th, of that year, stated that when the case came before the magistrates, the defendants considered, from the nature of their tenure of the Market Place, that they were not liable to repair it, but that the subject had been carefully looked into, and they admitted their liability. At the same time he repudiated the alleged wilful neglect, and complained that the greatest fault rested with the proprietors of the different houses in the Market Place, for breaking up the surface for the repairing of drains and not properly replacing the materials. The Market Place was kept better cleaned after this, but it was not until 1867 that it was repaved at cost of nearly £100, which was collected for the purpose by Mr. Coulson and Mr. Page.

Uttoxeter Market Place formerly contained an ancient market cross with a flight of twenty-four steps round it, resembling, probably, the old market cross at Repton. It is mentioned in the last century in a book of travels by "a gentleman," but it was removed either at the close of the last century or at the beginning of this. The neighbourhood of Uttoxeter has had a wayside cross, for in the parish a lane was anciently, and may now be called "Cross Lane," in the same way that a place near Ellastone is called "Ousley Cross," where the pedestal of it remains looking much like a trough, whilst near to a portion of the cross serves the purpose of a gate post. Roadside crosses were numerous in former times, and I have seen the pedestal of one close by the roadside not far from Sheen on the right hand side of the road betwixt Longnor and Hartington.

The accompanying beautiful engraving of crosses of the twelfth century shows the interesting character market and wayside crosses sometimes assumed.

Besides the fortnightly cattle market on every alternate Wednesday, Uttoxeter has cattle fairs on May the 6th, September 19th, November 11th, and 27th; colt fairs, September 1st and 19th; cheese fairs, March 12th, September 3rd, and November 12th.

For many years Uttoxeter had an annual show of fat cattle. The last was held in a field in Short Lane, December 12th, 1855, and was one of the most successful of any that had taken place. At the last annual dinner the chair was taken by H. Meynell Ingram, Esq.

The Staffordshire Agricultural Meeting took place for the first time, at Uttoxeter, in September, 1857. The trial of implements was made on land on the High Wood, in the occupation of the late Mr. Bakewell, of the Moor House Farm. In every respect, although the day turned out exceedingly wet, the meeting, both as to the extent and fineness of the stock exhibited, and the interest attaching to the inventions in machinery displayed for dairying and agricultural purposes, as well as for largeness of of attendance, was the best of any annual meeting which had, up to that time, taken place. It was successfully held at Uttoxeter again in 1864, when the sum of £221 5s. 0d. was taken for admission. On these occasions the large field at Dove Bank was used as a show yard, but at the annual meeting of 1875, it took place in a large field

WAYSIDE CROSSES.

in the Picknals. The attendance was very great, and the stream of people, quite filling Carter Street from side to side, who wended their way to the scene, after 12 o'clock, took about an hour and a half to pass. The number of tickets sold was, 450 at 2s. 6d. each, 8,474 at 1s. each, and 451 at 6d. each; in the whole 9,676 tickets were sold at the entrance of the show yard, making £498 14s. 6d. For this year the local committee paid over a guarantee of £200, and in addition, gave £100 in prizes, whilst the tradesmen of Uttoxeter gave £150 in prizes.

Owing to the cattle plague, Uttoxeter Smithfield was closed against the admission of cattle for sale on the 9th of December, 1865, until May, 1867, when it was re-opened for the sale of cattle by auction and license, but only under great restrictions, and this circumstance originated fortnightly sales by auction of all descriptions of stock, which continue to the present and are likely to be perpetuated. May fair of that and the preceding year, presented a most forlorn aspect, nothing but a few sheep being offered for sale. Subsequently, in 1867, the fortnightly cattle markets and the fairs were opened again in the usual way, all restrictions for the admission and sale of cattle being removed. The vicinity of Uttoxeter was most providentially free from the disease. The nearest place where it was stated it occurred was Leigh, at a farm near the river Blythe, in one lot of cattle only, most of which were killed and buried, but many persons of good judgment doubted whether it was the cattle plague.

We may proceed to notice that the trade of Uttoxeter is principally of a local description, like that of most other market towns situated in the centres of agricultural communities. In this respect it has, however, somewhat improved of late, but not in a way to add materially to the prosperity of the town. The Uttoxeter Brewery Company, whose business was started early in this century by Messrs. Earp and Saunders (Mr. Earp being also a spirit merchant and cheesefactor in 1818), * have extended

---

* In 1818 Mr. Saunders is only spoken of as a tanner and maltster, Bradley Street.

their operations, and made extensive additions to their premises, by which they are enabled to brew many times the quantity of malt they previously did. A new brewery was erected near Bridge Street Station in 1864, and for some time it was in operation, when its first owner failed, and after remaining inactive several years, it was bought in the year 1872 by Messrs. Gardner and Company (really by Mr. Stretch), and in their hands it has proved a successful undertaking, as, besides doing a good home business, they make large consignments of their ales to their Liverpool stores. In my youth the late Mr. Mills, maltster, had a small brewery in Church Street. Messrs. Crichlow, formerly Messrs. Cope and Crichlow, carry on a skin and tanning trade, and are manufacturers of glue. For many years a foundry was conducted at the Brookhouse by Mr. Bewley; and Messrs. Bamford erected one in Specal Street in 1871, for their own castings only, but since then they have also entered largely upon the manufacture of agricultural implements, and have taken out numerous patents for inventions and improvements, and during their throngest times employ some one hundred and thirty men and apprentices. A considerable business is done by a number of persons in preparing maw skins for cheese making.

One branch of manufacture formerly in Uttoxeter has gained for the town a remarkable notoriety, not only on account of its past importance, but also on the assumption, founded on a lack of correct information, that iron forges are in full work at Uttoxeter now, it being seriously asserted in books of reference down nearly to the present time that it is "surrounded by iron forges," which is enough to give a stranger the idea that it is one of the busiest places in the kingdom. Still, if the stereotyped remark does not hold true as to the present, it does, to some extent, as to the past, for in the fourteenth century it had two iron forges, and besides the manufacture of iron from its raw state, it is probable it was also a great centre for the conversion of it into articles and implements of husbandry for use in the honour of Tutbury generally, trade being very wisely equalized in those feudal times amongst the several towns of the honour, for their reciprocal benefit. In fact it was the only staple trade of the town, and most likely the people for the greater part got their livelihood either at the forges by making iron, or in the making of implements, or by the merchandise of the same, many persons probably being severally engaged in each.

Fortunately the site where one or more of these forges existed when in operation five hundred years ago is ascertainable, and it will not be uninteresting to point out the place. It is certain that when they existed it was by the side of some stream of water, and if refuse of such spots can be discovered in the vicinity of some flow of water near the town, it may justly be concluded that it was there that the manufacture of iron was carried on. Various mechanical contrivances are now employed, independent of a running stream, to produce the blast necessary to smelt iron, but in those days the only motive power for the purpose was that of a fall or current of water. The Hockley, or Muckle Brook, which has the name more northerly of Uttoxeter of Stony-ford Brook, is the only stream close to Uttoxeter, and it is by this, at the bottom of Pinfold Street, on the premises of Messrs. Crichlow, that the refuse of a forge or forges has been found. In the course of making foundations for buildings, excavating tan-pits, and digging holes for posts, Messrs. Cope came upon quantities of this refuse, known as slag, which leaves no doubt of the forges having been at that place. The meadow extending from there to the Hockley road was, doubtless, wholly occupied by these ironworks, for many years back it was covered by hillocks, and when the ground was levelled and drained, about seventy years ago, much ironworks refuse was observed; and, what may be geologically interesting, a number of owler trees were found lying at a considerable depth, where they had become prostrate when the land was a bog.

It is supposed that a mill or some such building, or perhaps another forge, existed at an early date higher up the brook, above the present Hockley fish pond (itself becoming a thing of the past), for when the railway was made by there the remains of such a place were discovered, and I just recollect seeing a large extent of ground covered with black fire refuse and several beams of wood. There is a piece of land there called "The Pool Meadow Shutt," and a pool at the place still must have been the "Pool of Uttoxhather," which was paid for as a fishery, and it may have been the pool of the mill.

Betwixt two and three hundred years ago there was a trade at Uttoxeter in fulling cloth, but whether this was of as high antiquity in the town as the bleaching and weaving which were established at Newborough, and wool combing at Tutbury at the time the ironworks were established at Uttoxeter, I have no means of showing, unless the non-mention of it in the documents in the office of the Duchy of Lancaster may be considered decisive against it. However, a fulling mill did exist in connection with this town at the beginning of the seventeenth century, and was owned or occupied by Sir Thomas Milward, chief justice of Chester. It was subsequently converted into a corn mill, when it was held by the heirs of Sir Thomas Milward and Walter Mynors, Esq., at the rent of £8 os. od. Entries respecting this mill are as follows :— "Sir Thomas Milward houldeth one ffulling mill now converted into a corn mill, late Kynedsleys and Shawcross, the millne and two small pieces of land adjoining, containing two roodes and one and twentie perches, at the rent of eigh pond." Again, "Walter Mynors, Esquire, and Sir Thomas Milward hould in ffre farm Uttoxeter millnes at the rent of £8 6s. 8d." Here mills appears in the plural, and it may therefore be supposed the present ancient corn mill may be included.

The fulling mill which was altered for the purposes of a corn mill stood at a place called Bangalore,* a name derived probably from the banging or beating of cloth in the stream, it being on the Tean Brook, betwixt the old

---

* Bangalore may be derived from *blangi* (wane) *bhang*, to break, and English breakers.

cotton mill house and the present old Uttoxeter corn mill. In the recollection of people living in 1872, an old mill actually stood at the spot, and was used as a rag mill. There is a powerful fall of water at the place, and large beams of oak timber lie in and at the side of the stream, with brickwork, and plainly indicate the exact site of the mill, whilst several poor cottages stood about the place until after 1845, as I very well recollect.

In the eighteenth century the family of Bladen were in business as woolcombers and woolstaplers, and amongst the indentures which are preserved in one of the chests in the vestry-room is one of the date of November 21st, 1730, mentioning that William Ford was bound to Samuel Bladen, of Uttoxeter, woolstapler and woolcomber. There is also one specifying that, in 1745, William Bladen, of Uttoxeter, son of John Bladen, webster or weaver, apprenticed himself to James Bladen, of Moddershall. The wool business is still carried on in the family, and jersey dyeing, and perhaps spinning and weaving, were connected with the business in olden times.

In reviving a little more of old Uttoxeter, it may be noticed that in the last century, and long into the present, the manufacture of jewellery was carried on to a great extent in the town; and it occasionally happens that the wonderful business, the extensive range of shops in which it was carried on, and other matters which appertained to the undertaking, are subjects of conversation amongst those whose reminiscences reach so far back. This, however, is, as old people die, less the case now than it was a few years ago. The buildings which formed the jewellers' shops, which were of the half-timber class, several stories high, resembling a factory, occupied an extensive site opposite to Silver Street, with a large yard in front coming up to the street, Silver Street doubtless taking its name from the fact of the jewellery business being in its vicinity. Two brothers of the name of Copestake, Thomas and Henry, are recollected to have been the proprietors of this business and of the premises, and also owners and occupiers of Uttoxeter Hall, a remarkable antique half-timbered

x

house adjoining. They did a considerable foreign trade, besides being under the patronage of the British Government, for whom they executed many important contracts, stars of honour of great value being amongst them. Altogether they employed about one hundred and forty men and eighty apprentices. Many of the lapidaries, who were also numerous, did the polishing of stones at their own homes, in various parts of the town ; and until 1872, when he died at a great age, there lived an old man in Uttoxeter who served his apprenticeship with the jewellers to the lapidary branch of the trade. It appears that the business left the town perhaps more than sixty years ago, in obedience to those changes, it is presumed, which are produced by competition, cheaper manufactures, or fictitious jewellery, and the application of mechanical contrivances, by which extensive undertakings are generally drawn to common centres, so that as the jewellery business from these causes declined at Uttoxeter, it gradually found its way to Birmingham. At the risk of some little repetition, I may state that, in referring to Wedgwood gem setting, Miss Meteyard, in her life of Wedgwood, was enabled from the Wedgwood accounts of the time of Josiah Wedgwood, to give some interesting information respecting the jewellery business at Uttoxeter, which I have not otherwise met with. She mentions that "A large number of these gems were set as rings, earrings, chatelains, bracelets and other such ornaments. At first, when gold was employed as a setting, the work was done in London by Nodes, the goldsmith. . . . For steel work, and later, when Nodes's prices were found too high, for gold work too, the gems were sent to Birmingham ; though from 1773, and for some years subsequently all the finer portion of these gold settings were the work of Thomas Copestake, jeweller, of Uttoxeter, in Staffordshire. Copestake was a man renowned throughout all these Midland counties as a lapidary, an engraver, and a goldsmith. He exported jewellery to Russia, and employed from one to two hundred hands in various branches of his trade. His house and workshops are said to have been picturesque in the extreme; the former being an old timbered hall lying just without the town; the latter, where the lapidaries had their sheds, whilst above were the shops of the smiths and setters. Copestake, who was a great admirer of Wedgwood works, was first employed by him to set seals, and from these he advanced to necklaces, bracelets and other ornaments. He also bought gems of Wedgwood to set on his own account, so that for some years the dealings between them were considerable; yet in spite of skill and an immense trade, Copestake from some unexplained cause was not a prosperous man. He eventually borrowed money of Wedgwood, and toward the close of the century in such reduced circumstances as to necessitate an unmarried daughter to set up frames for lacework in order to procure the means to live."

One of the Copestakes erected the powerful corn mills at Fole, now occupied by Mr. William Vernon, and in the ownership of his father.

Besides the jewellery trade, calico and linen weaving have been extensively carried on in Uttoxeter until about 1820, at several "jenny shops," at which about eighty or one hundred hands were employed, and I believe that some of the tablecloths which they manufactured were beautifully finished in resemblance of embroidery. One of the places occupied the whole of the north side of the triangular enclosure opposite to the Grammar School, and another, which remained unappropriated to any other purpose many years, and whose large extent I can speak of from personal knowledge, took up the whole space of the side of the yard and part of the garden of the premises now occupied as the Coach and Horses Inn, in Carter Street. *

And until about the same period there was a cotton mill at Tean Brook, where the farm house is, and which is the mill house or part of the mill. The site of the large pond is a little west of the house.

* In records of 1818, Robert Shawe, Sheep Market, is spoken of as a "linen and cotton manufacturer," and John Shawe, Carter Street, as a "manufacturer of sewing cotton and linen thread."

In those days, also, Stramshall corn mill was used as a cotton mill. I am unable, however, to show in what way and to what degree the mills were dependent upon the local manufacturers at the "jenny shops," but that they were there is scarcely a doubt, and, if so, it must have been to a good extent to have met the requirements of nearly a hundred persons engaged in manufacturing cotton and linen fabrics.

Of not much inferior importance was the lace trade, which was introduced by Miss Grace Copestake, sister of the Messrs. Copestake, jewellers, famous in "My Own Story," and who lived at Uttoxeter Old Hall, rendered famous by royalty having been entertained at it. Here she employed many young women of the town in embroidering lace, at which they were enabled to earn a guinea a week. She also let out quantities to the towns and places about. With these branches of trades and manufactures, giving employment to so many persons, it is surprising that Uttoxeter, which at the apparently less prosperous time of the civil war furnished such large sums of money for political purposes, was found to be so far oppressed by poor rates in 1788 as to have the common, in which the town had apparently communistic rights, enclosed, specially for the relief of the inhabitants burdened by them.

An extensive business has been carried on in Uttoxeter in clock case making in oak, and in solid mahogany, with inlaid ornamentation, large quantities being sent to Manchester, Birmingham, Macclesfield, Coventry, Wales, Chesterfield, and all the large towns. It began, however, to decline rapidly about 1850, and now, I believe, there is only one professional hand remaining, and in his old age, to eke out a living, he does jobs in other branches of woodwork. ✱

In my younger days there were several extensive tanneries in Uttoxeter and neighbourhood. One was at the Brook House, the business last being carried on by Messrs. Frost; another occupied an extensive space on

---

✱ Since this was written he has died.

the right hand side at the bottom of Bradley Street, at the bend into Silver Street, where Mr. William Perks has built a range of handsome residences, which have received the name of "The Crescent." This business was in the hands of a Mr. Shipley. There was also a tannery at the Leasows, which was carried on by Mr. Wigley, who, with his family, emigrated to Canada. There was likewise one at Scownslow Green, which belonged to a Mr. Towers. The late wealthy brothers, Messrs. John and Joseph Fox, Church Street; Mr. Bull, High Street; and Mr. Hobson, Bridge Street, who also occupied part of the premises now in use in the business of Messrs. Coulson, were extensive curriers. All these businesses, however, have disappeared, as has button making, and the manufacture of glass beads, both of which are recollected to have been in the town. The manufacture of singular and curiously hooped vessels called piggins or noggins, holding less than a pint measure, and long since superseded by pitcher basins, now so common in domestic use, has been discontinued generations ago. One of these articles, which was made in Uttoxeter, and was a heirloom of an Uttoxeter family more than two hundred years, is now in my possession. It consists of eight narrow oak staves or laggins only, including the handle. It is three inches and a quarter in length, outside, and five inches and a half wide. The handle is two-and-a-half inches in length. It has one wood hoop on it only, which is fastened by four notched buckles or straps, which pass through as many loops with notches in, so that when it was driven down to its intended place it became perfectly tight, and rendered the vessel secure against leakage. Wooden vessels for the dairy, especially milk pails, gauns, and round churns, were formerly hooped generally in a similar way with wood hoops, but the hoops were not so intricately constructed for these articles, having only one tongue to be notched on to the vessels with. But pails, gauns, round churns, buckets, cheese tubs, oval kimnels, and brewing vessels for private and public-house use, are now rarely required, tin and galvanized vessels having taken the place of some of the things named, and large breweries having rendered the others of no use. The manufacture and bending of wood hoops from cleft ash was formerly an important business in Uttoxeter, together with the making of wood measures, seed hoppers, and yokes for cows, instead of chains, but it has entirely disappeared, the last old maker having been Mr. James Tranter, who died in 1867. Mr. Tranter was also a large timber merchant, and the great quantities which he converted were sent to Manchester for sale. Mr. John Walker, cabinet maker and furniture dealer, Carter Street, is now the only wholesale converter of timber in Uttoxeter, and living in a woody district, having ample space, and a powerful saw mill in operation, he is enabled to send off a constant supply to the Manchester market by rail. Recently Mr. Cooper, of Ashbourne, has had the large warehouse at the old canal wharf altered into a stay factory, with steam power, and when all the internal arrangements are completed it is expected that about three hundred young women will be employed at it.

But these facts about the trade of Uttoxeter, will be wanting, if reference is not made to the bookselling and printing business. The former has been mentioned as having been introduced into Uttoxeter by Michael Johnson, but it was not until many years after that printing was brought into it. In connection with a notice in the *Graphic Newspaper*, of April 30th, 1881, of an engraving after "Dr. Johnson's Penance," a picture which was painted by Mr. Adrian Stokes, and exhibited at the Royal Academy, the following interesting remarks are made, showing how greatly the whole district, as well as Uttoxeter in particular, was indebted to the father of provincial booksellers residing at Lichfield. It says:—"at the time of Johnson's boyhood booksellers' shops in the provincial towns of England were very rare. There was not even one in Birmingham, where accordingly Mr. Michael Johnson (the philosopher's father), the Lichfield bookseller and stationer, used to open a temporary shop or stall, every market day. In this manner he occasionally resorted to several towns in the neighbourhood, Uttoxeter amongst others. That he was highly esteemed is shown by the following extract from a letter, written in 1716, from Trentham, by the Rev. George Plaxton, Lord Gower's chaplain :—"Johnson the Lichfield librarian, is now here : he propagates learning all over the diocese, and advanceth knowledge to its just height ; all the clergy here are his pupils, and suck all they can from him." The first professional printer in Uttoxeter was Mr. Richards, who established a printing office about the year 1782. Mr. Richards was a native of Coventry, and an apprentice in the Birmingham *Aris* and *Gazette* office, from which, at the expiration of his articles, he came direct to Uttoxeter and commenced business for himself. He soon married a Miss Askins, of the White Hart Hotel, whose father had kept the post office, and he succeeded to the office of postmaster, the delivery of letters then being made only three days a week, the mail coming to Uttoxeter from Lichfield, and the remuneration being a penny on each letter delivered. He continued printer and postmaster forty years, and was succeeded by his son Mr. Robert Richards, who held the appointment thirty-six years, until his death in 1869, and the business was continued by his widow till her death in 1881, when the post office was removed to the Market Place.

It is not to be expected that Uttoxeter printers have turned out of the press many works beyond such as have been of local import; and yet it may not be without interest to collectors of local literature, which is often illustrative of local events, to enumerate some of the pamphlets and small books which have come into existence through the medium of Uttoxeter printers. Perhaps the earliest specimens of printing done in Uttoxeter are the two pieces of poetry reprinted in connection with this book—one being on "Peace," and the other on his "Birthday," by Samuel Bentley, the printer of both being Mr. Richards. I have also seen a poem on "Patriotism" —the Patriotism of Sunday Schools,—a rather superior poem, also from the press of Mr. Richards, and, if I recollect rightly from the pen of one of the Saddlers. Mr.

Richards also printed for a London house an exceedingly well printed edition of "La Perous's Voyages," with plates, and an Arithmetic, as well as a tale by a Mrs. Holebrook, of Sandon, the title of which I cannot discover. Amongst the books printed by the late Mr. Thomas Norris, have been three editions of Uttoxeter Church Hymn Book, now superseded by Hymns Ancient and Modern, and an edition for Marchington Church. For the Rev. Dr. Bevin, formerly of Leigh, he printed a Catechism and a Scripture History, and a collection of letters and other religious pieces by persons in humble life, collected and edited by Mr. Blagg. These are the productions of persons who were living in the neighbourhood at the time, and considering by whom they were written, must be highly regarded for their ability and piety. "The Simple Wreath of Christian Flowers," by the Rev. H. W. Armstrong, vicar of Uttoxeter, was also from this press. It is a small collection of original poems, of which only two copies were on large paper. Mr. Norris also printed a "Lecture on Botany," and another able and lengthy one on "The Philosophy of History," and also an address delivered at a great Reform Meeting at Cheadle, all by the Rev. J. P. Jones, vicar of Alton, on the 31st of October, 1837. The two lectures, as will be noticed further on, were delivered in Uttoxeter by the reverend gentleman. For the late Miss Robotham, owner of Lea Hill estate, he printed a poem on Alton Gardens, with some other pleasing verses added. More recently he published a sermon, by the Rev. John Cooke, on the death in 1856 of the late Mr. John Vernon, founder of free Sunday Schools in Uttoxeter, and a "Farewell Sermon," by the late vicar of Uttoxeter, the Rev. C. F. Broughton. He also printed a small book of poems, and another little volume of very pleasing and readable sketches, entitled "Pictures of the Lowly," written by Mr. George Wakefield, who has recently also published through Messrs. Bemrose a similar volume of sketches, entitled "Sketches of Character," amongst which "Willy Beech" and the "Model Working Man," will be read with much interest. Mr. Norris also produced a number of large lithographic illustrations of Uttoxeter Church; St. John's Hospital, Alton; and of Alton Towers, and his successor, Mr. Brocklehurst, who had been a colonist in Australia and Africa, and whose restless and adventurous mind led him again from a settled business in the town to America, published at much expense, in tinted lithography, a view of Uttoxeter Market Place. The late Mr. Kelly printed two "Statements," being large pamphlets by Mr. Rushton, solicitor, which had respect to Alleyne's Grammar School. He also printed an able sixpenny pamphlet, written by the late Mr. Gould, solicitor, at a time when there was a great deal of discussion betwixt church parties in the town, it having reference to the subject in dispute, and besides other smaller things, a poem entitled "The River Dove and Human Life compared," by Mr. Geo. Wakefield. The late Mr. F. Davis printed several sermons for the Rev. H. Abud, vicar. It should be noticed that Miss Craven, of this town, has published a volume of "Fire Side Musings" through a Manchester printer, and also that, through the same medium, Mr. W. T. Birch, a native of Uttoxeter, published a similar volume entitled "Home Reveries." Several attempts have been made at originating newspapers in Uttoxeter, one having the name *Uttoxeter New Era*, which was started by Mr. Kelly, in 1855, and the other the *Uttoxeter Advertiser*, originated in 1882, by Mr. Ryder.

It will be useful to make memoranda of costly architectural works which have been executed by the late Mr. S. Crichlow, of this town. Of these may be mentioned "The Lonsdale Memorial Church," at Lichfield, except the tower, under Mr. Fowler, of Louth; St. Paul's, Burton-on-Trent, at a cost of £25,000, the gift of Mr. Bass, M.P., under Mr. Seal, of Doncaster; new porch, south aisle and organ chamber to Blythfield church, under Mr. Street; under the same architect, he added a new chancel in Early English, to Tutbury church, and restored the west end and nave; he built Heanor church in the early English style, under Messrs. Stevenson and Robinson; and he also erected the Free church, at Ashbourne, the gift of the late F.

Wright, Esq., of Osmaston; the architects being the same as the last named.

So lengthy a description having been presented of the trade of Uttoxeter, the notice may very properly be concluded by an account of a good number of Traders' Tokens which have been struck in the town. Their use appears to have originated in the time of Queen Elizabeth, in consequence of a great scarcity then existing of small change, and Arthur Leech, Esq., F.G.S., of Newcastle, in the proceedings of the North Staffordshire Naturalists' Field Club, informs us in an able paper on the subject that they are regarded under two heads, viz., "Early Tokens" and "Later Tokens." The Uttoxeter Tokens are of the latter class. Mr. Jewett says "that they are simply called 'tokens' because they denoted, and were passed amongst the people as tokens, or pledges of a certain money value; that they were in fact metallic promissory notes for halfpence, pence, or farthings, or other value as the case might be." In the time of Queen Elizabeth they were often in lead, pewter, tin, latten, and even leather, and when returned to the issuers in numbers, were bought back with regular coin; and commodities could only be had for them from their issuers.* In my recollection a grocer of this town had a large issue of them, and similar signs are in use by innkeepers to this day, and entitle their holders at any time to the value in liquor which they represent.

The following traders' tokens (of which engravings are given of two as examples) of the seventeenth century were struck in Uttoxeter:—

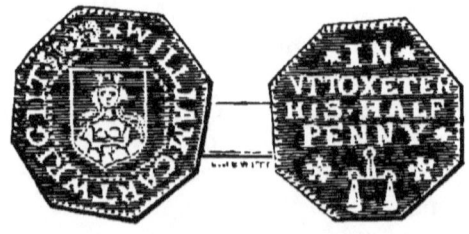

---

* Mr. Jewitt, L.S.A., and Boyne on English Tokens.

Obverse—WILLIAM CARTWRIGHT, 1668=within the inner octagon, in a shield, the Mercers' Arms.

Reverse— IN VTTOXETER HIS HALF PENNY. A pair of scales between two flowers.

This is an octagonal token.

The Mercers' Arms are *gules* a Demi-virgin couped below the shoulders, *proper*, vested *or*, crowned with an Eastern crown, her hair dishevelled and wreathed about the temples with roses of the second, issuing from clouds, and all within an orle of the same, *proper*. The orle of clouds is frequently, as in this instance, omitted.

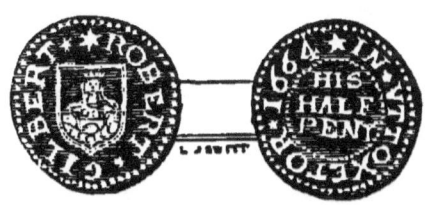

Obverse—ROBERT GILBERT=In the field, without an inner circle, the Mercers' Arms, in a shield.

Reverse—IN VTTOXETOR . 1664=In the field, HIS HALF PENY. within the inner circle,

Obverse—IOHN HALSEY . 1668=In the field without an inner octagon, the Mercers' Arms, in a shield.

Reverse— * IN * VTTOX * ETER * HIS HALF PENY. The lines divided by rows of dots.

Obverse—WILLIAM LAYTHROPP=In the shield, the Royal Arms. No inner circle.
Reverse—IN VTTOXETER 1663=In the field, HIS within the HALF inner circle, PENY.

The issuer of this token was probably an innkeeper, the Royal Arms being the sign of his hostlery, the "King's Arms."

Obverse—WILLIAM . LEESE . 1668=The Grocers' Arms.
Reverse—IN VTTOXETER HIS HALF PENY=In four lines across the field.

This is an octagonal token.

The Grocers' Arms are *argent*, a cheveron *gules* between nine cloves, six in chief and three in base, *sable*.

Obverse—JAMES LOYED.
Reverse—VTTOXETER . HIS HALF PENY, 1660.

JOHN LEESE, the arms defaced.
IN YTTUXET 1663.

Obverse—IEFFERY POWER . OF=St. George and the Dragon.
Reverse—VTTOXETER . 1666=In the field, within HIS the inner circle, HALF PENY.

This was probably an innkeeper's token, the sign being the "George and Dragon."

Obverse—WILL . WAKELIN . 1663=In the field, HIS within the HALF inner circle, PENY.
Reverse—VIVE . LE . ROY . IN . VTTEXETOR=In the field, within the inner circle, a crown.

Probably an innkeeper's token, the issuer keeping the "Crown."

It ought not to be considered inappropriate to make some reference to modes of conveyance with which Uttoxeter was, like many other places, compelled, in former times, to be content. No doubt plenty of people with conveyances could be had for hire either to take goods from the town or fetch them in, and during the civil war of the seventeenth century it is quite clear from local records that the hiring system was much in use. At the same time dealers would often be ready to deliver goods, whilst tradesmen of the town would be compelled to a great extent to fetch from distances what they required, and also to deliver goods in the same way. This is illustrated by the fact that the large clock-case makers of the town were obliged to pile their manufactures on carts and deliver them as far off as Birmingham, Wales, Chesterfield, Macclesfield, and other places equally distant. The Pickford waggons would be a great relief, and when the branch canal from Cauldon was made the joy of the people of Uttoxeter knew no bounds, and its opening was a day of great festivity. Lime kilns were erected at the wharf, a dock-yard for the construction and repair of boats was opened, and a works in the same vicinity were commenced for the manufacture of pyrolignious acid, or crude wood vinegar. Still coal was brought to the town regularly over the backs of mules and donkeys, as I recollect, on what might be called pack saddles, and this caused a considerable business in breeding mules in the neighbourhood of Alton and Cheadle, and I find that a William Summerland, of this town, was a mule dealer in 1818. But the North Stafford Railway has altered all this, and superseded the once useful canal, as well as the numerous coaches which came to the town, of which about seventy years ago, there were these :—

FROM THE WHITE HART INN.

The " Light Post," to London, every evening at half-past six; to Liverpool, every morning at half-past four o'clock.

The " Express," to Manchester, every day at twelve o'clock; to Birmingham, every afternoon at three o'clock.

The "Accomodation," to Derby, every Tuesday, Thursday and Saturday, at half-past eleven in the forenoon; to Newcastle, through the Potteries, every Monday, Wednesday and Friday, at half-past one o'clock.

From the Red Lion Inn.

The "Telegraph," to Sheffield, every Sunday, Tuesday and Thursday, at eleven in the forenoon; to Birmingham, same days, at half-past one o'clock.

The "Private Mail" (from the Post Office), for letters, parcels and *passengers*, to Rugeley, through Abbots Bromley, Admarstone, and Colton, every morning at six o'clock; returns every evening at five o'clock.

The large canal warehouse still exists, and after being used for a long period as a cheese warehouse, has, as previously mentioned, been converted into a stay factory, but the basin which was constructed in front of it for the reception of boats has been partially destroyed, and a saw mill and timber yard now occupy the bottom.

CHAPTER XI.

LIBRARIES AND LITERARY INSTITUTIONS.

The mention of books and printers almost naturally recalls again to mind the name and times of that fine old worthy, Mr. Michael Johnson. But much as he plodded weekly to Uttoxeter with books, there could not have been very much literature in the town generally in his day, and consequently but a limited variety of books for readers. Indeed, at the beginning of this century, and for some time after, books were very rare in Uttoxeter. The first circulating library in the town, of which I can obtain any knowledge, was established early in the century by a Mrs. Gent, in the Market Place, and about 1830, a Mr. John Bowers Smith, established one at the bottom of High Street. This desirable example was followed by Ann Norris and Son, establishing a more extensive one, to which readers had recourse during many years. Perhaps, however, few readers are prepared to say what one of its most frequent visitors has asserted, that "he had read all the books in it, and some of them several times over," although they were very numerous. White, in his *Gazetteer of the County*, remarks that a News' Room was opened in 1831, and that a Book Society was established about 1824, being doubtless what was more fully described as, "Uttoxeter Permanent Book Society," the members of which numbered about thirty-six, or forty at the utmost, when it was in its most flourishing state. Amongst the subscribers were the Earl of Shrewsbury, Lady Tamworth, Sir Thomas Cotton Sheppard, Sir T. Wheler, Colonel Marshall, the clergy of the neighbourhood and other respectable people. Later on in its history a supply of books was made to it from Mudie's library. The terms of membership were an entrance fee of a guinea, and an annual subscription of the same amount. Although the Book Society continued in existence a great many years—perhaps more than forty years—it ultimately, for want of sufficient support, became necessary to break it up, and the books were removed to the offices of Mr. Flint, and after remaining there a number of years in neglect, they were sold by auction at the Town Hall, in 1879, and proved to have formed one of the choicest libraries of modern books that could possibly have been brought together during the time of its existence.

From the consideration of Circulating Libraries to that of Mechanics' Institutes is but a step. The first in Uttoxeter was formed in or about the year 1839, under the title of "The Uttoxeter Society for the Diffusion of Useful Knowledge and Mechanics' Institute," and its meetings were held in a large room over the shop of the late Mr. Norris, in the Market Place. The opening lecture, which was an able disquisition on "The Philosophy of History," was delivered by the late Rev. T. P. Jones, of Alton, and it was printed in 1841, with a dedication to the late Robert Blurton, Esq., of Smallwood Manor, both being members of the local committee of the London Society for the Diffusion of Useful Knowledge. It had a small beginning, for its first catalogue of books, printed in 1844, did not number more than seventy-one distinct works of one hundred and twenty-eight volumes; but great discretion was exercised in their selection, for at that time a better collection, for the extent to which it went, could not have been formed for the purpose, all the works being so well calculated to please, instruct and educate. Yet this society did not realize general public support, and in

1845, a rival one was commenced with the title "The Uttoxeter Literary and Scientific Institution," which now exists under the name of Mechanics' Institute. The Society for the Diffusion of Useful Knowledge, if it was not over prosperous before, had now to yield entirely to the increased energy and spirit evinced in the inauguration and management of the Literary Institute, and its library was sold to the committee of the new undertaking for £20.

The rooms of the new society were, in the first instance, in the Market Place, but as the number of members increased, a more commodious and convenient place became necessary, and the large building in High Street, formerly a bank, but now the offices of Messrs. Welby and Wilkins, solicitors, were rented and used for several years for the library and reading rooms. The institution has a room now at the Town Hall, which it has occupied since 1853. At this period the society had attained gratifying success, and the treasurer had in hand the sum of £60, a great part of which was expended in buying furniture for the new rooms, for then it had two rooms—one for the library and another for a reading room. At that time it was declared by Dr. Hudson, in a work on Mechanics' Institutes, to be the most prosperous one in the kingdom. Although it was declared so flourishing by this gentleman at the time he wrote, it could not really have been so to the extent represented, from the amount of population in comparison with that of larger towns; neither could it really have carried the palm when judging of it on those principals of self-support which are the only just criteria for measuring the innate vitality and relative superiority, in a financial sense only, of such societies. In thus looking at the institution at that period, it ought to be remembered that it received many handsome donations from some of its patrons, as from the late Joseph Mallaby, Esq., of Loxley Park, and support to an extent, and in a way, of which the public will never be made acquainted, by its then worthy president, the late Thomas Bladon, Esq., of Old Field House. But of course,

Y

such external support could not always be expected. Once fairly started, and its advantages being so evident to the whole town, it ought, with proper management, to have held on its way prosperously to the benefit of the locality. This, however, was not the case, and when the novelty of the institution had somewhat subsided in 1859, it was found to be so involved in debt, that the only question was whether it should be allowed to die a natural death, or whether some extraordinary effort should be made to retrieve its former prestige. Perhaps one of the causes of its decline were the worse than profitless soirees and lectures, which invariably involved a serious loss. But gloomy as its condition had become, there was yet a healthy feeling in its favour, and this led to the determination to hold an annual fete for the benefit of its funds, it being rightly judged that great numbers of persons would, especially in connection with such a purpose, be pleased with a day's rustication on the greensward and amid the fine glades of some nobleman's park, or more private lawns, and accordingly the first was held in Loxley Park, by the kind permission of its owner, the late T. C. S. Kynnersley, Esq., and proved a success. The proceeds of this, with a public subscription, and the benefit of a soiree given by ladies and gentlemen of the town, proved sufficient to meet the claims against the institute, and to leave a surplus in hand, which, had due regard been had to the proper management of the large fete, might have been handsome. A fete was also held at Doveridge, in the front of the hall, east, and although the day was wet, preventing so large an attendance as at the one in the previous year, it produced a balance of £14, after deducting all expenses. After that another unfortunate soiree and several expensive lectures again tended to involve the institute in debt, which at Christmas, 1861, amounted to nearly £40, and a second time it presented an almost certain prospect of a final close. Phœnix-like, it, however, after some modifications in its construction and management, and a little kindly assistance, again rose into life, and surmounted the almost stifling incubus of debt standing against it, and it has since progressed to the general satisfaction of its members. Much of its successful re-establishment was due to a series of Penny Readings in 1867-8, by which, each season, some £50 was realized, so that in January, 1869, the committee had a fund of £100. Since the first fetes were held others have taken place at Sudbury Park, Alton Gardens, Woodseat, Sandon Park, and Barrow Hill, and by these means the managers have been enabled to maintain the institution in a good condition, by the supply of journals and newspapers, and by the purchase of books, including the circulating library of the late Mr. Norris. Space forbids to trace the history of the institute year by year, but it may be mentioned that in the year 1876, the funds amounted to £130 5s. od., being an excess of £25 over the previous year, and that, after allowing therefrom the value of a handsome testimonial to its late librarian for many years, Mr. Robson, in 1880, its funds were considerably over £100.

Since then, annual fetes and other amusements, on behalf of trifling, if not almost personal objects, have deprived the institute of much assistance, and, I am afraid, almost given it its death blow.

Since its formation the Literary Institute has had for patrons, Sir Percival Heywood, Bart., the late John Mallaby, Esq., and Lord Waterpark; and the following gentlemen have been presidents—A. A. Flint, Esq., the late Thos. Bladon, Esq., the late W. J. Fox, Esq., G. Cooper, Esq., and the late Rev. John Cooke acted for many years as vice-president. The Rev. H. Abud, vicar and rural dean, has occupied the position of chairman of the committee and spared no pains to be useful to the institute for a long period.

The late Joseph Bladon, Esq , was a great benefactor to the library, and amongst the books which he presented to it were a copy of the "Encyclopedia Brittanica," and one of "Knight's Pictorial History of England." It must not be omitted to be observed that since then her Majesty the Queen has been graciously pleased to present the institute with a copy of "The Early Years of the Prince

Consort," and with one of "Our Life in the Highlands," to both of which she has added her autograph. One of the works is enclosed in a glass case for its permanent preservation, and is opened where the autograph can be observed.

The Town Hall, besides comprising rooms which were purposely included for the Literary Institute, contains offices also for the police department and savings bank, the latter of which, in consequence of other modes of investing small sums of money, particularly in the post office savings bank, was closed in May, 1881, the investors receiving their several investments in full. The building owes its existence to the then proprietors of the tolls, which passed into their hands by purchase a little while before the hall was erected in 1853, its situation being in High Street, where it has a frontage of ninety feet four inches. It contains on the ground floor an entrance hall, twenty feet six inches by sixteen feet two inches, approached under a stone portico; a lobby (separated from the entrance hall by a glass screen), twenty feet six inches by eighteen feet four inches, which leads into the large room or hall, which is sixty-eight feet four inches long, thirty feet wide, and thirty-four feet high, for the use of the magistrates, public meetings, and lectures. A gallery runs round the two sides and south end; at the opposite end is an orchestra. On the ground floor is also the great staircase to the upper rooms; also on it is the late savings bank room, the magistrates' consulting-room, reading-room for the subscribers to the Literary Institute, and the police office. These are approached by two doors, one on each side of the principal entrance. The last mentioned department is kept totally distinct from the other portions of the building, and is entered by a passage at the side of the hall. On the first floor, immediately on the landing, is a large ante-room, from which the galleries round the great hall are approached; the ladies' retiring-room, thirty-five feet six inches by sixteen feet; the library belonging to the institution, twenty-three feet by fourteen feet; the honorary members' reading-room, twenty-nine feet six inches by seventeen feet; the female singers' retiring-room; and the sitting-room and three bedrooms of the police department. Under the ground floor is cellaring, which is let to the Brewery Company. There are also prisoners' cells under the police department. The architect was Mr. Fradgley, and the builder the late Mr. W. Evans, of Ellastone. The cost of the building was between £3,000 and £4,000.

The corner stone of the Town Hall was laid by Lord Waterpark, on the 26th of August, 1853, the trowel being presented to his lordship by Dr. Taylor. After this the architect deposited a bottle containing the various current coins of Her Majesty's reign, in an orifice cut for the purpose in the foundation stone, and the place was covered with a brass plate, bearing the following inscription:—" The corner stone of this Town Hall, erected by the following proprietors, was laid on the 25th day of August, 1853, in the sixteenth year of the reign of Queen Victoria, by Henry Manners, Lord Waterpark."

The names of the original proprietors, all of whom are deceased, were—Mary Sneyd Kynnersley, Ann Fox, Herbert Taylor, Joseph Mallaby, Thomas Rushton, John Vernon, and Thomas Bladon.

The Smithfield Market at the back of the Town Hall belongs to these, or succeeding proprietors, and was arranged at the time the Town Hall was built. It occupies 1a. 1r. 5p. of ground. The stalls and pens will contain eight hundred head of cattle, eight hundred and forty sheep, and two hundred and twenty-five pigs. The entrance for cattle is from Smithy Lane; for sheep and pigs in High Street. The disposition of the stalls was made by Mr. John Etches, of Harley Thorn Farm, near Stone. The Smithfield cost about £1,500.

The Town Hall was opened November 29th, 1854, under circumstances of a deeply interesting character. Then was progressing the ever memorable Crimean war, which left so many widows and orphans of soldiers to the mercy of their country, and the opening was made the public occasion of an appeal on behalf of the patriotic fund. The hall was densely crowded. The chair was taken by Clement Thomas Sneyd Kynnersley, Esq. The object of the meeting was introduced by Herbert Taylor, Esq., M.D., which was the opening of the hall in connection with so patriotic a cause. Various resolutions were proposed by the late John Vernon, Esq., the Rev. H. Abud, the late Joseph Bladon, Esq., the late Joseph Mallaby, Esq., the Rev. Peter Holland, Catholic Priest ; the Rev. John Cooke, Congregational minister; the Rev. William Parkinson, Wesleyan Minister; Thomas Bladon, Esq., Thomas Rushton, Esq., A. A. Flint, Esq., and others The amount collected in the town, with the proceeds realized at the opening of the Town Hall, for the patriotic fund, was the sum of £250. This was a large sum to raise in Uttoxeter for such a purpose, considering that £100 had been collected in the previous January for the poor of the town during the extremely severe weather.

An addition to useful public buildings of the town was made in 1871 by the erection of a Temperance Hall in Bridge Street, which was opened by W. S. Allen, Esq., M.P., of Woodhead Hall. An exhibition of pictures, objects of antiquity, old and modern pottery, and curiosities in general, was made to aid in the reduction of the debt on the building. Colonel Fitzherbert and Colin Minton Campbell, Esq., made the largest and most valuable loans, Mr. Campbell, with other art pottery, lending a magnificent vase, worked in coloured clays, of the value of £150. Several very excellent exhibitions have been held at the Town Hall since in connection with the Young Men's Improvement Society, which is under the management of Mr. Dams, of this town. The successful stimulus to industrial endeavour, intellectual improvement, and moral culture which this gentleman has been the means of promoting amongst the young men of the town over many years in connection with this society cannot be sufficiently appreciated.

CHAPTER XII.

PUBLIC SCHOOLS.

ALLEYNE'S GRAMMAR SCHOOL.

This school was founded May 24th, 1558, by Thomas Alleyne, Allyn, or Allen, priest and clerk, who founded and endowed it, and constituted the Masters, Fellows, and Scholars of Trinity College, Cambridge, trustees of his charity. The extent to which it was endowed was £13 6s. 8d. per annum; but in 1847 Trinity College, Cambridge, consented to raise it to £144 annually with the advantage to the town of seven free scholars, including whom, with five boys in the classical and five in the English school, there are altogether on the foundation fifty boys, the headmaster also being allowed to take in boarders. In 1855 documents were discovered which revealed the extent of the property of Mr. Allen, and it was conceived Uttoxeter had a right to a greater beneficial interest in it. An information was consequently laid against the college, and the cause, Attorney-General *v.* Trinity College, Cambridge, was heard before the Master of the Rolls on January 29th and 30th, 1856. The prayer was, that the court would declare the Uttoxeter and other schools entitled to the increased income of the testator's estates, or to some share thereof, and that a proper scheme might be framed for the management of the property of the said charity, for the regulation of the Uttoxeter and other schools, and for the management of the said school generally. The Master of the Rolls decided, February 7th, 1856, that the college was entitled to the beneficial interest of the surplus which had accrued in the case, and added that a great deal might be said whether the college was the trustee of the schools, with trusts to be properly performed, and if so, that the trust was to form a free grammar school, not to be solely for Church of England purposes, and that would be a trust to maintain the school sufficiently, having regard to the neighbourhood and its wants. He also thought that rules and regulations might be made for the government of Uttoxeter School, and admission of scholars into it, which might extend the benefit and make it unnecessary to interfere.

The informants, however, were heard before the Master of the Rolls, Sir William Romilly, on the 2nd of August, 1856, who dismissed the information. The suit was not fruitless, though partially unsuccessful, for it was the means of securing a more liberal mode of admission to the advantages of the school, of increasing the number of free scholars, and of greatly extending the limits as to the reception of pupils in the foundation, as well as a handsome new building for the school.

The legal proceedings incurred an expense of about £700, towards which Mr. Rushton gave £150; Mr. Joseph Bladon, £50; the Executors of the late Mr. John Vernon, £150; Mr. Thomas Bladen, £50; and Mr. G. G. Bladon, £50. But some of these gentlemen afterwards, but particularly the Executors of Mr. Vernon—gave additional sums for the same purpose.

The estate of the donor, according to one of the "Statements" of Mr. Rushton, was of great extent and value. In land there are about one thousand three hundred, or one thousand four hundred, acres, several manors, numerous dwelling-houses and buildings, and several tenements in London, some being on Ludgate Hill. These estates are let principally on leases. The rents *reserved* therein, amount annually to above £413 in money, eighty-five quarters of malt, and about three hundred of wheat. As fines were taken in the granting of nearly all the leases (thus anticipating the proceeds) the amount of the reserved money and corn rents bear not the slightest proportion to the actual rental of the estates; and it is admitted that the fines on granted existing leases amounted to £9,488 6s. 8d. The oldest of these was granted in 1837, and the remainder in 1842.

The following is a copy of Mr. Allen's will :—

"WILL OF THOMAS ALLYN, MAY 20TH, 1558.

"Will of Thomas Allyn, clerk, parson of the Parish Church of Stevenage, in the County of Hertford, respecting his personal estates only, appoints John Langley, citizen and goldsmith, of London (who married testator's cousin Joannes), and Thomas Allen, of Shirland, in the county of Derby, his executors.

" He appoints his god-son, Edmunde Kympton, of Weston, in the county of Hertford, gent., and his cousin, Christopher Edwards, citizen and haberdasher, of London, supervisers and overseers of his testament.

" The executors to do nothing without the counsel, advice, and consent of the said Edward Kympton'

" May 24th, 1558, the said testator made a will concerning his real estate, of which the following is a copy :—

" In the name of God, Amen, the 24th day of May, in the year of our Lord, 1558, and in the fourth and fifth years of the reign of our most gracious Sovereign Lord and Lady, Phillip and Mary, by the grace of God King and Queen of England, Spain, France, both the Sicilies, Jerusalem, and Ireland, Defenders of the Faith, Archduke of Austricke, Duke of Burgundy, Myllayne, and Brabant, counties of Hasburge, Flanders, and Tyrole. I. Thomas Allyn, clerk, parson of the Parish Church of Stevenage, in Stevenage, in the county of Hertford, having an earnest zeal, desire, and mind to set up and maintain for our soul's good and laudable works, as may and shall be to the honour and glory of Almighty God my Maker, Saviour, and Redeemer, do make, declare, and ordain this my last will, touching and concerning the law, order, and disposition of all and singular my manors, messuages, lands, tenements, and heriditaments, with all and singular their appurtenances whatsoever they be in the realm of England, in manner and form following :—that is to say, I give, devise, and bequeath unto the Masters, Fellows, and Scholars of Trinity College, in Cambridge, of King Henry the Eighth's foundation, all that my manor of Wheston, with the appurtenances thereunto belonging in in the county of Leicester : and all that my manor of Wry, Hellsham, with the appurtenances, in the county of Kent : and all and singular other my manors, lands, tenements, heriditaments, in the county of Leicester, and in the county of Kent, and in the county of Hertford aforesaid, and in the county of Stafford, and in the city of London, amounting to the clear yearly value of four score pounds, or thereabouts ; and all and singular deeds, evidences, charters, court-rolls, muniments, and writings, concerning the said manors and other premises, or any part or parcel thereof, to have and to hold the aforesaid manors, lands, tenements, heriditaments, deeds, charters, witnesses, muniments, and all other the premises and their appurtenances, unto the Masters, Fellows, and Scholars and their successors, *to their only proper use and behoof for evermore*, to the intent hereafter followeth :—that is to say, that they, the said Masters, Fellows, and Scholars, with part of the rents, revenues, issues, and profits, coming and growing of all the same manors, lands, tenements, and other the premises with the appurtenances, shall from the day of my death for evermore, keep, find, and maintain three separate Grammar Schools, one of them at Uttoxeter, in the county of Stafford, the second at Stone, in the county of Stafford, and the third at Stevenage aforesaid, in the said county of Hertford : and shall contract and pay every year to every schoolmaster of the said three mentioned schools, £13 6s. 8d. of lawful money of England, and in their several wages and stipends : and also make and ordain, note, and covenant statutes, orders, rules, and constitutions, for and touching the direct order and good government of the schoolmasters and scholars, and for learning of good authorers, and praying for me their founder morning and evening, with the psalm of '*De profundis*,' and other suffrages thereunto occasioned with the collect Inclinademine, Amen, &c. : and I will that Marcus Petrus Danus shall be the schoolmaster of the school to be kept at Stevenage aforesaid, and have the teaching of the scholars there during his whole life, with the consent of the Masters of the said college for the time being, he doing his duty therein as to that office appertaineth.

"And I will and devise that the Masters. Fellows, and Scholars, and their successors, with part of the said rents, issues and profits coming and growing of the manors and other premises, with the appurtenances, shall, from and after my decease, keep, find, and maintain for ever one honest chaplain, being of good name and fame, and being unpromoted of any and unto any spiritual benefice or service, and having no pay, or stipend, or wages, to say and sing mass two days in every week at the least, perpetually: that is to say, upon the Wednesday and Friday, and oftener when he is so disposed, within the Parish Church of Sudbury, in the county of Derby, and in that mass to pray for my soul, my father and mother's souls, for my brother and sister's souls, and all Christian souls, with the psalm of '*De profundis*,' and the collect of suffrages thereunto accustomed, and shall contract and pay to the said chaplain yearly for his salary or wages £13 6s. 8d. of good and lawful money of England, or more or less as the said Master, Fellows, and Scholars, and the chaplain for the time being can agree: and I will that Sir Robert Glasyer, now my chaplain, have that service during his life, if he will so long serve there.

" And I will and devise that the said Master, Fellows, and Scholars, and their successors shall with part of the rents and revenues aforesaid, keep and sustain once in the year for me perpetually four several obiits or anniversaries solemnly by note, with all divine service accustomed for all dead folks to be done for my soul and all Christian souls, whereof the one to be kept and done in Stevenage aforesaid, the others in Thornell aforesaid, and the third in Shirland, in the county of Derby aforesaid, and the fourth at Sudbury, in the county of Derby, at about such time of the year as I shall fortune to die, on which Placibo and dirge solemnly by note on evening, and mass and requiem solemnly by note on the morrow following, spending and bestowing yearly at every of the said obiits forty shillings of good and lawful money of England : that is to say, every priest that shall help to sing dirge on night, and sing or say mass on the morrow twelve pence, and to every clerk helping to sing dirge on the evening and mass on the morrow sixpence, at every of the said obiits, *and the overplus and residue of the said several sums of money to be dealt and distributed to the needy and poor householders of every of the said parishes, the same time by the discretion of the parson, churchwardens of every of the said parishes for the time being.* ∗

"And I will and devise, give and bequeath yearly, for evermore, to four old poor men, being householders and dwellers in Stevenage aforesaid, to pray unto Almighty God for the wealth of my soul, and all Christian souls, the sum of £5 6s. 8d. equally amongst them to be parted and divided : that is to say, to every of them £1 6s. 8d. of good and lawful money of England, to be paid and delivered to every of them at four times of the year : that is to say, at the feast of the nativity of St. John the Baptist, St. Michael the Archangel, the birth of Our Lord God, and the annunciation of our blessed lady St. Mary, the Virgin, or within twelve days next ensuing every of the said feasts, by even portions, the first pay thereof to begin at the first of the said several feasts which shall first and next happen after my decease : and I give and bequeath for and towards the finding or exhibition of one poor

---

∗ The obiits, of course, are done away with, but it appears to be a question if this clause of the will does not imply as much as a perpetual charity to the poor of these places, whether they have it or not.

scholar within the same college yearly for evermore, forty shillings of lawful money of England: and I give, grant, and will unto James Allen, of Sherland aforesaid, one annual rent of £10 of lawful money of England, yearly going out of my said manor of Wheston, with the appurtenances, and out of all other my lands, tenements, and heriditaments in Wheston aforesaid, and Blaby, and Counties Thorpe in the aforesaid county of Leicester, to have, levy, and receive the said yearly rent of £10 to the said *James Allen, and his heirs and assigns for ever*, and to be paid at the feasts of the year: that is to say, at the feast of St. Michael the Archangel, and the annunciation of our blessed Lady, St. Mary, by even portions, to be paid, the first payment thereof to begin at the last of the said two feasts which shall first and next happen after my decease. And I will that if it shall happen the said yearly rent of £10 to be behind in part or in all after any the said feasts at the which that ought to be paid by the space of one month, and that being lawfully asked, then I will that it shall be lawful for the same James Allen, and his heirs and assigns in the said manor of Wheston, and other the premises in Wheston, Blaby, and Counties Thorpe, with the appurtenances, to enter and distrain, and the distress so taken to bear, lead, drive, and carrying, and the same to retain and keep until the said James, his heirs and assigns, of the said yearly rent and every parcel thereof, with the arrears of the same (if any such shall fortune to be) shall be unto the said James Allen, his heirs and assigns, fully contented and paid.

"And I heartily pray the said Masters, Fellows, and Scholars of the said college, to demise, grant, and let to farm the said manor and all other premises in Wheston, Blaby, and Counties Thorpe, unto the said James, his executors, administrators, and assigns, for the term of fifty years next ensuing after the day of my death, yielding and paying unto the said Masters, Fellows, and Scholars, and their successors yearly during the said term of fifty years the yearly rent of £20, with the reasonable covenants to be contained in the said lease. And I will that the said James shall yearly default, abate, and deduct £10 of this said yearly rent of £20 for his and their said yearly amount of £10 during the said term of fifty years.

"And I will that the Masters, Fellows, and Scholars, and their successors, shall well and efficiently uphold, repair, and maintain all the manors, edifices, and buildings in and upon all and singular the premises from time to time when and as often as need shall require for evermore.

"And I will and devise that the said Masters, Fellows, and Scholars, and their successors, with part of the said rents, revenues, issues, and profits of the said manor, lands, tenement, and other the premises, shall as well content and pay unto the said James Allen, his heirs and assigns, the said amount rent of £10, before by this my last will and testament given and willed unto the said James, his heirs and assigns, as also the said sum of £5 6s. 8d. before given and bequeathed to the said four old poor men of the said parish of Stevenage for evermore. And I will that my said executors shall have and receive all the rents and services of all the said manors, lands, and tenements, and other the premises, that shall be due for the same, at the feast of St. Michael the Archangel next after my decease.

"Also I will that Nicholas Jacendeze shall have and enjoy during his life, all that tenement wherein he now dwelleth, situated and being in Stevenage aforesaid, and all such lands, meadows, and pastures now let him, and occupied with the same, the same Nicholas yielding and paying for the same during his life to the said Masters, Fellows, and Scholars, and to their successors, such yearly rent as heretofore he hath used to pay, anything before expressed to the contrary notwithstanding, in witness whereof I, the said Thomas Allen, clerk, have ratified and allowed this my present last will and testament in the presence of Edward Kimpton, gent.; Sir Robert Glasyer, chaplain; John Huckyll, John Clerke, Thomas Clerke, Edward Clerke, Robert Norris, Thomas Robynson, and divers others.

"Proved by John Langley and James Allen, the executors, in the Prerogative Court of the Archbishop of Canterbury, on the 7th February, 1558."

LIST OF ANNUAL SUMS DIRECTED BY THE WILL OF THOMAS ALLEN TO BE PAID OUT OF HIS REAL ESTATES.

	£	s.	d.
Uttoxeter: Schoolmaster	13	6	8
Stone: do.	13	6	8
Stevenage: do.	13	6	8
Sudbury: Chaplain to say mass	13	6	8
(Or so much as the Chaplain, Masters, Fellows, and Schoolmasters agree to.)			
Stevenage: Obiit	2	0	0
Thornhill (Yorkshire): Obiit	2	0	0
Shirland: Obiit	2	0	0
Sudbury: do.	2	0	0
Stevenage: Four poor men	5	6	8
Trinity College, Cambridge: Exhibition of one poor scholar	2	0	0
James Allen: Perpetual annuity	10	0	0
	£78	13	4
For repairs yearly	1	6	8
Estimated clear rent	£80	0	0

Mr. Allen, in the will of his personal estates, directs the residue thereof to be sold, and the money accruing therefrom to be given, disposed, and distributed in alms and deeds of charity, to and amongst the needy and poor people, for the wealth of his soul and all Christian souls.

Having possession of a copy of the regulations of Alleyne's Schools in writing as far back as perhaps early in the seventeenth century, and taken from first copy written by Mr. Allen, they ought to be introduced here, as they will, from their curious and interesting nature, be perused with much interest, especially as they have never before been in print, nor any copy been known previously to exist.

Maister Thomas Allen

HIS ORDERS OF HIS
GRAMMER SCHOOLES.
IN
STEVENAGE, STONE, AND UTTOXETER.

My dearly beloved children whom I love in Christ and tender you as myselfe, I desire and charge you upon payne of punishment to observe and keepe my orders appointed to be kept in the sd schooles.

I will that all the children within the towne of Stevenage, and Stone * and within two or three miles compasse of the same, which have learned the booke of the eight parts of speech in English commonly called the accidence perfectly without the booke, and verry perfectly can saye the declensions, and can give anie persons in the verbe part when they be examined, and have alsoe learned the concords of Grammer commonly called the English Rules, without the booke perfectly : shalbe admitted into this schoole and noe others within the compasse and space here before named.

Item I will that my schoolemaisters of those schooles shall and maye take all manner of Children without the compasse of Two or Three miles of this schoole to his owne proffitt and advantage.

Item I will that all the schollers of theise my schooles shall come into the schoole before seaven of the clocke in the morning from michlms till our ladie daye in lent, And from our ladie daye in lent untill michlemas againe they shall come into the schoole before six of the clocke in the morninge *sub pena virgæ*.

---

* *Note in the margin of MSS :* Uttoxeter by some chance is left out in the originall.

𝕴tem my schollers shall goe to dinner at eleaven of the clock and come into the schoole againe before one be stricken, *sub pena virgæ*. And they shall goe home at five of the clocke at afternoone.

𝕴tem I will that in the morning they shall say *miserere* Psalme kneeling, a *pater noster* and *Credo in deum, et hanc orationem: domine sancte pater omnipotens æterne deus qui nos ad principium &c* and at the end of the Collect as followeth O most mercyfull father maker of Heaven and earth wee most humblie beseech thee for Jesus Christ sake to have mercy upon us and give us grace to increase in vertue and learning to the perpetual fame and thankfullness of our founder Maister Allen, and especially to the proffit of thy Universall Church, and Glorie of thy holy name who livest and raignest one god world without end Amen.

𝕬t one of the Clock before they begin lessons all the schollers kneeling shall saye the ten commandments of Almightie god in Latine &c as they did in the morning.

𝕴tem at five of the Clock before they depart out of the schoole they shall saye the psalme of *Deus misereatur* givinge thankes for their founder as in the morning. *sub pena virgæ*.

𝕴tem their communication shalbe Latine in all places among themselves, as well in the streets and their playes, as in the schoole. *sub pena virgæ*.

𝕴tem they shall Rest from the schoole on the thursday in the passion weeke till munday after lowe ✱ sundaye ymediately and noe longer: *sub pena expulsionis*, except lycence be obteyned of my schoolemaister for a reasonable cause.

✱ " Upon the octave, or 1st Sunday after Easter day, it was a custom of the ancients to repeat some part of the solemnity which was used upon Easter day: from whence this Sunday took the name of Lowe Sunday, being celebrated as a fast, though of a lower degree than Easter day itself."— *Wheatly on the Common Prayer.*

Item my schollers shall play all wittson weeke, and noe longer, *sub pena expulsionis* excep lycence be asked and obteyned of my schoolemaister.

Item they shall play one afternoone everie weeke if their maister doe thinke their dilligence doe deserve it, or else not: and that afternoone to be when the schoolemaister doth thinke most convenient, and my schollers most worthie to have it.

Item I will that if anie of my schollers use sweareing or unhonest gaines, or evill companie of anie men or women or wenches to the hinderance of his learning he shall be expulsed forth of my schoole, except he amend upon good admonition given to him, and to his friends of his faults by my schoolemaister.

Item I will that all my schollers shall behave themselves gently to all kinds of persons of every degree, *sub pena virgæ*.

Item I will that all my schollers shall love and reverence my schoolemaister and gently receive punishment of him for their faults. *sub pena expulsionis.*

Item I will that all my schollers at their first entrance into my schoole shall give Two pence apeece to a poore scholler appointed by the maister to keepe the schoole cleane and to provide rods.

*   *   *   *   *   *

Item I will that my schoolemaister shall make good orders, or change fashions in my schoole to the preferment of my schollers if need require that to be done.

FINIS.

The tercentenary of Alleyne's Grammar School took place in 1858, and was duly observed. The New Grammar School, which was erected in 1859, is pleasantly situated at Dove Bank, adjoining the residence of the Headmaster, then the Rev. W. Harvey, M.A. The present excellent Headmaster is Thomas Allen, Esq., M.A. The death of Mr. Harvey took place very suddenly on the 4th of February, 1864. He was held in the highest esteem as a model teacher, and the love which his old scholars bore towards him induced them to erect a handsome mural tablet to his memory in the school. A marble tomb was also raised over his grave in the cemetery, with a granite cross at the head, at a cost of about £100, by the inhabitants of the town. Harvey prizes were also founded at the same time, £150 being collected for the purpose, and invested in railway stock to produce £7 per annum. The prizes in books from this foundation, and from the bequest of Mr. Phillips, are distributed each Christmas on the breaking up of the school.

The original building of the school was in Bridge Street, and it stood about one hundred yards up in the street from the bridge, on the west side. It was a plain brick building of a remote date. The same street is also, or rather used to be, called Schoolhouse Lane, from the circumstance of the school having been situated there, and Dean's Row, through the tithe barn, which belonged, together with the houses there, to the deans and canons of Windsor.

An antique sun dial, formerly on the south end of the old school house, is preserved in the wall of the interior of the New Grammar School.

NATIONAL SCHOOL.

The National School in 1818 was in Carter Street, and was taught by a female named Temperance Goodhall. *
A school was first built in Bradley Street in 1829, being only 24 feet by 12 feet. The present schools were erected in 1855, and since the large boys' school has been erected on the site of the then master's house, and two adjoining houses have been purchased, one for the master, and the other for the mistress of the girls' school. The master is Mr. Tortoishell, and the mistress Miss Bennett. In 1881 the schools were enlarged by the whole being brought to the side of the street.

* " Parson and Bradshawe's Directory," 1813.

NORMAL SCHOOL.

This is called "The New Day School," the schoolroom being the largest room in the town, except the Town Hall. It has a class-room connected with it of considerable extent. The building is in High Street, and it was first erected for a Wesleyan Sunday School.

Mr. BLADON'S SCHOOL.

This school was in Pinfold Lane, and was erected by the late Joseph Bladon, Esq., and conducted at his expense. It was well furnished with every school requisite, and had a playground attached, where every necessary apparatus existed for the exercise and amusement of children. Since his death, however, it has been closed, and converted into houses.

CATHOLIC SCHOOL.

This is in Balance Street, connected with the chapel of the Roman Catholics, and is exclusively for secular instruction.

CHAPTER XIII.

UTTOXETER CHARITIES.

Inquisitions respecting Uttoxeter Charities have been held at the following places :—1690, October 24th, at Lichfield Close ; 1727, May 10th, at Uttoxeter ; and in the same year at Wolsley Bridge. The following account of Uttoxeter Charities is carefully abridged from the Charity Commissioners' Report. Time and circumstances have, doubtless, made alterations necessary in the mode of applying some of the gifts :—

JOHN DYNE'S CHARITY.

This is a gift by will, bearing date January 12th, 1644. It consists of the Talbot public-house and premises, and a croft, called " Botham Croft," containing 1a. 2r. 29p., which produce a rent of about £68 per annum. The money is applied in apprenticing poor boys of Uttoxeter to trades, a premium of £8 being given with each boy, payable by yearly instalments of £2. One half of the charge of the indenture is also paid from the funds of the charity. By consent of the Charity Commissioners the Old Talbot Inn was sold in 1876, and was purchased by Mr. Stretch, proprietor of the New Brewery, for £1,400.

GIFTS OF BAGNALL AND OTHERS.

This is a gift by indenture of feoffment, bearing date June 1st, 1686. It consists of a close of land called "The Parks," comprising 6a. 2r. 7p. The rent is £18 a year.

GIFTS OF OKEOVER AND OTHERS.

Dorothy Okeover and others, by will, dated May 6th, 1627, gave to the poor of Uttoxeter £40 as a constant standing stock. Stephen Spencer, by will, dated August 27th, 1625, for the same object gave £10, to be disposed of in land. On June 20th, 1727, Richard Heaton also gave to the poor of Uttoxeter £40. These three sums were employed in purchasing for the poor of Uttoxeter three closes of land, called "Thorney Fields" and "Russell's Spring," containing in the whole 15a. 1r. 29p., which are let at about £25 per annum.

GIFTS OF SAMPSON ALKINS AND SIMON WAKELIN.

The former by indenture dated December 2nd, 1670, and the latter by will dated September 3rd, 1697. The property is the "Red Hills," abutting on Pool Meadow, and is a field containing 2a. 1r. 2p., and is let at £10 a year.

DYNE'S LANE.

Dyne's Lane belongs to Uttoxeter Charities, it having been purchased since 1727, by several sums of money then in the hands of the trustees undisposed of, and arising out of charity lands. The land consists of about 20a., producing a rental of about £30 a year, which forms part of the annual distribution to the poor.

ELLEN MIDDLETON'S GIFT.

This was by will dated August 29th, 1657, and consists of "Wilg's Croft," or "Willig's Croft," of 1a. or. 2p., producing a rent of £5 a year, which is applied to the benefit of poor widows.

ROBERT COXE'S GIFT.

This was by will dated October 22nd, 1621, and is 40s. a year, payable out of "Munk's Field." The land belongs to the Vicarage, it having been purchased by Queen Anne's Bounty. It is employed in the purchase of shoes.

GILBERT'S GIFT.

Robert Gilbert's will, dated February 12th, 1648, left 20s. for shoes for two poor men yearly. The money is paid yearly out of the Nag's Head (now the Vine) public-house.

CHAMBERLAIN'S GIFT.

Francis Chamberlain devised on the 22nd October, 1651, the annual sum of 13s. 4d., out of land in Botham Field, for honest widows and widowers.

MIDDLETON'S GIFT.

Richard Middleton, by will, dated February 6th, 1668, gave to James Wood a yearly rent-charge of 40s. out of Dove Close, or Bushby's Great Close, to be expended in shoes for the indigent.

BLOUNT'S GIFT.

Mrs. Mary Blount, by will, dated April 23rd, 1594, bequeathed £100 to the town of Uttoxeter, to the help and relief of such persons as should fall into decay by fire, or death of cattle, sickness, or otherwise, providing such persons found securities for the repayment of such sums as might be lent. By lying in hand the sum increased to £140, which Walter Mynors, Esq., *for his love to the town*, was pleased to take for a yearly rent-charge, from the close called the Smetholme.

POKER'S GIFT.

William Poker, by will, dated January 8th, 1636, left a parcel of ground, 1a. or. 23p. in extent, called the Mitch, for the poor of Uttoxeter and Marchington. The rent is £4 per annum, which is laid out in loaves on Good Friday.

MYNOR'S GIFT.

William Mynors, Esq., of Hallingbury Hall, by will, dated October 27th, 1666, gave £100 to be put forth in the purchase of land, the moiety of the profits thereof to be for the apprenticeship of poor children in the Woodlands, and the other moiety for the relief of the poor living near Hallingbury Hall. Nicholas Mynors, for the use of the £100 granted a rent-charge yearly of £5, issuing out of messuages and lands at Gorsty Hill, in the parish of Cheadle, for the uses aforesaid.

SHALLCROSS'S CHARITY.

William Shallcross, by will, dated May 25th, 1719, gave 20s. yearly, to be paid to the vicar on St. Thomas's day, for a sermon on that day; and a rent-charge of £5 yearly, to be distributed on the same day to poor housekeepers having no pay from the parish, deducting a land tax of 10s. 6d. The amounts arise from premises in the parishes of Stoke and Uttoxeter.

AFTERMATH AND MEADOWS.

These are the Broad Meadow and Netherwood Meadow, comprising together about one hundred and twenty acres, besides seven acres of land *anciently enclosed* from Broad Meadow. *Time out of mind* the profits of the aftermath and meadow were applied to the repair of Dove Bridge,* and other bridges and causeways, and public uses in Uttoxeter, but did not then amount to more than £7 per annum, as the inhabitants allowed them to lie common part of the year, and took the benefit to themselves when they should have kept them enclosed, only taking sixpence a cow, and a shilling for a horse, contrary to a decree made October 24th, 1690, after which time Dove Bridge was made a county bridge. By a decree of the Charity Commissioners, founded upon the inquisition taken May 10th, 1727, it was determined that, for the future, the aftermath should be made the best use of for the repair of the bridges in the town, the surplus to go to the general charities. On the 8th of August in each year the right of the trustees to the aftermath commences, and the gates are locked and the cattle excluded till the last week of the same month, when horses are taken at 7s. each, and cows at 4s. each, and young stirks in proportion. From three hundred to four hundred head of cattle are then turned on the aftermath for a fortnight annually. This ought to be stated as belonging to past arrangements, for the aftermath is now sold by auction, and makes more than in the old way. The average produce of the ley is about £50 a year. The sum of £10, or thereabouts, is for the repair of bridges (four foot bridges) in the Woodlands over Netherland Lane Brook; a cart bridge at Quee Lane; and two footbridges near Will's Lock. The expenses of the waterworks from Bramshall are about £30 annually, any residue being applied to the charities.

---

* Dove Bridge, which consists of six arches, was built in the 13th century. During the Spring of 1864, it underwent repair, including the removal of decayed stone at the bed of the river, and the substitution of fresh stone work in its place. In 1874 the arch nearest Uttoxeter was re-built, but evidently without the superintendence of an architect, for it was omitted being re-built again with ribs underneath as it was before in resemblance of the extreme east arch. The parapet has been re-built sometime.

The water with which the town is thus supplied, springs up in a plantation a little west of Bramshall Park. The spring is a very powerful one and never failing. Its situation is low on the gravel, with a deep gravel bed capping the higher surrounding land, and before it was conducted to Uttoxeter it must have flowed down Bramshall Hollow. Some two hundred and fifty years ago the wells of the town were supplied by the water running along the streets. There was a tradition that this was particularly so in Bradley Street, and the whole of its course was laid open in 1866, when waterpipes were laid down from the newly constructed reservoir in the strip of land known as "Abraham's Walk." It is believed the wells were uncovered, there being no pumps in the town at the remote period referred to, nine pumps being for the first time erected by public subscripton about the year 1774. One of these wells, or in this instance a pond rather, was found in the year just named, when the late Mr. William Perks constructed a deep culvert from his property at the bottom of Bradley Street, along Silver Street. The old water course, already mentioned, was found to lead right to the place about the centre of Silver Street, rather on the west side, and that both the water course and pond were in use in the seventeenth century was evident by old Brosley pipe bowls—one with masks round the lower part of the tube—and pitchers with the comb ornamentation on, being found in them. A fish hook was also found in the pond, and also a cleft oak stake shod with iron, and driven into the bottom of the place, clearly showing that it was also a fishery. The cover for the well in the Market Place was a little dome about three or four feet high, and water was laded out of it. This was so recently as to have been in the recollection of aged persons with whom I have conversed. The late conduit which was built over the same well from a design by the late Mr. Garner, builder, of Uttoxeter, was constructed in the year 1780, and it was surmounted by an interesting sun dial for the four cardinal points. The sun dial bore the following inscription in Roman letters in Latin:—"*Mentiri non est meum. Fugio fuge. Moriendo vivo. Resurgam.*" These sentences in English are, "It is not mine to lie. I flee, flee thou. In dying I live. I shall rise again." The desire for a public weighing machine and house, led to the old conduit being taken down to make way for the present building which is after a design by Mr. Fradgley, architect. It was stated that the reservoir and filter bed with the laying down of fresh cast-iron pipes, involved an expense of about £1,200, which was derived from the sale of land to the N. S. Railway Company, and from a charity. The water was enclosed from its source across the fields and by the toll gate, and along the side of Kiddlestich Lane and through some other fields in and after 1869. In 1884 the filter bed was enlarged.

CATHERINE MASTERGENT'S GIFT.

Catherine Mastergent, by will, dated March 20th, 1646, gave a yearly rent charge of £3 6s. 8d., to be paid out of Pool Meadow to three poor widows of Uttoxeter, of honest and religious conversation, in the purchase of gowns, and after to others, the best of the inhabitants of Uttoxeter: and also her barn in Carter Street, with all belonging to it, to be employed for the habitation for three poor widows, directing them to be made into habitations after her decease. The houses have since been rebuilt by subscription.

WRIGHT'S GIFT.

John Wright, by will, dated March 23rd, 1729, gave £10 yearly, for ever, out of Snape's Field, Hatchet Wood, and Tinker's Lane Croft, subject to a deduction of £1 for one poor widow occupying the Almshouse he left by the same will in Carter Street.

WILLIAM LATHROP'S GIFT.

William Laythrop, by will, devised, in the year 1700, four dwelling-houses in Carter Street, and two parcels of land in Broad Meadow and the Netherwood, in Uttoxeter, in trust, as to the houses, for the use of poor widows; and as to the rent of the land, to be applied in the repair of the said houses, and the overplus, if any, in the purchase of fuel. The land is one acre in each of the said meadows, an acre of enclosed land on Balance Hill, and a rent of £1 0s. 6d. out of a close in Rye Croft Lane. The income is about £14 0s. 6d. yearly. Lathrop's Almshouses were re-built in 1848, at a cost of £300, the builder being Mr. W. Perks, of Bradley Street.

A William Lathrope, of Uttoxeter, died 28th April, 1664. His father was Humphrey Lathrope, of Crakemarsh. The Hare MS., 6104, has the following:—"John Lathrope of 'ye Priory, neere Lincolne,' had issue Thomas, 'Bramshall,' who had three daughters, Elizabeth, Jane, and Mary."*

PYOTT'S GIFT.

Mrs. Margery Pyott, by indenture, dated March 1st, 1622, left a field called Mansholme, comprising 6a. 2r. 14p. The rent thereof amounts to about £23 a year, to be applied in providing twelve twopenny loaves, to be distributed at the church, to twelve poor men or women of Uttoxeter who should have been that morning at church, the overplus, except 5s. for the trustees for their trouble, to be for the relief of such poor persons of Uttoxeter as should be unable to attend. The trustees do not receive the 5s. Mr. Jeremiah Ives was one of the trustees.

RUSSELL'S CHARITY.

Edward Russell, of Chester, by will, dated June 7th, 1666, devised 50s. out of land in Great Broughton, county of Chester, and other land lying in Great Broughton, for providing bread for the poor of Uttoxeter, his native place, some part of it to be distributed every Sunday, as the

---

* See the "Staffordshire Collection," published by the William Salt Archæological Society.

churchwardens should think proper. Fourteen penny rolls are considered satisfactory to this gift. He left a similar sum yearly to the poor of Chester.

CLOWNHOLME'S GIFT.

Thomas Clownholme, by will, dated June 8th, 1702, gave to the poor of Uttoxeter a rent-charge of 20s., to be given in bread on St. Thomas' Day. The land from which it arises is Goose Croft.

HARRISON'S GIFT.

Edward Harrison gave yearly, for ever, out of a tenement at Spath, £1, to be given to the poor of Uttoxeter on Candlemas Day.

BARN'S GIFT.

William Barns, in 1697, devised £2 a year, for ever, to the poor of Uttoxeter Woodlands, on St. Thomas' Day, out of land on the High Wood. It was not invested in the trustees of Uttoxeter Charities till 1860, when application was made for that purpose to Sir W. B. Riddall, Bart., at the County Court, and granted. Previously those who held the land disposed of the charity.

According to the deeds of Mr. Dester, late of Netherland Green, Mr. Barns left the above-mentioned subject to the payment of £2 annually to a Mr. William Bladon and his heirs, and a farm at Gorsty Hill he bequeathed to a Mr. Redfern.

BEQUEST TO THE POOR OF UTTOXETER BY MISS ELIZABETH JOHNSON, OF BURTON-ON-TRENT.

Miss Elizabeth Johnson, of Burton-on-Trent, by will, dated 24th December, 1861, for the love her mother had for Uttoxeter, devises as follows :—" I direct my executors, hereinafter named, to purchase the sum of £200, at £3 per cent., consolidated bank annuities, in the names of the official trustees of charitable funds, upon trust, to divide the annual income arising from the same amongst six poor men and six poor women, inhabitants of Uttoxeter, every Christmas, to be selected by and at the discretion of the churchwardens for the time being of the said parish of Uttoxeter."

GIFT OF JOSEPH BLADON, Esq.

The late Joseph Bladon, Esq., of Old Field House, built almshouses at the bottom of Pinford Lane, and they are occupied by old widows, who pay, as an acknowledgement, a penny a week, which is returned. He also left £50 a year for five years, to be distributed, after his death, amongst the poor, but whether more than one of the sums have been available for the purpose has not transpired.

GIFT OF WILLIAM PHILLIPS, Esq.

William Phillips, Esq., of Springfield House, in the parish of Uttoxeter, by will, dated September 12th, 1863, and whose demise took place on the 21st October of the same year, gave and bequeathed the sum of £800 to the vicar and churchwardens of Uttoxeter, and their successors, in trust, and the annual income thereof to be applied in the purchase of suitable clothing, bed linen, and blankets, to be distributed by the discretion of the major part of them from year to year, for ever, amongst the poor of the same parish of Uttoxeter, and in such shares, at such times, and in such manner as the said vicar and churchwardens should think fit.

The same testator, by the same will, devised £100, producing £3 10s. a year, to the Masters and Fellows of Trinity College, Cambridge, for the use and benefit of Alleyne's Grammar School, in Uttoxeter aforesaid, in such manner as the said Masters and Fellows should decide.

And also by the same will, the sum of £400 to the vicar and Churchwardens of Burton-on-Trent, the income thereof to be applied in the purchase of fuel, clothes, meat and bread, for the poor of that parish, from year to year, for ever.

UTTOXETER POOR LAW UNION.

This union comprises the parishes of Blythfield, Abbots Bromley, Boylestone, Bramshall, Croxden, Cubley, Doveridge, Draycot-in-the-Clay, Field, Gratwich, Kingstone, Leigh, Marchington, Marchington Woodland, Marstone Montgomery, Rocester, Somershall Herbert, Sudbury, and Uttoxeter. The master of the union is Mr. Sargeant ; the clerk thereof is Mr. F. Hawthorn.

PETTY SESSIONS.

These used to be held alternately at a large room at the White Hart Hotel and at the Red Lion Hotel. They are now held every alternate Wednesday at the Town Hall. The late Lord Waterpark presided at these sessions during a period of about thirty years. His lordship, in various other ways, gave his influence and time for the promotion of the interests of the town, which, he frequently stated, it gave him great pleasure to do, when so called upon. Sir Percival Heywood, Bart., Lord Waterpark, Capt. Dawson, Capt. Duncombe, Charles Tyrrel Cavendish, Esq., A. W. Lyon, Esq., and other gentlemen are amongst the magistrates who sit on the bench. A. A. Flint, Esq., is the magistrates' clerk and the coroner for North Staffordshire.

THE BANKS.

At this time there are two banks in Uttoxeter. The oldest is a branch of the Burton, Ashbourne and Uttoxeter Union Bank, in Carter Street, the principal manager being

Mr. John Hare, and the assistant Mr. Fletcher. More than sixty years ago it was open only on a Wednesday, in the Market-place. At that time Thomas Hart, Esq., had a bank, which he continued nearly to the end of his life. Mr. James Bell also had a bank at the now offices of Messrs. Welby and Wilkins, solicitors. The undertaking was a failure ultimately, perhaps fifty years ago, and its affairs were not wound up till 1863, by its only surviving trustee, the late Mr. Francis Cope, making the last dividend just before his death. The other bank at present in Uttoxeter is a branch of the Dudley, Birmingham and Midland Banking Company.

CHAPTER XIV.

NOTICES OF PLACES IN THE NEIGHBOURHOOD OF UTTOXETER.

LOCHELER, OR LOCKESLEID.

Loxley, in the parish of Uttoxeter, on the west, is an old Saxon name, and a place of considerable interest. It was a grant from the Crown to Robert de Ferrars, first Earl of Derby, who died in 1184. By the second Earl William, it was granted to his younger son Wakelin, and it was held by a Robert, an Alan, a Thomas, and Henry. From an inquisition taken after 1297, it appears that Loxley manor was held by the heirs of Thomas de Ferrars, who was the youngest son of William, third earl of Derby, who did homage for Chartley, which was exchanged by Thomas with his brother for Loxley. There is a blank here in this branch for one generation at least, and therefore the second Thomas, whose daughter Johanna, as sole heiress, brought Loxley to the Kynersleys by marriage in 1327 with John de Kynnardsley, must have been of a third generation from the first Thomas. In existing deeds there are evidences of a William and a Robert holding Loxley. William Earl de Ferrars, grants in or near Lockesleid " Will'o, filio Will'i, filiolo meo." In a deed

of Lord Bagot, "Robert de Ferr', avunculus com, de
Ferr," grants "eight bonatas in Lochesl' to Osbert,
homini meo de Lockesleid;" yet besides this Robert
"avunculus" there was a Robert de Ferrariis de Lokesle,
co-witness with Robert avunculus de Monastic. (Angl.
II. 506.) The above John de Kynardsley is mentioned
in a deed of 1330, as "Dominus de Lockesley." He
was descended from the family of Kynardsley of Kynardsley
Castle, in Herefordshire, where they were seated at and
before the time of the Conquest. His two immediate
ancestors were, William, seated at Kynardsley Castle, and
William, lord of the manor of Wyebridge. John
Kynardsley and three brothers were advanced with estates
(most by returning to John or issue) by an uncle, "dom's
John de Kynardesley, cleric 's Thomæ com, Lancaster,"
and rector of Stoke. The estate has descended in uninterrupted succession from father to son (except in
instances, when in default of issue, brother succeeded
brother), to Clement Kynersley, Esq., who died in 1815,
having devised this estate to his nephew, Thomas Sneyed,
Esq., a son of his eldest sister, Penelope, by John Sneyed,
of Belmont, Esq., and who, in compliance with the will
of his uncle, Thomas Sneyd, took the name of Kynersley
in addition to his own. He died by an accident in 1844.
His eldest son and heir, Clement John Sneyd Kynersley,
dying in 1840, he was succeeded by his grandson, the
eldest son of C. T. S. Kynersley, who was born in 1833,
and since deceased. Thomas Kynersley, twenty-two,
Charles I.; Craven Kynersley, seventh, George II.; and
Clement Kynersley, tenth, George III., were sheriffs.

Some of the land now belonging to Loxley estate
was of recent acquisition in the early part of the reign of
Charles I., and is then spoken of in writings in the ensuing words:—"Thomas Kynnersley, Esq., houldeth by
fealty Knight service and suit the manor of Little Loxley,
and he houldeth freely one part of the reputed manor of
Little Bromshulfe, in three parts to be divided, and certain
other lands sometimes Walter's land by the yearly rent of

xviiis." The ancient Loxley inheritance is mentioned in these words:—" The said Thomas Kynnersley, Esq., houldeth divers lands and tenements, the *ancient lands* of Kynnersley, at the rent of xxxiiis. iiiid." The hall is referred to in the same records as "The Ould Hall," and "The Ould Hall Meadow." The ancient residence was probably superseded by the hall which was partly demolished by Thomas Sneyd Kynersley, Esq., who built the present edifice, which is of stone. The preceding house was of red brick with stone dressings and pediment, Ionic pillars with elaborately carved Corinthian capitals. The front hall is a noble room with a gallery. The arms of the principal families in the Kingdom in 1608, are painted round the room, and those of the Royal family over the fire-place, which is supported by ancient and beautifully carved oak pillars. A painting of the old hall, as well as one of Ashcombe Hall, is also over the fireplace on a panel. A little beneath the row of almost innumerable coats-of-arms, there are old paintings let in antique oak panelling of the wainscotting, of the apostles and disciples of Christ. In the hall are also preserved a number of ancient family portraits. The Corinthian capitals, the beautifully carved volutes and floral designs in stone, the stonework of the open parapet of the old hall, the armorial bearings of the family cut in stone, and a fine grotesque mask in the same material, all having been ornamental portions in the front of the old mansion, have been built into a grotto which stands in the Long Walk. In the windows of the grotto were also inserted small square panes of glass from the same ancient residence, bearing the arms of the Ferrars in the form of horse-shoes, and which were doubtless executed before Loxley came to the family of Kynnersley. The elaborately carved oaken door in oak-leaf work, probably of the decorated period, in the grotto, was the front door of the old hall. When I saw this interesting place some nine or ten years ago it looked very forlorn, and the last piece of coloured glass with a horse-shoe represented on it bid fair to follow others which have been broken to pieces within the last twenty-five years. Loxley Hall has not been occupied by the representatives of the family of Kynnersley for many years, but has been rented successively by Joseph Mallaby, Esq., Colonel the Hon. Thomas Stanley, and now by Dr. Mould, of Cheadle, near Manchester, as a convalescent home for wealthy patients, who are under the care of Dr. Fletcher, of Uttoxeter.

Loxley Park and Paddock, with a small intake, comprise 212a., and the Hall, pleasure-grounds and gardens, about 7a. or. 2p.

Loxley has attained a degree of celebrity as having been the reputed birthplace and scene of the marriage and of many of the bold exploits of Robin Hood, who, it is believed, was no other than a Robert de Ferrars. It is supposed he may have had the name of Hood from being hooded, and that of Huntingdon from engaging in hunting, and although Norman by blood, it is thought not improbable that he might take up the popular cause. There is in existence in the family of Kynnersley, an ancient horn having the proud name of Robin Hood's horn, and which was formerly in the possession of the Ferrars, of Chartley, and then of the branch of the same family at Loxley, and so passed to the family of Kynnersley by the marriage of the heiress of Ferrars with John de Kynardsley. It has the initials of R. H., and three horse-shoes, two and one in a shield, that being the way in which the arms were borne by the first Thomas de Ferrars of Loxley, and probably by a Robert, who preceded him apparently towards the close of the twelfth century, and as they were on the coloured glass of which I have spoken, the traditionary connection of the horn with the name of Robin Hood is interesting. The horn is mounted with silver ferrules, and has a silver chain attached to it for suspension. As will be perceived by the engraving, ornamentation is also carved upon it, including a star, which may be emblematic, having long and short radiations alternating, and all cut in notches.

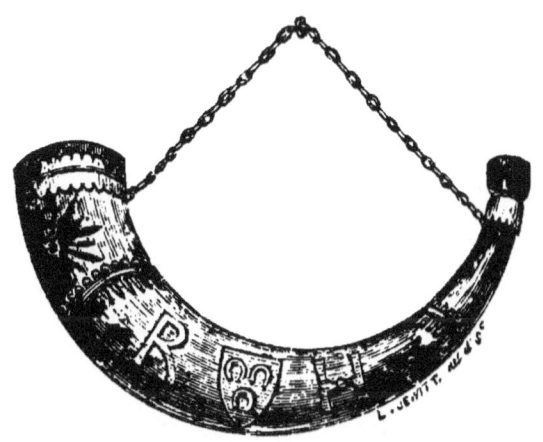

ROBIN HOOD'S HORN.

With respect to the marriage of Robin Hood at Loxley, an old chronicle states that after his return there from a visit to his uncle Gamewell, in Warwickshire, after certain enquiries concerning his men,

> Cloranda came by,
> The queen of the shepherds was she,

with whom he fell in love, when,

> Sir Roger, the parson of Dubridge was sent for in haste:
> He brought his mass book and bid them take hands,
> And joined them in marriage full fast.

According to the traditions of the neighbourhood, the honeymoon was spent at the beautiful demesne of Loxley; and many engaging stories have been related by the old gardener of Loxley a hundred and ten years ago—the maternal grandfather of a friend of mine, Mr. G. Foster, of Endon—respecting both the rendezvous and doings of this celebrated outlaw. These lines are supposed to have reference to the gallant freebooter, on his return to Loxley after the marriage with his wife:—

> Bold Robin Hood and his sweet bride,
>   Went hand in hand into the green bower;
> The birds sang with pleasure in those merry green groves;
>   O, this was a most joyful hour,

Mr. Foster, whom I have mentioned above, was born at Loxley Green, and is the author of an essay on " The History of Astonomy," published in 1839, in a magazine entitled *Espalier*, and edited at Hanley. It appeared under the signature of "Newtonian." He has also contributed numerous local sketches, pleasingly written, to the *Staffordshire Sentinel*.

The family of Kynnersley now reside at the Highfields.

BLOUNT'S HALL.

About a mile to the west of Uttoxeter is Blount's Hall, where the Blounts had a seat. This ancient family is said to have taken its origin from the Blondi in Italy, and they from the Roman Flavii, so called from their fair hair. Le Blond, lord of Guines in France, came over with the Conqueror; two of whose sons, Sir Robert and Sir William, were the progenitors of all the Blounts in England. * The branch at Blount's Hall were descended from John Blount, third son of Sir William Blount, Knight, who had lands in Burton and Rollestone. Edward Blount, tenth, Edward II., died without issue, and his property passed to Elizabeth, daughter of Walter Blount, youngest brother of Thomas. Sir Thomas Pope Blount was the founder of Trinity College, Oxford. In Clerkenwell Church was inscribed on a stone, " Ann Blunt, daughter of Walter Blunt, of Blunt Hall, and sister to Lady Paulet, and to Lady Sidenham, died 24th April, 1503." John Blount, of Blount's Hall, 1527, was High Sheriff for this county. Erdeswick, who commenced writing his "View" in 1593, states that Blount's Hall had then been lately built. As it is evident there was a hall there a very long period previously, it may be understood to mean that it had been recently then rebuilt. The old hall, which stood where there is a moat, was, we are told by Dr. Harwood, taken down in 1770. When the estate was held by Sir Henry Blount, early in the seventeenth century,

---

*Erdeswick's " Survey of Staffordshire," 1820.

it comprised 563a. 2r. 8p. Blount's Hall and land are described in the *Local Terrier*, so often referred to, in these words :—" Sir Thomas Pope Blount, Knight, houldeth freely by him and his heirs certain lands and tenements being the ancient lands of the Blounts." And again :—" One capital messuage called or known by the name of Blunt's Hall, being environed with a moat, with a dere-house, barns, stables, courts, and yards, and one close of pasture land adjoining. Mr. Gorenge, Tenant. All these lands (except this half) are now the inheritance of Sir Henry Blount, and doe contain in the whole 563a. 2r. 8p." Blunt's Hall—the house which now has that name—and such land as yet remains to it, amounting to 52a., belong to the representatives of the late Mr. William Bathew, who died in 1872, and they were bequeathed to his father by a Mr. Spencer. They now belong to Mr. Dunnett, of Uttoxeter.

STRAMSHALL.

Straguicesholle, Stranshall, Stronshall (Stramshall), is about a mile slightly to the north-west of Uttoxeter. In the twentieth year of the Conquest it was held by Abricus, and afterwards Roisia de Verdun was lady of Stramshall. A church was built there in 1852, by Mr. Evans, from a design by Mr. Fradgley, architect, of Uttoxeter.

KINGSTONE.

Kingstone, which is about four miles west of Uttoxeter, belonged to the Gresleys, and was sold in the sixteenth century, by Sir Thomas Gresley, to Sir Edward Aston. It now belongs to the Earl of Shrewsbury and Talbot. Kingstone Hall is near to the church, and is a timber house covered with plaster. Kingstone old church was taken down in 1860. This church was the burying place of Sir Symon Degge in a chapel on the north side which he built himself. Part of the rood screen remained. One of the bells bore this inscription: "Ora prohnobis Sancte Jacobus" (pray for us St. James); on a second bell, "Ora prohnobis Sancte Edwarde" (pray for us St. Edward); and on the third, "God Save the Queen, 1595." A new church was erected at Kingstone in 1861, at some distance east of the old site, by the Earl of Shrewsbury, in 1861. The architect was Mr. Brandon, of London; the builder, Mr. Evans, of Ellastone. It was opened and consecrated by the bishop of the diocese, October 21st, 1861. Of the family of Bakewell, of Kingstone, was Mr. Thomas Bakewell, said 'to have been a geologist. He was a soap boiler there, and on his premises being burnt down he gave up the business and left the village. Leese Hill is a member of Kingstone, and was the inheritance of the Tixalls and Normans; but afterwards it came by marriage to Henry Goring, of Kingstone. Wanfields belonged to the Manloves, and was bought by Rowland Manlove, by the wealth he obtained in the naval service under Sir Walter Leveson; it having previously belonged to Sir Walter Chetwynd. It was enjoyed by his son Alexander, in 1660. Dr. Wilks, who made extensive collections towards a History of Staffordshire, in 1725, married Rebecca Manlove, of Leese Hill. Wanfield subsequently came to the family of Lawrance, and till 1871, the time of his death, was owned by Humphrey Lawrance, Esq., whose only issue is a daughter married to William, eldest son of William Bathew, of Blunt's Hall, and who has taken the name of Lawrance.

BROMSHULFE AND GROTEWICHE.

Bramshall. Robert de Stafford held Bramshall of the king, in the twentieth year of the conquest. The Erdeswicks, Willoughby de Brooke, and Sir Faulke Greville, have been lords of it. A great portion of it belongs to Loxley estate. Mrs. Lassitter occupies the old manor house in which she was born, and which has been traced to have been, with the farm, in the family of the late Roger

KINGSTONE OLD CHURCH.

Warner, that lady's father, successively, about four hundred years. The old church at Bramshall, built in the time of Edward III, was taken down in 1835, and the present one was built from a design in the Batty Langley Style, by a person of the name of Laycock, head carpenter to the late Lord Willoughby de Brooke, at his lordship's expense. The tower of the old church appears to have been of wood, and to have stood considerably more south than the present edifice. It did not contain any monuments, but in the east window of the present church is preserved some coloured glass of the arms and figures of some of the Verneys—a lady and children—and these names, Alice, Jane, Lady Verney. Gratwich, near to, was a manor of the Chetwynds and Gorings, and had an old church, recently superseded by a new one in brick.

LEGHE AND FEELDE.

Leigh, which is about six miles north-west of Uttoxeter, was held in 1114, by Ormus, from Galfrid, Abbot of Burton, at 100s. rent for sixteen years. The church is cruciform. It contains an altar-tomb, with recumbent figures of Sir John Aston, and the lady Johanna, his wife, grandaughter of Judge Littleton. The church was restored in 1845, when "some mouldings" Mr. Garner states of the Anglo Norman style were dug up. An incised slab having a cross within a circle lies in the churchyard. A beautiful memorial cross has been raised to the memory of the late rector, the Rev. L. Bagot, at the north-east angle of the church.

There is an old house at Leigh, at the angle of the road from Withington to the church, containing some very interesting mural decoration in plaster of a remote date. It exists on the wall opposite to the fire place. Centrally is a figure of a cherubim, and branching on each side from underneath the wings are representations of the vine—leaves and fruit, the whole being enclosed in a border, whilst bosses are represented over a door at each side the scene. I think it must have been the reredos or back of an altar of a private chapel at perhaps the beginning of the seventeenth century, or an earlier place where mass was said.

Withington and Nobut are in this parish, in the former of which hamlet there is a nice timbered house going to ruin, on which, some years ago, I made out the date 1644. Till about 1835, or thereabouts, there was a compact brewery, since converted into cottages, at Nobut Hall, as well as a large bakery which supplied a great deal of bread to Uttoxeter. Field, in the same parish, was held in fee from Burton Abbey by Sir John Bagot In the time of Henry I. it was given by Geoffrey, abbot of Burton, to one Andrew, in fee farm, for 20s. per annum. Sir Harvey Bagot built a house there for his seat. In 1680, a Swilch Elm was felled at Field of gigantic size. It took two able men five days to stock it. It was one hundred and twenty feet long. Its girth in the middle was twenty-five feet six inches. There were sixty-one loads of firewood in it. To saw it asunder two saws were fastened together, with three men at each end, and eighty pairs of naves were got out of it, and eight hundred feet of sawn timber, in boards and planks; and the sawing, as the price of labour then was, cost £12. It contained ninety-six tons of solid timber. It size was attested by Lord Bagot and all the workmen by their signatures. * Field Hall is occupied by W. Mountfort Blurton, Esq.

CHARTLEY—CHARTLEY CASTLE.

Chartley Castle, six miles west of Uttoxeter, was built in 1220, by Richard Blunderville, Earl of Chester, on his return from the Holy Land, and an impost was levied upon all his vassals to defray the expense of building. After the death of the founder, the castle and estate fell to William Ferrars, Earl of Derby, whose son Robert forfeited them by his rebellion. Afterwards he was allowed to

---

* Plott's "Staffordshire."

retain them. They were subsequently carried by marriage to the family of Devereux, and then to those of Shirley and Townsend, and Lady Northampton gave up all she could of Chartley, namely, the estate, to one of her uncles, the then Earl Ferrars, to whose descendants it now belongs. Of the castle, which has been in ruins from before the time of Leland, there remain fragments of three round towers, in two of which there are loopholes so constructed as to allow of the arrows being shot diagonally into the ditch. The keep was circular, and about fifty feet in diameter. The ancient manor house was curiously made of wood, the sides carved, and the top embattled, and the arms of the Devereux, with the devices of the Ferrars and Garnishers, were in the windows, and in many parts within and without the house. For some time it was the prison of the unfortunate Mary, Queen of the Scots, who wrought a bed that was in it. On her way to Stafford, in 1575, Queen Elizabeth visited it. It was burnt down in 1781, but an engraving of it appears in Dr. Plott's "Natural History" of the county. The park is a thousand acres, and the breed of the wild beasts of Needwood Forest are preserved in it to this day. It is traditionally said that Robin Hood found asylum at Chartley Castle; and its founder, Randall of Chester, is thus named in connection with the famed Robin, by the author of "Piers Plowman"—

> I can perfitly my paternoster, as the priest it singeth;
> I can rhyme of Robin Hood, and Randall of Chester.

Does the coupling together of these two names favour the idea of a Robert de Ferrars being no other than a Robin Hood?

This item appears in Mr. Lightfoot's "Survey"— "Robert, Earl of Essex, held freely the Castle of Chartley, by the rent of ijs."

There has been a Roman camp at Chartley, for from the ground at the castle I have Roman pottery, and on the east side a part of it remains perfect.

BROMLEY.

Bromley, which took its name of Abbot's Bromley from there having been an abbey in the neighbourhood, is about six miles a little south-west of Uttoxeter. It had formerly a number of valuable privileges, now neglected, including a market on every Tuesday, and three annual fairs, viz., the Thursday before mid-lent Sunday, May 22nd, and August 24th, for horses and cattle. The market cross on oak pillars remains. The hobby-horse dance was celebrated there thrice a year two hundred years ago. The custom consisted in a person carrying between his legs the figure of a horse composed of thin boards. He bore in his hands a bow and arrow, which last entered a hole in the bow, and stopping on a shoulder in it, made a sort of snapping noise as he drew it to and fro, keeping time with the music. Five or six individuals danced along with this person, each carrying on his shoulder a reindeer's head, three of them being painted white and three red, with the arms of the chief families who had at different times been proprietors of the manor painted on the palms of them. In connection with these was a pot, preserved by one of four or five persons called the "Reeves," in which cakes and ale were put. The cakes and ale were purchased by the money collected, and some of the money went towards the repair of the church, and some towards the support of the poor. These antique relics were used in perpetuation of the custom in 1866, and for several years thereabout. They were kept in the church, but of late they have been removed from it. The church was restored in 1855, at a cost of £4,000, when the floor was lowered to show the base of the columns. One of the windows contains painted glass of a man in coat armour.

The Rev. W. Carey, translator of Dante, was clergyman here in 1834.

When fairs were held at this place all the inhabitants possessed a right by custom to sell ale on such days. All that was required was, for those who choose to avail themselves of the privilege, to place a bough of some tree over the door of the house.

At the conquest one Bagod held Bromley of one Robert de Stafford; and, in the time of Henry II., one Symon Bagod was owner thereof.

WOODFORD.

This is about a mile-and-a-half south of Uttoxeter. Soon after 1297 there was a Stephen de Wodeford, who held four parts of Marchington. In the 31st year of the reign of Henry VI., Woodford belonged to Ralph Woodford, grandson of Sir Robert. In the seventeenth century it is stated:—" Walter Jeffreys holdeth freely one messuage, and divers lands called Woodford farm, by the yearly rent of iij., in lieu of a sparrow-hawk, at Michas, late Heath's Land."

Thomas Jeffreys, of Uttoxeter, died April 28th. 1664. Their arms are:—*Sable*, a lion rampant between three scaling ladders *or*. Crest: On a rock *argent*, a castle *or*, charged with a trefoil stippled *gules*. *

In the eighteenth century Woodford belonged to the Webbs, but when Samuel Bentley wrote it belonged to Lord Bagot. It belonged afterwards to Mr. Lasbrey, of Uttoxeter, and has since passed to -- Duncombe, Esq. The house is a large Elizabethan building.

THE WOODLANDS.

The Smallwood estate and Manor House belonged till recently to Thomas Webb, Esq., to whom they came by will from Robert Blurton, Esq. A short time back the estate was purchased by G. A. Hodgson, Esq., who is completing a large and most attractive mansion on the site of the old house in brick and terra-cotta. At Berisford Green, near here, there was a residence which belonged to

---

* See "Staffordshire Collections."

the Rugeleys, and some of the estate was lately owned by Mr. Dester. The amount of land belonging to Thomas Rugeley there in the sixteenth or seventeenth century was 16a. 2r. 20p., and is represented as being in the parish of Uttoxeter. But long before it was held by this family, it was owned by Thirkell's, the first of whom in this country was Roland Thirkell (son of Robert Thirkell, of Grenworth, and brother to Robert Thirkell, Knight), who married Rose, daughter of John Mynors, about the reign of Edward IV. The property passed to the Rugeley family by Roland Rugeley, of Shenton and Smallwood, marrying Elene, daughter and sole heiress of James Thirkhill, of Smallwood.* The family is extinct. A beautiful new church was erected in the Woodlands, near the Manor House, in 1859, chiefly at the expense of Mr. Webb. Knypersley, near Gorsty Hill, is one of the seats of the Mynors, and belongs to the representative of the late John Mynors, Esq., of Eaton. The house is of timber, and remains tolerably perfect as it was built.

In the Woodlands, at Gorsty Hill, a new Wesleyan chapel was built in 1877, by J. E. Lightfoot, Esq., J.P., of Accrington, in memory of his son-in-law, the Rev. W. Bunting, at a cost of about £300. Uttoxeter was the birthplace of Mr. Bunting, who was highly esteemed for many excellent qualities, which are finely portrayed in a memoir prefixed to a volume of his sermons published after his death. The land on which the chapel is built was the gift of the late John Mynors, Esq. Mr. Lightfoot is the owner of much landed property near the Woodlands, and of a large block of houses in Uttoxeter. Before the chapel was built, the Wesleyans preached at Scounslow Green from 1822.

SINGULAR INSTANCE OF GENEROSITY.

"In September, 1801, W. T. Mynors, Esq., of Knypersley, near Uttoxeter, died without a will, and his large property, consisting of landed estates. devolved upon his eldest son, the then W. T. Mynors, Esq. By this circum-

* Third volume "Staffordshire Collections," edited by William Salt Archæological Society.

stance eight younger children were left unprovided for. But he immediately made over to his younger brothers and sisters three considerable estates of the stated value of £10,000, which were about two-thirds of the whole property. When remonstrated with for doing so, he having a large family of his own, he replied, ' I have enough, and am determined that all my brothers and sisters shall be satisfied.' "—*Evangelical Magazine*, Oct., 1802, pp. 401–2.

MERGHANSTONE.

Marchington is about four miles south of Uttoxeter. It was granted by the founder of Burton Abbey, Wulfric Spot, to one Wulfag, but at the Conquest it was held of the king by Henry de Ferrars. In the thirtieth year of the reign of Henry VIII., Thomas Kynnersley, of Loxley, possessed it by inheritance from the Ferrars, and it has since passed through a variety of owners. In Marchington church there is an altar-tomb, date 1592, to Walter Vernon, of Hound Hill. Henry Chawner, Esq., of Hound Hill, lately founded almshouses at Marchington, which have been erected from a design by Mr. Fradgley, architect, of Uttoxeter. The Bank House, near this village, is a timbered house, which remains perfect as built about the year 1622.

HOUND HILL.

The earliest deed with respect to Hagenhull, Hoenil, or Howenhull, is of the time of Henry III., when Sir Henry Hanbury married the daughter and heiress of Hound Hill. In the time of Henry VIII., it was sold to Humphrey Vernon, third son of Henry Vernon, Knight, of Haddon, in the county of Derby. Hound Hill joins Marchington, which is a township in the parish of Hanbury. In 1012 the Saxons, oppressed by the Danes, embraced King Ethelred's plan for their extermination, and Hound Hill is named by Hollingshead as the opening scene of the tragedy. The following are the words of this ancient historian respecting it :—" Egelred being greatly advanced, as he thought, by reason of the marriage, devised upon presumption thereof, to cause all the Danes within the land to be murthered in one day. Hereupon he sent privie commissioners into all cities, boroughs, and towns within his dominions, commanding the rulers and officers in the same to dispatche and flee all such Danes as remained within their liberties at a certain day prefixed, being St. Ryce's day, in the year 1012, and in the thirty-fourth year of King Egelred's raigne (the 12th of November). Hereupon (as sundry writers agree), in one day and hour this murther begannne, and according to the commission and instructions, executed ; but where it first beganne the same is uncertain ; some say at Wellowyn, in Hereforth, some *at a place in Staffordshire called Hown Hill*, and others in other places, as in such doubtful cases it commonly happens." There is a tradition of a battle having been fought at Hound Hill, which may be thought confirmatory of this old writer, and to this these words have reference :—

> Don't let us lie here like hounds upon a hill,
> But march into the town ;

though there is evidently also a play upon the names of Hound Hill and Marchington in them. A bronze key has been dug up at Hound Hill. A key in similar metal, but not of so good a form, has been found in the Chapel Gardens, Uttoxeter.

DRAICOTE.

Draycot, six miles south of Uttoxeter, was held by Henry de Ferrars, in the twentieth year of the Conquest, and in the second year of Edward II. Thomas, lord of Boylestone, held it from the Ferrars, by the service of hunting ; and in the sixteenth Edward III., it belonged to one Richard Draycot, and by his second wife it passed to his posterity, and in right of one of them, Johanna, to her husband, William de Pipe. It belongs now to Lord

Vernon. Near Draycot, in the Greaves, Mr. Thomas Hollis, Queen's ranger, found, in 1848, a British torque of pure gold, formed of eight twisted wires or rods, each itself formed of three other wires, and having two chaste perforated ends, and weighing fifteen and a half ounces. It was worn round the neck. It is shown in the accompanying plate.

NEWBOROUGH.

Newborough, a new borough established by Robert de Ferrars soon after the Conquest, although there might have been a village there without trade before. At Agardsley, an hermitage was granted to the priory of Tutbury, by William de Ferrars, Earl of Derby. At the former place a Roman coin, of base silver, has been found —obverse, two heads with wreathes; reverse, figures, with four horses in a chariot, and the word "Rowa" underneath. It is in the possession of R. Garner, Esq., F.L.S., of Stoke.

HANBURY.

Hanbury, from "hean," high, is an ancient place, the inhabitants being called *civis hean* or *hen*, signifying old. During the Saxon Heptarchy it was granted by Ethelbert, A.D., 674, to his niece, the pious Wurburga, daughter of Wulphere, where she erected a nunnery of which she was abbess. Her body was buried here, but on the place being afterwards overrun by the Danes, it was conveyed to Chester, where there is a splendid shrine to her, and Hanbury Church is dedicated to her. The church was erected from remains of the nunnery and priory. About 1842, when it was undergoing repairs, some early English raised cross slabs were discovered, and Mr. Fradgley, architect, had them safely placed in the interior of the church in the west wall. The tower of the church was restored in 1883. The church contains a number of monuments—a recumbent figure to

Charles Egerton; figures to the Agards; one of an ecclesiastic, in engraved brass; a monument to Ralph Adderley, and an early effigy in chain armour.

FELEDE.

Faulde is a little to the south-east of Hanbury, and is eight miles from Uttoxeter, south. It belonged to John de Curzon, by gift of William de Ferrars, Earl of Derby, and he dying without issue, it was carried in marriage by his sister to Nicholas, son of Adam de Burton, of Tutbury, who was living in the time of Edward II., and was witness to Burton Abbey Roll, in 1321. A William Burton, says one authority (Mr. Shaw), was Abbot of Rocester; another says of Croxden. Another William was standard-bearer to Henry V. William Burton, author of the "History of Leicestershire," was a descendant, and died at Fauld, and was buried at Hanbury, April 6th, 1645. Robert Burton, author of the "Anatomy of Melancholy," was another descendant. Fauld has had a church.

TOTEBERIE.

Tutbury is supposed to have taken its name from being dedicated to the Saxon deity, Tuisto; but it is more likely to have received its name from an altar there to Tutas, the god of the Gauls. It is supposed there was a castle at Tutbury, as one of a line of forts belonging to the Celts. Offa, or Kenulph, kings of Mercia, it is conjectured, had a palace here; but it is certain Ethelred, another of these kings, made the castle there, the place of his residence. Previous to the Conquest it also belonged to Ulfric Spott, founder of Burton Abbey, and was perhaps his place of residence. At the Conquest it was given to Henry de Ferrars. It was repaired by Thomas, Earl of Lancaster, and was rebuilt by John of Gaunt, when it became a place of great splendour. Bull-running and the minstrels' court were instituted by him.

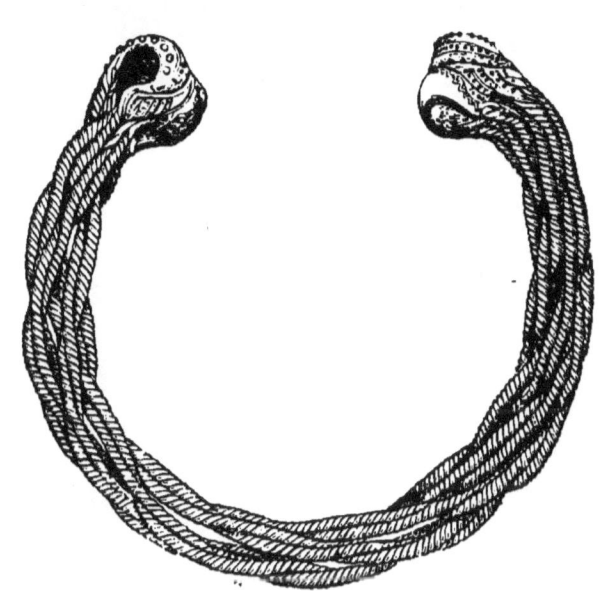

BRITISH TORQUE.

Amongst other places this fortress became a prison of Mary, Queen of Scots. In 1831, the rich contents of the chest, which was lost in the Dove on the flight of Thomas, second Earl of Lancaster, on his rebelling against Edward II., was found, on clearing the bed of the river, and proved to consist of a complete series of the early English coins. A further find was made in 1883. The total quantity found first was one hundred thousand. A priory was built at Tutbury by Henry de Ferrars, it being commenced about 1080. The present church is the nave of the priory, the west doorway and window being unrivalled specimens of Norman architecture. The arch of the doorway recedes from the face of the church three feet ten inches, and consists of seven principal mouldings, all richly adorned with zigzag, beak-head, flowered, and other devices. There are many other specimens of Norman device about the building. This church was restored in 1866, and in the course of clearing the plaster from the walls an early inscription was found in painted letters to a Ferrars, but was unfortunately destroyed.

SUDBERIE.

The parish of Sudburie, which includes Hill Somershall and Aston, was part of the grant of Henry de Ferrars. At an early period it came to the Montgomery family. In the reign of Henry VIII, these manors were brought by a co-heiress of Sir John Montgomery, to Sir John, son of Sir Henry Vernon, of Haddon Hall. This branch of the family, however, became extinct, when they went to Walter Vernon, of Hound Hill, descended from one of the elder brothers of Sir John Vernon, who married the co-heiress of Montgomery. Sudbury Hall, the architect of which was Inigo Jones, is the seat of the present Lord Vernon, who is descended from this branch. The name is derived from a town and district in Normandy. There was a church and priest at Sudbury at the Conquest. The present church contains two ancient effigies of females of the Montgomery family, and several beautiful monuments to members of the Vernon Family. The late Lord Vernon privately published an edition of Dante in three folio volumes. He organised the Sudbury Rifle Corps, which included Uttoxeter, and at great expense he constructed in the Park a fine rifle butts and shed. Augustus Henry Lord Vernon, his son, who commenced the extensive cheese and butter factory at Sudbury, died suddenly in London in 1883, whilst preparing to bring a motion the same evening before the House of Lords.

DUBRIDGE, BROUGHTON, MARSTON, SOMERSHALL, EATON.

The manor of Doveridge, which is about a mile and a half east of Uttoxeter, belonged to Edwin, Earl of Mercia. After the Conquest it was given by Bertha, wife of Henry de Ferrars, to the priory of Tutbury. It was in 1552 granted to Sir William Cavendish. Sarah, a wife of his descendant, was in 1792 created Baroness Waterpark. The late Lord Waterpark was a member of Parliament in the Liberal interest. The family is descended from the same branch as the Dukes of Devonshire. Doveridge Hall, now occupied by the Hon. S. C. Allsopp, Esq., M.P., was built in the last century (about 1770), and has a fine prospect. Doveridge had a church and priest at the time of the Norman Survey. The present church contains architecture of different periods—Anglo-Norman, Early English, and of the decorated period, the east window being of the Perpendicular style. The church was restored in 1866, not externally, but by scraping the plaster off the walls, and round the arch of the west wall a floral design, representing the honeysuckle, was discovered painted of a dark blue or purple colour. The church contains a monument to Sir Thomas Milward; a fine one to the Fleetwoods; and there is an early incised slab representing a priest, supposed to be of Robert Knifton, founder of a Chantry there, 1393. In the inside of the north wall there is an arched recess in which, perhaps, there was an effigy, or it might be called the Holy Sepulchre. There is a piscina for holy-water. A part of the ancient churchyard cross was found in the village in 1866, and was brought back to the churchyard, where the ancient circular steps of it remain. The ancient yew tree in the churchyard is about twenty-two feet in girth, and the branches extend about sixty-two feet, and it has been stated that it has been growing fourteen centuries. Doveridge had a market, granted by the Priory of Tutbury in 1275, and a hiring market is held there now. Michael Thomas Sadler, M.P., and author of several political treatises, was born at Snelstone in 1780, and his friends afterwards lived at Doveridge, where he was educated till he was about fifteen. Mr. Harrison, his schoolmaster, was a remarkable man, and gave him a good knowledge of Latin, Greek, and French, and the rudiments of Italian and German, as well as Mathematics and Algebra. At West Broughton, William Parr, Earl of Essex, had an estate in 1544. In the reign of Queen Elizabeth the manor belonged to the family of Palmer. It has had a church. Marston belonged formerly to the Montgomeries. Its ancient church was fearfully mutilated, the north aisle having been destroyed, and the old pillars and arches became exposed in the north wall. The original south doorway had a circular arch, and the capstones from which it sprung are of the early Norman style. This edifice, however, has been excellently restored, including the north aisle. and the Norman doorway opened. This, as well as the other places named here are east and south-east of Uttoxeter. * Somershall Church has been

---

* Somershall lies a little south-west of Marston, and there is the picturesque old residence of Colonel Fitz Herbert, who is the owner of the hall and its accompanying estate. The original part of the hall is cruciform, being the eastern portion, and the following inscription, carved in oak, was formerly over the entrance-hall door :—"ANNO DNI. 1.5.6.4., I HON FYTZ HEBERT AND ELEN HYS VYFE. IHS." The western portion of the hall, with the high dormer windows, was the residence of the Montgomery family at Cubly. It was taken to pieces, conveyed to Somershall, and re-erected as an addition to Somershall Hall. The interior, in the upper rooms. bears out the fact that the two parts have been distinct. The Rev. Reginald H. C. Fitz Herbert has recently published twenty-two charters which have been preserved at Somershall from 1272—1464, and of which I have made use.

restored. An ancient cross stands in the churchyard. Near to the hall is an oak forty-one feet round at the base, and at the height of three feet, twenty-seven feet in girth. The house of Sir Thomas Milward, Chief Justice of Chester, was at Eaton, and over the door was placed the following inscription :—" V.T. placet Deo, sic omnia siunt, Anno Domini, 1576. Junii 12." The cellars remained till recently, and a bare tunnel communicated with them from a distance. *

NORBURY.

Norbury, which is about north-east of Uttoxeter, in the time of the Saxon dynasty, belonged to Siward, the great Saxon Thane. It was confiscated from him by King William, and given to Henry Ferrars. Sir William Fitz Herbert, Knight, was lord of Norbury in 1252, to whose ancestors it was granted in 1125. The Fitz Herberts, of Tissington, are descended from the family at Norbury. Norbury Hall was built thirteenth, Edward I., and was occupied by the family till 1648. Norbury had a church at the Conquest. The present church is ancient, and is remarkable for its numerous richly-coloured glass windows, with memorial devices, and for its architecture. It also contains a number of altar-tombs. In the yard of Norbury old hall, the interesting remains of a private chapel, of an early period, are in existence.

ALVETON.

At Alton there was a castle before the Conquest, held by one Lunan, or, as Erdeswick says, by one Juvar.

---

* Sir Thomas Milward and other members of his family are referred to in the poetical works of Bancroft, a Derbyshire poet, and also in the poems of Sir Aston Cockayne. Sir Thomas was the son of John Milward, a captain of the City of London, and first governor of the corporation of the silk trade. Captain Robert Milward, who whilst serving in Spain, killed in single combat a Spaniard, was drowned in the Trent. The portraits of the captain and his brother, John, hung at each side of that of their father the Judge, who was represented at full length in his robes. It is stated that the eldest son of Sir Thomas cut off the entail of the Eaton estate from his only son, and it was sold to Godfrey Clark, Esq., of Chilcote. The deposed grandson retired to a village in Staffordshire, where he died at an advanced age.‡

‡ *Gentleman's Magazine*, vol. lxi., page 993.

The castle, of which there are now but slight remains, was built by Bertram de Verdun. A battle was fought at Bonebury, in the year 716, betwixt Coelred, King of Mercia, and Ina, King of the West Saxons, who had invaded Mercia. Brompton, the abbot of Jourvall, says, "Ina, king of the West Saxons, raised a great army, fought Ceolred at Bonebury; when yet Ceolred (by the advantage of his strong fortifications) so warmly received him, that he was glad to withdraw on equal terms, neither having much to brag of victory." The fortress was of an irregular figure, encompassed with a single, and in some places with a double ditch, the whole encompassing about one hundred acres of land. Alton Towers was built on a portion of the site of Bonebury, where the old lodge—well remembered by old people—stood, and now forming an undistinguishable part of the present princely mansion. At this entrenchment a Saxon sword and a Celt of an earlier date, have been dug up. The sword was given to Sir Joseph Banks, president of the Royal Society. It is, perhaps, deserving mention, that at the foundation of these early earthworks an abundance of wood charcoal was observed, when they were totally destroyed at the erection of the towers, with the exception of a small part near the Flag Tower. The improvements at Alton were begun by Charles, Earl of Shrewsbury, a considerable part of Alton Towers and their decoration, with many works in the gardens having been executed after the designs of Thomas Fradgley, Esq., Architect, of Uttoxeter. Amongst these were the (exterior) east end of the chapel; the ceiling; the richly-carved chapel-tower; the chapel Gothic benches; the sacristy; the elaborate ceilings, the marble chimney-pieces, doors, &c., of the music-room; the Poet's Corner; the interior of the two libraries (including the bookcases); and of the State bedroom and dressing-rooms. Also the black oak corridor, the chapel corridor, and the corridor leading to the new dining-room; the ceiling and heraldic cornice of the late Earl's family dining-room; the clock tower (except the angle turret). In the gardens he designed the Harper's cottage, the conservatory adjoining the cromlech, as well as the cromlech; the fountain at the bottom of the gardens, never finished, and which was to have been of stone in three stories, and on each eight fountains; the spiral fountain; the drawings for the temple at the entrance of the gardens, containing the bust of the founder of the gardens and Towers; the Italian lodge near the smelting mill, and that at the top of Barberry Dell. * This gentleman saw one of the remaining towers of the fine old ruins of the castle fall In Alton church some fine remains of Norman architecture, consisting of a magnificent row of arches, and a splendid pointed arch, were brought to light recently during a process of restoring. It is a pity St. John's Hospital was erected on the site of the castle, as it might have done quite as well on some other eminence, and the ruins of the castle have been allowed to remain as a relic of the past.

TEAN.

In the twentieth year of the Conquest, Tain, or Tean, belonged to Robert de Stafford, and has since passed through a great many families. At Over Tean, Major Ashby, in 1728, found, at some depth in his garden, an earthen vessel which he assigned to the Roman period, but which was doubtless Celtic. The garden has the name of Willy Wall Well, which exists on the west side of the Tean Brook, almost opposite to Hall Green. At Upper Tean a field is called Tumulus field, and a large oblong stone lying flat there probably marks the site of a cemetery of the Roman period. Heath House, the residence of J. C. Philips, Esq., is on the east side of

---

* Amongst other works designed by Mr. Fradgley have been Marchington Alms Houses, Rocester Bridge over the Dove, Hanbury Schools, Uttoxeter Town Hall (plain according to instructions), Draycot-in-the-Clay Schools, Stramshall Church, Uttoxeter National Schools, Cauldon Low Schools, the Grammar School Abbot's Bromley, the Independent Schools, and the Old Brewery Offices, all receiving the approval of the Privy Council.

Tean, and Heybridge is at the entrance of Tean, and is the mansion of W. Philips, Esq., late a sheriff of the county. These gentlemen are the owners of the extensive tape works at Tean, which were established in 1747, and are now the most extensive in Europe.

CROXDEN, OR CROKEDON.

Croxden, six miles north of Uttoxeter, is remarkable for the fine ruins of an abbey, consisting of the west front, south transept, and part of the cloisters, founded there for the Cistercian order of monks, in 1176, by Bertram de Verdun. Thomas, the first abbot, wrote a commentary on the Bible. The curious diary of Richard de Schepeshead, thirteenth abbot, is in the British Museum. The heart of King John was buried here; and it was the burying place of the Verduns. A crucifix, with an image of the Saviour, was found, broken, amongst the ruins, by the late Mr. Carrington, who repaired it, and it, with a representation of a knight in coat armour, are preserved. Croxden parish church (alas! recently superseded by a new one), was coeval with the abbey, and its ancient single bell of the fourteenth century, having become cracked, was brought to Uttoxeter and sold to the late Mr. James Vernon, ironmonger, who broke it up. This was a great pity, as it was so interesting. It had an alphabet round it, a groat of the 25th, Edward III., the obverse and reverse of it being shown, was let, during the process of casting, in the rim, and there was a mark on the side in the form of a cross reversed, intended either as a sacred symbol, or the founder's mark. The alphabet, which is in curious mediæval characters, is as follows :— "A B C D. K M N O P. A B C D. E F G H I K. E F G H I K." The inscription on the groat was as follows :—" Posvi deum adjuiorum mex" within the outer circle. Within the inner circle, " Civites, London."

CHECKLEY.

In the twentieth year of the Conquest, Checkley, or Cedla, was held of the king by Otha; and in King John's time it came to the Ferrars. The church is of the fourteenth century. The west wall within has had some ancient and curious paintings, which have been destroyed by scraping the walls. Some of the windows have interesting stained glass; and there is also in it an altar-tomb, of the date 1524, to Godfrey Foljambe, with an effigy of himself and wife. The font, which is Norman, is shown in the accompanying engraving.

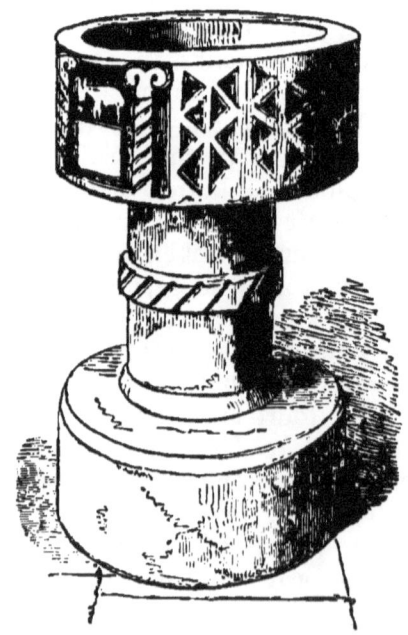

NORMAN FONT.

In the churchyard are three tapering stones, two of which bear defaced ornamentation and human figures represented in basket-work. They have been said to be monumental and Danish, and to have been originally set

DANISH STONES.

up to preserve in memory a great battle said traditionally to have been fought between the Danes and the English, in which the latter were victorious; and that one of the armies was totally unharmed; and that the stones represent three bishops who fell in the engagement. Tradition also states that a field called "Naked Field," and a place known as "Dead Man's Green," (written in the old register at Checkley, "Tetterton Green") represent the scene of the battle, where the dead strewed the ground, and where a human skeleton has been dug up. A battle may have taken place at Checkley; but it is doubtful whether the stones have any connection, in any way, with it, notwithstanding that such is the popular belief. They are pillarstones of the Saxon, if not of the Norman period, although I think of the former, of the ninth century, having on them a great variety of interlaced ornamentation, with the exception of one which is plain, the ornamentation, if it ever bore any, being worn away. They are described by the sexton as standing in troughs, or, more correctly in the sockets of pedestals. A considerable quantity of human remains have been found in the course of draining near to, on the Park Hall farm.

Dr. Whittaker, in an interesting note in his "History of Walley," where he is speaking of the division of the Northumbrian and Mercian kingdoms, contends that Calclinth, which was under the control of Offa, King of Mercia, was held at Checkley, and not at an obscure place near Manchester, called Culcheth, as hitherto believed, and thereby does much towards explaining the old and singular traditions of the village, though it is not as a consequence necessary to follow Dr. Plot in his opinion about the intent of the stones. Dr. Whittaker writes :—
"It is strange indeed that the attention of no antiquary has been directed to Checkley, in Staffordshire, as the real scene of this quarrelsome and opprobrious assembly. But upon every hypothesis Checkley was far within the limits of Mercia : and it is highly improbable that a council in the decrees of which so powerful and spirited a monarch as Offa had so near an interest, would be permitted to

assemble anywhere but in his own territories. Let us see, however, on what grounds the evidence in favour of Checkley, rests. First, the initial "C," in Saxon, was pronounced as *ch* in church. Thus Cheadle was altered in the orthography only to Chad. Calclinth then would be pronounced as Chalclinth, and the last consonants very indistinctly. Invert the letters (c and i) in the middle of the word, and we have Chacli, or Checkley. Dr. Whittaker in supporting this hypothesis, on the constant tradition of the village about a battle, and the slaughter of three bishops! and the memorials in the churchyard said to be to their memory, proceeds—"Compare these circumstances with the character of that council, which is called in the *Saxon Chronicle*, ' Gefhtfullic,' a word yet retained in the Lancashire dialect, which would be, literally translated, ' flitting,' and the violence with which it is known to have been conducted, and there can be no doubt that the tradition is an exaggerated account of that event, whence it must follow that Calclinth is Checkley."

The Saxon word appears to be in these letters – "Gef'htfullic," and translated as above would imply that the council (in this instance of so very violent a character) was not always held at one particular place, but occurred periodically at different places.

By the side of Checkley Church lies the effigy of a crusader.

The Rev. Dr. Langley, of Checkley, translator of a portion of "Homer," wrote an account of Checkley, and the manuscript passed to the Rev. Simeon Shaw, historian of a portion of the county.

In the constable's accounts at Checkley, there are several entries specifying payments to the High Constable for maimed soldiers. In 1629, 4s. 6d. ; March 29th, 1633, 4s. 8d.; March 16th, 1633, 4s. 8d.; December 20th, 1666, 9s. od. Spent when I met the High Constable at Beamhurt, 8s. od.; paid to maimed soldiers 2nd April, 9s. od.

ROWCESTER.

I have already spoken of Rocester as a Roman station, and there are also some evidences of its importance in the time of the Saxons. A field at the entrance of Rocester, from Barrow Hill, is named Lyggets, from the Saxon word Lyd, which means to cover or protect, says Mr. Wood, in his "History of Eyam," and implies there was a strong gate there across the road entering Rocester, at which there was a nightly watch.

At the Conquest, Rocester was held by Robert de Stafford. In 1140, Richard Bacon founded a monastery of Black Canons there. Rocester churchyard contains a perfect raised cross slab and two others much defaced;

CROSS SLAB.

and also the shaft of an ancient cross, with tooth ornamentation betwixt moulded corners. The following engraving gives some idea of the ancient earthwork near the church :

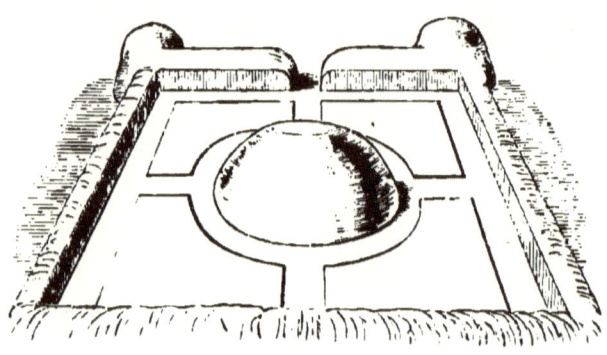

EARTHWORK.

The church, which was taken down in 1871, was in the Italian style, and a gothic structure was immediately raised on its site, and opened by the bishop of the diocese, on Friday, September 28th, 1872, its architect being Mr. Christian, of London. The cost of the structure was £4,000, towards which the patron of the living, C. M. Campbell, Esq., of Woodseat, gave £400, and the fine east window. Other large donors were Sir Percival Heywood, Bart., Captain Dawson, and Messrs. Houlsworth. Mr. Campbell also gave the organ, Mrs. Dawson the beautifully inlaid altar, and Mrs. Webb, of Clownholme, the books. The tower of the previous church remains, but it has had gothic windows put in, and been embattled and surmounted by a spire. In course of taking out the new foundations a few relics only of the old abbey were discovered, including a slender shaft, a small scolloped Norman cap, a number of encaustic tiles of the 13th century, with some earlier, of which I have examples and drawings, and a brass with "Thomas" engraved upon it in old English letters.

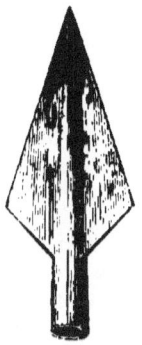

SPEAR HEAD, FOUND AT ROCESTER.

Rocester is of much importance in consequence of its large factory, which was erected in 1772 by Mr. Arkwright, and which, in 1818, was the property of Mr. Bridone, or Briddon, a son of whose has been many years one of Uttoxeter rural postmen : subsequently that of Messrs. Houlsworth, who recently sold it to A. W. Lyon and T. Webb, Esqs., who have put entirely new works in it by which they are enabled to carry the cotton through all stages of manufacture.

In the parish of Rocester, at Dove Leys, is the seat of Sir Percival Heywood, Bart., which was burnt down by fire in 1873, and rebuilt as it was before. If the situation is not elevated it is very beautiful, pleasant, and picturesque.

Barrow Hill House, having very fine and commanding prospects, is in the same parish. The late Mrs. White collected there a fine library of books, in choice condition, and some rare and valuable paintings of the old masters. This estate is now the patrimony of Captain Dawson.

Another lovely spot in Rocester parish is Woodseat, the mansion and grounds of the late lamented Colin Minton Campbell, Esq., whose fine museum of rare examples of antique art pottery is extremely valuable. Woodseat House was erected a little before 1774 by Thomas Bainbrigge, Esq. From 1829 the estate was subject to litigation till 1860, after which it was sold in divers lots, the house and land now attached to Woodseat being bought by Mr. Campbell, who added two wings to the residence, and otherwise expended large sums in improving and decorating it, and in increasing the attractions of the gardens and grounds. Space forbids me entering upon a detailed account of the litigation in which this property was involved, but the following notice of a grandson, of military distinction, of Thomas Bainbrigge, of Woodseat, will be interesting to peruse :— General John Hankey Bainbrigge died March 15th, 1881, at his residence, Robais Manor, Guernsey, in his ninetieth year. He was second son of Lieutenant-Colonel Phillip Bainbrigge, who was killed commanding the 20th Regiment at the battle of Egmont-op-Zee, in Holland, and was grandson of Thomas Bainbrigge, of Woodseat and Rocester, Staffordshire, who, as High Sheriff of Derbyshire, in 1760, proclaimed King George III, on his accession to the throne. General Bainbrigge entered the 20th Foot in 1808, and was transferred to the 41st as captain in 1844. With the former regiment he served in the Peninsular, being present at Vimiera, Corunna, Vittoria, and the Walcheren expedition, and attained the rank of General in 1877. He married his cousin Sophia, daughter of Mr. Bonamy Dobree.

Mince Pie Hall, near to, is a curious building, and was originally intended as the mansion for Woodseat estate, and was consequently erected before the present principal residence there, but not pleasing its owner, it was discarded for the purpose for which it was intended, and Woodseat House was built in its place on a finer site and in a different style. Mince Pie Hall consists of two wings having a south and eastern aspect respectively, and at the angle there is a prospect tower, containing rooms, and which gives such peculiarity to the place. It is built in brick with stone dressings, is in the Italian style, and is rusticated with rectangular joints, the rusticated arches of the windows having elbowed voussoirs.

Abbots Clownhome is near Rocester on the Derbyshire side of the Dove, and there are situated the residences of Mrs. Webb, and the late A. W. Lyon, Esq., the largest collector of paintings of any gentleman within a great distance. These valuable works of art were sold in London in 1883, and realised over £7,000. "The Scottish Raid," by Rosa Bonheur, sold for £1,837 10s.

Denstone, in Rocester parish, was held before the Conquest by Juvar. At the Conquest it was held by the king, and subsequently it passed to the Verduns and Furnivals. In the sixteenth, seventeenth, and eighteenth centuries it belonged to the family of Madeley, whose descendants removed to Uttoxeter, where one was a physician. It is now owned principally by Sir Percival Heywood, Bart., to whose munificence the first erection of a church there is due. Denstone has become noted, and will become more so, in consequence of the middle class school or college, which has been erected there in a conspicuous and healthy situation. The conception of the erection of a college there arose with Sir Percival Heywood, who gave the site and contributed largely towards its cost.

Prestwood is also near Rocester, and in 1307 a curious suit was instituted by Adam de Prestwood against Richard de Wallop, of South Hampshire, at a Court of Afforcements at Leek, for stealing the prosecutor's horse and appurtenances from the Inn at Prestwood (qy., that at Quexhill now standing?), and a jury condemned him to be hung. By the influence, however, of the Vicar of Leek, in which town he had no chattels, a commission was brought from the Bishop of Lichfield, which claimed Richard de Wallop as a clerk and member of the church, and he was consequently delivered over safely to the vicar and the gaol of the bishop. ∗

CRACKMERES.

Before the Conquest, Crakemarsh was the demesne of Algar, Earl of Mercia, and was part of the grant by the king to Henry de Ferrars. Robert de Ferrars gave

---

∗ "Notes and Queries."

Crakemarsh to his daughter Maud, on her marriage with Bertram de Verdun. It was in the possession of the Delves from the time of Edward I., one of whom, John, son of John de Delves, whose seat it was, was one of four squires with James, Lord Audley, at the battle of Poictiers.* John Delves, of Uttoxeter, amongst other persons, was convicted and attainted of High Treason, A.D., 1482.† There is a field near Bridge-street, Uttoxeter, called both Delves' Hall and Delves' Hall meadow, in old writings, and probably a branch of the family lived there. Bertram de Verdun called Crakemarsh, or a place at it, his "Grove," meaning a place of devotion. Crakemarsh had formerly a church, and in a *Terrier* of 1774, some ground there is called, along with the Rectory Glebe, "The Chapel Yard." It was standing in the last century, and an old man was living about twenty-five years ago who recollected both it and the gravestones standing about it as well. Sir Thomas Cotton Sheppard, Bart., of Crakemarsh Hall, died in 1847, and Lady Cotton Sheppard, who was the donor of four lifeboats to the National Lifeboat Institution, died in 1872. By marriage with the only daughter of Thomas Hart, Esq., it became the property of the late Hon Richard Cavendish, and then his heir, also deceased. It is now occupied by Charles Tyrrel Cavendish, Esq., J.P.

NEEDWOOD FOREST.

Needwood Forest, in 1656, covered nine thousand two hundred and twenty acres of land, and contained forty-seven thousand one hundred and fifty trees, including huge oaks, limes, wych-elms, &c., and ten thousand cord of hollies and underwood. Before it was de-forested it contained twenty thousand head of deer. The Swilcar Oak, at six feet high, is twenty-one feet four inches in girth. It is sixty-five feet high, and contains one thousand

---

* " Froisart's Chronicles."
† " Rolls and Journals of House of Commons," vol. i., p. 167.

feet of timber. In 1658 one half of the open forest, four thousand six hundred and ten acres and twenty-four poles, and one-tenth part of the timber was allotted and allowed to the Freeholders in lieu of all their rights, but the division did not take place till 1778, when Marchington, Marchington-Woodlands, Hound Hill, Stubbey Lane, Moorton, Draycot, Coton, Fauld (or Fawld), Hanbury, and Hanbury Wood-end participated in the allotments, but not according to the original boundaries made in 1658, as they could not be discovered. *

FINIS.

www.ingramcontent.com/pod-product-compliance
Lightning Source LLC
Chambersburg PA
CBHW051234300426
44114CB00011B/731